Applying Six Sigma Using SigmaXL

1th Edition

ISBN: 978-1-7349210-9-0

This book is printed on acid-free paper.

Printed in standard color.

Global Six Sigma USA

TABLE OF CONTENTS

Acknowledgement

Writing a book using material developed for Six Sigma methodology is not an individual's undertaking. Many distinguished colleagues have supplied ideas and updates to create material used in this book. The authors wish to thank the following individuals for their ideas and efforts: Eric Edwin, Jeff Jackson and Richard Lynch. Without their inputs this book may not have been created.

We also wish to thank SigmaXL Inc. for the support they provide. SigmaXL is a company that has shown a strong customer focus. No issue has ever been too small or large for their support team. The website's knowledge database and their technical support are unmatched.

Finally, we wish to thank our 30,000 plus students from over 6,000 organizations who allow us to continue doing what we love to do, teach. Without their kind comments and helpful suggestions this would simply be a job, and not a passion.

To find out more about SixSigma.us and the services offered, go to:

www.6sigma.us

Introduction

Welcome to **Applying Six Sigma Using SigmaXL**. This book is specially designed to be an easy-to-understand and easy-to-use resource for Six Sigma practitioners of all experience levels. It is filled with explanations and hands-on demonstrations of the common and useful features in SigmaXL.

The authors understand that even experienced Six Sigma practitioners can use a SigmaXL refresher from time to time, especially since the program offers such a wide array of features and functionality. Just as importantly, experience has shown us that those new to Six Sigma need a solid reference resource as well.

That's why we decided to write this book. It is written for the purpose of serving Six Sigma practitioners regardless of whether they are working on their first project or their one thousandth project. Of course, those new to Six Sigma will likely need access to a variety of resource materials so there's no claim that this is the "only book needed" or some other such statement.

For those outside of Six Sigma, this book offers plenty of information to meet basic needs. The practice of data analysis crosses many different industries and boundaries, so the concepts and ideas presented here are easily transferable to other applications.

Six Sigma and SigmaXL: A Powerful Combination

The Six Sigma process improvement methodology, more than any other methodology, demonstrates the critical importance of proper collection and analysis of data. From its roots in the manufacturing environment, the power of Six Sigma has found its way into virtually all areas of business, regardless of product, service, industry, or profession.

Some of the strongest proponents of Six Sigma methodology can be found in non-manufacturing disciplines. Why? Because the companies that use Six Sigma reap tremendous money savings, and they quickly recognize the value of this methodology. In fact, many of these non-manufacturing entities enjoy even greater savings than those typically generated in a manufacturing environment.

SigmaXL® Statistical Software is an exceptional tool for data analysis, especially when used with the Six Sigma methodology. Their website states:

Established in 1998, SigmaXL Inc. is a leading provider of user-friendly Excel Add-ins for Lean Six Sigma graphical and statistical tools and Monte Carlo simulation. SigmaXL has over 100,000 users in more than 180 countries.

Our flagship product, SigmaXL®, was designed from the ground up to be a cost-effective, powerful, but easy to use tool that enables users to measure, analyze, improve and control their service, transactional, and manufacturing processes. As an add-in to the already familiar Microsoft Excel, SigmaXL® is ideal for Lean Six Sigma training and application, or use in a college statistics course.

SigmaXL® and all other trademarks and logos for the Company's products and services are the exclusive property of SigmaXL Inc. All other marks referenced remain the property of their respective owners. See www.sigmaXL.com for more information.

How This Book Is Constructed

The text in this book follows the **DMAIC** (**Define Measure Analyze Improve Control**) phases of Six Sigma methodology. While the book's flow is DMAIC in nature, its applications are not limited to this particular process. Data analysis is the same no matter what process is used. Furthermore, this book is not designed to analyze manufacturing projects differently than transactional projects. If something can be measured, it can be analyzed.

Throughout the book, various data sets are presented to demonstrate specific statistical analysis tasks and tools. SigmaXL uses Excel file extensions.

This book explains how to use SigmaXL in a process improvement project. It is assumed that the user understands how to use Excel.

Datasets

The datasets used in this book can be downloaded at: ***www.6sigma.us/ApplyingSixSigmaUsingSigmaXL*** ***or email*** to ***SigmaXL@dmaic.us***

Using SigmaXL

Once downloaded, SigmaXL can be automatically opened when starting Excel. Once purchased, go to; **File** > **Options** > **Add-ins**. Under **Manage**; select **Excel Add-ins**. Click **GO**. Choose **SigmaXL**, then click **OK**.
SigmaXL will now be loaded every time Excel is opened.
Since SigmaXL is an Excel Add-In, it uses **Excel Worksheets**.

To perform an action on the data, the cursor must be placed within the desired values. When this is done, and the user selects an action, the following dialog box appears:

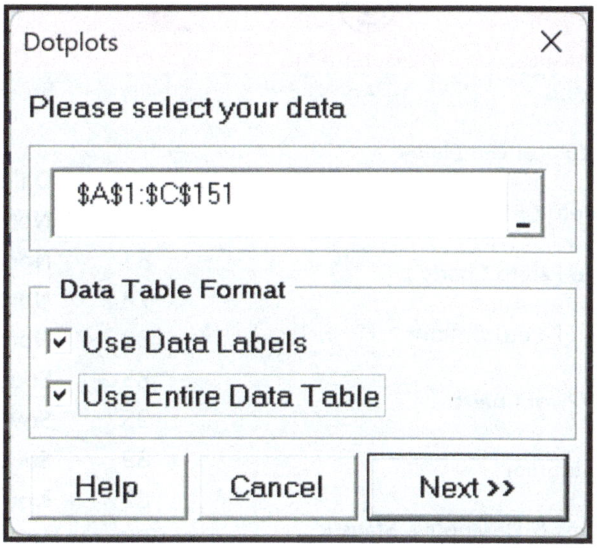

Select both options; **Use Data Labels** (if they exist), and **Use Entire Data Table**. Then Click **Next**.

> **Hint:** When SigmaXL looks for the **Entire Data Table**, it looks at the active cell(s), and selects all congruent columns that contain information. An empty column is considered the end of the Data Table.

> **Note:** Throughout the remainder of this book, this dialog box will not be mentioned. It will be assumed that the user fills it out properly.

Menu Commands

Menu commands will be shown in the following format;

Main Menu Item > Sub Menu Item (1) > Sub Menu Item (2) ....

For instance, to create a Dot Plot of the data, highlight the desired values and select;

SigmaXL > Graphical Tools > Dotplots.

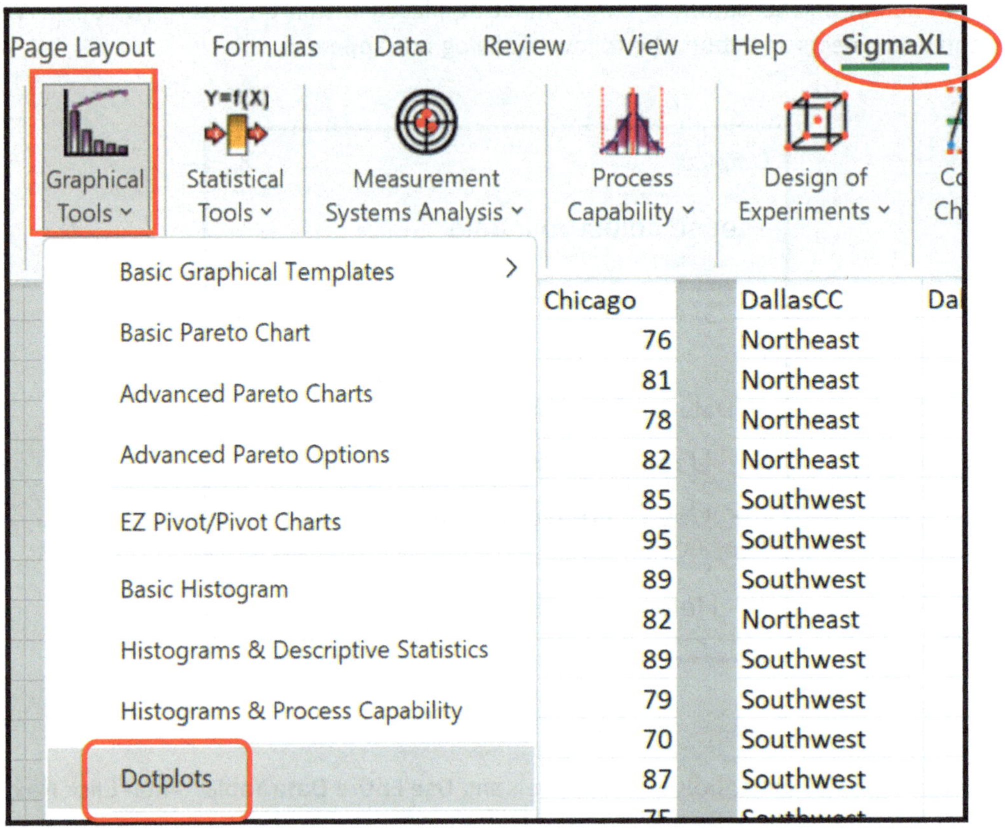

The user would click on **SigmaXL,** in the Main Menu bar, then click **Graphical Tools** (the sub menu), then **Dotplots**, (the second sub menu).

Dialog Boxes

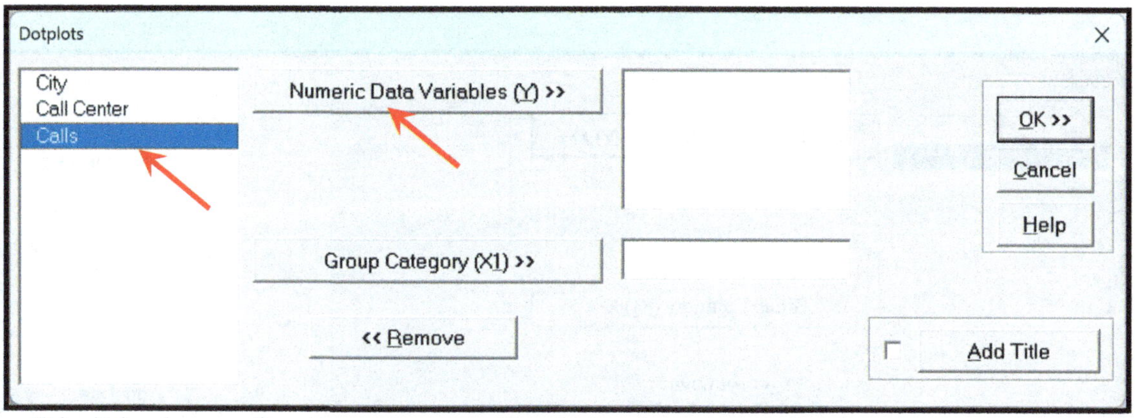

SigmaXL's dialog boxes allow the user to specify which column to use for the requested actions. Some dialog boxes allow a single column entry, while others allow for multiple columns.

As an example, to select the column **Calls**, click on the column heading within the display on the right, then click **Numeric Data Variables (Y)**.

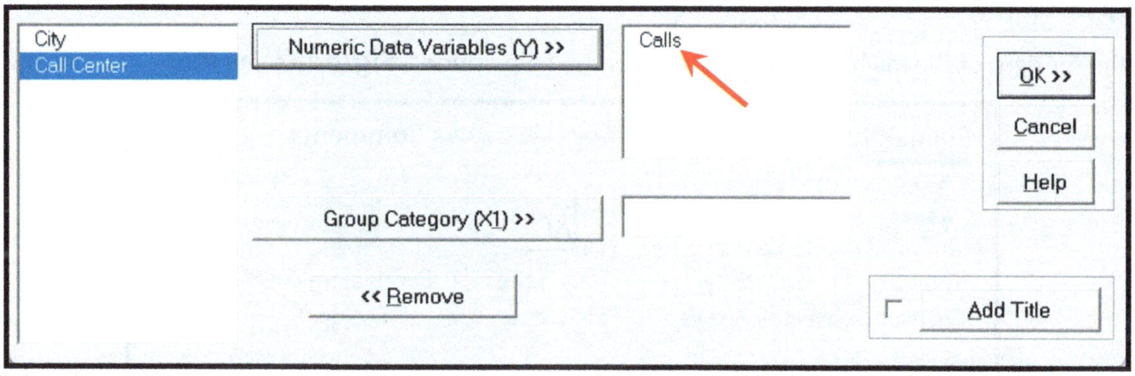

Calls has been removed from the columns listing on the left and is now in the **Numeric Data Variables** box. The Dotplot will be created using that column. More information for the dialog boxes will be presented throughout the units.

Selecting the column Call Center, which is text for the Numeric Data Variables, results in the following

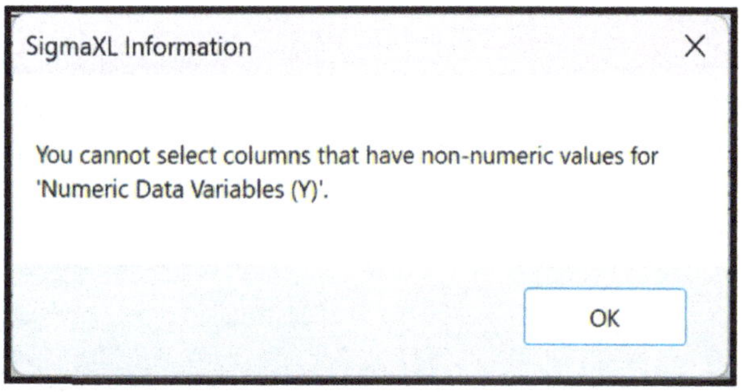

warning. Click **OK**, then select a column with numeric data.

Some tabs within the Dialog box will display information when the cursor hovers over the tab. In this example, hovering the cursor over the **Remove** tab shows the explanation; 'Highlight the item to

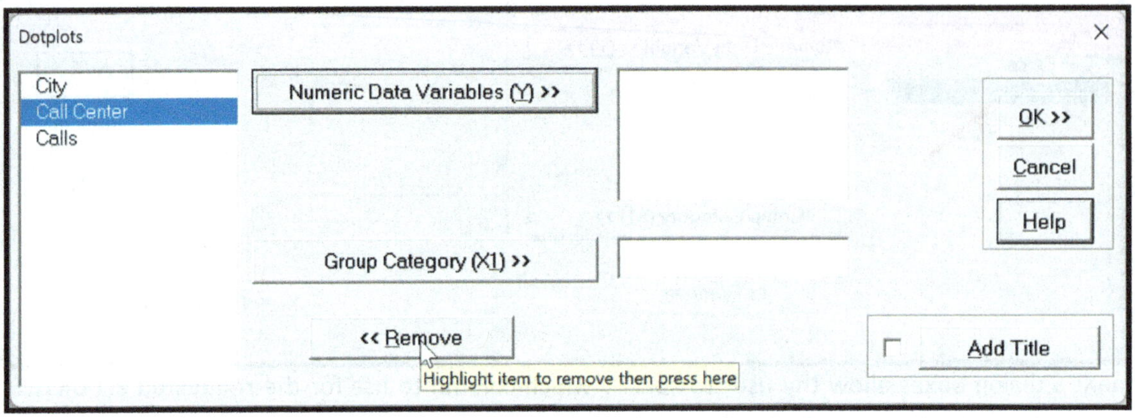

remove then press here'.

Help options:

On the far right of the main SigmaXL menu bar is the help option. ***SigmaXL > Help***

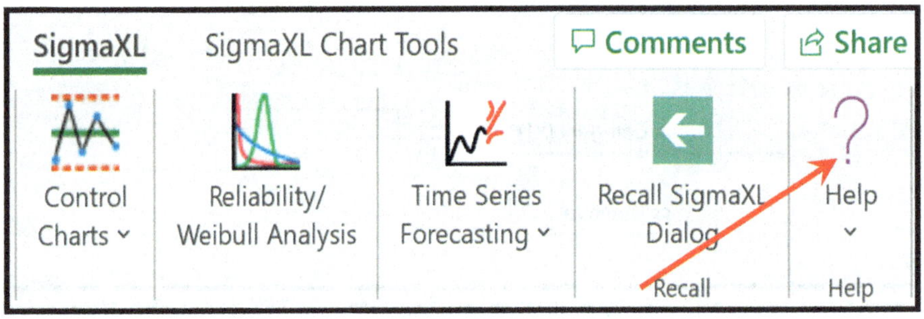

Selecting the **Help** option produces more choices. Select the desired option.

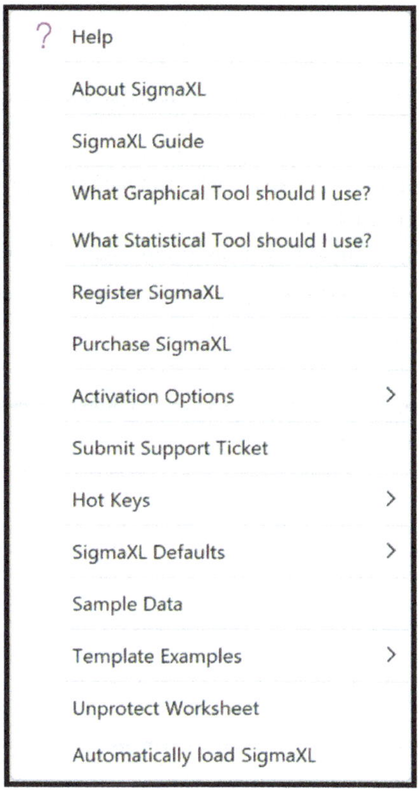

Every dialog box contains a ***Help*** button. When selected, it redirects the user to the SigmaXL website for online help.

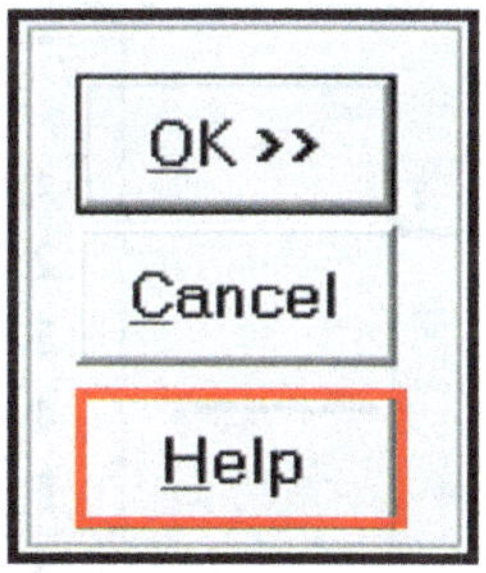

Input Data

Typing Data into SigmaXL

Hint: Best practices:

1. Column headings should be placed in row 1 of the worksheet.
2. Each column should have a unique name.
3. Do not name a column **Data**. SigmaXL will produce a warning notice.

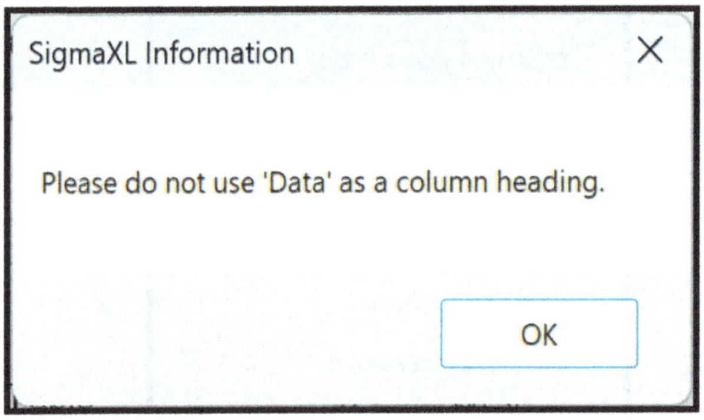

Typing information directly into a cell is easy, but there are times when it becomes tedious. For instance, instead of typing in a single value over and over to populate a column, use the following method to populate the entire column.

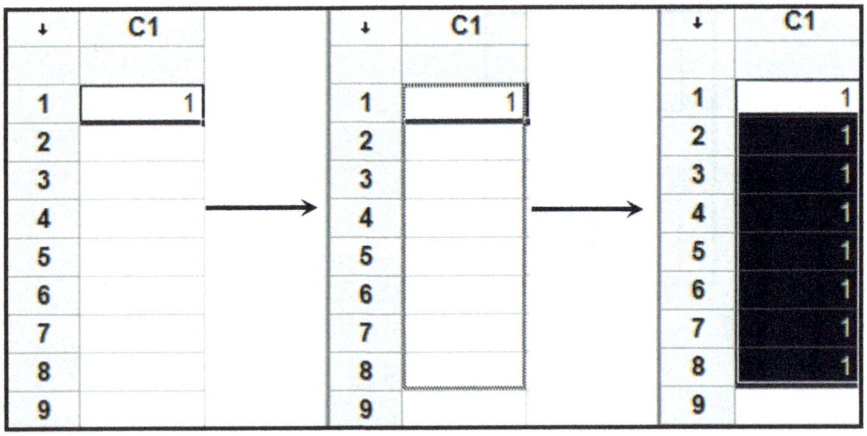

To accomplish this task, perform the following steps:

- Type the value into one cell.
- Select the cell.
- Place the cursor over the lower right corner of the cell. (Cursor becomes a + sign.)
- Click and hold the left mouse button, then drag down to the final cell of the repeated values.
- Release the left mouse button. The value 1 populates all of the selected cells.

To continue a sequence of numbers, perform the following steps:

- Type in the first few values of the sequence.
- Highlight the cells that define the sequence.
- Place the cursor over the lower right corner of the last cell.
- Click and hold the left mouse button, then drag down to the final cell to be populated.
- Release the left mouse button. SigmaXL fills in the sequence values.

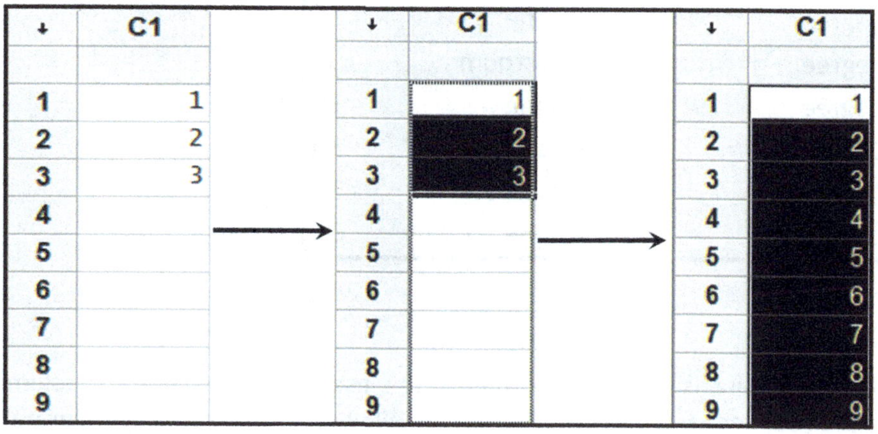

To repeat a pattern of text or data, highlight the pattern, then select: ***Edit > Copy Cells*** (shortcut key Crtl + c). Next, highlight the destination cells and select ***Edit > Paste Cells*** (shortcut key Crtl + v).

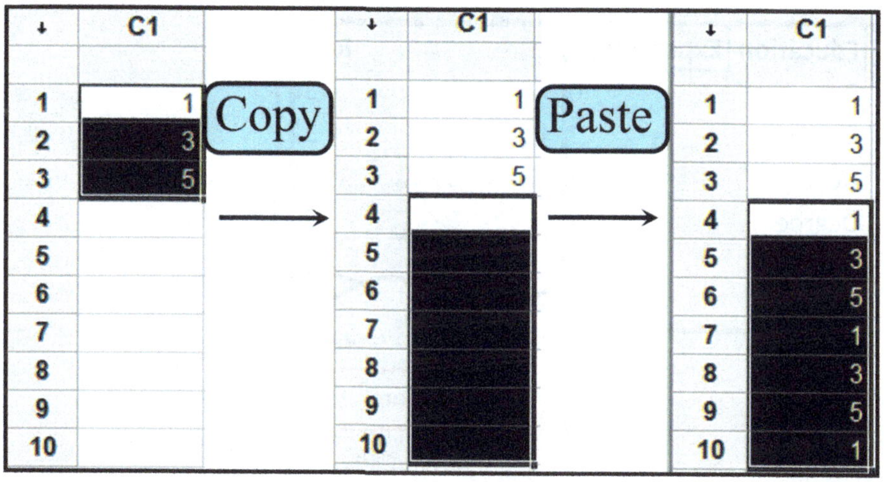

The sequence is copied to the highlighted cells. Notice that if the highlighted cells do not allow for the completion of the sequence, the sequence simply stops.

As an alternative to the menu command: ***Edit > Copy Cells***, once the sequence is highlighted, right-click inside the worksheet and select ***Copy Cells***, then highlight the cells for the sequence and again, right-click, then select ***Paste Cells***.

Column Name (Headings) and Descriptions

Column Names

Excel allows for column names or headings to be placed anywhere in the worksheet. The recommended method for using SigmaXL is to place the column headings in row 1.

Education	Experience	Training	Error Rate
Degree	0	Online	36
Degree	3	Classroom	32
Degree	1	Online	38
Degree	2	Classroom	30
Degree	5	Classroom	26
Degree	7	Online	37

Column Descriptions

A column or worksheet filled with data is meaningless unless the user knows what each column represents. A description for each column, as well as the worksheet, allows information to be accurately transferred from one user to the next.

To add a description for the column **Experience**, Right-Click on the column heading and select,

New Note.

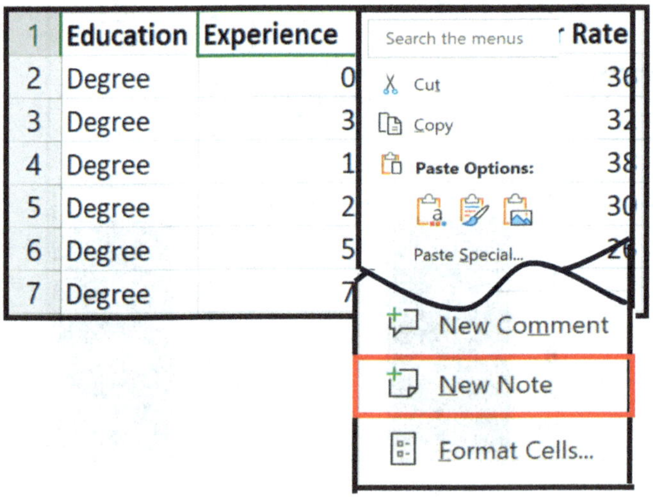

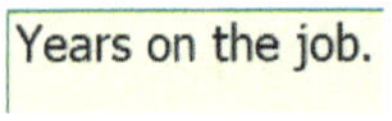

Type in the appropriate information, then click anywhere within the spreadsheet to close the note.

> **Hint:** Column Notes.
>
> While it is possible to place notes in any cell of the Spreadsheet, it is recommended to keep them associated with the column headings.

A red diamond appears in the cell indicating a note exists. To view the note, hover the cursor over the red diamond. The note is displayed.

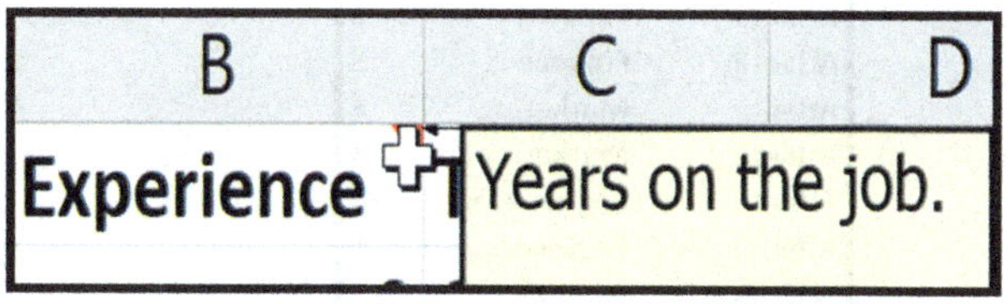

Worksheets

Use the following worksheet to explore SigmaXL's functions.

Select the SigmaXL Worksheet: ***Time Card Errors***

Subset

There are 4 methods available to subset a worksheet.

1. Category Subset
2. Random Subset
3. Numerical Subset
4. Date Subset

This demonstration will use **Category Subset**.

To subset the worksheet, **Time Card Errors**, select:

SigmaXL > Data Manipulation > Category Subset

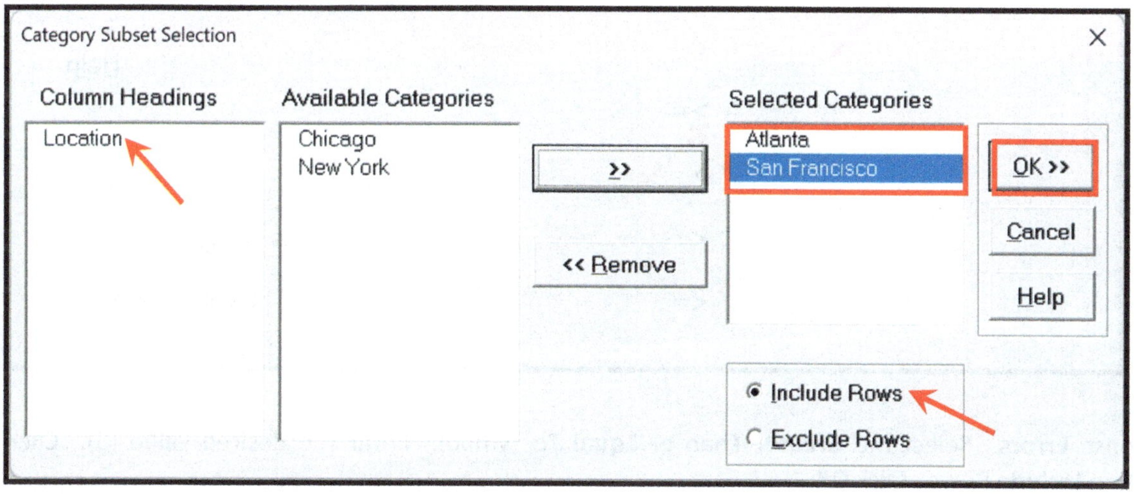

Select Location the choose Atlanta and San Francisco. Click the option **Include Rows**. Click **OK**.

Location	Department	Errors
Atlanta	HR	3
Atlanta	HR	6
Atlanta	Finance	6
Atlanta	Finance	8
Atlanta	Marketing	8
Atlanta	Marketing	4
Atlanta	Engineering	9
Atlanta	Engineering	4
Atlanta	Safety	4
Atlanta	Safety	7
San Francisco	HR	10
San Francisco	HR	7
San Francisco	Finance	10
San Francisco	Finance	10
San Francisco	Marketing	4
San Francisco	Marketing	3
San Francisco	Engineering	10
San Francisco	Engineering	6
San Francisco	Safety	8
San Francisco	Safety	3

A new worksheet; **Category Subset (1)** is created. It includes all rows for Atlanta and San Francisco.

To create a subset based on values, return to the Time Card Error worksheet and select;

SigmaXL > Data Manipulation > Numerical Subset

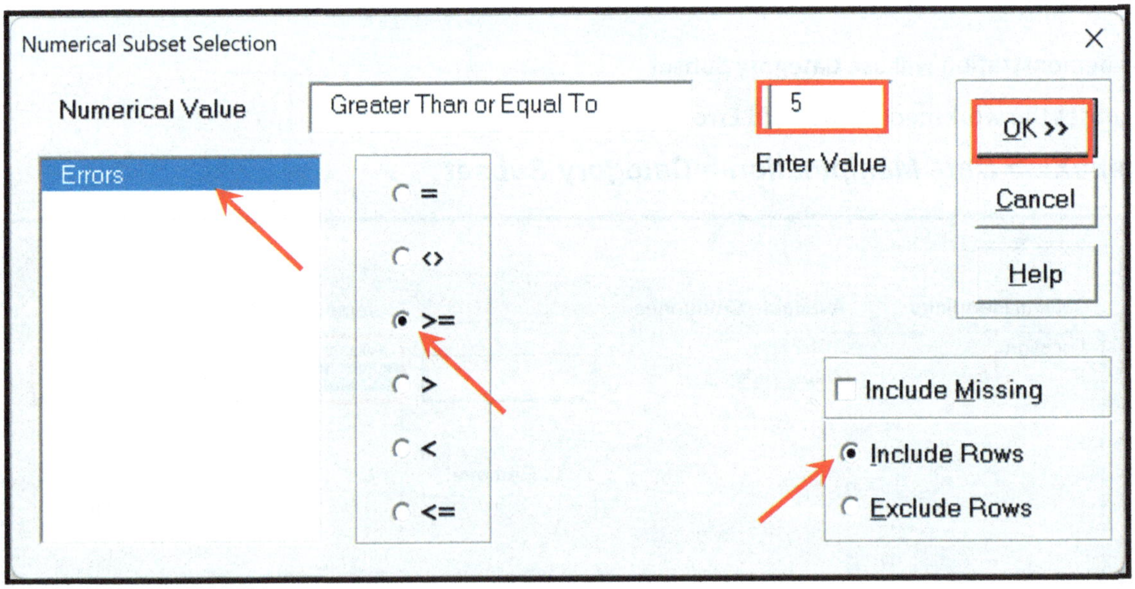

Choose **Errors**. Select the **Greater Than or Equal To** symbol. Enter the desired value (5). Click the option **Include Rows**. Click **OK**.

The new worksheet; **Numerical Subset (1)** is created. It contains all rows with Error values greater than or equal to 5.

Location	Department	Errors
Chicago	HR	11
Chicago	Finance	7
Chicago	Marketing	7
Chicago	Marketing	7
Chicago	Engineering	8
New York	HR	5
New York	HR	6
New York	Finance	7
New York	Finance	6
New York	Marketing	6
New York	Engineering	8
New York	Safety	7
Atlanta	HR	6
Atlanta	Finance	6
Atlanta	Finance	8
Atlanta	Marketing	8
Atlanta	Engineering	9
Atlanta	Safety	7
San Francisco	HR	10
San Francisco	HR	7
San Francisco	Finance	10
San Francisco	Finance	10
San Francisco	Engineering	10
San Francisco	Engineering	6
San Francisco	Safety	8

Columns

Stacking Columns

Columnwise is a format in which each column represents either an output or an input pertaining to the process under investigation.

For instance, look at the cycle time for a particular activity. One approach is to assign each associate to a separate column and populate with his/her data. The columnwise method, on the other hand, would put cycle time data for all operators in one column, with a separate column containing the associate's name or some other designation.

SigmaXL's **Stack Columns** function makes it easy to change a worksheet from being a non-columnwise configuration into a columnwise.

Use the following worksheet to perform these actions.

SigmaXL Worksheet: ***Columns***

The worksheet contains cycle times for 3 associates; each associate is listed in a separate column. To create the columnwise format, the columns must be placed one on top of the other.

Menu command: ***SigmaXL > Data Manipulation > Stack Columns***

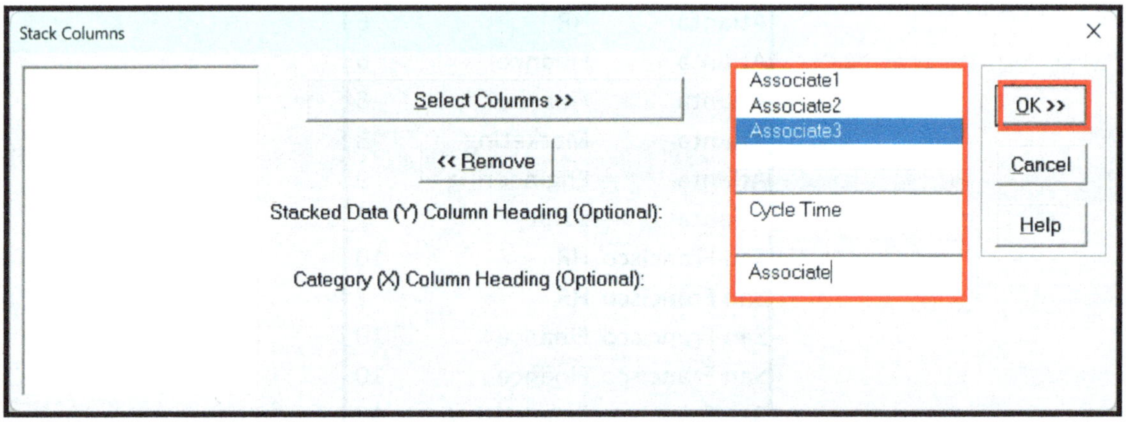

Select the columns to stack (**Associate1**, **Associate2** and **Associate3**).

Add a column heading for the data (**Cycle Time**).

Add a heading for the Category (**Associate**). Click **OK**.

Associate	Cycle Time
Associate1	51
Associate1	54
Associate1	50
Associate1	42
Associate1	49
Associate1	44
Associate1	33
Associate1	32
Associate1	46
Associate1	45
Associate1	37
Associate1	41
Associate1	45

A new worksheet **Stacked (1)** is created. Only the first 13 rows are shown.

Unstack Columns

SigmaXL also offers a method to do the opposite of the stack process. This is the unstack data option. With this method, the designated column is separated into a number of new columns depending upon the number of unique entities in the specified column.

Use the new worksheet **Stacked (1)**.

This command will take the previously stacked Cycle Time information and unstack it based on the associates. (This action will essentially undo the actions performed previously.)

Menu command: ***SigmaXL > Data Manipulation > Unstack Columns***

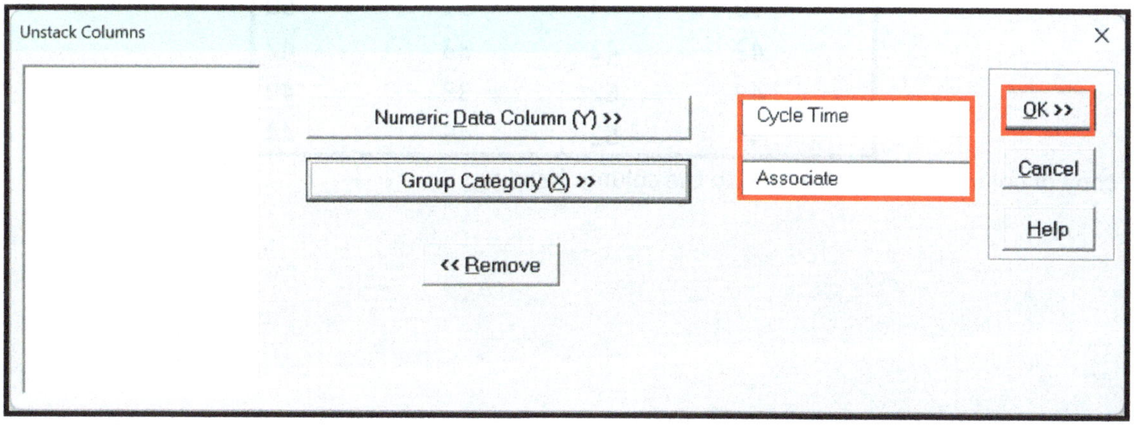

Select **Cycle Time** for the Numeric Data Column (Y).

Select **Associate** for the Group Category (X). Click **OK**.

Here are the first few rows of the final table.

Associate1	Associate2	Associate3
51	41	55
54	34	45
50	44	51
42	42	33
49	62	38
44	52	46
33	50	46
32	36	44

The cycle time information is separated based on the associate.

> ***Hint:** Use caution in selecting the Unstack option. Selecting the wrong **Group Category (X)** column could produce a worksheet with a large number of columns, each with only one or two readings.*

Copy Columns

When a column is copied, the new column contains the same heading as the old. This can lead to confusion with future actions. Once copied, change the heading. This can be accomplished by simply adding a suffix, such as _# (underscore and number) to the column name.

Associate1	Associate2	Associate3	Associate1_1
51	41	55	51
54	34	45	54
50	44	51	50
42	42	33	42
49	62	38	49
44	52	46	44

The copy of column 1 has a _1 added to the column heading.

Format columns

To change the format of cells in a worksheet, highlight the desired cells, then Right-Click and select ***Format Cells***.

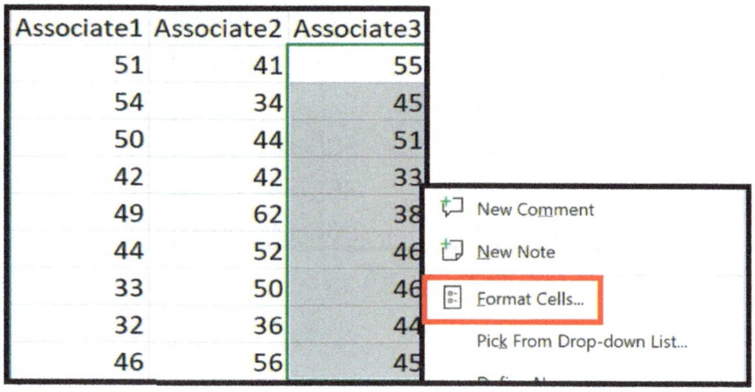

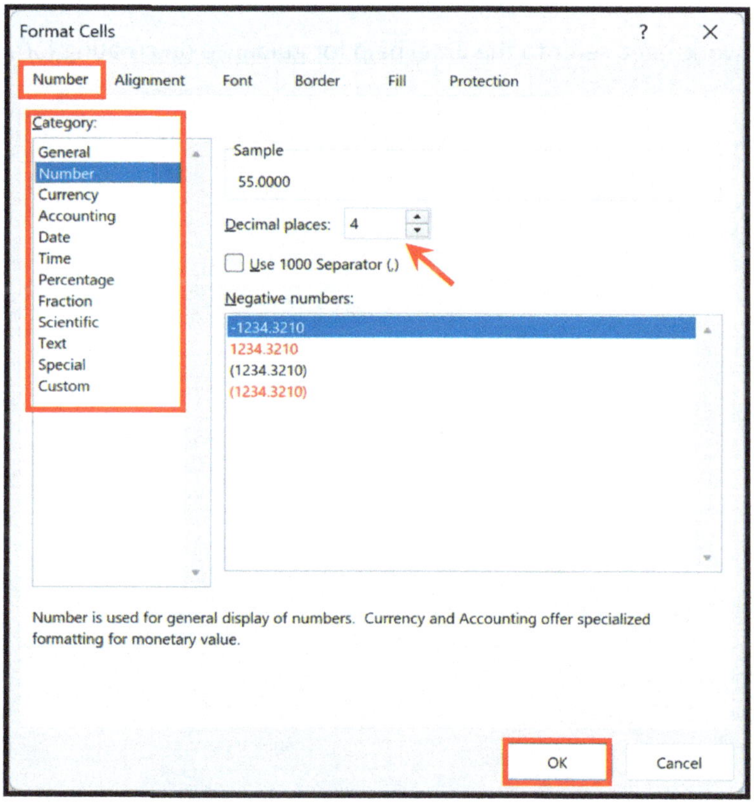

Select **Number**, then choose the Category (**Number**).

Finally, make the desired changes (**Decimal places - 4**) then click **OK**.

Associate1	Associate2	Associate3
51	41	55.0000
54	34	45.0000
50	44	51.0000
42	42	33.0000
49	62	38.0000
44	52	46.0000
33	50	46.0000
32	36	44.0000
46	56	45.0000

The cells are reformatted.

Assigning Formulas

Formulas may be assigned to single cells, or whole columns.

Since these are Excel worksheet, refer to the Excel help for guidance on creating formulas.

Random Data

Columns of data based on different distributions are useful in simulations or '(**what – if**') scenarios. To create random data, select: ***SigmaXL > Data Manipulation > Random Data***.

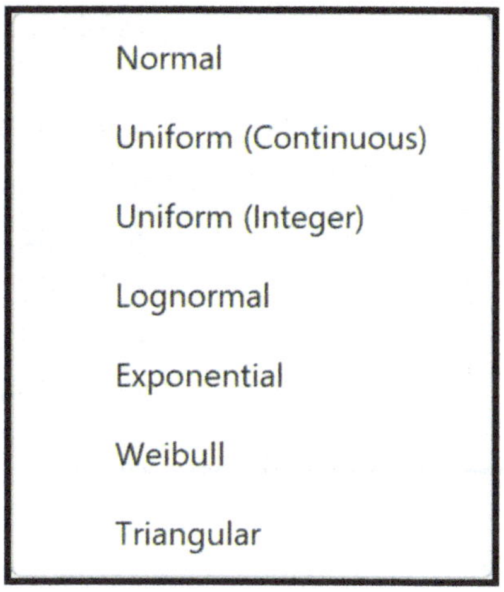

Select the desired distribution (**Weibull** for this demonstration).

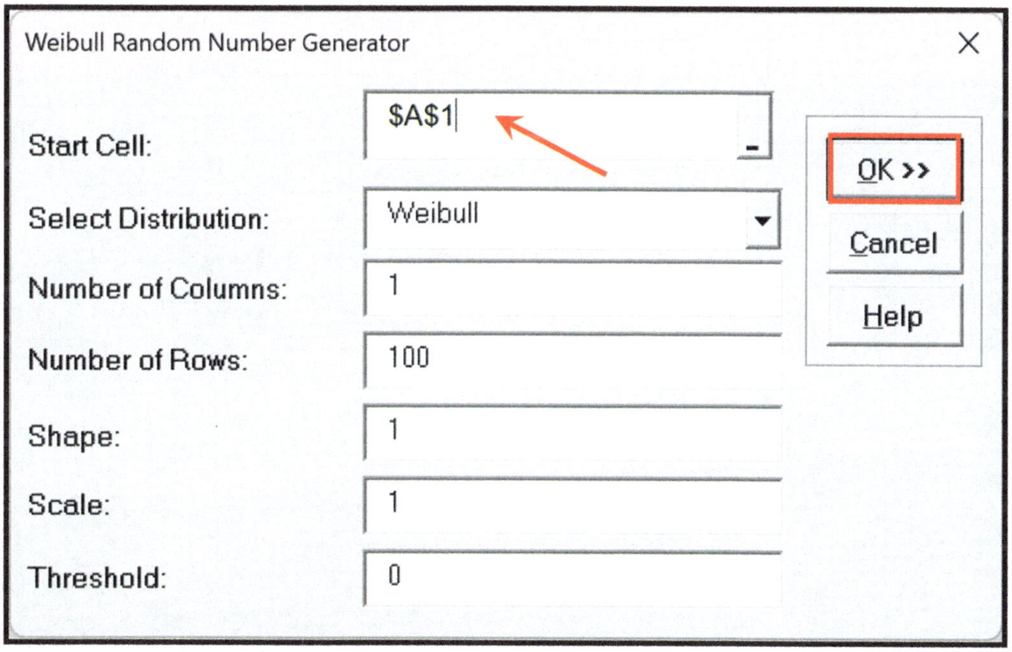

Fill in the required information then click **OK**.

A new worksheet with the random numbers is created. (**SigmaXL Random Data (1)**)

1. Weibull Shape: 1 Scale: 1 Thresh: 0
0.303525159
0.302171369
1.370943179
1.142984656
4.906421028
0.282471938
0.651231676
0.519504007
0.106380275

Copy the data to the desired worksheet.

Data Manipulation

SigmaXL allows data manipulations in many different forms. This section covers the following:

- Convert to Discrete
- Text to Numeric
- Standardize Data

SigmaXL Worksheet: ***Data Manipulation***

Convert to Discrete

If numeric data appears in a column left justified and the column heading has a **–T**, SigmaXL considers the values to be text and no statistical analysis is possible. This issue often appears if a file is opened from another program into SigmaXL.

Select; ***SigmaXL > Data Manipulation > Convert to Discrete***

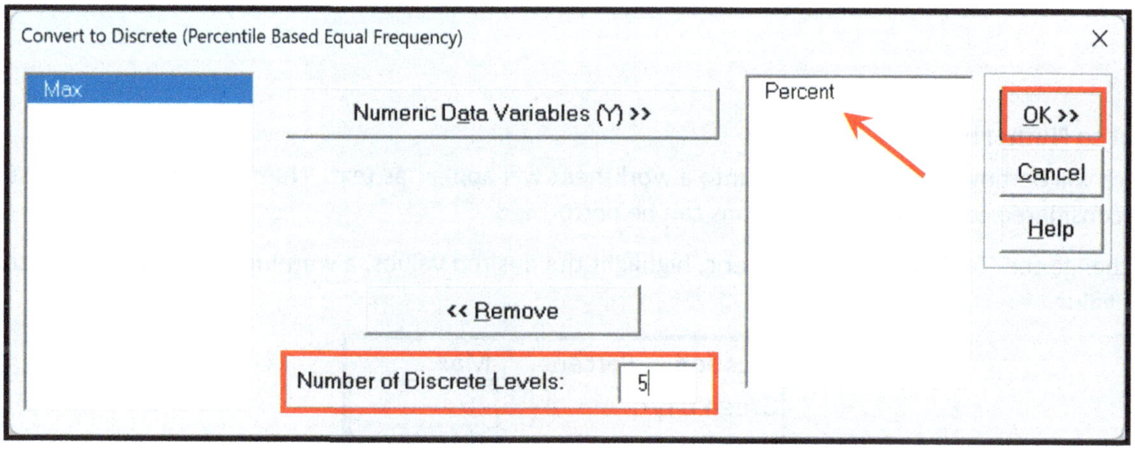

Select **Percent** for the Numeric Data Variables (Y).

Set the Number of Discrete Levels to **5**. Click **OK**.

To correct this issue, change the data type.

The new worksheet, **Convert to Discrete (1),** contains the original column of data plus the associated

Percent	Percent_discrete
4.5	3
6	4
2.3	1
8	4
4.2	2
3.1	2
4.5	3
6	4

Percent_discrete. This column indicates which group the value falls into.

Text to Numeric

There will be times that data copied into a worksheet will appear as text. Numbers that are left justified are considered text, and no calculations can be performed.

To change the 'Text' number to numeric, highlight the desired values, a warning sign appears next to the first value.

Location	Percent	Max
Green Bay	.5	40
Green Bay	6	34
Boston	2.3	42
Boston	8	47
Austin	4.2	55
Austin	3.1	32
Seattle	4.5	48

When the cursor is placed over this sign, a pull-down option appears. Open the pull-down and select **Convert to Number**.

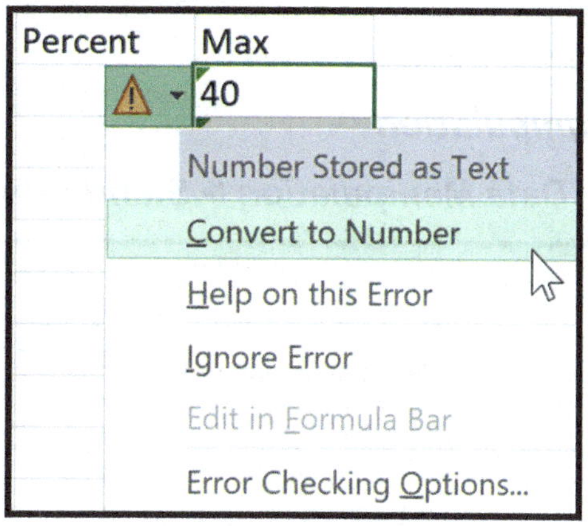

Values are now right-justified, and therefore they are considered to be numeric values.

Location	Percent	Max
Green Bay	4.5	40
Green Bay	6	34
Boston	2.3	42
Boston	8	47
Austin	4.2	55
Austin	3.1	32
Seattle	4.5	48
Seattle	6	72

Standardize Data

Standardizing Data provides two options. The first uses the data mean and standard deviation, the second simply identifies the highest value as 1, and the lowest as -1. It will then give the remaining values their appropriate value based on the -1 to 1 scale.

SigmaXL Worksheet: ***Data Manipulation***

Menu command: ***SigmaXL > Data Manipulation > Standardize Data***

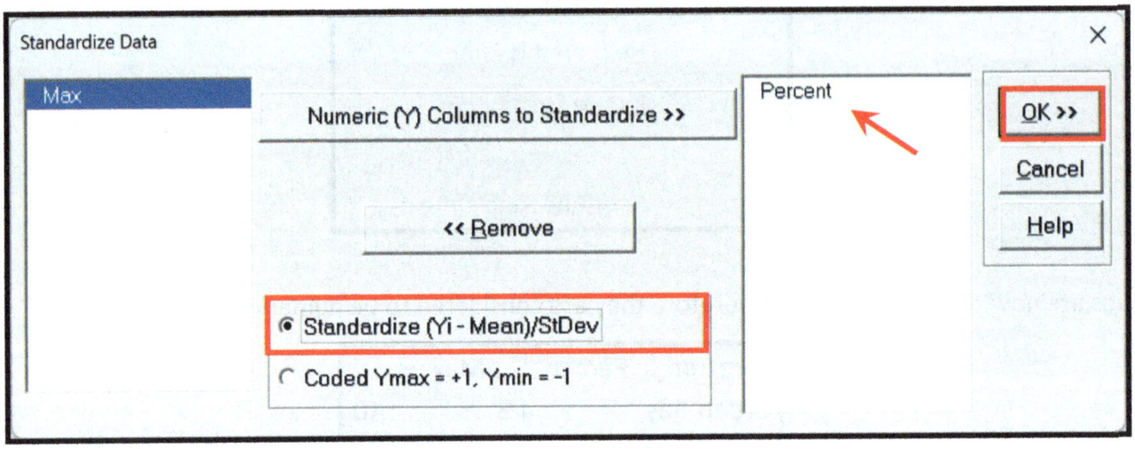

Select **Percent** as the Numeric (Y) Columns to Standardize. Choose the first option. Click **OK**.

A new tab is created, **Standardize (1)**. The worksheet shows the original values and the results of the standardization.

Percent	Percent_Standardize
4.5	-0.100464961
6	0.690078997
2.3	-1.259929434
8	1.744137608
4.2	-0.258573753

Repeat this process with the second option:

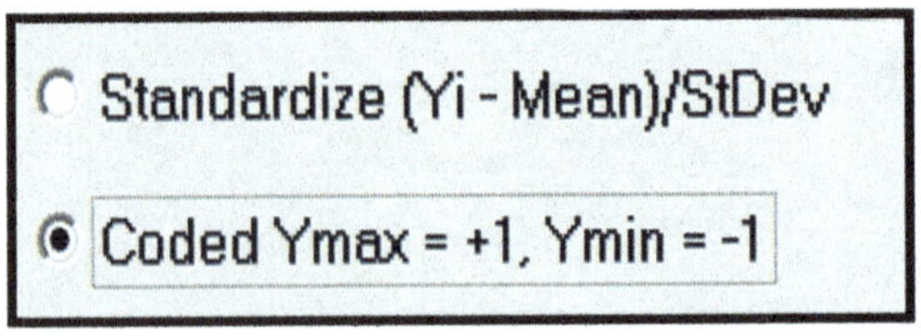

Percent	Percent_Coded
4.5	-0.147058824
6	0.294117647
2.3	-0.794117647
8	0.882352941
4.2	-0.235294118
3.1	-0.558823529
4.5	-0.147058824
6	0.294117647
2.1	-0.852941176
7.5	0.735294118
4.2	-0.235294118
4	-0.294117647
4.5	-0.147058824
6.3	0.382352941
1.6	-1
8	0.882352941
4.6	-0.117647059
3.1	-0.558823529
4.5	-0.147058824
5.7	0.205882353
2.3	-0.794117647
8.4	1
4.2	-0.235294118
3.7	-0.382352941
4.5	-0.147058824
6.9	0.558823529
2.3	-0.794117647
7.1	0.617647059
5	0
2.8	-0.647058824
5.7	0.205882353
2.5	-0.735294118

The maximum value of 8.4 is coded with a 1. The minimum value of 1.6 is coded with a -1. The value 5 is coded 0, because it is half way between 1.6 and 8.4. The other values are provided values that relate their relative position between -1 and 1.

Hot Keys

There are 2 important **Hot Keys** in SigmaXL. They are **F3** and **F4**.

Command	Keys	Description
Recall Last Dialog Box	F3	Displays the last used Dialog Box. (May require Fn+F3 on some computers.)
Activate Last Sheet	F4	Returns user to the last active worksheet. (May require Fn+F4 on some computers.

Define Phase

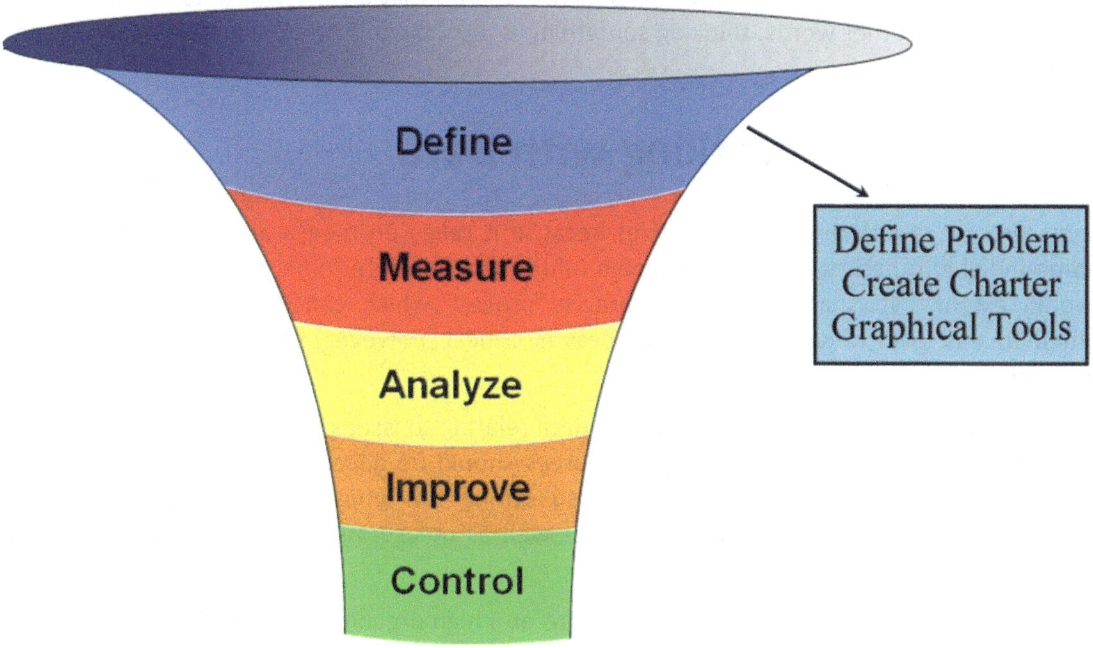

Define Phase

Six Sigma practitioners believe this is the critical phase of any Six Sigma project. Why? Because selecting the right project and accurately scoping that project form the basic foundation for the ultimate success of the project. This is also the phase where those new to Six Sigma first encounter a major difference between Six Sigma and other process improvement methodologies.

In the past, organizations relied on 'gut feelings' and anecdotal observations as the primary sources of information to create a project definition. Perhaps this method occasionally bore fruit, but in the majority of cases it likely caused the entire project to go astray. The issue is that 'gut feelings' and anecdotal observations are simply not reliable sources of information on which to base a critical improvement project. In other words, thinking something is a problem is one thing, being able to show it with data is something else.

Working with Data

The Six Sigma process is different (and effective) because it relies on measurable data. This usually requires some initial and basic analysis of available information to determine where a problem exists and its overall extent. It is a detailed and precise process which can be frustrating for those unaccustomed to this level of scrutiny. The process is critical, however, to accurately defining the problem at hand.

In the Define phase, team efforts focus on exploring data relating to issues within an organization. This allows the team to determine where and how resources should be allocated to produce the desired improvements. Specific metrics are also established during this phase, allowing for an accurate determination of the business case for proceeding as well as measuring the ultimate success of the project.

While the initial project selection process typically begins at a high organizational level, it is then scoped down to a level appropriate for either a Black Belt or Green Belt to pursue. An effective method often used to aid in scoping a project is to create a series of graphs based on available data. Graphs are an excellent visual representation of the information under investigation. They allow team participants to observe the information in new ways.

In addition, graphs can demonstrate clearly whether there have been recent changes in the metric, and/or if the variation in the metric are due to a second factor. Graphs are also used to visualize and demonstrate whether changes in the process instituted by the team have improved or degraded the metric. This chapter includes samples of several different graphs using SigmaXL.

Project Charter

Following project definition, the next step is to create a Project Charter. A project charter is a written road map, used to define the issues identified and clearly state how the team will proceed through the project.

There are many different types and styles of project charters, but they all have similar requirements and specific components.

State the Practical Problem under consideration. It is important for every improvement team to understand exactly what it is they are working on, and defining the **Practical Problem** is one way of achieving this objective. This is where the basic issue at hand is explained and described.

2. Project Description: what is the "Practical Problem"	Problem and goal statement (project's purpose)

Examples might include:

- Customers are dissatisfied with our on-time delivery.
- Department 47 creates too much scrap.
- Invoices have too many errors.
- Customers complain about the wait times when they call in.
- Claims take too long to process.

Next, each general issue needs a; **Problem and goal statement**.

Using the examples above, potential statements include:

- Customer on-time delivery is currently averaging 74%. The goal of this project is to raise the on-time delivery to 95%.
- Department 47's scrap costs are 33% of sales. The goal of this project is to reduce this to 10% of sales.
- The current 12.8% of the invoices have errors. The goal of this project is to reduce this to 1%.
- The current customer wait time is 5.5 minutes. The goal of this project is to reduce the wait time to 45 seconds.
- The current claims process takes 21 days. The goal of this project is to reduce the claims process to 5 days.

Assign Metrics to the problem. At this point, each general issue must also have a metric assigned to it that ties into the overall practical problem. Using the examples above, potential metrics might include:

- Measure Percent on-time delivery, or actual time to deliver.
- Measure scrap as a percent of product or as a gross weight.
- Measure the number of errors per invoice, or the number of errors per line on an invoice.
- Measure customer's wait times.
- Measure time to process a claim.

3. Objective:	What improvement is targeted and what will be the impact on Rolled Throughput Yield (RTY), Cost of Poor Quality (COPQ) and Capability index C-P, back orders, costs? The "Statistical Problem" - the measurable variable(s	Project Y's	Baseline	GOAL	Entitlement	units
		Metric 1				%
		Metric 2				$/A
		Metric 3				units/A

The Charter includes three categories of metrics: baseline (the current situation), goal (the level that indicates a successful project) and entitlement (the best that can be expected or perfection). Along with the critical metrics, another type of metric is important to consider. These are referred to as **secondary** metrics. Secondary metrics are those that the team needs to keep-an-eye on. For instance, if a team is tasked with reducing a cycle time by 30%, their secondary metric would be defects. It's easy to reduce cycle times if defect levels are allowed to soar. So, in this case, whatever is the defect's baseline, this would also be the goal. By reducing cycle time, the team cannot allow the defects to increase.

Use the first project as an example, where the primary metric is on-time delivery. This primary metric could be improved by sending out partial shipments or keeping a large inventory of finished goods on hand and available for shipping. Stepping back from the primary metric, however, neither of these solutions is acceptable because they would create other, much greater problems elsewhere in the organization. Therefore, a secondary metric might include: inventory levels, or percent shipments complete.

For another example, look at the third project where the primary metric is measuring the number of errors per invoice. This primary metric could be improved by ensuring multiple individuals inspect each invoice, but again, this solution is not acceptable. It would greatly increase the cycle time for each invoice, causing a negative impact elsewhere in the organization. The secondary metrics in this case could be: cycle time and man-hours per invoice.

Refine the Project Scope. At this point in the process, many projects are far too broad to be accomplished within the target of four to six months. The scope is simply too large and must be reduced, generally by performing some preliminary analysis on primary metric. Simple graphs are quite useful in helping to refine the scope of a project.

6. Project Scope:	Which part of the process will be investigated and excluded.

Scope reduction begins with looking at data taken from the process in question, or from customer surveys if applicable. If this kind of data is not readily available then the team should start collecting it.

Examples of useful types of data to collect include;

- Cycle times
- Defects
- Count of issues
- Sales volume
- Number of new clients per month

Before data analysis can begin, it is important to determine the critical metrics. Critical metrics come from internal customers (individuals or groups within a company who receive or are affected by a process output) or external customers (those who receive the output of a process but are not part of the company). Once critical metrics are determined and data is gathered, the team can determine if the results indicate a problem does indeed exist.

It is important to remember that during this Define phase, only an initial assessment is performed. More detailed analyses occur later on in the Measure and Analyze phase; it is these later analyses that will associate specific critical inputs (X's) with the critical outputs (Y's), allowing proactive process control to occur.

The Define phase, then, should set in motion the path to improvement.

Graphs

Graphs are critical to the Define phase because they are quite often the best way to analyze data related to the processes under investigation. Of course, there are many different methods for analyzing preliminary data, and Six Sigma teams should not hesitate to use other methods as well. However, graphs are particularly useful because they add a visual component to the process.

No single graph is right for every occasion and situation, so the team should have a good understanding of:

a) different kinds of graphs, and

b) when and where it is appropriate to use each type of graph.

This portion for the Define section will discuss the following types of graphs:

- Dot Plot
- Histogram
- Box Plot
- Scatter Plot
- Run Chart
- I-MR Chart
- Pareto Plot

Dot Plot

Tool Use

Use a Dot Plot to display data values within bins. It provides an excellent visual representation for the data set's center and range. It also provides a satisfactory indication for the shape of the distribution.

Data Type: A Dot Plot requires numeric data

Worksheet: **Tear**

The data represents the tear strength of a new material from different vendors.

Menu command: ***SigmaXL > Graphical Tools > Dotplots***

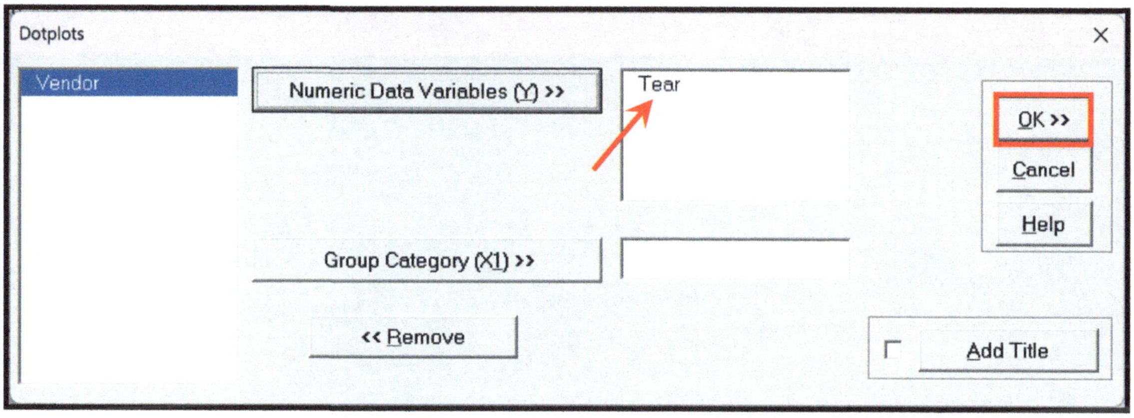

Select Tear for the Numeric Data Variable (Y). Click OK.

A new tab is created, labeled **Dotplot (1)**.

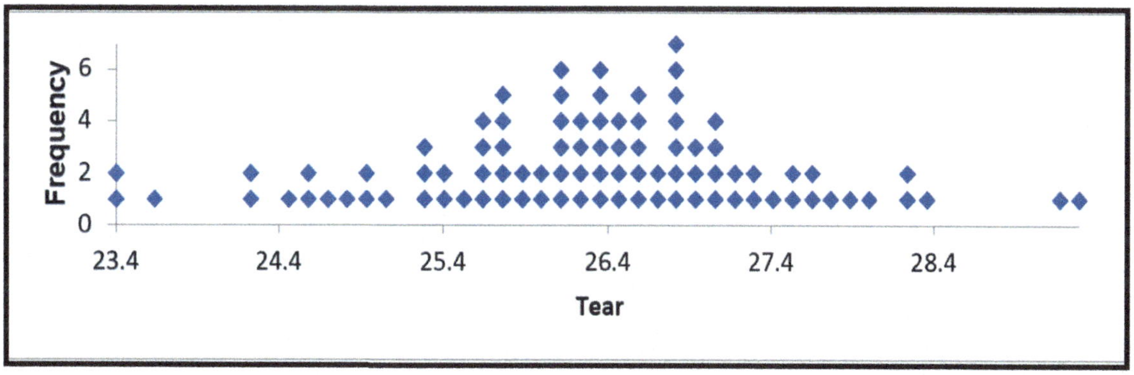

The X-axis is divided into bins. Each dot represents a value within that bin. If more than one value falls within the bin, the dots are stacked upon one another.

The graph shows the approximate range. The minimum is approximately 23.4 and the maximum is approximately 29.0. Therefore, the range is approximately 29.0 – 23.4 = 5.6.

An estimate for the center is approximately 26.5.

Following an initial look at the process data, it might be desirable to determine if the vendors have different tear values. To accomplish this, it is necessary to show which values are associated with which vendors.

The Vendor information is in column A. There are three Vendors. If they have different tear values, a graph showing each vendor's values next to one another would be useful. A **Dot Plot** showing this information is an option.

Dot Plot with Groups

Menu command: ***SigmaXL > Graphical Tools > Dotplots***

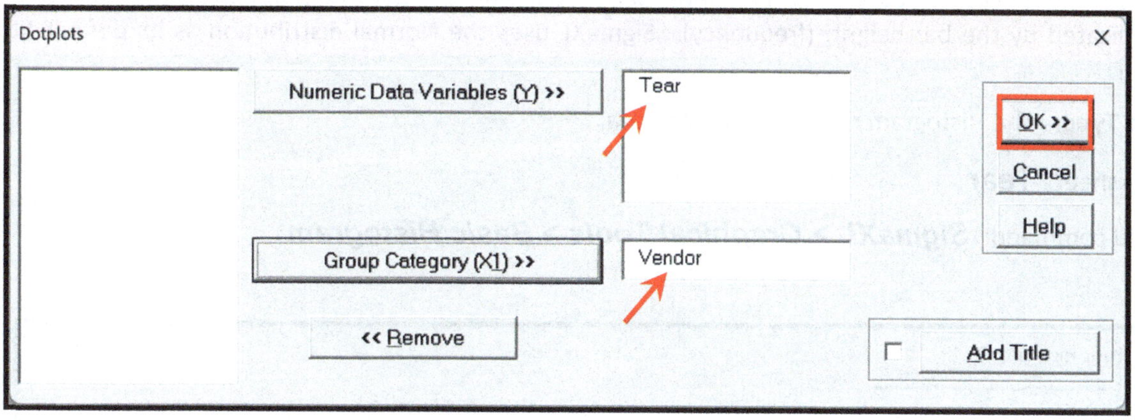

Select **Tear** for the **Numeric Data Variables (Y)**, then select **Vendor** as the **Group Category (X1)**. Click **OK**. A new tab **Dotplot (2)** is created.

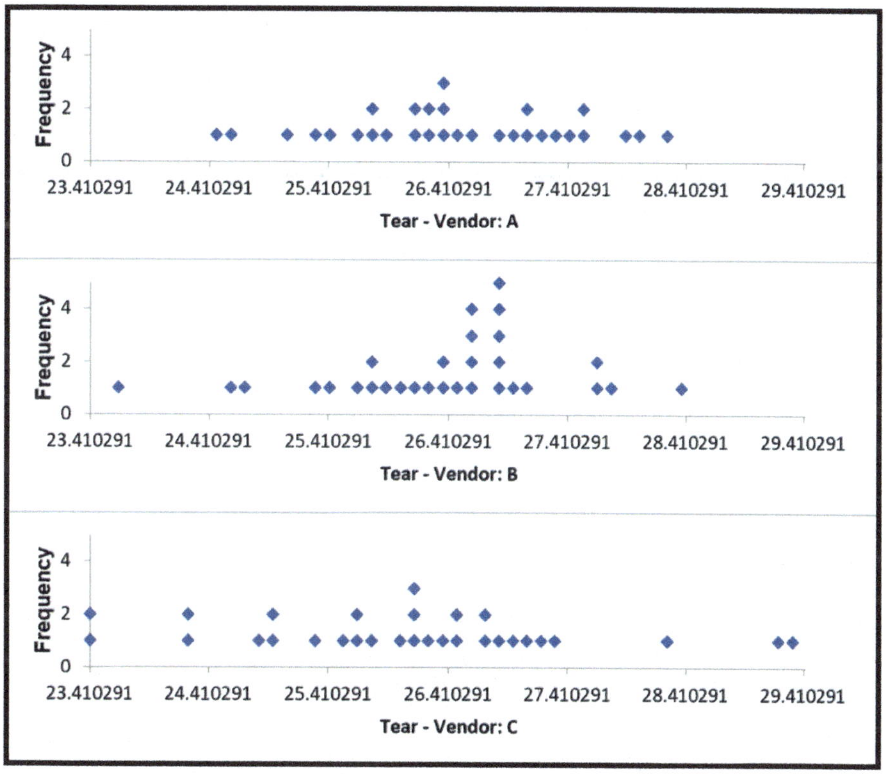

The graph shows the same information as the original Dotplot, only now the data is separated by Vendor.

Histogram

Tool Use: Use a Histogram to show the general shape, center and spread of data. It does not provide individual data values. Data are binned into non-overlapping groups. The number of values in each bin is indicated by the bar height, (frequency). SigmaXL uses the Normal distribution as its default fitted curve.

Data Type: The Histogram requires numeric data.

Worksheet: **Tear**

Menu command: ***SigmaXL > Graphical Tools > Basic Histogram***

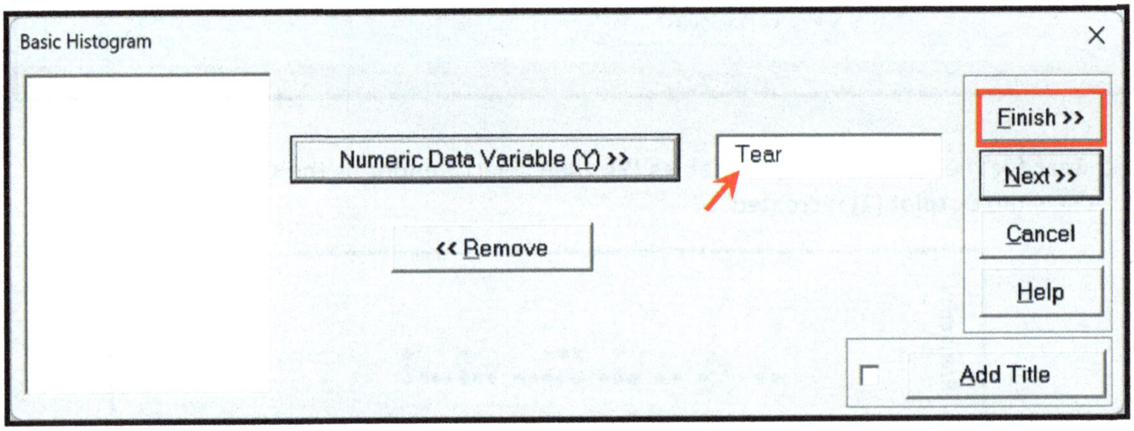

Select Tear for the Numeric Data Variable (Y). Click OK.

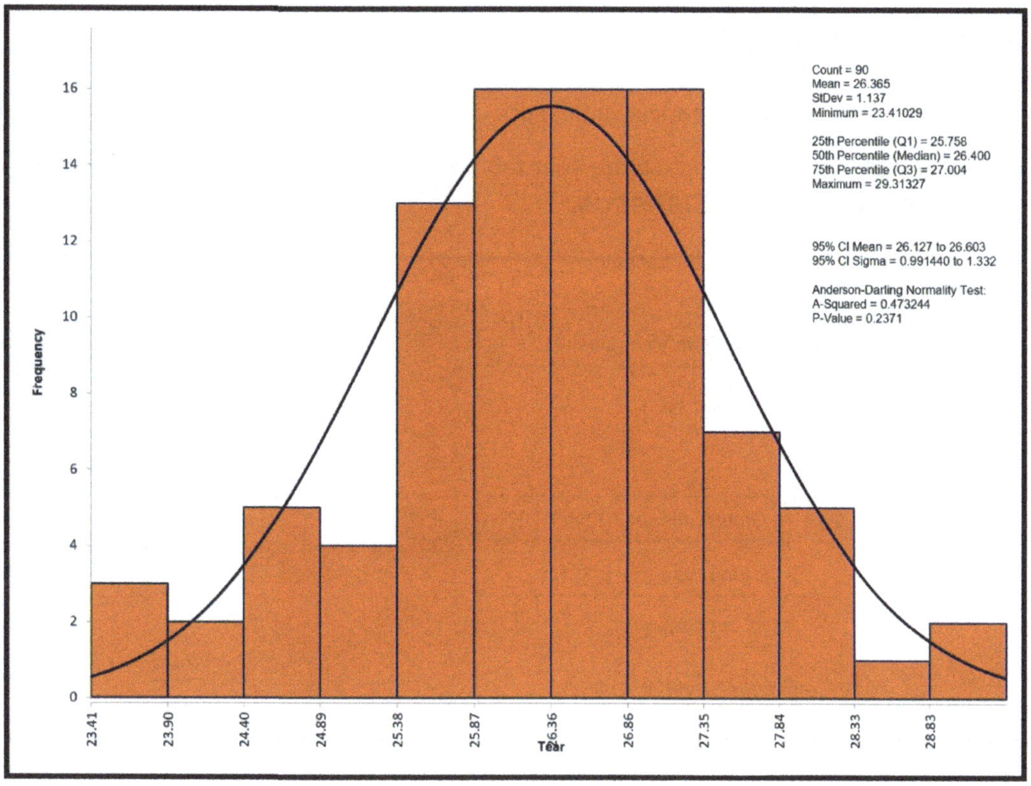

The histogram with summary information is displayed in a new tab.

The summary information is shown below. Details regarding these values are discussed throughout the book.

Count = 90
Mean = 26.365
StDev = 1.137
Minimum = 23.41029

25th Percentile (Q1) = 25.758
50th Percentile (Median) = 26.400
75th Percentile (Q3) = 27.004
Maximum = 29.31327

95% CI Mean = 26.127 to 26.603
95% CI Sigma = 0.991440 to 1.332

Anderson-Darling Normality Test:
A-Squared = 0.473244
P-Value = 0.2371

Histogram with Groups

Histograms can be split using a categorical value, such as Vendors. This allows for direct comparisons.

To divide a histogram by group, return to the Tear tab and select: ***SigmaXL > Graphical Tools > Histogram and Descriptive Statistics.***

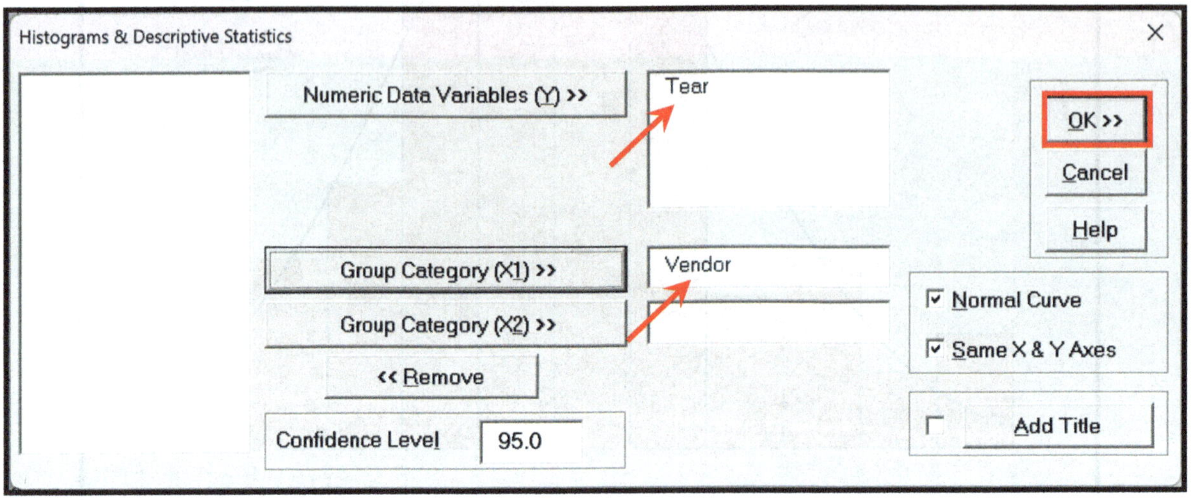

Select **Tear** for the **Numeric Data Variable (Y)**, and **Vendor** for the **Group Category (X1)** value. Leave the other options as shown. Click **OK**.

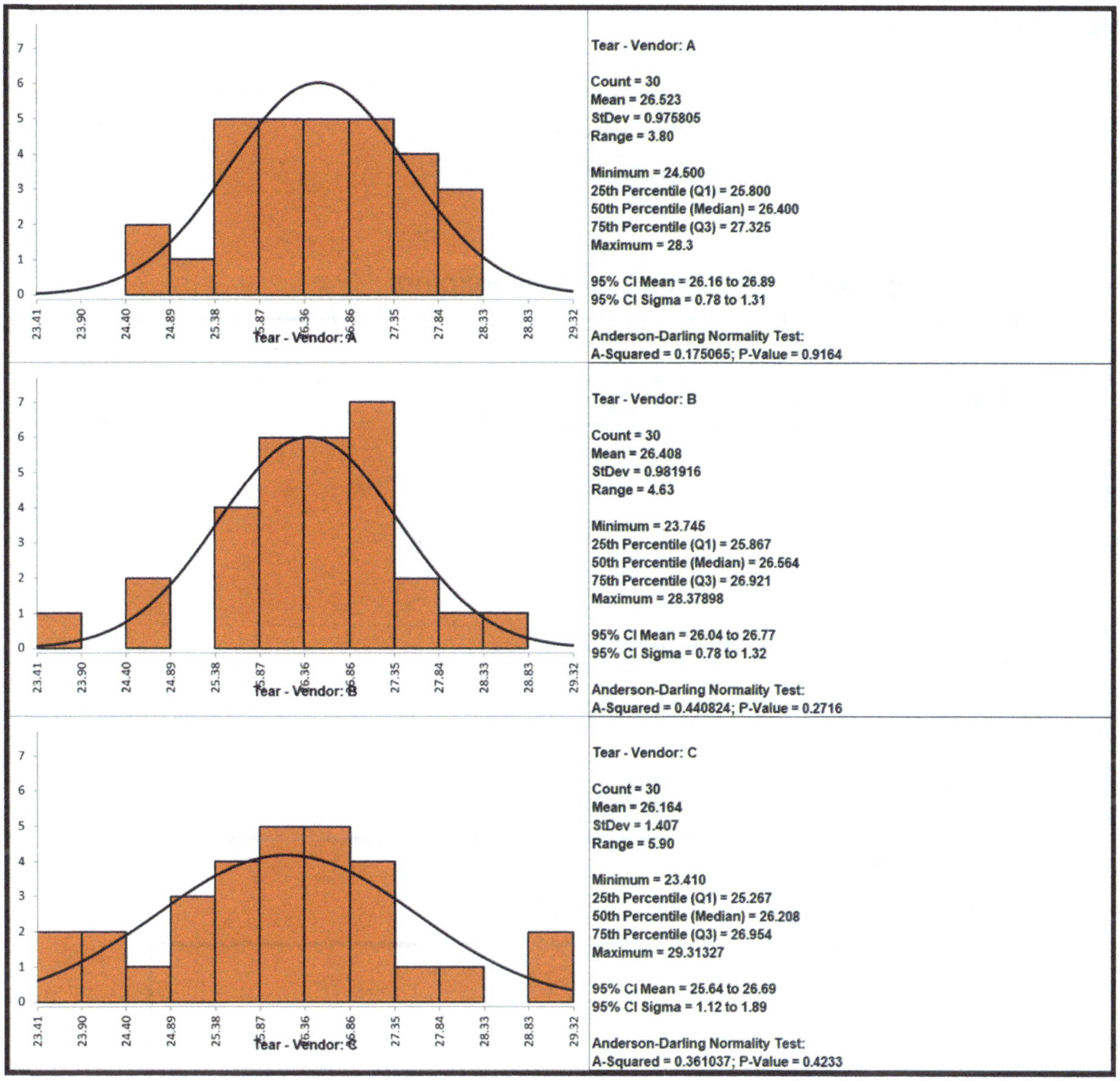

Using the same X and Y axes, allows for a direct comparison for each vendor.

Hint: Basic Histogram vs. Histogram and Descriptive Statistics:

The **Basic Histogram** option allows the user to control the Bin Width, Starting Value, Number of Bins, whether the Descriptive Statistics are shown, but does not allow for groups.

The **Histogram with Descriptive Statistics** allows for grouping, but not customization of the graph.

If customization is not required, the **Basic Histogram** can be created using the **Histogram with**

Box Plot

Tool Use Box Plots are considered a 5-value summary of the data. The 5 values are the; Minimum, 1st quartile, Median (2nd quartile), 3rd quartile and Maximum.

Data Type: Box Plots requires numeric data.

Worksheet: **Tear**

Menu command: ***SigmaXL > Graphical Tools > Boxplots***

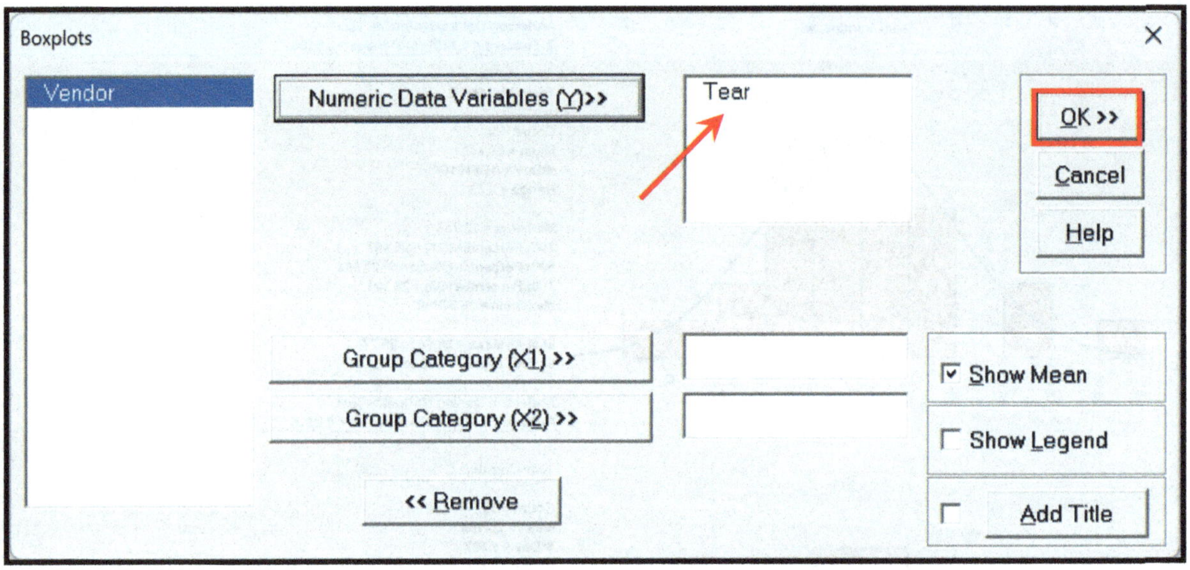

Input Tear as the Numeric Data Variables (Y). Click OK.

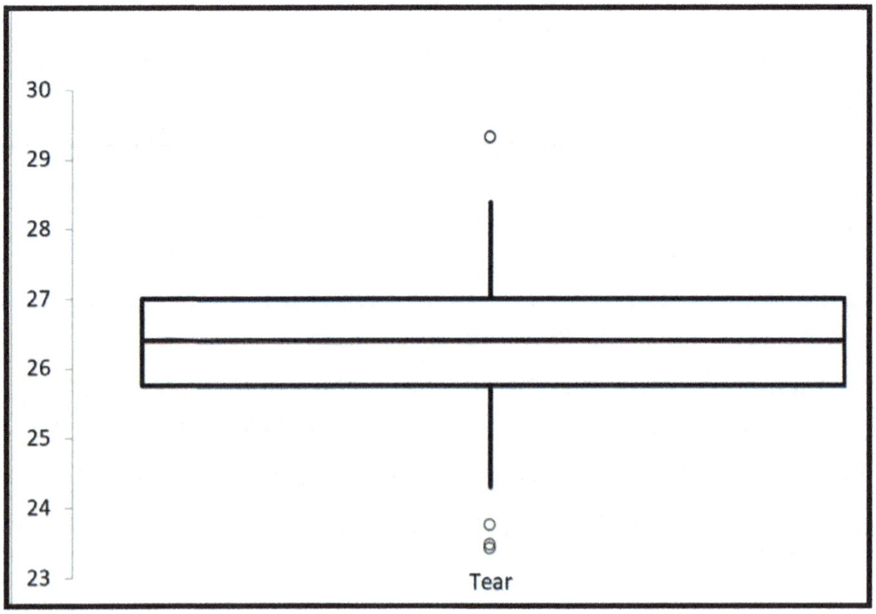

The Box Plot (also known as a Box and Whiskers plot) is so named because the design forms a box representing the middle 50% of the data.

The upper portion of the box represents the value below which 75% of the data resides.

The line inside the box represents the Median (the middle or 50% value).

The bottom portion of the box is the value below which 25% of the data resides.

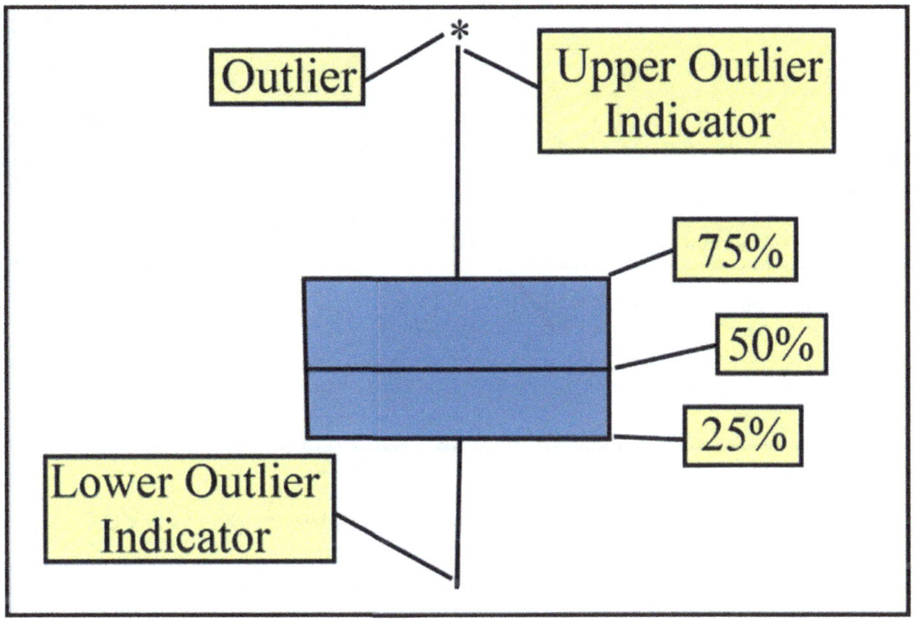

The whiskers extend to the upper and lower values, unless the value extends beyond the predetermined limit referred to as the **outlier indicator**.

Any value beyond a length of 1.5 times the box height (referred to as the **IQR** or **Inner Quartile Range**) will be considered an outlier.

Remember this is a designation only. An outlier does not refer to a bad or incorrect value, only one that is different than the rest of the values in the data set.

Outliers should be investigated to be sure an error wasn't made in the recording or collection of the value.

Box Plots with Groups

The Box Plot will also display different groups of data for a side-by-side comparison.

Menu command: ***SigmaXL > Graphical Tools > Boxplots***

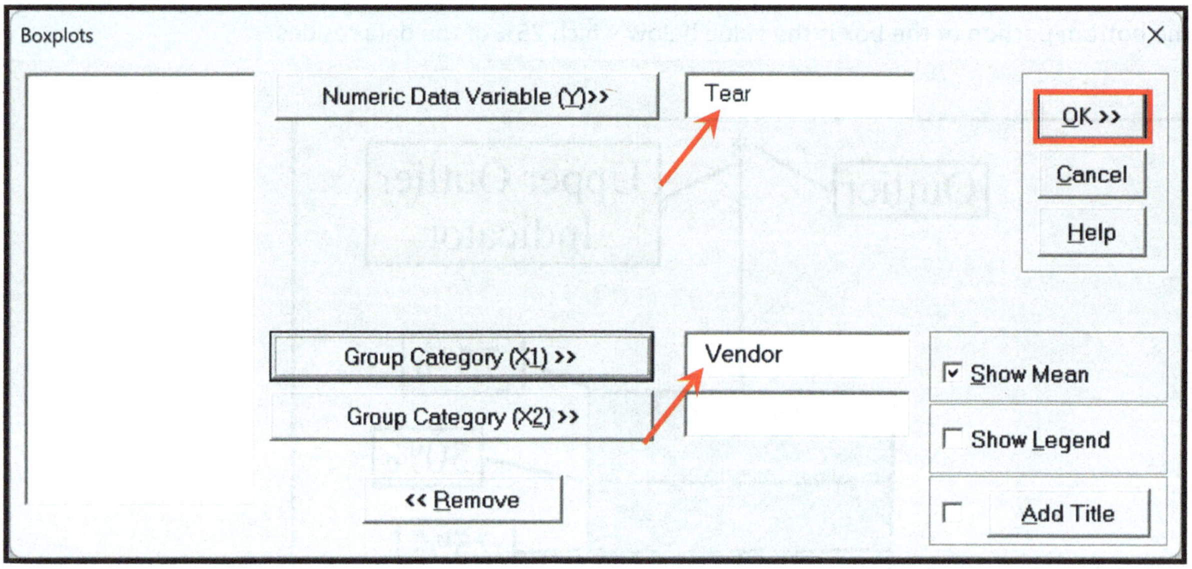

Input Tear as the Numeric Data Variable (Y). Select Vendor for the Group Category (X1). Click OK.

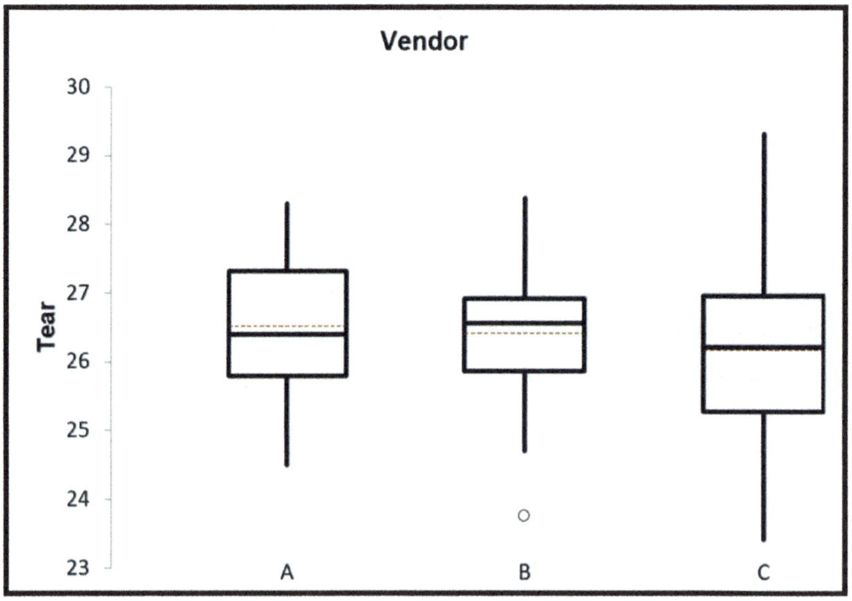

The Box Plots are displayed side by side for easy comparison.

The analytical tools to make this determination are covered in the Analyze chapter.

Run Chart

Tool Use: The Run Chart displays data in time sequence. It will display shifts, trends or cyclic events that might help the team determine sources of variation.

Note: SigmaXL assumes data is arranged in a time sequence from earliest to recent.

Data Type: The Time Series Plot requires numeric data.

Worksheet: ***Start Up***

Menu command: ***SigmaXL > Graphical Tools > Run Chart***

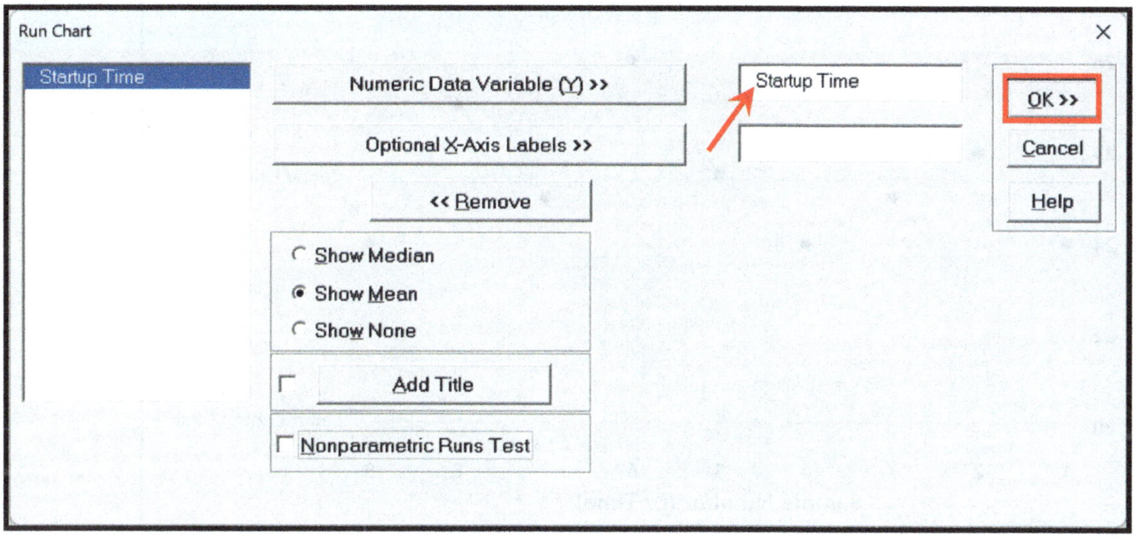

Select **Startup Time** as the **Numeric Data Variable (Y)**. Select the other options as shown, then click **OK**.

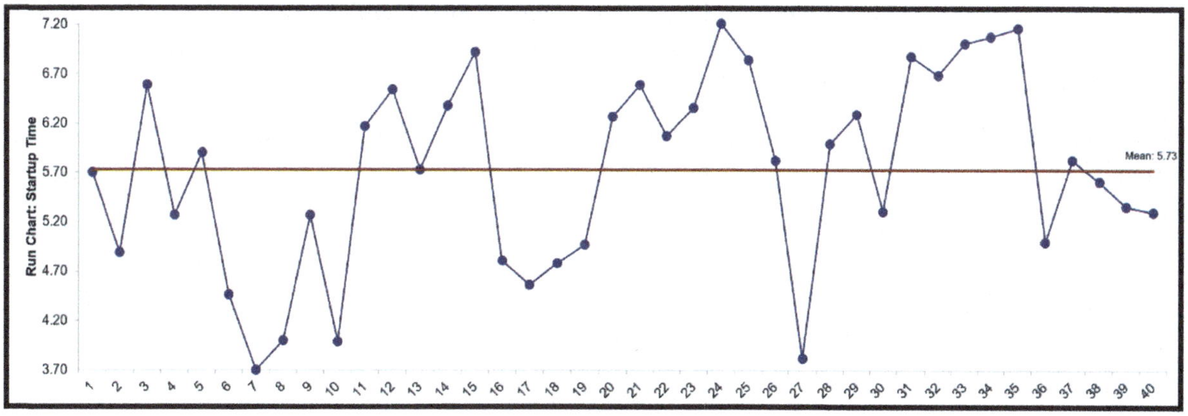

The user must look at this data verses past data to see if changes have occurred in the process.

Individuals Control Chart

Tool Use: The Individuals Control Chart mimics the Time Series Plot, but contains two additional lines.

Data Type: This Chart requires numeric data.

This is an example of an **Individuals Control Chart**:

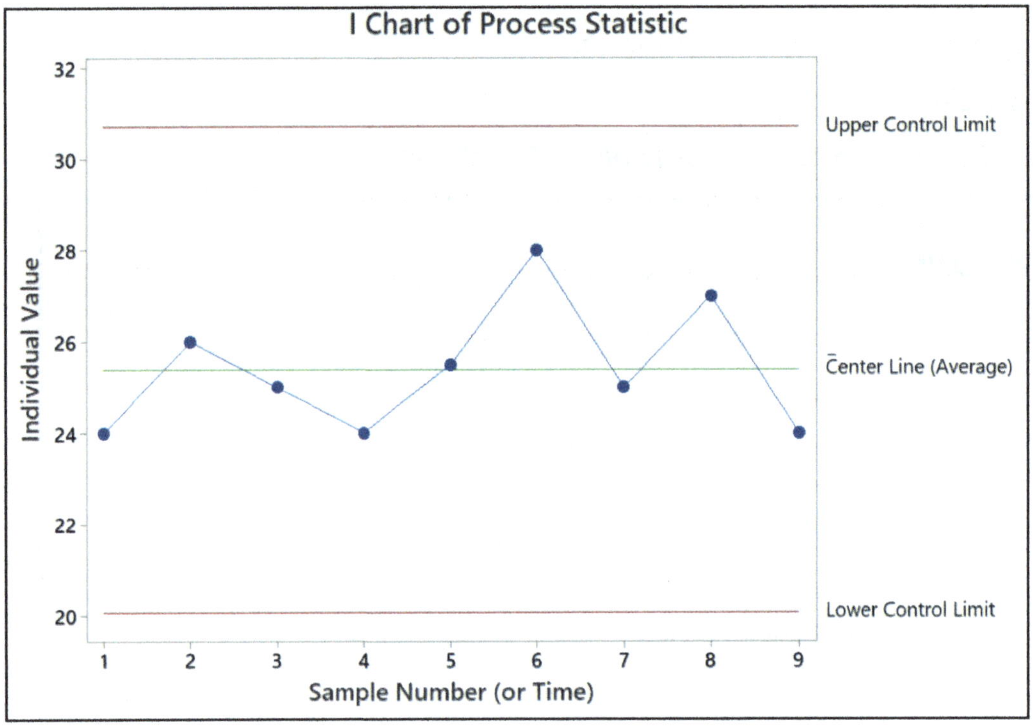

The **Center line** is the average of the selected values. It is expected that the values follow a random pattern around the Center Line.

The upper and lower lines are called the **Upper** and **Lower Control Limits**. These values are calculated based on the sample data. The lines represent the values between which almost 100% (99.73% to be exact) of the values are expected to reside.

Values outside of these limits indicate a potentially abnormal condition existed during those time periods.

Creating an Individuals Chart

Worksheet: ***Start Up***

Menu command: ***SigmaXL > Control Charts > Individuals***

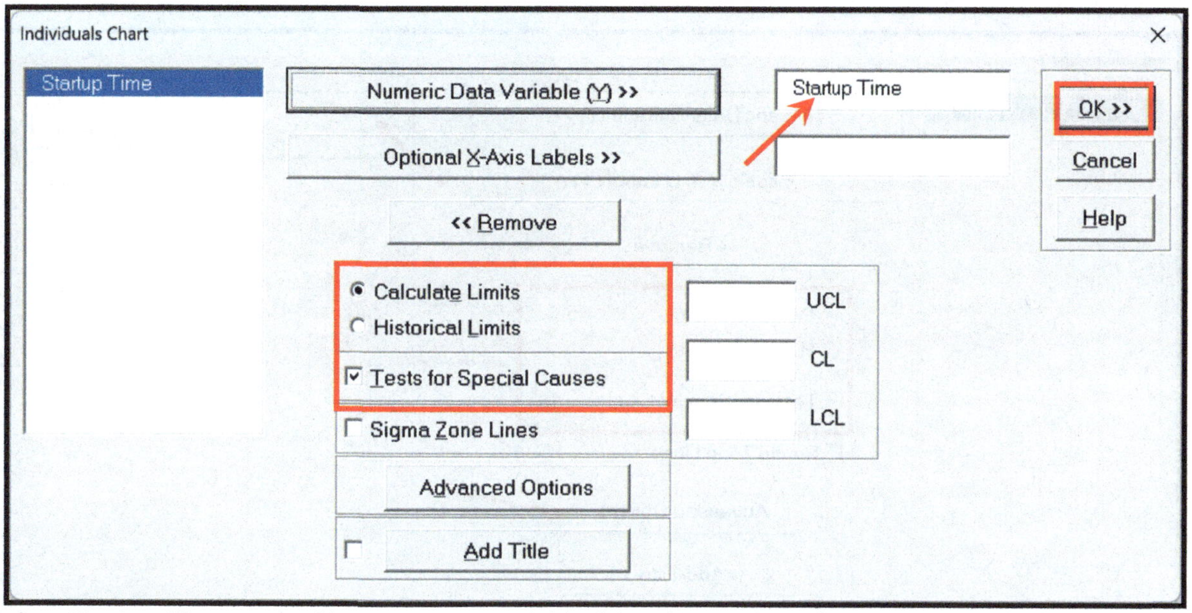

Select **Startup Time** as the Numeric Data Variable (Y). Choose the other options as shown, then click **OK.**

The Individuals Chart looks like a Time Series Plot with the addition of the Control Limits.

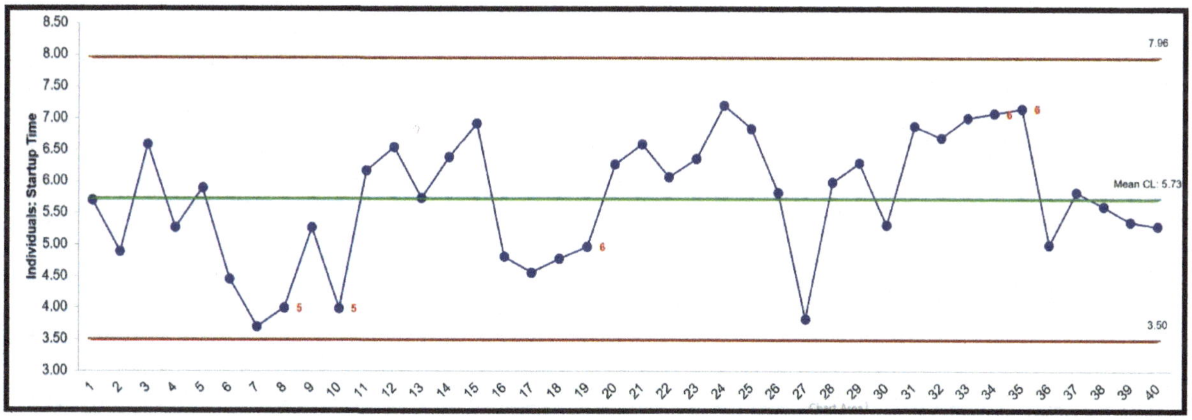

Note: Refer to the **Control** Chapter for detailed information regarding Control Charts.

For now, simply understand that any point above the upper red line, the Upper Control Limit (UCL) or below the lower red line, the Lower Control Limit (LCL) indicates a possible issue during that time period.

In this example, several values are above the UCL; these points should be investigated.

Another advantage of the Individuals chart is the ability to compare groups. In the Startup Time worksheet, the second column represents two locations. To compare the locations, return to the **Individuals** input screen.

Menu command: ***SigmaXL > Control Charts > Individuals***

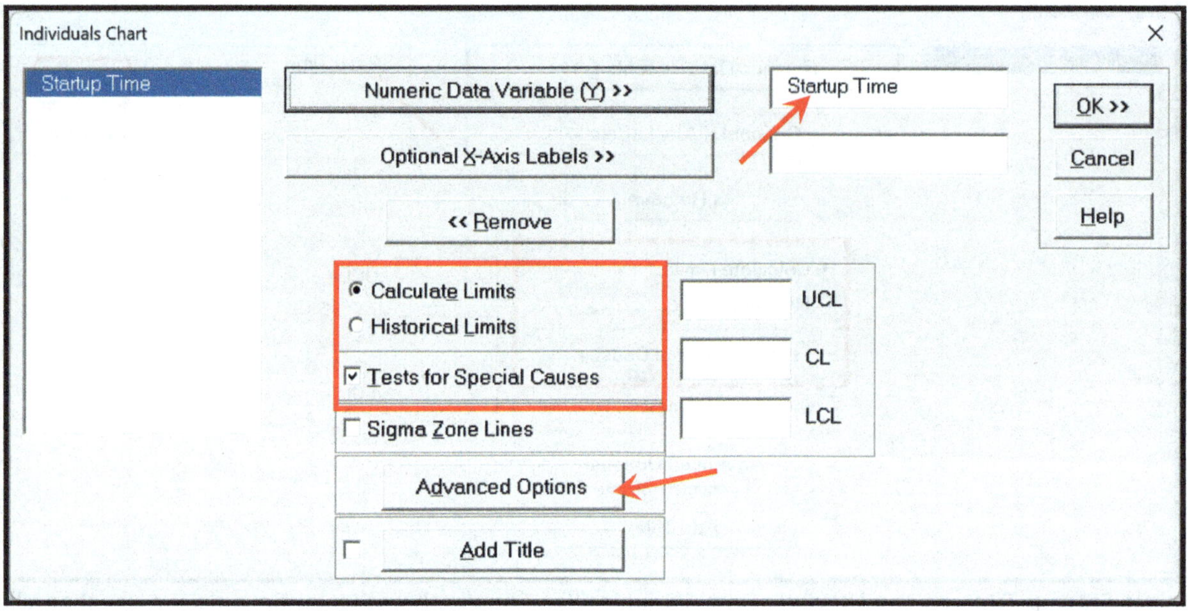

Inputs are the same. Select **Advanced Options**.

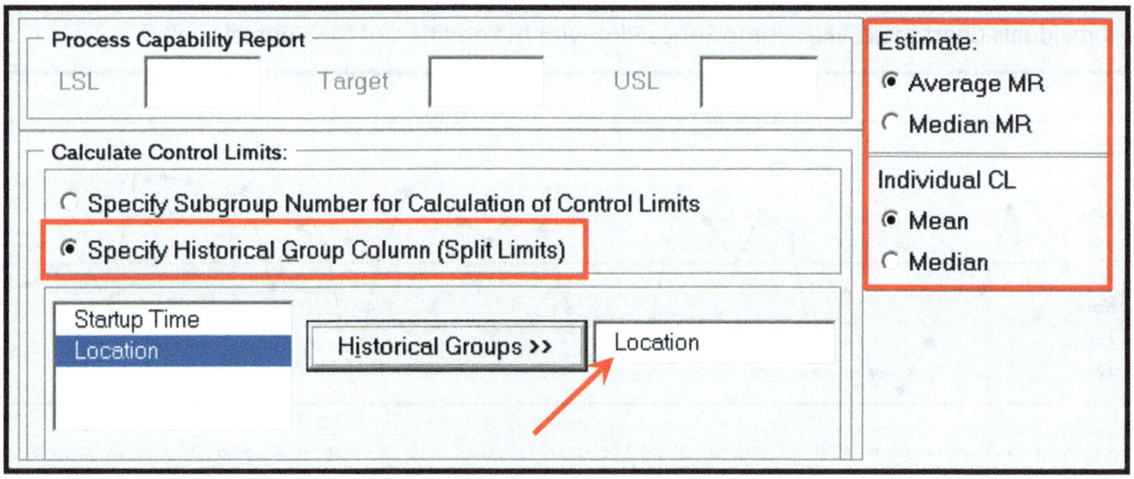

The dialog box opens the advanced options as a single dialog box. This is the lower half of the dialog box.

Choose; **Specify Historical Group Column (Split Limits)**. Select **Location** as the **Historical Groups**. Determine the desired **Estimates**. (More information will be supplied in the Control Chart portion of the text book.)

Click **OK** (at the top of the dialog box).

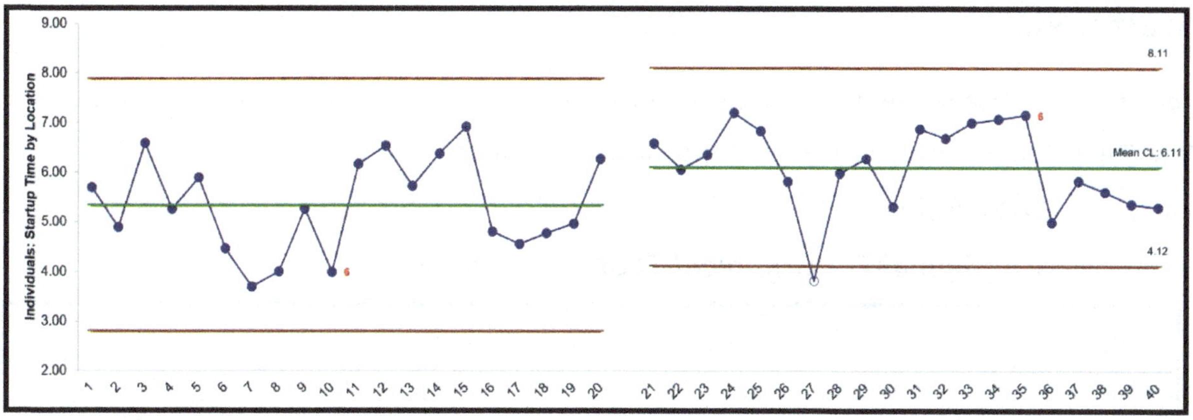

Location A is on the left, and B is on the right. There is a difference between the means; (the center lines for the groups are not the same). Whether this difference is significant requires analytical tools that will be discussed in the Analyze chapter of this book.

Notice that the mean for Location A is shown on the right side of the graph. To find the mean value for Location B, hover the cursor over the mean line in the chart. The mean value (Center Line) appears next to the cursor.

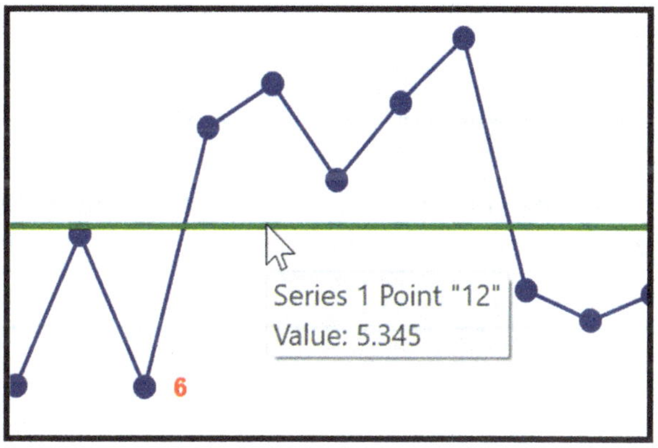

Scatter Plot

Tool Use: Use a Scatter Plot to determine whether a relationship exists between two variables.

Data Type: A Scatter Plot requires numeric data for both inputs.

Worksheet: ***SnowRain***

Menu command: ***SigmaXL > Graphical Tools > Scatter Plots***

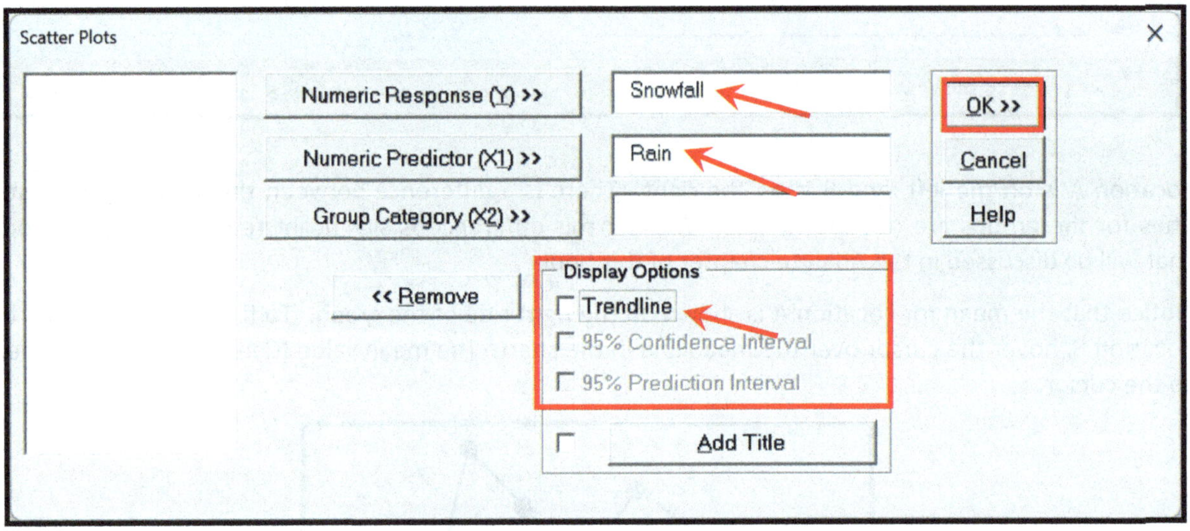

Select **Snowfall** as the **Numeric Response (Y)** and **Rain** as the **Numeric Predictor (X1)**. Deselect the **Trendline** under **Display Options**. (Information regarding trendlines will be provided in later chapters.

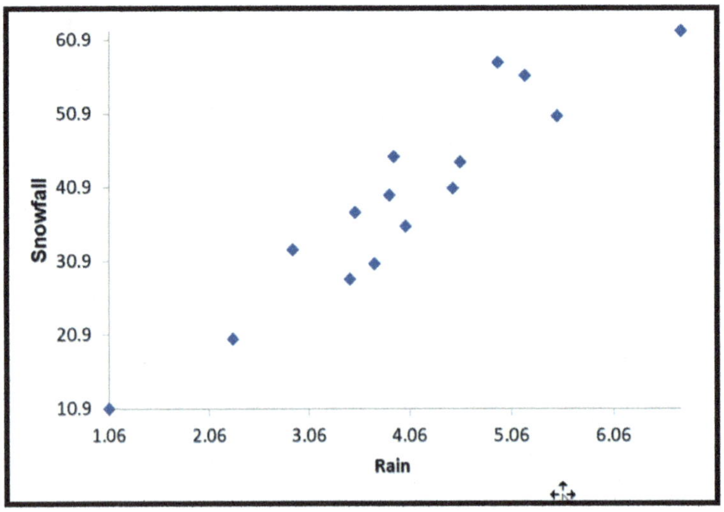

Click **OK**.

The relationship between Rain and Snowfall is clear; higher Rain levels correspond to higher levels of Snowfall. Further analysis of this relationship is provided in the Regression portion of the Analyze chapter.

Pareto Charts

Tool Use: The **Pareto Chart** is a sorted bar chart; (sorted left to right, highest to lowest). It is commonly used to indicate the frequency of issues. It is easy to understand, and is an excellent way to shed light on the major issues or problems facing a company. Use a Pareto Chart to help prioritize issues related to the project.

Data Type: A Pareto Chart requires counts of issues in different categories.

Data for a Pareto Chart is collected in one of two ways:

1. Record each issue as a separate entry in the worksheet (referred to as **Raw** data) or
2. Perform a summary analysis and present the information as a summary table.

Both methods are demonstrated in this section.

Basic Pareto Chart

Worksheet: ***Pareto***

Using a Summary Analysis: In the Pareto worksheet select the data in columns A and B. (Data has been summarized.)

Menu command: ***SigmaXL > Graphical Tools > Basic Pareto Chart***

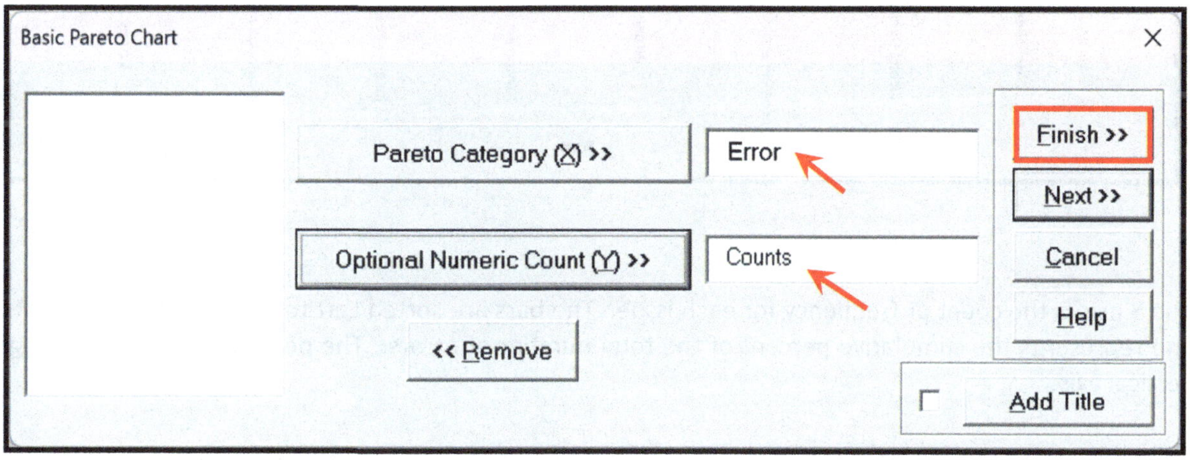

Input Error for the Pareto Category (X). Select Counts for Optional Numeric Count (Y). Click Finish.

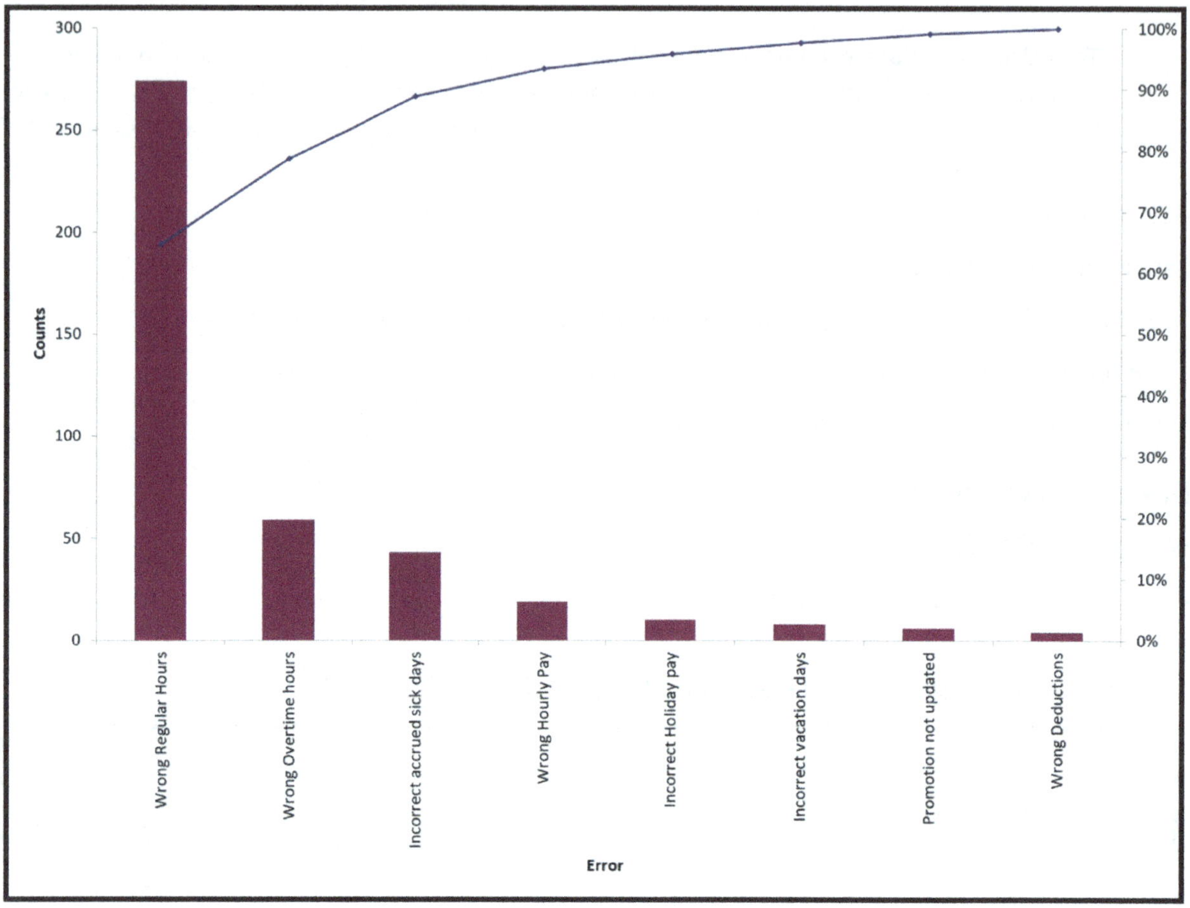

The Y axis is the count or frequency for each issue. The bars are sorted Left to Right (High to Low). The line represents the cumulative percent of the total number of errors. The percent scale is on the right vertical axis.

Hint: To prevent confusion, when selecting categories for defects, try to create an exclusive, comprehensive list. This means that each defect found will fall into one and only one of the categories. If this is not possible, have a category labelled, **Unknown,** to capture issues that do not fall into the defined categories. However, if this category is selected, the user should explain why it doesn't fit into any of the current categories. Then this issue can be added as a future category.

Issues with Excessive Number of Categories

The Pareto Chart is used to demonstrate the **'80/20'** rule. This states that 80% of the problems are caused by 20% of the issues. Projects usually revolve around the 20% of issues that cause 80% of the problems.

For some processes the number of categories might be large. Trying to display a large number of categories on a Pareto Chart leads to an excessive number of bars, many of which have low counts. Companies are not concerned with these issues.

To prevent the minor issues from interfering with an informative Pareto Chart, once 95% of the counts have been identified, all remaining issues go into a category labelled; **Other**. This bar will be placed on the far right of the Pareto Chart.

To demonstrate how to create a chart with this bar, return to the Basic Pareto Chart dialog box.

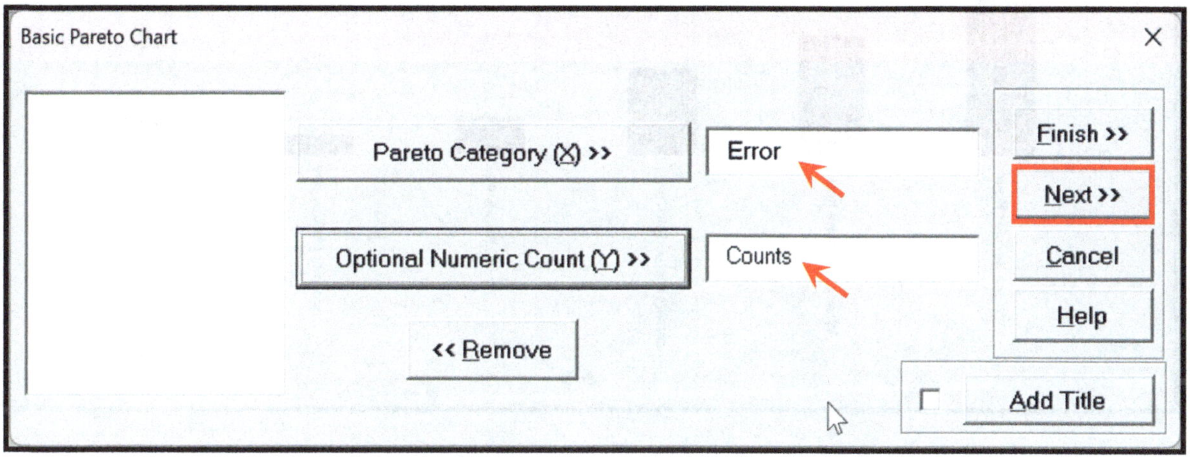

Input Error for the Pareto Category (X). Select Counts for Optional Numeric Count (Y). Click Next.

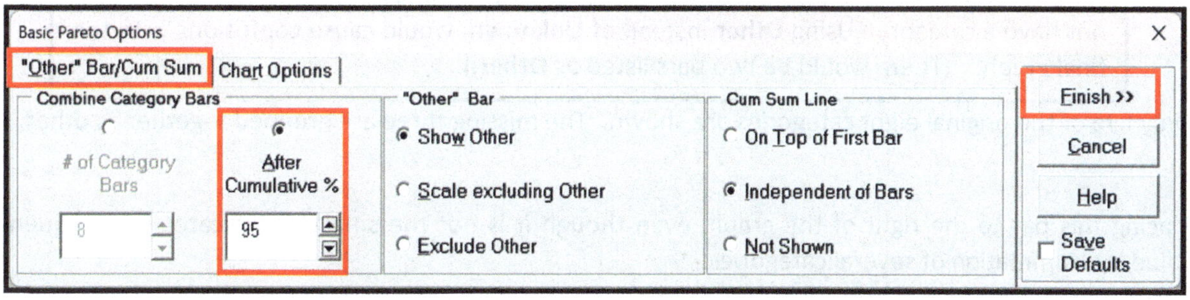

Choose the tab; **"Other" Bar/Cum Sum**. Click the **After Cumulative %** option and change the percent to **95**. The other two options, **"Other Bar"** and **Cum Sum Line** should be left at the default settings. Click **Finish**.

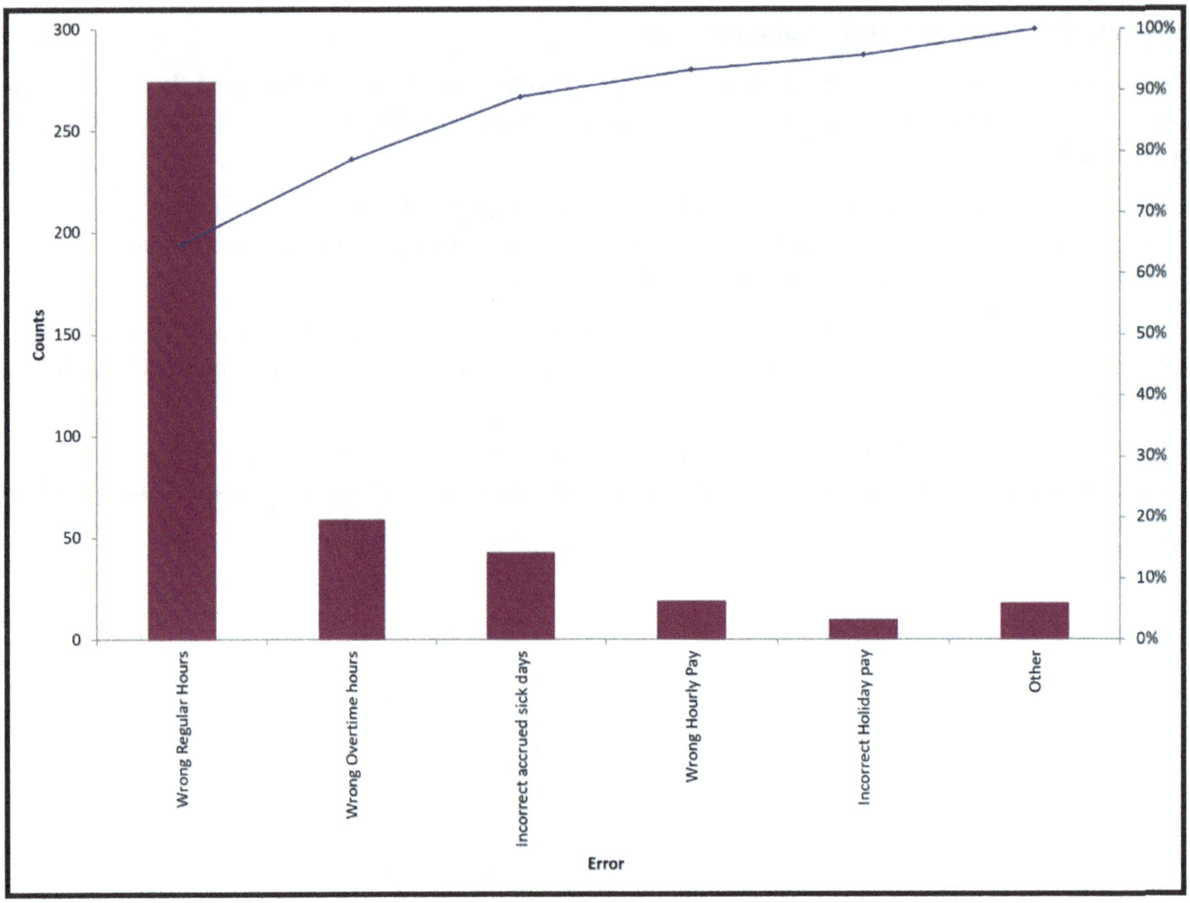

> **Hint:** This is why it was suggested to use a category of **Unknown** for those issues that did not have a category. Using **Other** instead of **Unknown**, would cause confusions with the final graph. (There would be two bars listed as **Other**.)

Only five of the original eight categories are shown. The missing three are grouped together as other.

Placing this bar to the right of the graph, even though it is not the smallest, indicates this frequency value is a summation of several categories.

Advanced Pareto Chart

Second Level Pareto's

While the Basic Pareto option works well to create a single, cumulative view of the data, it cannot separate the information based on a second factor.

Return to the **Pareto** worksheet. Columns **F** and **G** list issues from exit interviews as to why someone left a company. Column **F** is the 'Raw' data format, no summary has been performed. Column **G** shows a second variable, **Department**.

To demonstrate how to create a Pareto chart by department, begin with a cumulative Chart (one without the groups). Using columns F and G, select;

SigmaXL > Graphical Tools > Advanced Pareto Chart

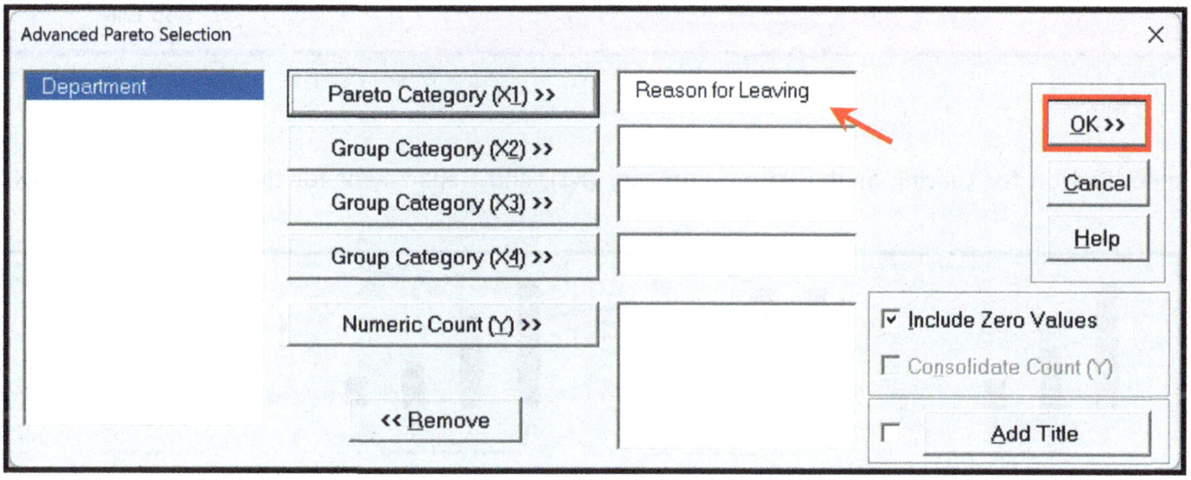

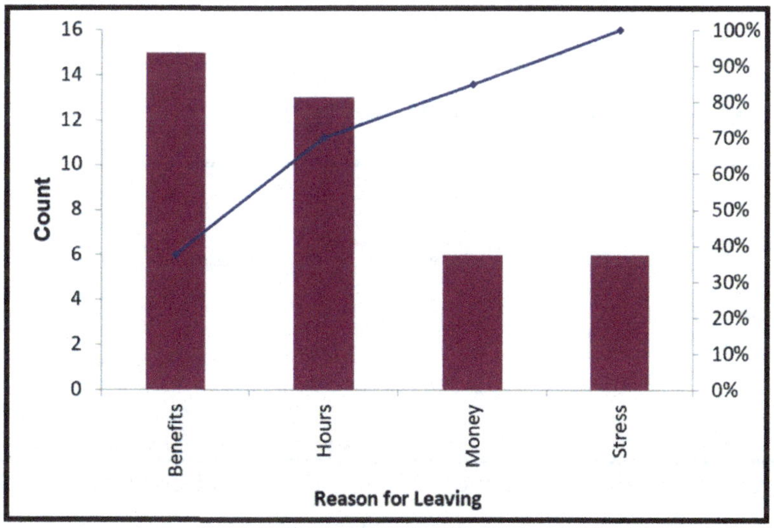

Select Reason for Leaving as the Pareto Category (X1). Click OK.

The Pareto Chart shows the four groups. Next, return to the input Dialog box.

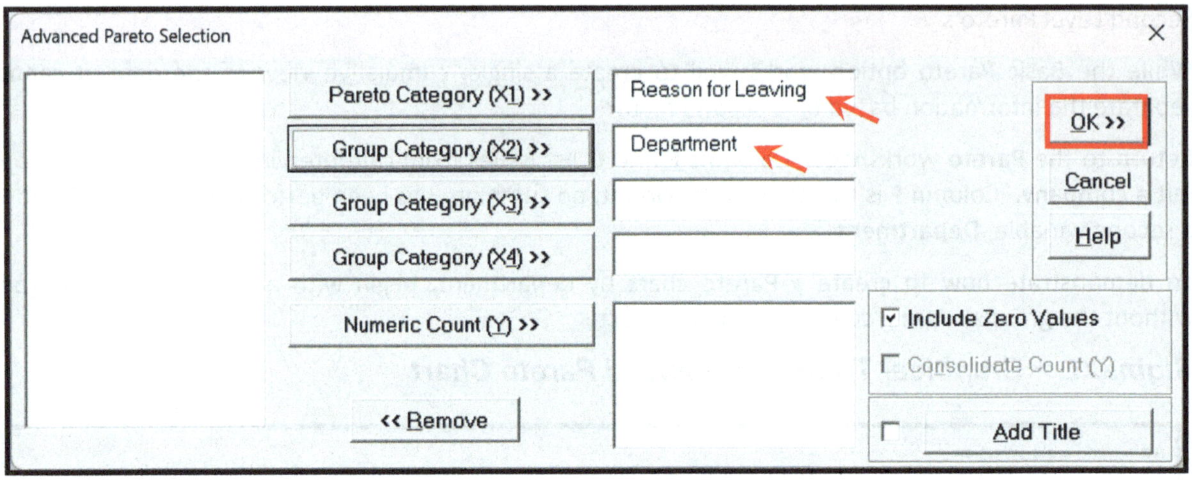

Select Reason for Leaving as the Pareto Category (X1), and Department for the Group Category (X2).

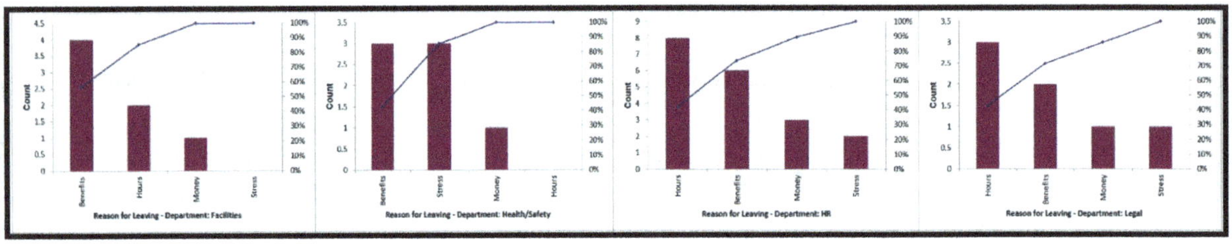

Click OK.

A close examination of the graphs shows different orders to the categories, and different Y axis scales. This makes it difficult to compare the groups.

To alleviate this issue, use the **Advanced Pareto Options** tool. Select:

SigmaXL > Graphical Tools > Advanced Pareto Options

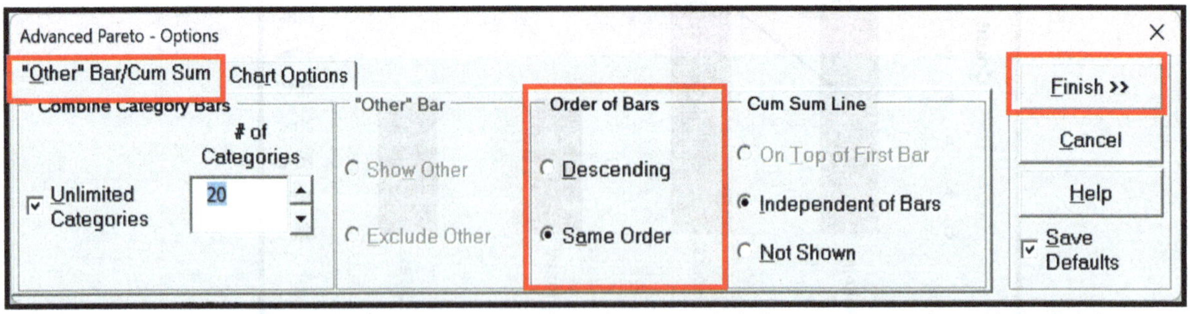

Select the **"Other" Bar/Cum Sum** tab. Go to Order of Bars and click on **Same Order**. Click **Finish**.

This will send the user to the **Advanced Pareto Selection** dialog box.

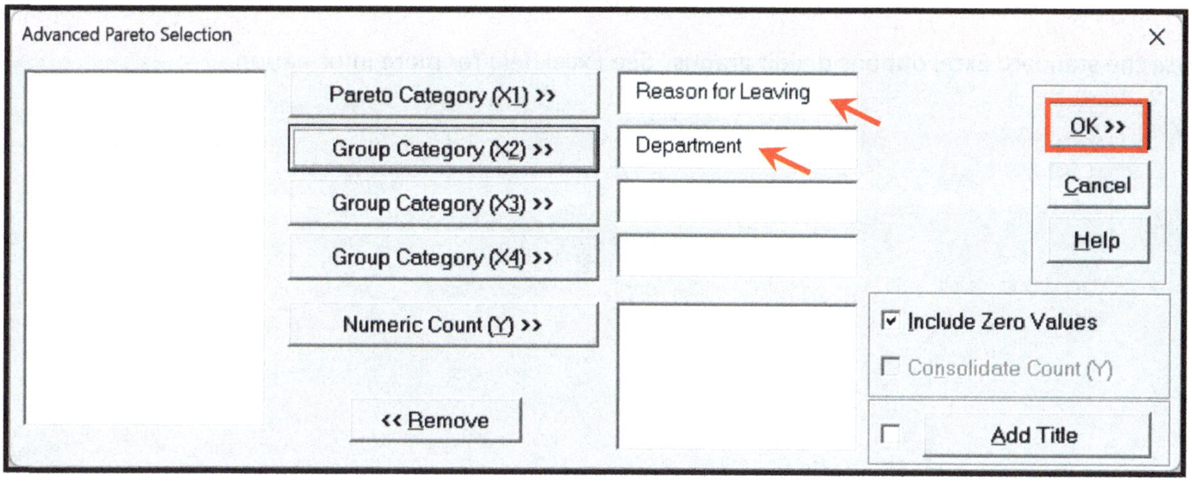

Input the X1 and X2 values as shown previously. Click **OK**.

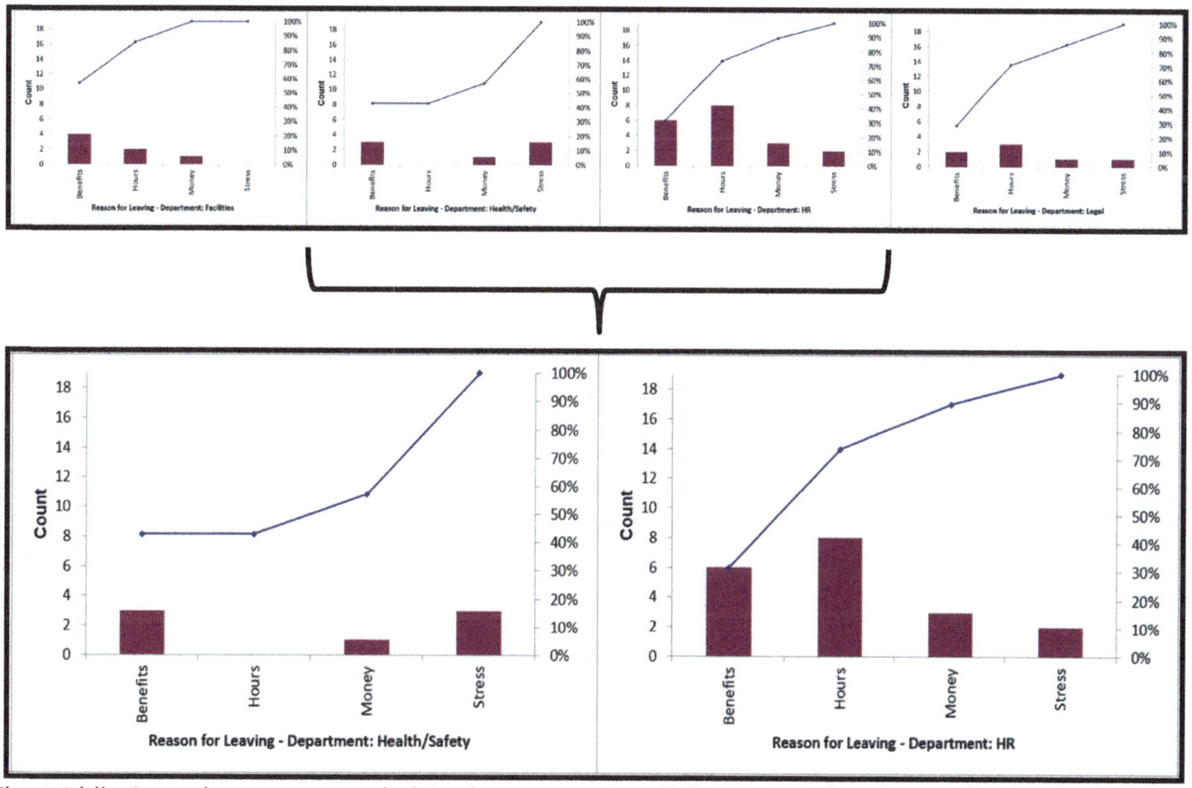

The middle 2 graphs were expanded to show the order of the bars, and the values for the Y axis. They are now the same for all Departments. Comparisons are easier to visualize. The order of the bars follows the cumulative Pareto Chart.

Editing Graphs

Use the standard Excel options to edit graphs. See Excel help for more information.

Measure Phase

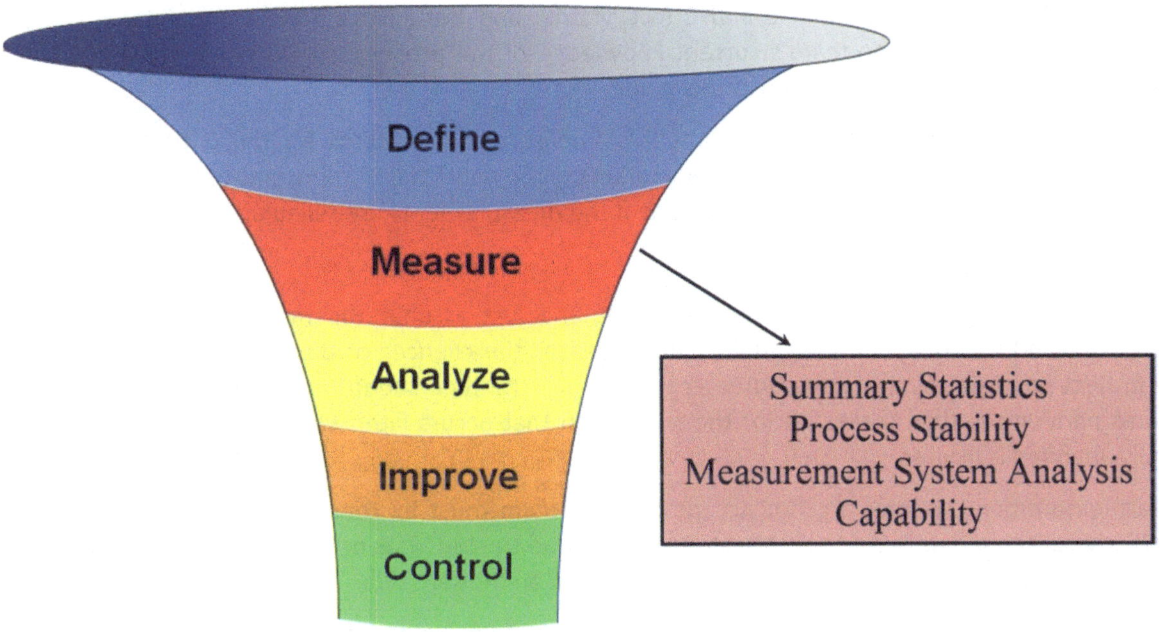

Measure Phase

The Measure phase of a Six Sigma process produces a number of important outcomes. The top two are:

- Determine the critical outputs (Y's) the project intends to improve
- Determine the inputs (X's) that affect the critical outputs

Knowledge-based tools are critical to this part of the process, as they are used to analyze various inputs and determine their appropriate categorization. Some of the commonly used knowledge-based tools include the Process Map; the Cause and Effect Matrix; and the Failure Modes and Effects Analysis (FMEA). These tools use the team's current knowledge of the process, so while statistical analysis is possible it is generally not emphasized at this point.

In addition, the team performs an assessment of measurement systems for the critical Y's. This is necessary to verify the project team is indeed working on an issue that is important to the company, and it requires a critical look at the data to determine if the measurements are reliable.

The Importance of Assessment

It may be tempting to skip over this assessment and just assume the measurement systems are appropriate and accurate; however, doing this increases the chances of discovering later on that the true project issue was simply a measurement problem. The time spent in checking the measurement systems early, more than makes up for the frustration that occurs later when it's discovered the data initially analyzed is useless.

If the measurement systems are not acceptable, the team must fix them and collect new data. All previously collected data is suspect at best, and cannot be trusted. It is not unreasonable to completely disregard previous data and wait for new data, just to be on the safe side.

Once assessment is complete and measurement systems are found to be acceptable and accurate, the team can move on to assessment of the Y's. This assessment includes analyzing the Y's for stability and capability.

Throughout this book, our assumption is that the user will analyze their own sample information of a particular process of interest to their organization.

Tools and Outcomes

Common tools used in the Measure phase fall into two categories: Statistical Tools and Outcomes. Some examples of each include the following:

Statistical Tools	Outcomes
Summary Statistics	Baseline Capability
SPC (Statistical Process Control) for process stability	Project Goals
MSA (Measurement Systems Analysis)	Measurement Systems assessment
Capability Studies	

Summary Statistics

Statistical analysis and summary statistics serve an important purpose - to provide estimates of the population (process) parameters under investigation. Depending on the specifics of an issue, this may be as simple as estimating the defects found in customer orders, or as complicated as understanding the relationship among several factors in the manufacturing of a computer chips.

In this chapter, use of the term **statistic** refers to sample values (average, range, standard deviation, etc.), and the term **parameters** refers to the population values these statistics are estimating. To put it in simple terms, sample statistics are used to estimate population parameters.

Throughout this book population parameters are written as bold font Greek letters. Sample statistics are written as bold letters. The following chart is set up as a reference:

Sample Statistics ⟶ Estimate ⟶ Population Parameters

Sample Statistics	Population Parameters
Average (Mean)	Mean
$\bar{X}$	μ
Standard Deviation	Standard Deviation
$\mathbf{s}$	σ
Variance	Variance
$\mathbf{s}^2$	σ^2

This chapter also contains simple mathematical formulas for some common statistics, but it is not necessary to know how to perform these calculations. What is important, though, is to understand what each statistic represents and how to use it properly.

Statistical Terms

Central Tendency

Values that define the center of datasets include the **Mean**, **Trimmed Mean**, **Median**, and **Mode**.

Mean (Average)

The sample mean, or average, is a commonly used statistic. To calculate the mean, simply sum all of the values in a dataset and divide by the number of values in the dataset. For example, if the dataset contains five values (5, 8, 2, 6 and 4), the sum is 25. Twenty-five divided by 5 produces an average of 5.

The formula for determining the mean is written as follows:

$$\text{Mean } (\overline{X}) = \frac{1}{n}\sum_{i=1}^{n} X_i$$

Trimmed Mean

The trimmed mean is based on a calculation similar to that used to find the mean. The only difference is that before performing the arithmetic operation, a percentage of the values on either end of the dataset are eliminated. For example, to calculate a 90% trimmed mean, first remove 5 % of the upper values and 5% of the lower values. The mean is then calculated on the remaining 90% of values in the dataset.

The trimmed mean is a useful statistic to use when there are suspect values on either end of the dataset. The formula for trimmed mean is the same as that used to determine mean, after removal of the desired percentage of points.

Median

The median is simply the center value of a dataset. To determine the median, arrange the values in an ascending order and determine the center; that is, the value with an equal number of data points above and below it. Go back to the example dataset used in the definition of mean. The sorted numbers are 2, 4, 5, 6, and 8. The value 5 is the median because there are two values above it (6 and 8) and two values below it (2 and 4).

If the dataset contains an even number of values, then the median is the average of the center two values. For example, say the dataset contains the values 4, 4, 7, 2, 6, and 11. When these values are sorted in ascending order, the dataset appears as 2, 4, 4, 6, 7, and 11; the middle two values are 4 and 6, and the average of these two values is 5, so the median is 5. Even though the value 5 is not in the dataset, it is still the median of these values.

There are two variations on the formula used to determine median – one for an odd number of values in the dataset and one for an even number of values in the dataset.

When the number of values is odd:

Median (sorted data) = (n+1)/2 where n is the number of data points.

When the number of values is even:

The median is the average of the n/2 and n/2 + 1 data values.

Comparing Mean and Median

While mean and median both indicate central tendencies, their respective benefits differ slightly. It is important to understand these differences in order to use the appropriate metric for the issue under investigation.

The Mean is a commonly used statistic, but it is problematic when there are outliers in the dataset; that is, when some data points are far removed from the majority of data. Because the mean uses all data points in a set, outliers have an excessive influence on the final value. The Median, on the other hand, is not used as often as the mean. However, it offers the significant benefit of eliminating the problem of outlier influence.

Here is an example of how this works. Suppose the dataset contains the values 5, 9, 2, 8, and 6; the mean is 6 and the median is also 6. Now, replace the value 9 with the value 99 – a significant outlier. The new mean is 24, but the median remains at 6.

So, which is better, mean or median? The answer is; **it depends**. The mean is used in other calculations and is the statistic of many comparison studies, so it should not be neglected; however, keep in mind the possible effects of outliers in the data set.

The best approach is to calculate both mean and median, then compare them. Symmetric datasets will produce two values close to one another, while dataset with outliers will produce values farther apart from each other. If there is a significant discrepancy between the mean and median, the team should investigate further using graphs and a thorough examination of the data.

Mode

Mode is defined as that value which occurs most often. For a symmetric dataset the mode is a good indicator of the center, but small datasets often contain multiple modes. Unimodal, bimodal and trimodal describe the number of modes in a dataset.

For example, a unimodal dataset contains a single major peak, while a bimodal dataset contains two major peaks. In terms of descriptive value, these terms are useful in determining if a dataset contains data from a single population (unimodal) or is potentially contaminated with data from multiple populations (bimodal or trimodal).

Spread

Values indicating the spread of data include the Range, Variance, Standard Deviation, and Coefficient of Variation (CV).

Range

Range represents the spread of a dataset. It is simply the highest value minus the lowest. The formula is:

Range = High value – Low value.

This is an easy value to calculate, but it has a couple of limitations. First, it ignores all but two data values, and second, it doesn't indicate how the rest of the data is distributed. For example, if a dataset contains 100 values, the range provides information on two of the data points. It does not, however, indicate how the remaining 98 values are grouped.

Variance (σ^2 (population), s^2 (sample))
Variance uses all data point to indicate the data's spread. It is defined as the average squared deviation from the mean. Datasets with larger variances have a larger spread compared to those with smaller variances. Formulas for the sample and population variances are:

Sample Variance:

$$s^2 = \frac{\sum_{i=1}^{n}(x_i - \bar{x})^2}{n-1}$$

Population Variance:

$$\sigma^2 = \frac{\sum_{i=1}^{N}(x_i - \mu)^2}{N}$$

Because the difference between the data values and the mean is squared, there are implications with outliers. As with the mean, outliers will have a large influence on the variance. It doesn't matter if the outlier value is low or high; because the difference is squared, it will always add to the variance.

An important property of variance is referred to as the additive property. This results in the total variance for a process being the sum of variances for the individual components (assuming the components are independent). The equation is:

$$\sigma_{Total}^2 = \sigma_1^2 + \sigma_2^2 + \sigma_3^2 + \cdots + \sigma_n^2$$

A more thorough examination of the additive property of variances will occur in the Measurement System Analysis (MSA) section.

Standard Deviation (σ (population), s (sample))
Standard deviation is the square root of the variance. It is a metric used to express information in the same units as mean value. Why is this useful? Because the squared units used in variance make it difficult to visualize the spread of values, and standard deviation helps overcome this difficulty. The formula for standard deviation is:

Population Standard Deviation: $\sigma = \sqrt{\sigma^2}$

Sample Standard Deviation: $s = \sqrt{s^2}$

Coefficient of Variation (CV)

The final value used to indicate spread is the Coefficient of Variation, or CV. It shows the spread relative to the sample mean. The formula is:

$$CV = \frac{s}{\bar{x}}$$

A common problem in datasets with high means is that they tend to have high variances. The CV makes it easier to compare unrelated datasets because the calculation produces a dimensionless value, better showing the relative spread of the datasets.

Shape

Values indicating the shape of data include skewness and kurtosis.

Skewness

Skewness indicates the relative size and direction of a dataset's asymmetry, sometimes described as a tail in the dataset. A positive skew indicates a tail to the right, or in the positive direction, while a negative skew indicates a tail to the left, or in the negative direction. A dataset with normal (or symmetric) distribution will have a skew value of 0.

The formula for skewness is fairly complicated, so it will not appear here. Instead, it can be found in the SigmaXL help menu.

Kurtosis

Kurtosis indicates the flatness of a dataset. A negative kurtosis indicates a flat distribution while a positive kurtosis indicates peaked distributions. A normal distribution will have a kurtosis of 0.

Using SigmaXL to Display Statistics

SigmaXL allows users to control the display of various statistics:

- Summary information on critical Outputs (Y's) produces a wide variety of values representing the center, spread and shape of data
- Summary statistics, (along with graphical analysis), display vital information before proceeding with the process improvement project

Descriptive Statistics

Data Type: Summary statistics require numeric data.

This example looks at the amount of time each of 3 customer service representatives take to check in customers at a large casino.

Worksheet: ***Check in Time***

Menu command: ***SigmaXL > Statistical Tools > Descriptive Statistics***

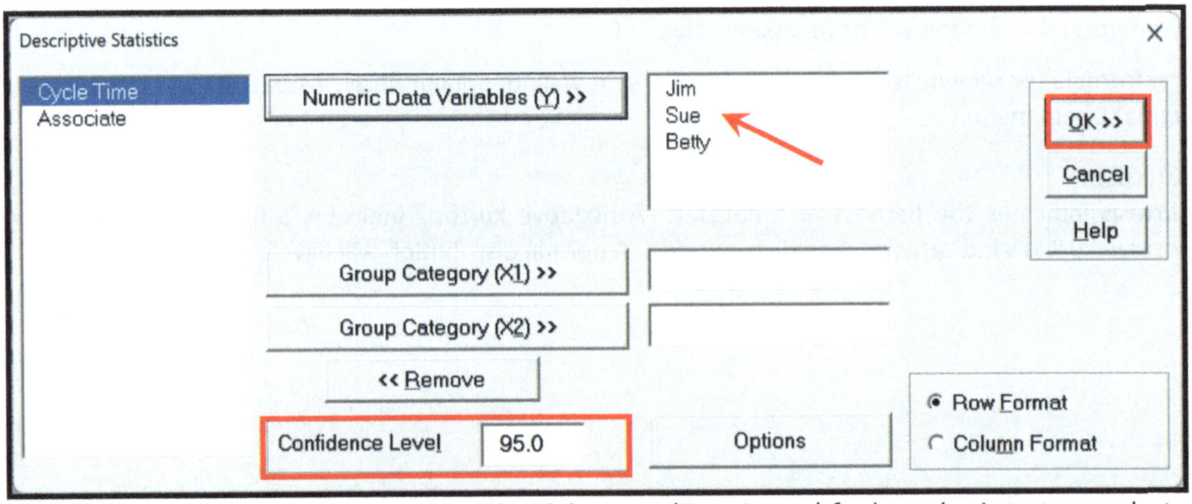

Input **Jim, Sue, and Betty** as the variable. The alpha error (Type I error) for hypothesis tests on selected statistics, is controlled through the Confidence Level. For an alpha value of .05, keep the level at **95.0**. The lower right corner contains the output display option. The information can be presented in either Row, or Column format. Keep the **Row Format** option. Repeat the analysis using the **Column format**, then decide which works best for your situation. Click **OK**. (For more information regarding the statistics, click the **Help** button in the dialog box.)

Note: For more information regarding the statistics, click the Help button in the dialog box.

Hint: Use the output from this function with caution when giving presentations. This tool presents a great deal of information in a manner that may be confusing if the audience is not well-informed about statistical values. Depending on the situation, this output may not be the appropriate choice for communicating with a broad audience.

Summary statistics for each person are shown. For the normality test, the test of skewness and kurtosis, p-values below the specified Type I error are highlighted in red.

Descriptive Statistics	Jim	Sue	Betty
Count	50	50	50
Mean	295.43	323.89	360.65
StDev	23.497	39.631	34.519
Range	93.273	183.28	152.00
Minimum	256.05	239.84	295.85
25th Percentile (Q1)	278.42	302.45	341.92
50th Percentile (Median)	294.09	319.98	356.62
75th Percentile (Q3)	310.40	351.04	375.91
Maximum	349.32	423.11	447.85
95.0% CI Mean	288.75 to 302.11	312.63 to 335.15	350.84 to 370.46
95.0% CI Sigma	19.628 to 29.28	33.106 to 49.386	28.835 to 43.015
Anderson-Darling Normality Test	0.305253	0.246540	1.026568042
P-Value (A-D Test)	0.5554	0.7431	**0.0097**
Skewness	0.394587	0.079796594	0.733742
P-Value (Skewness)	0.2289	0.8035	**0.0332**
Kurtosis	-0.252717	0.018880668	0.800239
P-Value (Kurtosis)	0.8157	0.8032	0.2133

The **95.0% CI Mean** and **95% CI Sigma** are the 95% confidence intervals for each associates population mean and standard deviation.

To access additional statistics, return to the dialog box, use the same inputs and click the **Options** button.

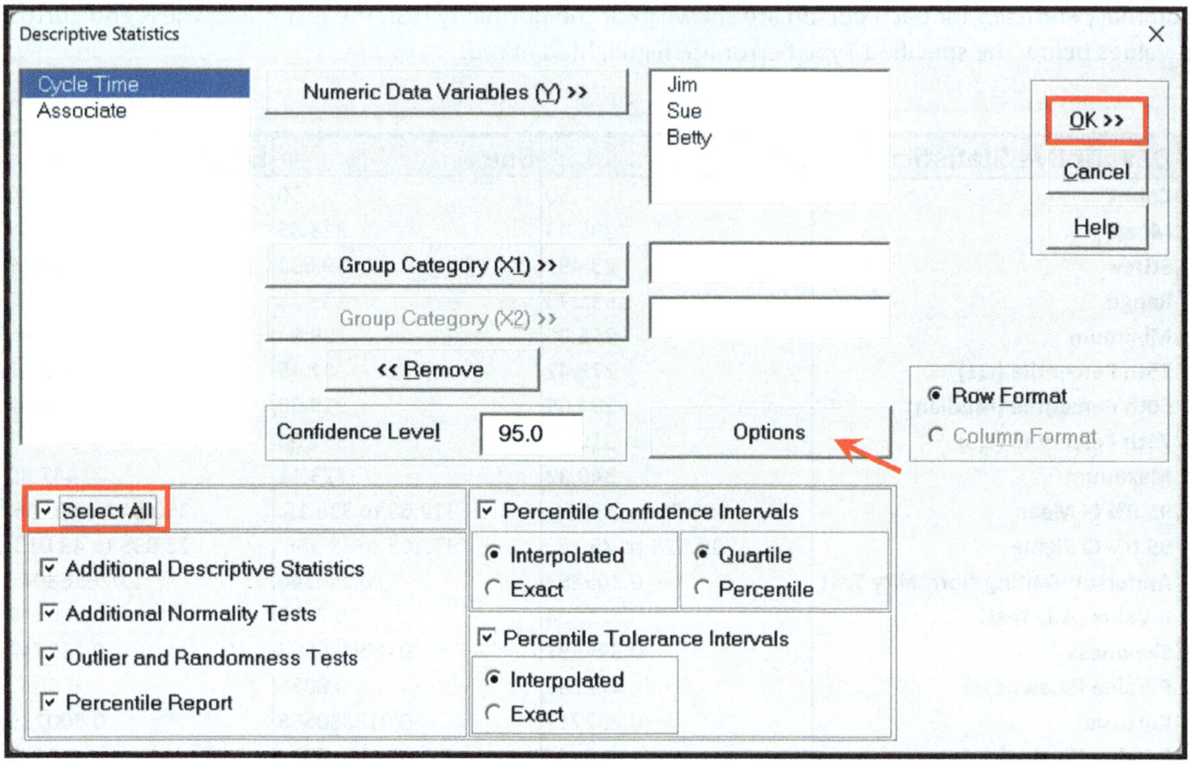

Choose **Select All**. (The other option is to select the desired statistics from the list.) Click **OK**.

The additional tests are shown.

Additional Descriptive Statistics			
5% Trimmed Mean	294.55	324.00	358.92
Standard Error of Mean	3.323	5.605	4.882
Variance	552.11	1570.7	1191.5
Coefficient of Variation	7.954	12.236	9.571
StDev (Within, Short Term)	24.472	40.688	33.206
Additional Normality Tests			
Shapiro-Wilk/KSL	0.972120	0.987491	0.937719
P-Value (Shapiro-Wilk/KSL)	0.2817	0.8711	0.0110
Doornik-Hansen	1.769	0.351081	4.544
P-Value (Doornik-Hansen)	0.4129	0.8390	0.1031

Quartile Confidence Intervals (Interpolated 95.0%)			
25th Percentile (Q1)	273.63 to 283.55	283.43 to 307.89	327.54 to 351.09
50th Percentile (Median)	283.18 to 302.58	307.21 to 334.04	350.57 to 363.47
75th Percentile (Q3)	302.28 to 319.91	333.67 to 368.46	362.91 to 390.09
Percentile Tolerance Intervals (Interpolated 95.0%)			
50%	273.71 to 313.33	294.13 to 358.15	327.96 to 379.02
80%	258.02 to 342.46	248.3 to 389.85	308.25 to 439.39
90%	256.05 to 348.98	239.84 to 416.88	297.93 to 447.85
95%	Min. sample size = 93	Min. sample size = 93	Min. sample size = 93
98%	Min. sample size = 236	Min. sample size = 236	Min. sample size = 236

Descriptive Statistics	**Jim**	**Sue**	**Betty**
0.135	256.0510189	239.8366433	295.8517777
0.5	256.0510189	239.8366433	295.8517777
1	256.0510189	239.8366433	295.8517777
2.5	256.4185748	241.1966883	298.6046126
5	257.7370993	246.4747383	307.1739871
10	262.7919907	272.3568792	313.3639035
15	273.6469282	284.7846656	327.6070125
20	275.7630443	296.1274604	333.3944849
25	278.4194479	302.4549673	341.918811
30	281.1677137	304.7803074	347.3186505
35	283.0888565	306.8090188	349.6547114
40	286.3924414	310.9428074	352.5610645
45	289.9600558	312.2661965	354.0859357
50	294.0936996	319.9771955	356.6175984
55	297.2030697	324.8438919	361.2802087
60	301.7191902	331.6681788	362.4628945
65	303.0677691	334.851088	365.4633122
70	307.5088419	347.218413	372.3316363
75	310.3960266	351.0407143	375.9053401
80	314.9919599	358.8308836	381.8851191
85	319.1579456	368.2151551	390.0147744
90	329.5201676	376.2912518	422.8356053
95	344.9456247	391.340094	440.9098891
97.5	348.8640474	414.8776915	446.3816737
99	349.3235359	423.1143153	447.8548807
99.5	349.3235359	423.1143153	447.8548807
99.865	349.3235359	423.1143153	447.8548807
75 - 25 (50%, Interquartile Range IQR)	31.97657869	48.58574702	33.98652918
90 - 10 (80%, Interdecile Range IDR)	66.72817692	103.9343727	109.4717018
95 - 5 (90%, Span)	87.20852536	144.8653558	133.7359021
97.5 - 2.5 (95%, +/- 1.96 Sigma Equivalent)	92.44547253	173.6810031	147.777061
99 - 1 (98%)	93.27251694	183.277672	152.003103
99.5 - 0.5 (99%)	93.27251694	183.277672	152.003103
99.865 - 0.135 (99.73%, +/- 3 Sigma Equivalent)	93.27251694	183.277672	152.003103

Outlier and Randomness Tests			
Outliers (Boxplot Rules)	No outliers found.	No outliers found.	Potential (1.5*IQR) outlier upper count = 4. Note that if the outliers are removed, Anderson Darling P-Value = 0.386. Excluding the outliers, data are inherently normal.
Grubbs Outlier Test	Grubbs' Test P-Value = 0.944. Fail to reject null hypothesis: "There are no outliers in the data set." Note that Grubbs' Test assumes normality and tests only if the maximum or minimum is an outlier.	Grubbs' Test P-Value = 0.497. Fail to reject null hypothesis: "There are no outliers in the data set." Note that Grubbs' Test assumes normality and tests only if the maximum or minimum is an outlier.	Grubbs' Test P-Value = 0.462. Fail to reject null hypothesis: "There are no outliers in the data set." Note that Grubbs' Test assumes normality and tests only if the maximum or minimum is an outlier.
Randomness Runs Test	Nonparametric Runs Test (Exact) P-Value = 0.884. Fail to reject null hypothesis: "data are random," so conclude that the assumption of randomness (independence) is not violated.	Nonparametric Runs Test (Exact) P-Value = 0.671. Fail to reject null hypothesis: "data are random," so conclude that the assumption of randomness (independence) is not violated.	Nonparametric Runs Test (Exact) P-Value = 0.062. Fail to reject null hypothesis: "data are random," so conclude that the assumption of randomness (independence) is not violated.

For more information regarding the additional summary information, refer to the online help at www.Sigmaxl.com. Go to Help and Support, SigmaXL Guide.

Graphical Summary

To create a graphical summary of a data set, SigmaXL uses a **Histogram & Descriptive Statistics** option.

Worksheet: ***Check in Time***

Menu command: ***SigmaXL > Graphical Tools > Histograms & Descriptive Statistics***

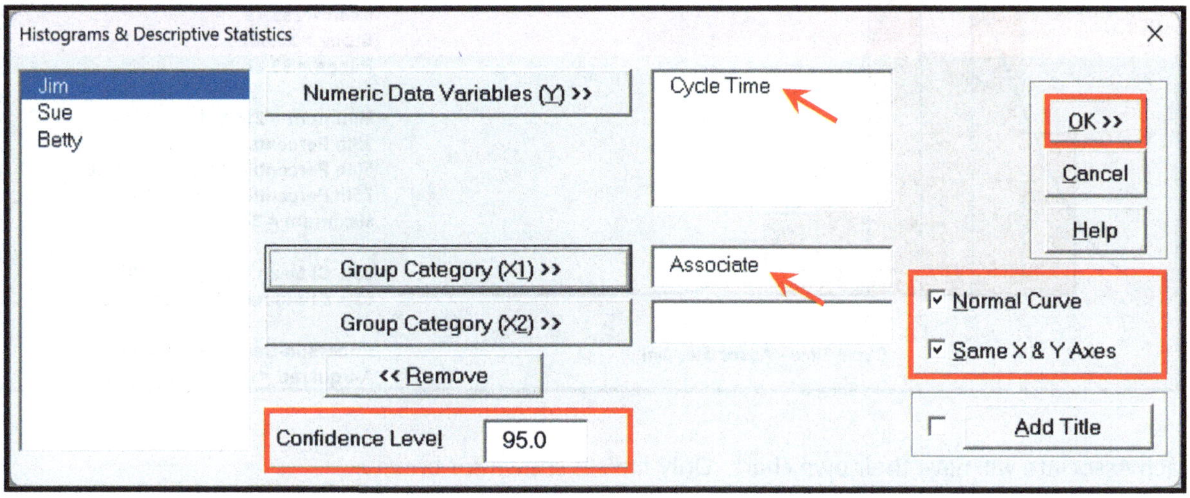

Input **Cycle Time** as the variable.

The user can change the confidence level by simply typing a desired value in place of the default value (95.0).

Click **OK**.

The graph shows a histogram with the normal curve based on the sample information. This type of graph will appear in the Analyze chapter.

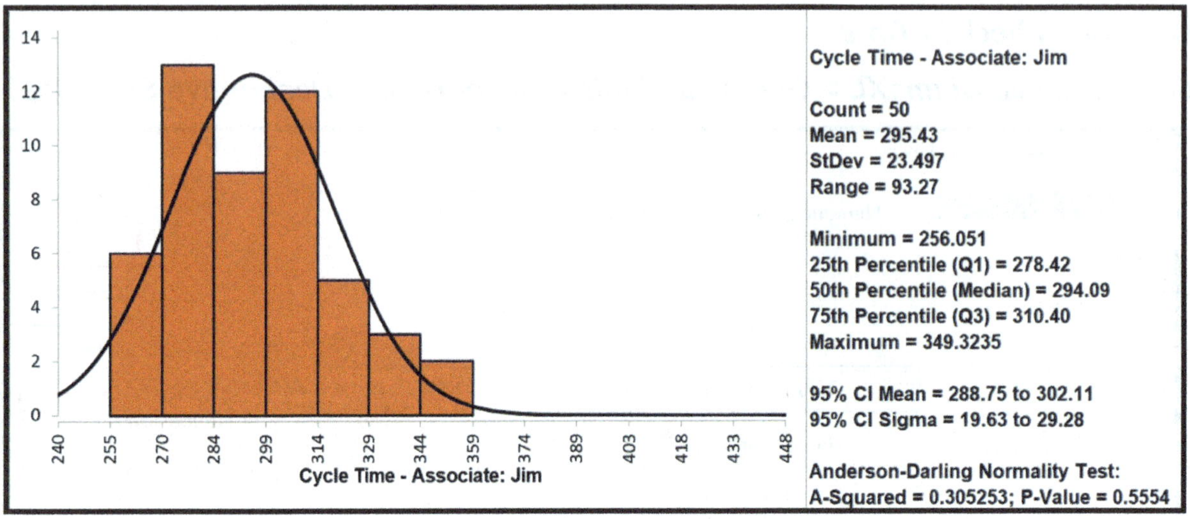

Each Associate will have their own chart. Only Jim's is shown for brevity.

The analytical portion of the graph includes the Anderson-Darling Test, the Mean, StDev (Standard Deviation), Range, along with the sample size (Count).

Finally, Confidence Intervals for the population Mean and Standard Deviation (Sigma) are shown.

Checking Process Stability – SPC (Statistical Process Control)

Before beginning any improvement activity, a team must determine process stability. This is important because an unstable process may occur as a result of multiple processes contaminating each another. What's more, to establish a baseline on an unstable process will create misleading information.

To determine the stability of a process, use an SPC chart. This is a specialized run chart with statistically based control limits. More information about control charts is presented in the Control chapter.

Tool Use: Use an SPC chart to determine if a process is running under a Common Cause variation (stable condition), or if a Special Cause variation (unstable condition) exists. If special cause variation exists, the sources of variation should be found and eliminated.

Data Type: SPC charts can use either continuous or discrete data.

A stable process has a constant mean and a constant standard deviation or spread. Running under a common cause variation condition allows the process owner to make predictions on future process output. This is an example of a stable process:

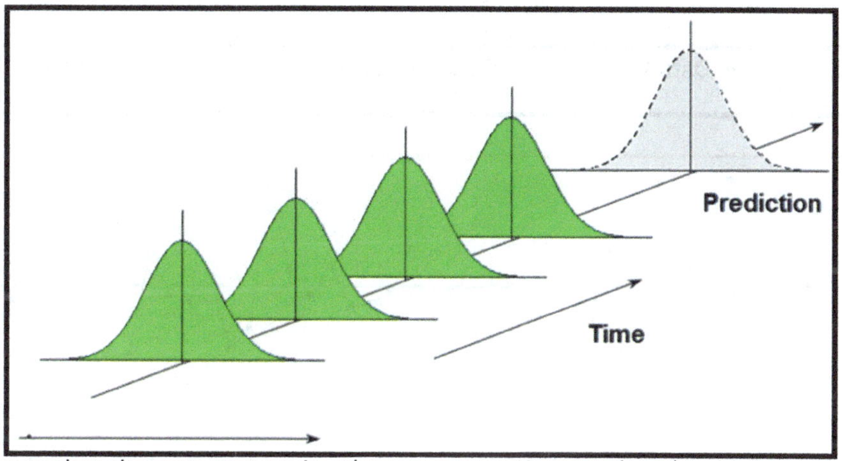

This demonstrates that the output remains the same over time so there's a high degree of predictability as to what will happen in the future.

*For the purposes of this chapter, the discussion of Control Charts will be quite limited. A closer examination will occur in the **Control** chapter.*

A popular control chart used during an initial investigation is the I-MR chart (Individuals and Moving Range Chart; it uses either continuous or count data collected as individual values. At least 25 data

Note: Refer to the Control Phase unit for more information regarding Statistical Process Control.

points should be used to assess process stability.

Worksheet: ***Check in Time***

Menu command: ***SigmaXL > Control Charts > Individuals & Moving Range***

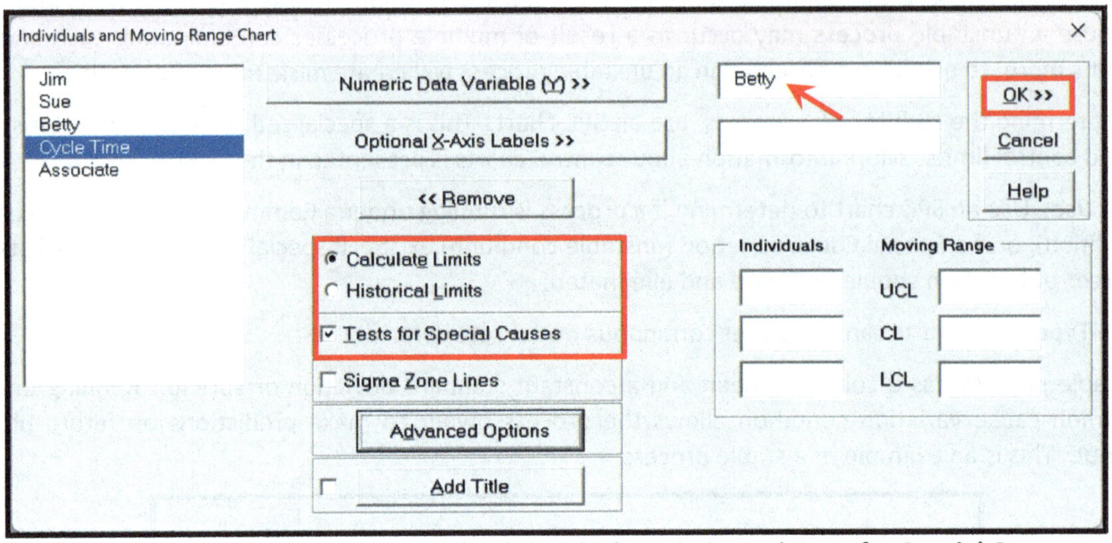

Select **Betty** as the Numeric Data Variable (Y). Click **Calculate Limits** and **Tests for Special Causes.**

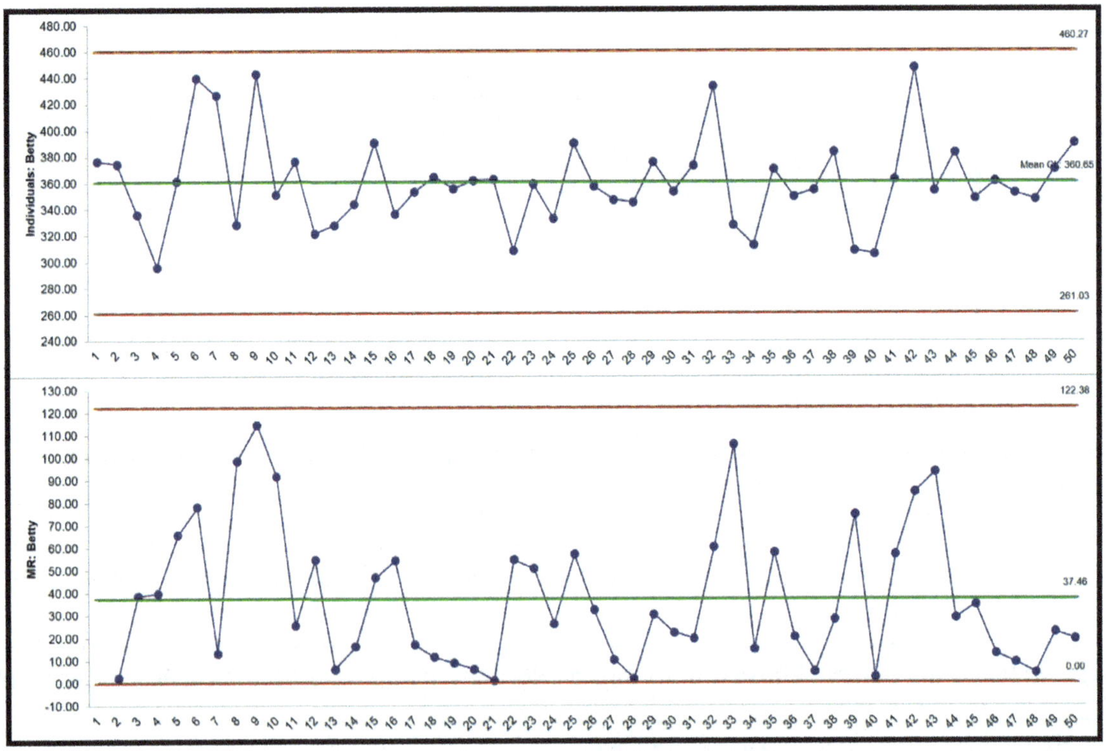

Examine the graph. If no points are outside the control limits (red lines) and no obvious shifts have occurred, the process is stable. Additional discussion regarding Control Charts and unstable processes occurs in the Control chapter.

Measurement Systems Analysis (MSA)

Continuous Data

Tool Use: Perform a Measurement System Analysis (MSA) on all critical outputs (Y's). Any inadequate measurement system must be corrected; if not corrected, the team cannot accurately measure improvements. A similar MSA should be performed on all critical X's to determine their reliability as well.

Data Type: An MSA can be performed on either continuous or discrete (attribute) data. This chapter includes examples that will:

1) Follow the lines of a traditional MSA for manufactured parts
2) Demonstrate an MSA for a transactional process
3) Show how to perform an analysis of files in a database

Overview: Before proceeding with any project, teams must use an MSA to determine if the available data (or collected data) is trustworthy. If the measurement system is poor or even flawed, the data it produces is suspect at best.

Remember, an MSA is not simply a test of the equipment; rather, it includes tools, procedures, operators and environment. The MSA creates values associated with Repeatability and Reproducibility to address all of these issues.

Types of MSA studies include:

1) GR&R Study (Gauge Repeatability and Reproducibility)
2) Attribute MSA
3) Audits

In a perfect environment, the observations in a dataset represent the true process variation. However, in the real world, the values represent not only the process variation but also the variation caused by the measurement system.

This is represented by the following: (Long and short term process variation will be discussed in more detail in the process capability section.)

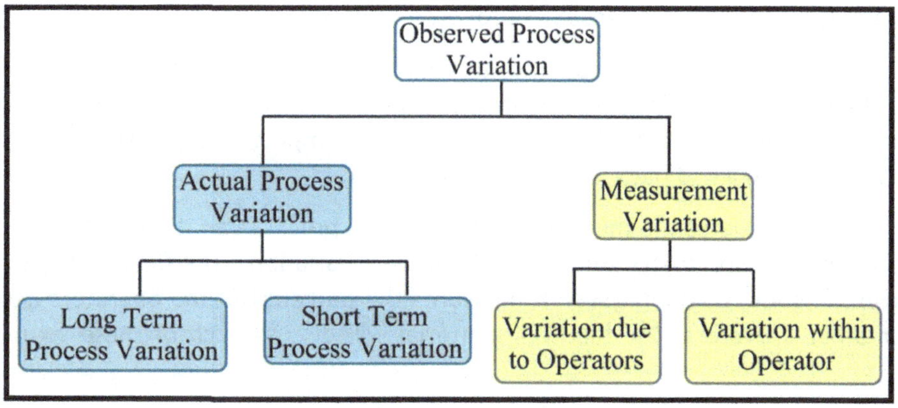

Variation in a measurement system contains two components – variation due to operators (Reproducibility) and variation within operator (Repeatability).

Issues in the first group (variation due to operators) are usually the result of slight differences in technique from one operator to another. To resolve issues of this kind conduct a thorough review of procedures and institute best practices.

Issues in the second group (variation within operator) may be a result of the operator not performing procedures consistently, or a result of the tool itself.

The purpose of an MSA study is to determine variation caused by the measurement system, and to assess its impact on the observed process variation.

If measurement variation is small relative to process variation, then the measurement system is adequate to proceed with the improvement project.

However, if measurement variation is large relative to process variation, the measurement system needs to be improved. If improvements are not made, it will be impossible to accurately measure process variation reduction due to Six Sigma team efforts.

It is also important to assess measurement system variation relative to process specifications. SigmaXL produces metrics for both situations.

> ***Hint:*** *Avoid issues related to a particular tool by having the tool serviced and calibrated by the manufacturer before performing the MSA.*

Metrics: To assess a measurement system, it is necessary to develop metrics linked to the system in terms of the process and customer specifications as well as to the system itself. MSA output metrics include the following:

1. Standard deviation of the measurement system. $\sigma_{\text{measurement system}}$
2. Standard deviation repeatability. $\sigma_{\text{repeatability}}$
3. Standard deviation reproducibility. $\sigma_{\text{reproducibility}}$
4. P/T – the precision to tolerance ratio. (Also listed as %P/T
5. % R&R – the percent Repeatability and Reproducibility
6. % Agreement – the percent agreement for studies of attribute data.

The first three of these metrics (Standard deviation of the measurement system; Standard deviation repeatability; Standard deviation reproducibility) assess the system itself. The fourth (P/T ratio) relates the measurement system to customer specifications. This is important because if the system is unable to distinguish a good from a bad part, it is of little use.

The fifth metric (%R&R) relates the measurement system to process variation. If this value is large, the system is unable to measure improvements in the process variation. The final metric (%Agreement) is used with attribute (good, bad) analyses. It measures the percent of time operators agree with either themselves or other operators. The following material will discuss each of these six metrics in more detail.

Accuracy and Precision

Accuracy and precision are two often misused terms when discussing measurement systems. In other disciplines they may be used interchangeably, but in Six Sigma they each have a separate, distinct definition.

Accuracy

Accuracy is defined as the difference between actual value and the average of multiple readings. It is also known as the systems bias. Bias can only be determined using a known standard, one that has traceable standards with known values. Analysis of bias in a measurement system is generally conducted by the equipment maintenance group.

Precision

Precision is defined by the spread of multiple readings; the smaller the spread of reading, the more precise they are, while the larger the spread the less precise they are.

This illustration demonstrates these concepts:

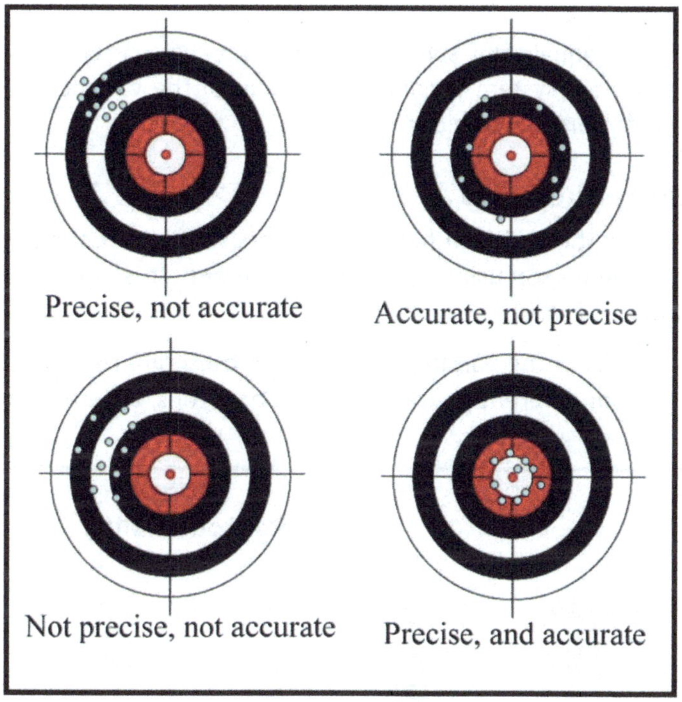

The upper left image is precise (tight cluster of points) but is not accurate (the average shot is off target).

The upper right is accurate because the average of all shots is close to the target, but the spread is large so it is not precise.

The Impact of Additivity Property for Variances

In the Summary Statistics section, variances were mentioned as being additive. This additive property is used to divide measurement system variation into its component parts.

In measurement system analysis, teams must calculate variances and standard deviations.

Using the additive property of variances, the following condition exists:

$$\sigma^2_{observed\ process\ variation} = \sigma^2_{true\ process\ variation} + \sigma^2_{measurement\ system}$$

and

$$\sigma^2_{Measurement\ System} = \sigma^2_{Repeatability} + \sigma^2_{Reproducibility}$$

The observed process variance equals the sum of the true process variance and the measurement system variance; the measurement system variance is the sum of the variance from repeatability and reproducibility. Values for all factors are provided by SigmaXL.

Repeatability and Reproducibility

Repeatability - Repeatability is the variation between successive measurements of the same sample, same characteristic, by the same person using the same instrument. It is also known as the *test- retest error*, and is used as an estimate of *short-term variation*.

Reproducibility - Reproducibility is the variation that results from different conditions used to make measurements. This results from different operators, different setups, different samples, and different

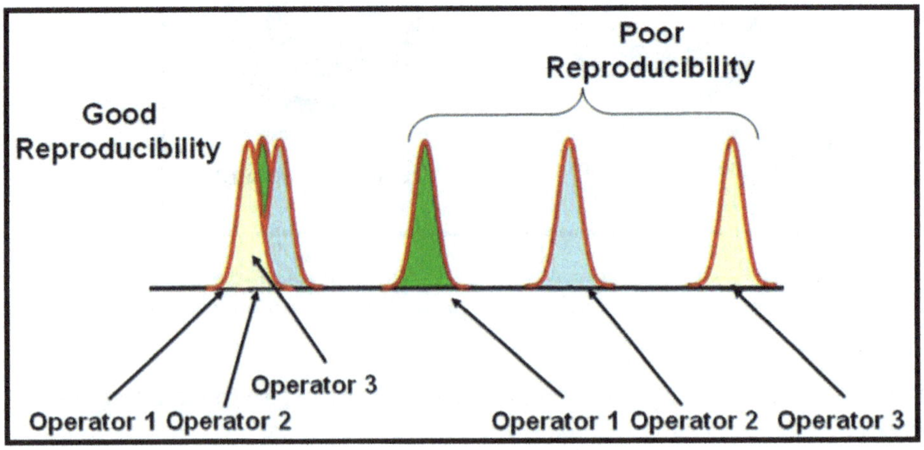

environmental conditions. It is also known as *long-term variation*.

Metrics

$$\%R\&R = \frac{\sigma_{\text{Measurement System}}}{\sigma_{\text{Observed Process Variation}}} * 100\%$$

%R&R: This metric relates measurement system variation to process variation. The formula:

%R&R indicates the measurement system's proportion of the total observed variation. This is a useful metric for the Project Leader because it reveals whether or not a measurement system is capable of measuring improvements in process variation. (In SigmaXL this is the % Study Variation or %SV.)

%P/T: This metric compares measurement system variation to process tolerance. If the value of this ratio is too high, it indicates the system is unable to distinguish between good product and bad product. The formula is:

$$\%\ P/T = \frac{6 * \sigma_{\text{Measurement System}}}{\text{USL} - \text{LSL}} * 100\%$$

Note: The value 6 in the numerator was originally listed as 5.15 (99% of the area under the normal curve) in earlier approaches to Six Sigma process improvement; however, many companies are now moving to 6 (99.73% of the area).

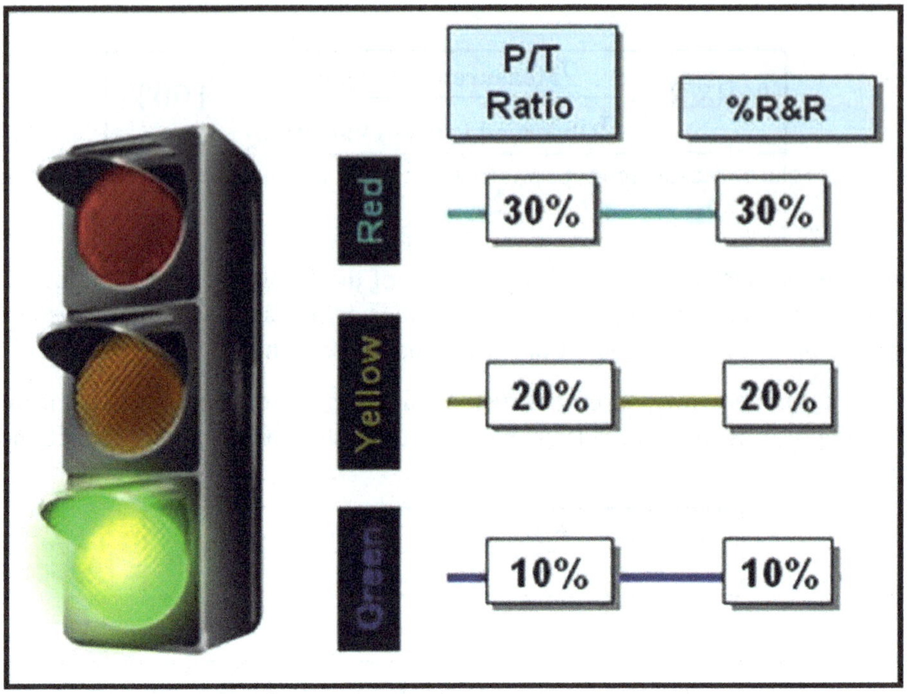

Guidelines for acceptable levels of P/T and %R&R values are shown below;

Typically, levels below 10% indicate an excellent system. Levels between 10% and 20% indicate the system is good for the current process, but as process variation decreases %R&R will increase, so it should be re-checked periodically. In fact, a dramatic decrease in process variation could cause a previously good measurement to become bad.

When levels fall between 20% and 30%, the system is still considered acceptable but improvement plans should be investigated. If levels are above 30% the system is not acceptable and should not be used with the current procedures.

Creating the MSA Worksheet

A typical MSA for manufactured parts consists of obtaining material from the production line, having several operators measure the items multiple times, and then analyzing the results to determine where the major sources of variation exist. It is important to use common sense when determining resource requirements to run an MSA.

A modified procedure will be used to separate the Trials for the MSA. The final worksheet will use 10 Parts, 3 Operators and 2 trials. Each trial will be created separately, then combined for the final worksheet.

Menu command: ***SigmaXL > Measurement Systems Analysis > Create Gage R&R (Crossed) Worksheet***

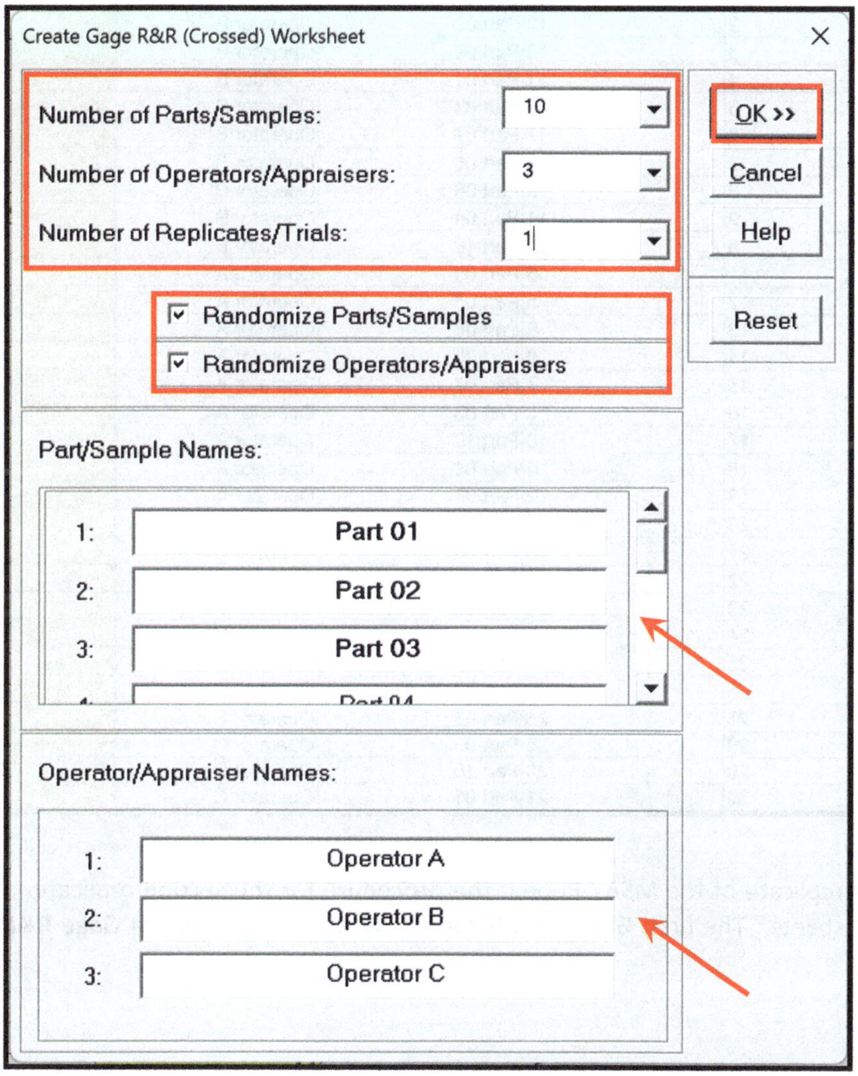

Select the number of **Parts (10)**, the number of **Operators (3)** and the number of **Replicates (1)**.

SigmaXL allows each part to have an identifier, and for each operator to be listed by name. For simplicity, the default values will be used.

The option, **Randomize Parts/Samples**, is the typical method of running an MSA study; additionally, using the option to **Randomize Operators/Appraisers** is an excellent way to eliminate issues associated with the same operator performing the initial measurement for each replication.

Select the options as shown, then click **OK**.

Gage R&R Study (Crossed) Worksheet				
Gage Name:				
Date of Study:				
Performed By:				
Notes:				
Run Order	**Std. Order**	**Part**	**Operator**	**Measurement**
1	15	Part 05	Operator B	
2	12	Part 02	Operator B	
3	19	Part 09	Operator B	
4	11	Part 01	Operator B	
5	13	Part 03	Operator B	
6	17	Part 07	Operator B	
7	16	Part 06	Operator B	
8	18	Part 08	Operator B	
9	14	Part 04	Operator B	
10	20	Part 10	Operator B	
11	6	Part 06	Operator A	
12	5	Part 05	Operator A	
13	8	Part 08	Operator A	
14	9	Part 09	Operator A	
15	7	Part 07	Operator A	
16	3	Part 03	Operator A	
17	10	Part 10	Operator A	
18	4	Part 04	Operator A	
19	2	Part 02	Operator A	
20	1	Part 01	Operator A	
21	28	Part 08	Operator C	
22	24	Part 04	Operator C	
23	26	Part 06	Operator C	
24	22	Part 02	Operator C	
25	29	Part 09	Operator C	
26	27	Part 07	Operator C	
27	23	Part 03	Operator C	
28	25	Part 05	Operator C	
29	30	Part 10	Operator C	
30	21	Part 01	Operator C	

This is the first replicate of the MSA. Repeat the procedure for the second replicate. Once completed there will be 2 sheets. The first; **Gage R&R (Crossed) WKS**, and the second **Gage R&R (Crossed) WKS (2)**.

Gage Name:	
Date of Study:	
Performed By:	
Notes:	

Run Order	Std. Order	Part	Operator	Measurement
1	15	Part 05	Operator B	
2	12	Part 02	Operator B	
3	19	Part 09	Operator B	
4	11	Part 01	Operator B	
5	13	Part 03	Operator B	
6	17	Part 07	Operator B	
7	16	Part 06	Operator B	
8	18	Part 08	Operator B	
9	14	Part 04	Operator B	
10	20	Part 10	Operator B	
11	6	Part 06	Operator A	
12	5	Part 05	Operator A	
13	8	Part 08	Operator A	
14	[illegible]	[illegible]	[illegible]	
15	[illegible]	[illegible]	[illegible]	
16	[illegible]	[illegible]	[illegible]	
17	10	Part 10	Operator A	
18	4	Part 04	Operator A	
19	2	Part 02	Operator A	
20	1	Part 01	Operator A	
21	28	Part 08	Operator C	
22	24	Part 04	Operator C	
23	26	Part 06	Operator C	
24	22	Part 02	Operator C	
25	29	Part 09	Operator C	
26	27	Part 07	Operator C	
27	23	Part 03	Operator C	
28	25	Part 05	Operator C	
29	30	Part 10	Operator C	
30	21	Part 01	Operator C	

Copy rows 1-30. **Do Not** include the headings.

Go to the **Gage R&R (Crossed) WKS (2)** worksheet and copy rows, 1-30. **Do Not** copy the column headings. Then paste these rows below row 30 in the **Gage R&R (Crossed) WKS** worksheet.

Pasted rows below row 30 of worksheet **Gage R&R (Crossed) WKS**.

Gage R&R Study (Crossed) Worksheet

Gage Name:	
Date of Study:	
Performed By:	
Notes:	

Run Order	Std. Order	Part	Operator	Measurement
1	23	Part 03	Operator C	
2	26	Part 06	Operator C	
3	21	Part 01	Operator C	
4	22	Part 02	Operator C	
5	30	Part 10	Operator C	
6	25	Part 05	Operator C	
7	28	Part 08	Operator C	
8	27	Part 07	Operator C	
9	29	Part 09	Operator C	
10	24	Part 04	Operator C	
11	18	Part 08	Operator B	
12	14	Part 04	Operator B	
13	11	Part 01	Operator B	
14	16	Part 06	Operator B	
15	17	Part 07	Operator B	
16	13	Part 03	Operator B	
17	12	Part 02	Operator B	
18	20	Part 10	Operator B	
19	15	Part 05	Operator B	
20	19	Part 09	Operator B	
21	9	Part 09	Operator A	
22	7	Part 07	Operator A	
23	1	Part 01	Operator A	
24	6	Part 06	Operator A	
25	4	Part 04	Operator A	
26	10	Part 10	Operator A	
27	2	Part 02	Operator A	
28	3	Part 03	Operator A	
29	8	Part 08	Operator A	
30	5	Part 05	Operator A	
1	15	Part 05	Operator B	
2	12	Part 02	Operator B	
3	19	Part 09	Operator B	
4	11	Part 01	Operator B	
5	13	Part 03	Operator B	
6	17	Part 07	Operator B	
7	16	Part 06	Operator B	
8	18	Part 08	Operator B	
9	14	Part 04	Operator B	
10	20	Part 10	Operator B	
11	6	Part 06	Operator A	
12	5	[illegible]	Operator A	
13	8	[illegible]	Operator A	
14	9	[illegible]	Operator A	
15	7	[illegible]	Operator A	
16	3	[illegible]	Operator A	
17	10	[illegible]	Operator A	
18	4	Part 04	Operator A	
19	2	Part 02	Operator A	
20	1	Part 01	Operator A	
21	28	Part 08	Operator C	
22	24	Part 04	Operator C	
23	26	Part 06	Operator C	
24	22	Part 02	Operator C	
25	29	Part 09	Operator C	
26	27	Part 07	Operator C	
27	23	Part 03	Operator C	
28	25	Part 05	Operator C	
29	30	Part 10	Operator C	
30	21	Part 01	Operator C	

Pasted rows.

Number the **Run Order** column for the second Replicate, **31-60**. The MSA should be run according to the **Run Order** specified in the worksheet, this follows the desired randomization.

Run Order	Std. Order	Part	Operator	Measurement
1	23	Part 03	Operator C	
2	26	Part 06	Operator C	
3	25	Part 05	Operator C	
4	28	Part 08	Operator C	
5	30	Part 10	Operator C	
6	29	Part 09	Operator C	
7	22	Part 02	Operator C	
8	27	Part 07	Operator C	
9	21	Part 01	Operator C	
10	24	Part 04	Operator C	
11	12	Part 02	Operator B	
12	15	Part 05	Operator B	
13	17	Part 07	Operator B	
14	19	Part 09	Operator B	
15	20	Part 10	Operator B	
16	13	Part 03	Operator B	
17	16	Part 06	Operator B	
18	11	Part 01	Operator B	
19	18	Part 08	Operator B	
20	14	Part 04	Operator B	
21	4	Part 04	Operator A	
22	8	Part 08	Operator A	
23	6	Part 06	Operator A	
24	5	Part 05	Operator A	
25	7	Part 07	Operator A	
26	9	Part 09	Operator A	
27	1	Part 01	Operator A	
28	10	Part 10	Operator A	
29	3	Part 03	Operator A	
30	2	Part 02	Operator A	
31	16	Part 06	Operator B	
32	19	Part 09	Operator B	
33	11	Part 01	Operator B	
34	15	Part 05	Operator B	
35	12	Part 02	Operator B	
36	17	Part 07	Operator B	
37	13	Part 03	Operator B	
38	14	Part 04	Operator B	
39	18	Part 08	Operator B	
40	20	Part 10	Operator B	
41	1	Part 01	Operator A	
42				
43				
44				
45				
46				
47				
48	10	Part 10	Operator A	
49	9	Part 09	Operator A	
50	4	Part 04	Operator A	
51	21	Part 01	Operator C	
52	24	Part 04	Operator C	
53	23	Part 03	Operator C	
54	22	Part 02	Operator C	
55	25	Part 05	Operator C	
56	27	Part 07	Operator C	
57	30	Part 10	Operator C	
58	26	Part 06	Operator C	
59	29	Part 09	Operator C	
60	28	Part 08	Operator C	

Number the Run Order column 31-60

Repeat this procedure for the number of desired Replicates.

To show how to analyze the MSA, use worksheet; ***WaterMSA***.

Performing the MSA – (Gage R&R Study)

Worksheet: ***WaterMSA***

Menu command:

SigmaXL > Measurement Systems Analysis > Analyze Gage R&R (Crossed)

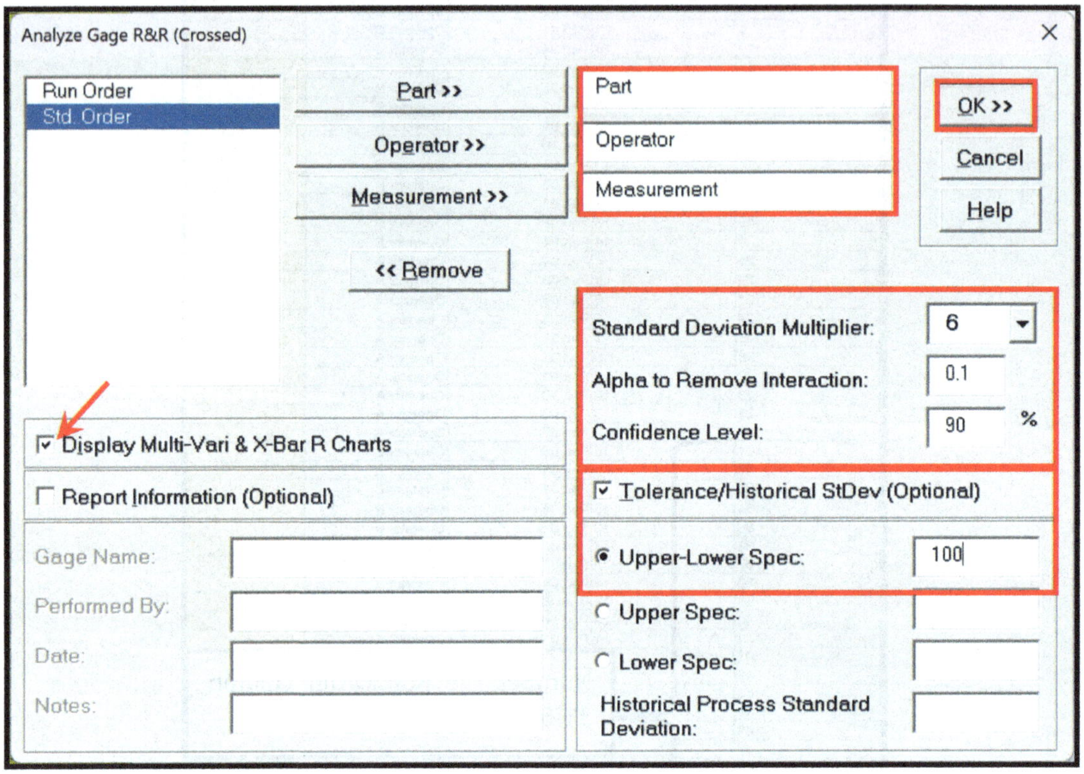

Insert the factors Part, Operator and Measurement. Choose; Display Multi-Vari & X-Bar R Charts. Keep

> **Note:** For the Multiplier, some companies use 5.15. Follow your company's policy for this

the default values for Standard Deviation Multiplier, Alpha to Remove Interaction and Confidence Level.

Check: **Tolerance/Historical StDev**. Choose, **Upper-Lower Spec:** then input the value **100**. This is the specification window for the process. Click **OK**.

Output: (Three worksheet are created)

Analyze Gage R&R, - shows the analytical results.

Gage R&R -Multi-Vari, - shows each Operators Measurements by Part.

Gage R&R – X-Bar & R. – shows an X-Bar & R chart for the average reading for each operator by part.

Analytical Output – **Analyze Gage R&R**

Process Tolerance (USL - LSL):	100
Historical Process Standard Deviation:	
Standard Deviation Multiplier:	6
Alpha to Remove Interaction:	0.1
Confidence Level:	90.0
Number of Parts:	10
Number of Operators:	3
Number of Replicates:	2
Design Type:	Balanced

Analysis of Variance with Part * Operator Interaction:

Source	DF	SS	MS	F	P
Part:	9	5170.3	574.47	331.07	0.0000
Operator:	2	159.10	79.550	45.845	0.0000
Part * Operator:	18	31.233	1.735	1.679	0.1018
Repeatability:	30	31	1.033333333		
Total:	59	5391.6	91.383		

Analysis of Variance without Part * Operator Interaction (P for Interaction >= 0.1):

Source	DF	SS	MS	F	P
Part:	9	5170.3	574.47	443.09	0.0000
Operator:	2	159.10	79.550	61.356	0.0000
Repeatability:	48	62.233	1.297		
Total:	59	5391.6	91.38305085		

The first section contains information regarding the MSA study.

The next two sections show the Analysis of Variance (ANOVA) table for the model with and without the interaction.

The **ANOVA** table is a statistical assessment of factors (parts and operators plus their interaction). Low p-values indicate that statistically there is a difference between levels within the factor; however, this does not indicate whether the measurement system is or is not acceptable.

Since the **p-value** for the **Parts*Operator** interaction is greater than the alpha to remove value of 0.10, SigmaXL produces an ANOVA table without the interaction.

For both situations, the output indicates there's a difference between parts. This is a good result. But it also shows a difference between Operators. This is not good. This indicates that the measured output is dependent upon the operator.

Two values of particular interest are the **%R&R** and **% P/T** ratios. The first metric, **%R&R** relates variability of a measurement system to process variation, while **%P/T** relates variability of a measurement system to the specification window.

There are two important questions to answer when reviewing a measurement system:

1. Is the system acceptable as a means of determining whether the product is within specification?
2. Is the system acceptable to measure improvements made to the variability of the process?

%P/T answers the first question and **%R&R** answers the second question. The quality of a measurement system is considered acceptable if **%R&R** and **%P/T** are below 30%, and excellent if those values are below 10%. To find these values, go to the next output.

Gage R&R Metrics	StDev	StDev Lower 90% CI	StDev Upper 90% CI	6 * StDev	% Total Variation (TV)	% TV Lower 90% CI	% TV Upper 90% CI
Gage R&R:	2.282	1.594	8.876	13.694	22.74	11.97	67.41
Operator (AV Appraiser Variation):	1.978	1.123	8.802	11.868	19.71		
Part * Operator (INT Interaction):	0	0	0	0	0.00		
Reproducibility (SQRT(AV^2 + INT^2)):	1.978	1.123	8.802	11.868	19.71		
Repeatability (EV Equipment Variation):	1.139	0.977204	1.371	6.832	11.34		
Part Variation (PV):	9.774	7.121	16.091	58.644	97.38		
Total Variation (TV):	10.03687165	7.473	16.731	60.221	100.00		

The **%R&R** is highlighted in blue, under the % Total Variation (TV) or **22.74%**.

Gage R&R Metrics	% Tolerance	% Tolerance Lower 90% CI	% Tolerance Upper 90% CI
Gage R&R:	13.69	9.56	53.25
Operator (AV Appraiser Variation):	11.87	6.74	52.81
Part * Operator (INT Interaction):	0.00	0.00	0.00
Reproducibility (SQRT(AV^2 + INT^2)):	11.87	6.74	52.81
Repeatability (EV Equipment Variation):	6.83	5.86	8.23
Part Variation (PV):	58.64	42.73	96.55
Total Variation (TV):	60.22	44.84	100.39

The **%P/T** is highlighted in blue, under the % Tolerance or **13.69%**.

The important outcome of a MSA is to understand where variation exists and determine if it is worthwhile to improve or replace the current system.

Remember, typical goals for **%P/T** and **%R&R** are as follows:

- **<10%** = Ideal
- **10%** to **30%** = Acceptable
- **>30%** = Unacceptable

The analysis to this point uses the standard deviation to determine the spread of the data. However, standard deviations are not additive. Using the variance property of additivity allows for a more accurate estimation of **%R&R**.

The **Component of Variation** (VarComp) table shows this information.

The **VarComp** table uses variances to calculate the portion each component of the measurement system contributes to the overall variation. This table takes advantage of additive property of variances.

Gage R&R Metrics	Variance Component	% Contribution of Variance Component
Gage R&R:	5.209	5.17
Operator:	3.913	3.88
Part * Operator:	0	0.00
Reproducibility:	3.913	3.88
Repeatability:	1.297	1.29
Part Variation:	95.530	94.83
Total Variation:	100.74	100.00

Since the variance is a squared value, the guidelines are not the same as for Repeatability and Reproducibility using standard deviations.

The goals for **%R&R** when using the variance are:

- **<1%** = Ideal
- **1%** to **9%** = Acceptable
- **>9%** = Unacceptable

If the Gage R&R portion of the % Contribution of Variance Component analysis exceeds this value, then determine which metric (Repeatability or Reproducibility) contributes the largest portion.

Remember, the Gage R&R % Contribution of Variance Component (5.17) is equal to the sum of the Repeatability (1.29) and Reproducibility (3.88) percentages.

The Reproducibility % contribution is equal to the Operator plus the Operator * Part interaction. Since the interaction has a value of 0, it was removed from the model. The Reproducibility (3.88) component is the same as the Operator.

The Variance Component method does not relate the values to the process specification. (There's no %P/T calculated with Variance Components.)

The output indicates that, while the MSA results are in the Acceptable level, it can be improved by

Gage R&R Metrics	NDC	NDC Lower 90% CI	NDC Upper 90% CI
Number of Distinct Categories (Signal-to-Noise Ratio: 1.41 * PV/R&R):	6.1	1.5	11.7

looking at the operator component. The total Gage R&R is 5.17%. The Operator makes up 3.88%. Working on methods to obtain more consistent agreements between operators could reduce the Gage R&R to 1.5% or less.

The final output shows the NDC (Number of Distinct Categories). The goal is to have this value >= 5.

> Note: Due to the complexity of calculations, SigmaXL must be loaded and appear on the menu in order for this template to function.

Graphical Output: **Gage R&R – Multi-Vari**

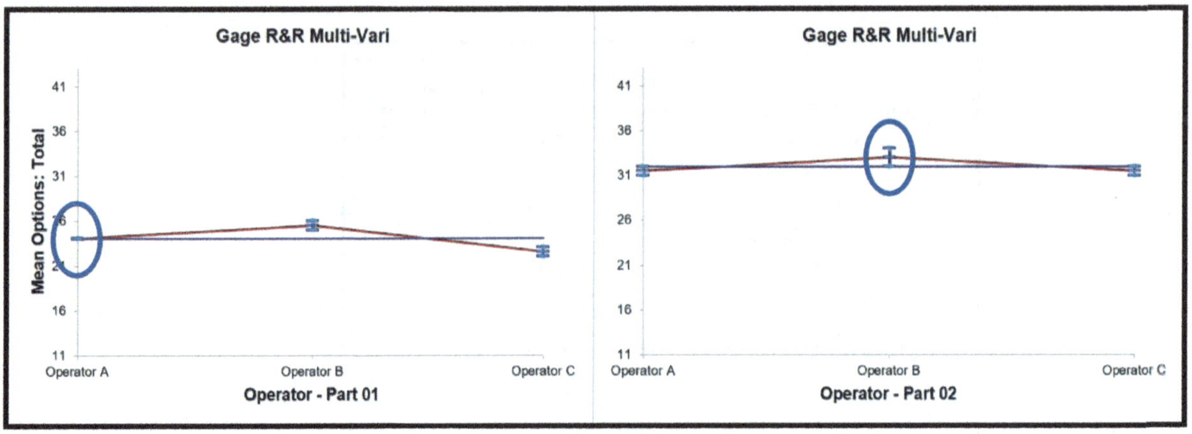

Only showing 2 parts of ten for brevity.

The Multi-Vari charts shows results for each part. The horizontal line is the part's average reading for all operators. For each operator, within that part, there are 3 lines; the top line is the maximum value for that operator, the lower is the minimum, and the middle is the average. The average for each operator is connected by the red line. For Part 1, Operator 1 had no variation. Both readings were the same. In the graph for part 2, Operator B had a wide range between the minimum and maximum values.

> Hint: To observe the maximum and minimum values for each operator, hover the cursor over the line representing the desired value.

Look for operator issues. Does one of the operators have higher readings than the other? Does one of the operators have higher ranges compared to the others? Do certain parts have higher ranges compared to other parts? (This might indicate a Part by Operator interaction.)

Graphical Output: **Gage R&R X-Bar & R**

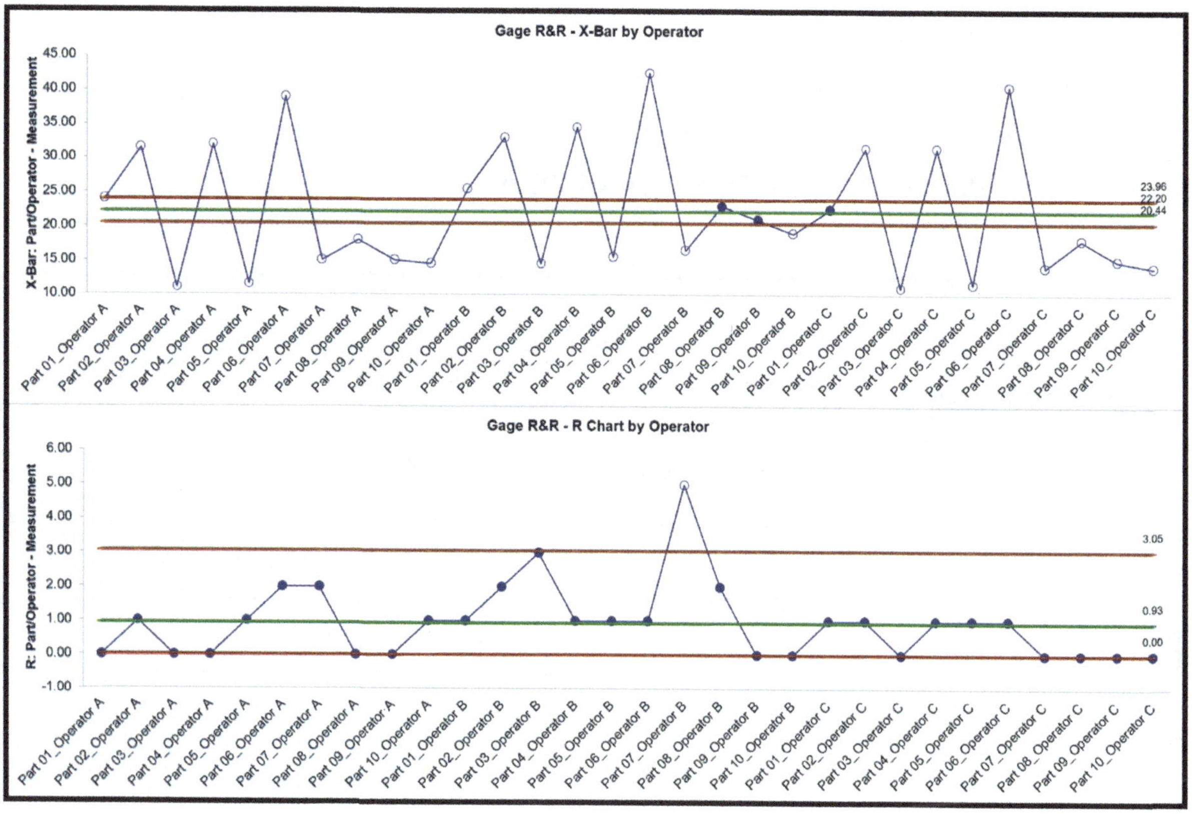

The X-Bar by Operator chart shows the average for each part by operator. The first 10 values are Operator A, the next 10 are Operator B, and the last 10 are Operator C. The pattern within each operator should be almost the same. Notice Operator B, the middle 10 readings. These seem to be higher than Operators A and C. This could lead to an operator issue.

All readings should in the X-Bar by Operator (top chart) should be ***outside*** the Control Limits. This indicates that the measurement system is able to distinguish the differences between samples.

If all, or most, of the readings are within the control limits, then either the study samples did not represent the true process variation, or it may indicate the measurement system is unable to distinguish differences between parts because the measurement system itself has too much variation.

The R (range) chart by Operator shows the ranges for each part by operator. Notice that operator B again seems to have higher values compared to A and C.

Additional Graphs:

Two-Way ANOVA Interaction Plots.

Return to the **WaterMSA** worksheet.

Menu command:

SigmaXL > Statistical Tools > Two-Way ANOVA

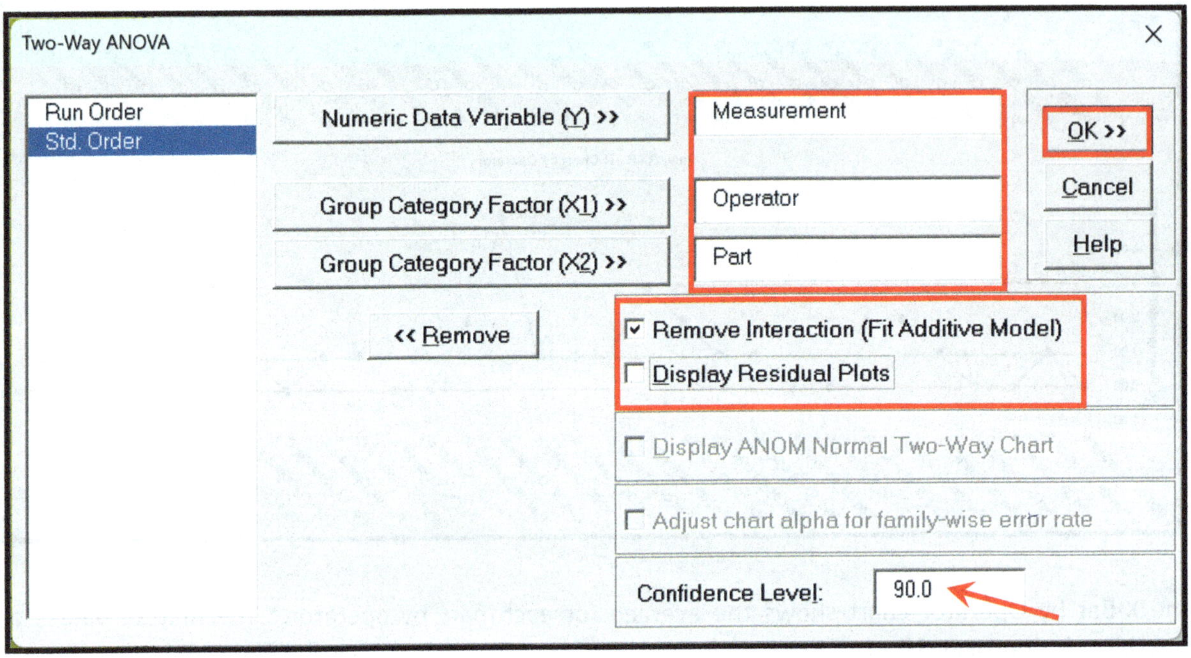

The output creates the; **Two-Way ANOVA** tab. This contains both analytical and graphical analysis. The reason to run this test is for the graphs.

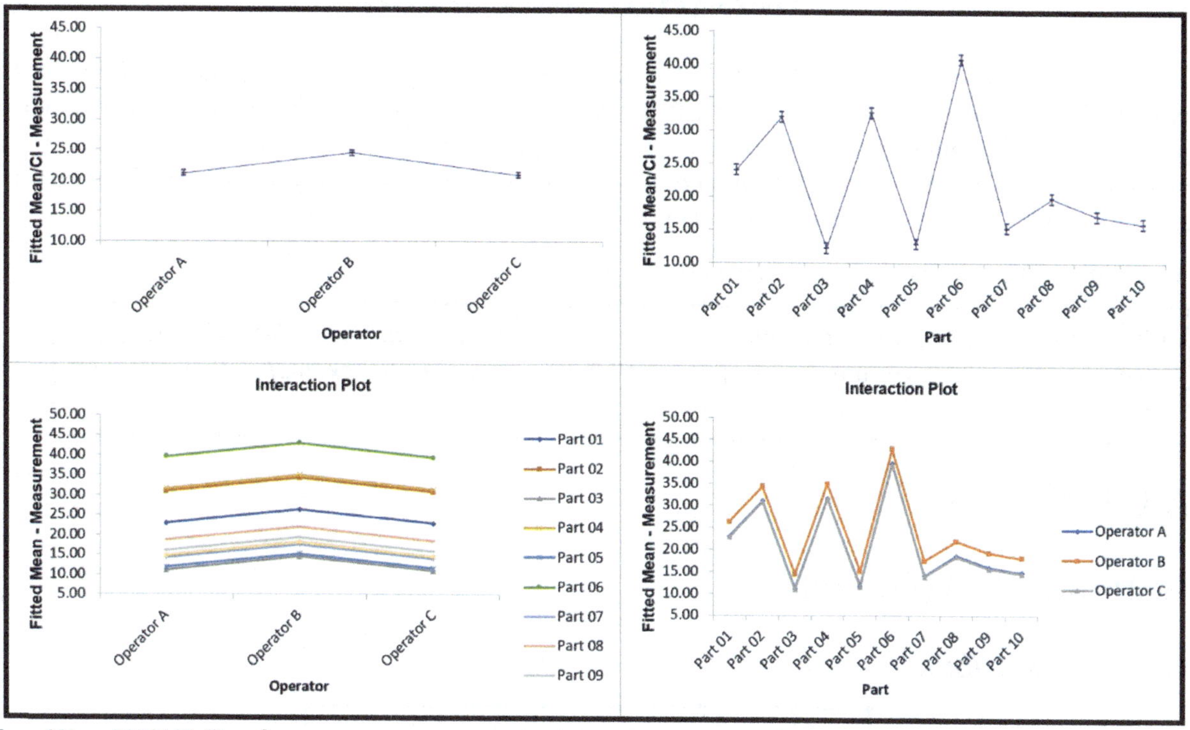

Two-Way ANOVA Graphs

The upper left graph shows the mean value with a 90% confidence interval (specified in the Input dialog box) for each operator. This is the average per operator for all 10 parts. The ideal situation is to have the connect line appear almost horizontal. Here we have operator B slightly higher compared to operators A and C.

The upper right graph shows the overall average with a 90% confidence interval for all 10 parts. If some parts have a higher range for the confidence interval, this might indicate there's an issue with measuring that part. This should be investigated.

The lower left graph shows the average reading per part for each operator. Horizontal lines would be ideal, but here operator B has higher readings for each part.

The final graph shows an overlaid plot of the part average by operator. Ideal situation would have all lines overlapping. This graph reinforces the idea that operator B has higher readings compared to A and C.

Repeatability of the measurement system is indicated by the difference between readings within each part for each operator. A larger average difference indicates the measurement system suffers from a repeatability (short term) issue.

Reproducibility is indicated by the difference between operators within each part. Operator differences are obvious, such as the case for parts 8 to 10 where operator 2 produces readings consistently higher than the other two operators.

Use the %R&R value for process improvement efforts, and the %P/T for acceptance of product to specification.

MSA (Attribute Data)

There are a variety of ways to perform an MSA for attribute data. The simplest is one which checks the system via a "Good" and "Bad" set of criteria for each item. The items can range from actual products produced in a manufacturing environment to assessment of inputs for order forms, invoices, or information obtained during check-in at a hotel. A more detailed MSA for attribute data is to assess the system in terms of the type of defect found in the process.

An attribute MSA may be applied to any part of a business.

> **Hint:** *Remember, attribute data contains less information than continuous data, therefore, an attribute MSA requires a sample size of at least 50 items or more. The example below contains only ten items for demonstration purposes.*

Attribute MSA

Attribute MSA (Binary)

Worksheet: ***Attribute***

Sample	Operator	Replicate	Rating
1	1	1	Good
2	1	1	Bad
3	1	1	Good
4	1	1	Good
5	1	1	Bad
6	1	1	Good
7	1	1	Good
8	1	1	Good

The first example contains a simple situation. In this study, ten items were selected for a Good/Bad assessment. Each of three operators looked at the items two times, and recorded them as either Good or Bad. No expert opinion as to whether it is Good or Bad, was provided. This is considered a Binary output.

The purpose of this assessment is to determine how often the inspectors agree with themselves and with each other.

To run the Attribute MSA (Binary) use the menu command:

SigmaXL > Measurement Systems Analysis > Attribute MSA (Binary)

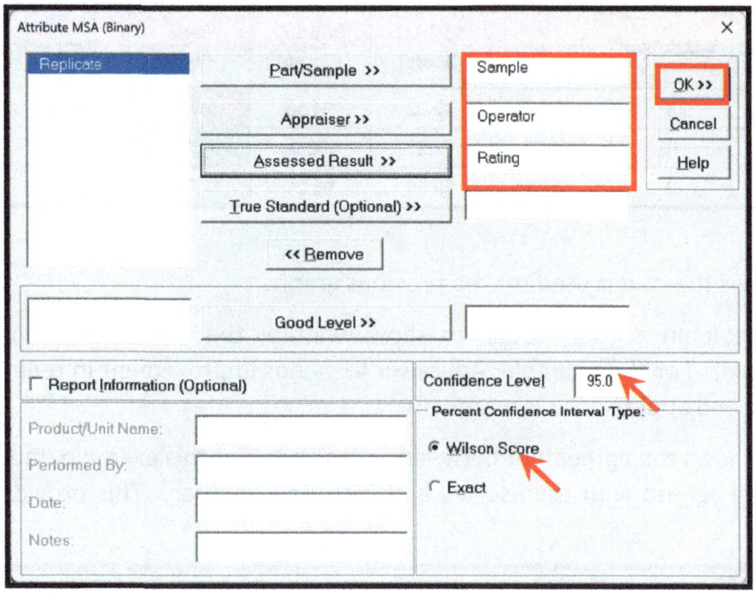

Fill in the **Part/Sample**, **Appraiser**, and **Assessed Result** as shown. Keep the Wilson Score. Finally, decide on a Confidence Level. Click **OK**.

Results:

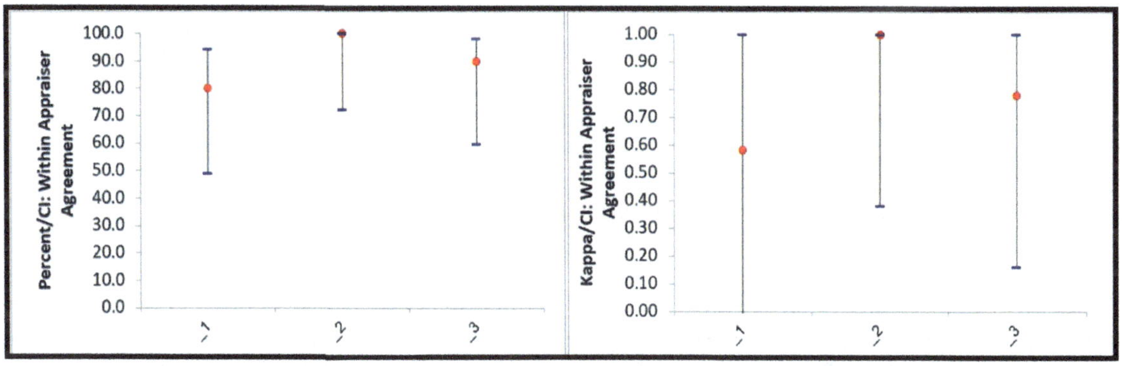

The graph on the left displays the Percent Within Appraiser Agreement. This is how often each appraiser agreed with themselves. The dot represents the sample value while the lines indicate a 95% confidence interval for the population.

For Appraiser #1, the agreement is 80%, while the confidence interval is approximately 50% – 95%.

For Appraiser #2, the agreement is 100%, while the confidence interval is approximately 70% – 100%.

For Appraiser #3, the agreement is 90%, while the confidence interval is approximately 60% – 98%.

The graph on the right shows the Kappa Value Within Appraiser Agreement. The sample value and confidence intervals have the same explanation as shown for the Percent Agreement.

Analytical Reports

Attribute Agreement Report:

Within Appraiser Agreement	# Inspected	# Matched	Percent	95% LC (Score)	95% UC (Score)	Fleiss' Kappa	Fleiss' Kappa P-Value	Flieiss' Kappa 95% LC	Fleiss' Kappa 95% UC
_1	10	8	80.00	49.02	94.33	0.5833	0.0325	-0.0365	1.0000
_2	10	10	100.00	72.25	100.00	1.0000	0.0008	0.3802	1.0000
_3	10	9	90.00	59.58	98.21	0.7802	0.0068	0.1604	1.0000

The first report shows the values used for the previous graphs.

The **Fleiss' Kappa** column is color coded to show whether the values are Good (**Green**), Marginal (Yellow) or Poor (**Red**). For this example, Appraiser #1 needs improvement in repeating an assessment. Appraiser #2 is fine, and appraiser #3 is marginal.

The second report shows the agreement between appraisers. For this example, there were six out of 10 where the assessors agreed with themselves and with one another. This provided a Kappa value of

Between Appraiser Agreement	# Inspected	# Matched	Percent	95% LC (Score)	95% UC (Score)	Fleiss' Kappa	Fleiss' Kappa P-Value	Flieiss' Kappa 95% LC	Fleiss' Kappa 95% UC
	10	6	60.00	31.27	83.18	0.6044	0.0000	0.4444	0.7644

0.6044. This is a RED situation. The appraisers are not agreeing with one another.

Several different methods are available to improve a visual quality inspection. These include:

1) Improve lighting
2) Magnification of item
3) Display photos of good and bad conditions
4) Refresher classes on the criteria

Processes with poor attribute MSA's should implement some of these improvements, then re-run the MSA.

If an operator did not agree with themselves, they couldn't agree with the other operators.

Note: The 95% Confidence Interval (CI) is an estimate for the Appraiser's population agreement value. In other words, for Appraiser 2, even though they agreed with themselves 100% of the time in this test, if they had looked at an extremely large number of items, their agreement could be anywhere between 74.11% up to 100%. The CI range is large because the sample size used in this assessment was only 10. A larger sample size (50) would produce a tighter range. For a simple Agreement Analysis, as shown in this example, Kappa does not add any additional useful Information. **Kappa** will be explained further in the next example.

For a simple Good vs. Bad analysis, it is important to have the Inspectors match themselves and the other Inspectors at 100%, otherwise good material will be scrapped and bad material will be passed on.

Attribute MSA with Known Attributes

The next example shows attribute data in which the operator must not only identify a defect, but must also classify the defect. This worksheet demonstrates the use of an Expert or Standard; in other words, the correct answer.

Up to this point, the tests have compared operators within and between themselves, but with no mention of whether they were correct. The Expert or Standard column contains the correct answer, so now the test will compare operators within and between themselves as well as with the expert answer.

Worksheet: ***Attribute_Standard***

Samples	Appraisers	Assessment	Standards	Replicate
1	1	Scratch	No Defect	1
2	1	No Defect	No Defect	1
3	1	Smudge	Mottle	1
4	1	Pickle	Pickle	1
5	1	No Defect	Smudge	1
6	1	Mottle	Pickle	1
7	1	Scratch	No Defect	1
8	1	Scratch	No Defect	1
9	1	Smudge	Smudge	1
10	1	Mottle	Pickle	1
1	1	Pickle	No Defect	2
2	1	No Defect	No Defect	2
3	1	Smudge	Mottle	2
4	1	Pickle	Pickle	2
5	1	No Defect	Smudge	2
6	1	Mottle	Pickle	2
7	1	Pickle	No Defect	2
8	1	Pickle	No Defect	2
9	1	Smudge	Smudge	2
10	1	Mottle	Pickle	2
1	2	Smudge	No Defect	1
2	2	Scratch	No Defect	1
3	2	Smudge	Mottle	1
4	2	Pickle	Pickle	1

To run the analysis, select:

SigmaXL > Measurement Systems Analysis > Attribute MSA (Nominal)

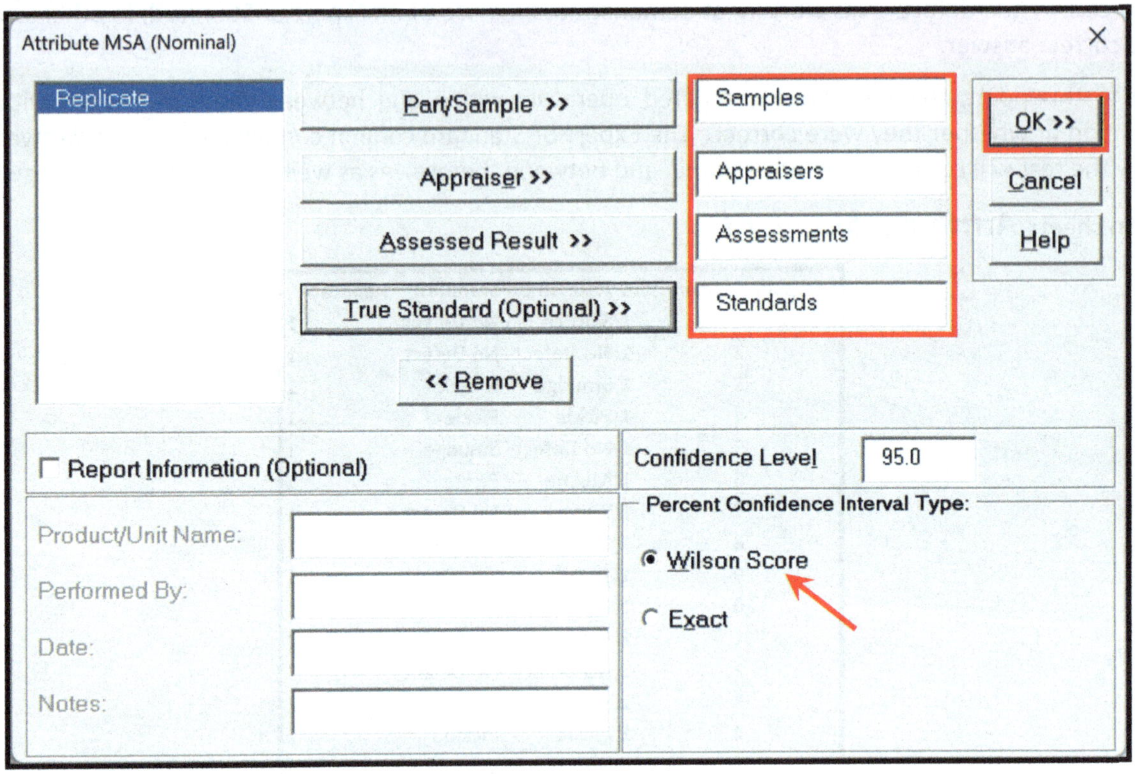

Fill out the dialog box in a similar manner to the previous example, but add the column **Standards** for the **True Standard (Optional)**. Click **OK**.

The output creates both graphical and analytical information.

Graphs:

Percent Within Appraiser Agreement

Percent Each Appraiser vs Standard Agreement

Percent Each Appraiser vs Standard Effectiveness

Kappa Within Appraiser Agreement

Kappa Each Appraiser vs Standard Effectiveness

Reports:

Attribute Agreement

Attribute Effectiveness

Attribute MSA Data

Graph: Percent Within Appraiser Agreement

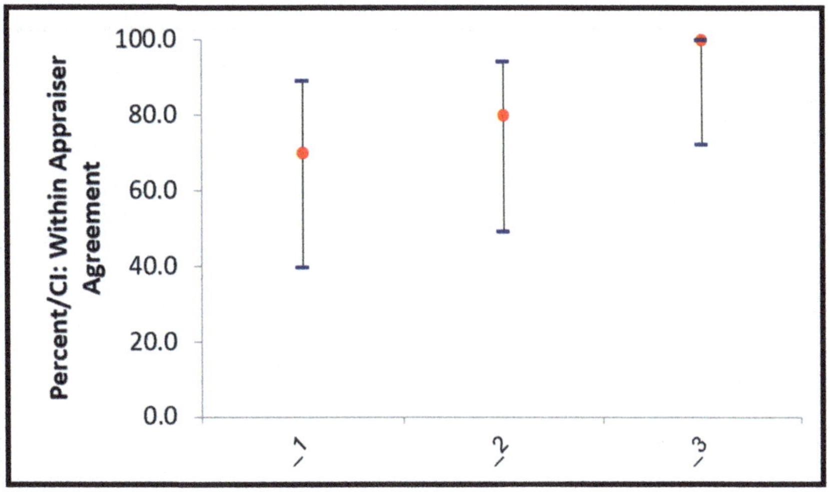

This is the same graph as shown previously. Each Assessor's percent agreement with themselves (the dot), along with the confidence interval. Anything short of 100% agreement indicates an operator has an issue with repeating the assessment (agreeing with themselves). In this example, only Appraiser 3 agreed with themselves 100% of the time.

> **Note:** *The 95% Confidence Interval (CI) is an estimate for the Appraiser's population agreement value. In other words, for Appraiser 3, even though they agreed with themselves 100% of the time in this test, if they had looked at an extremely large number of items, their agreement could be anywhere between 74.11% up to 100%. This range is large because there was a small sample size used in this Agreement Analysis.*

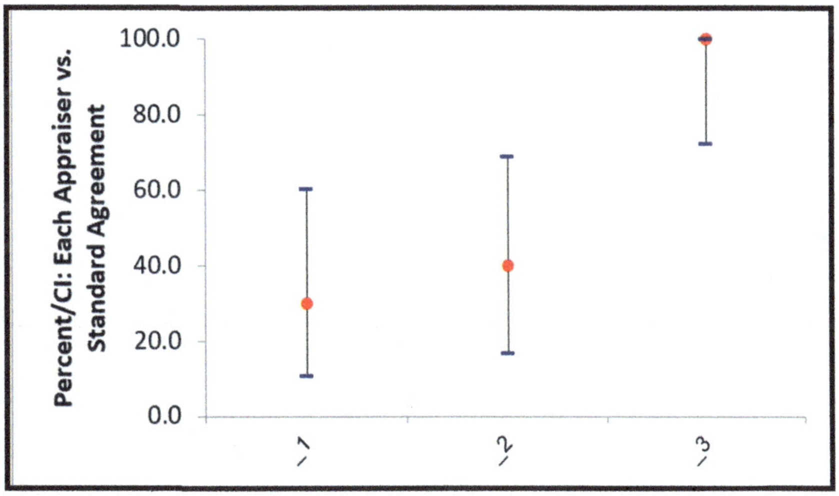

Graph: Percent Each Appraiser vs Standard Agreement

This graph shows how often the assessors agreed with the correct assessment. The Appraiser must agree with themselves before they can agree to the **Standard**.

Graph: Percent: Each Appraiser vs Standard Effectiveness

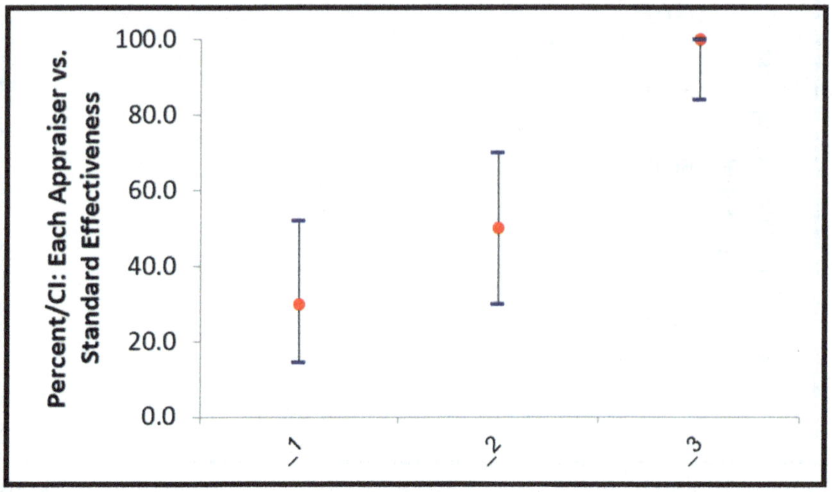

The **Attribute Effectiveness** treats each trial as an opportunity. Consistency across trials or appraisers is not considered. This has the benefit of providing a Percent measure that is unaffected by the number of trials or appraisers. Also, the increased sample size for # Inspected results in a reduction of the width of the Percent confidence interval.

Graph: Kappa Within Appraiser Agreement

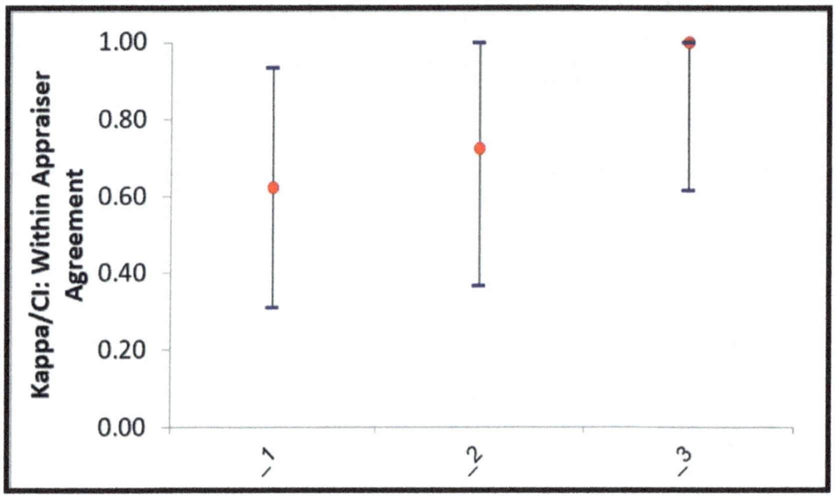

Kappa Analysis:

Fleiss' (Within Appraiser) Kappa Statistics shows each Appraiser's ability to determine a specific quality characteristic.

Kappa Calculation:

Kappa is calculated using the following equation:

$$Kappa = \frac{P_{observed} - P_{chance}}{1 - P_{chance}}$$

where:

$P_{observed}$ = Proportion of units classified in which the raters agreed

P_{chance} = Proportion of units for which one would expect agreement by chance

Kappa values less than 1.0 indicates which categories the Appraiser does not agree with themselves. Use this output to verify if an operator has trouble consistently identifying a specific issue.

Note: *While a Kappa of .75 is considered acceptable, anything less than 1.0 indicates an area for improvement.*

Results of the calculation are categorized as follows:

Kappa = 1.0	Kappa = 0.0	Kappa < 0.0
Perfect agreement.	Agreement the same as would be expected by chance alone.	Agreement less than would be expected by chance alone.

Each Kappa value has an associated p-value, based on the Kappa Hypotheses:

H_o: Agreement is due to chance

H_a: Agreement is not due to chance

It is generally agreed that a Kappa >.75 indicates an acceptable measurement system.

Kappa: Each Appraiser vs Standard Effectiveness

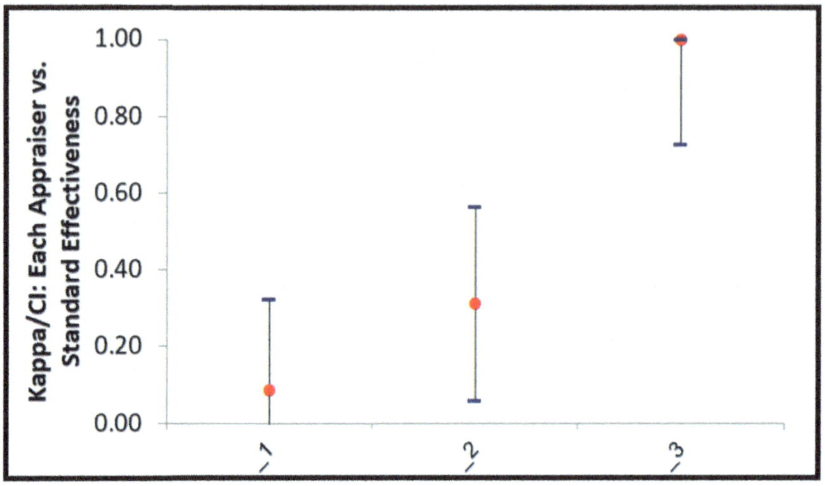

This graph shows a Kappa value related to the Effectiveness metric described previously.

Attribute Agreement Report:

Within Appraiser Agreement	# Inspected	# Matched	Percent	95.0% LC (Score)	95.0% UC (Score)	Fleiss' Kappa Overall Response	Fleiss' Kappa Overall Response P-Value	Fleiss' Kappa Overall Response 95.0% LC	Fleiss' Kappa Overall Response 95.0% UC
_1	10	7	70.00	39.68	89.22	0.6226	0.0000	0.3098	0.9355
_2	10	8	80.00	49.02	94.33	0.7241	0.0000	0.3684	1.0000
_3	10	10	100.00	72.25	100.00	1.0000	0.0000	0.6141	1.0000

Each Appraiser vs. Standard Agreement	# Inspected	# Matched	Percent	% LC ()	% UC ()	Fleiss' Kappa Overall Response	Fleiss' Kappa Overall Response P-Value	Fleiss' Kappa Overall Response % LC	Fleiss' Kappa Overall Response % UC
_1	10	3	30.00	10.78	60.32	0.0714	0.2833	-0.1727	0.3155
_2	10	4	40.00	16.82	68.73	0.3122	0.0080	0.0580	0.5665
_3	10	10	100.00	72.25	100.00	1.0000	0.0000	0.7271	1.0000

This report shows the data behind the graphs for both the percent values and the Kappa results for the **Within Appraiser Agreement** and **Each Appraiser vs Standard Agreement**.

It produces a color coated assessment for the **Kappa Overall Responses**.

The remaining portion of the report looks at each defect category producing a Kappa value along with

Fleiss' Kappa Response (MOTTLE)	Fleiss' Kappa Response (MOTTLE) P-Value	Fleiss' Kappa Response (MOTTLE) 95.0% LC	Fleiss' Kappa Response (MOTTLE) 95.0% UC	Fleiss' Kappa Response (NO DEFECT)	Fleiss' Kappa Response (NO DEFECT) P-Value	Fleiss' Kappa Response (NO DEFECT) 95.0% LC	Fleiss' Kappa Response (NO DEFECT) 95.0% UC
1.0000	0.0008	0.3802	1.0000	1.0000	0.0008	0.3802	1.0000
1.0000	0.0008	0.3802	1.0000	0.5833	0.0325	-0.0365	1.0000
1.0000	0.0008	0.3802	1.0000	1.0000	0.0008	0.3802	1.0000
Fleiss' Kappa Response (MOTTLE)	Fleiss' Kappa Response (MOTTLE) P-Value	Fleiss' Kappa Response (MOTTLE) 95.0% LC	Fleiss' Kappa Response (MOTTLE) 95.0% UC	Fleiss' Kappa Response (NO DEFECT)	Fleiss' Kappa Response (NO DEFECT) P-Value	Fleiss' Kappa Response (NO DEFECT) 95.0% LC	Fleiss' Kappa Response (NO DEFECT) 95.0% UC
-0.1765	0.7850	-0.6147	0.2618	0.0476	0.4157	-0.3906	0.4859
-0.1765	0.7850	-0.6147	0.2618	0.5693	0.0054	0.1311	1.0000
1.0000	0.0000	0.5617	1.0000	1.0000	0.0000	0.5617	1.0000

the 95% confidence interval. Only categories **MOTTLE** and **NO DEFECT** are shown here.

The rest of the Report shows the **Between Appraiser Agreement** and **All Appraisers vs Standard Agreement**.

Between Appraiser Agreement	# Inspected	# Matched	Percent	% LC ()	% UC ()	Fleiss' Kappa Overall Response	Fleiss' Kappa Overall Response P-Value	Fleiss' Kappa Overall Response % LC	Fleiss' Kappa Overall Response % UC
	10	1	10.00	1.79	40.42	0.3445	0.0000	0.2583	0.4307
All Appraisers vs. Standard Agreement	# Inspected	# Matched	Percent	% LC ()	% UC ()	Fleiss' Kappa Overall Response	Fleiss' Kappa Overall Response P-Value	Fleiss' Kappa Overall Repsonse % LC	Fleiss' Kappa Overall Response % UC
	10	1	10.00	1.79	40.42	0.4612	0.0000	0.3126	0.6098

The wide range for the confidence intervals is the result of a sample size of 10. Larger samples will create tighter confidence intervals.

Fleiss' Kappa Response (MOTTLE)	Fleiss' Kappa Response (MOTTLE) P-Value	Fleiss' Kappa Response (MOTTLE) 95.0% LC	Fleiss' Kappa Response (MOTTLE) 95.0% UC	Fleiss' Kappa Response (NO DEFECT)	Fleiss' Kappa Response (NO DEFECT) P-Value	Fleiss' Kappa Response (NO DEFECT) 95.0% LC	Fleiss' Kappa Response (NO DEFECT) 95.0% UC
0.4240	0.0000	0.2640	0.5840	0.3100	0.0001	0.1500	0.4700

Fleiss' Kappa Response (MOTTLE)	Fleiss' Kappa Response (MOTTLE) P-Value	Fleiss' Kappa Response (MOTTLE) 95.0% LC	Fleiss' Kappa Response (MOTTLE) 95.0% UC	Fleiss' Kappa Response (NO DEFECT)	Fleiss' Kappa Response (NO DEFECT) P-Value	Fleiss' Kappa Response (NO DEFECT) 95.0% LC	Fleiss' Kappa Response (NO DEFECT) 95.0% UC
0.2157	0.0474	-0.0373	0.4687	0.5390	0.0000	0.2859	0.7920

Each defect categories are also shown.

Attribute Effectiveness Report:

Each Appraiser vs Standard Effectiveness

Each Appraiser vs. Standard Effectiveness	# Inspected	# Matched	Percent	95% LC (Score)	95% UC (Score)	Fleiss' Kappa Overall Response	Fleiss' Kappa Overall Response P-Value	Fleiss' Kappa Overall Response 95% LC	Fleiss' Kappa Overall Response 95% UC
_1	20	6	30.00	14.55	51.90	0.0865	0.2357	-0.1488	0.3217
_2	20	10	50.00	29.93	70.07	0.3115	0.0078	0.0590	0.5641
_3	20	20	100.00	83.89	100.00	1.0000	0.0000	0.7271	1.0000

Fleiss' Kappa Response (MOTTLE)	Fleiss' Kappa Response (MOTTLE) P-Value	Fleiss' Kappa Response (MOTTLE) 95.0% LC	Fleiss' Kappa Response (MOTTLE) 95.0% UC	Fleiss' Kappa Response (NO DEFECT)	Fleiss' Kappa Response (NO DEFECT) P-Value	Fleiss' Kappa Response (NO DEFECT) 95.0% LC	Fleiss' Kappa Response (NO DEFECT) 95.0% UC
-0.1765	0.7850	-0.6147	0.2618	0.0476	0.4157	-0.3906	0.4859
-0.1765	0.7850	-0.6147	0.2618	0.5833	0.0045	0.1451	1.0000
1.0000	0.0000	0.5617	1.0000	1.0000	0.0000	0.5617	1.0000

The Effectiveness Report also has a color coding to highlight issues.

The individual defect categories are shown in a similar manner as demonstrated with the Attribute Agreement Report.

All Appraisers vs Standard Effectiveness

All Appraisers vs. Standard Effectiveness	# Inspected	# Matched	Percent	95% LC Score	95% UC Score	Fleiss' Kappa Overall Response	Fleiss' Kappa Overall Response P-Value	Fleiss' Kappa Overall Response 95% LC	Fleiss' Kappa Overall Response 95% UC
	60	36	60.00	47.37	71.43	0.4569	0.0000	0.3124	0.6014

The report for All Appraisers vs Standard Effectiveness has the same format as shown for Each Appraiser

Fleiss' Kappa Response (MOTTLE)	Fleiss' Kappa Response (MOTTLE) P-Value	Fleiss' Kappa Response (MOTTLE) 95.0% LC	Fleiss' Kappa Response (MOTTLE) 95.0% UC	Fleiss' Kappa Response (NO DEFECT)	Fleiss' Kappa Response (NO DEFECT) P-Value	Fleiss' Kappa Response (NO DEFECT) 95.0% LC	Fleiss' Kappa Response (NO DEFECT) 95.0% UC
0.1346	0.1485	-0.1184	0.3876	0.5694	0.0000	0.3163	0.8224

Effectiveness and Misclassification Summary	Standard (Mottle)	Standard (No Defect)	Standard (Pickle)	Standard (Scratch)	Standard (Smudge)
Appraiser Response (Mottle)	2	0	8	0	0
Appraiser Response (No Defect)	0	16	0	0	4
Appraiser Response (Pickle)	0	3	10	0	0
Appraiser Response (Scratch)	0	4	0	0	0
Appraiser Response (Smudge)	4	1	0	0	8

vs Standard Effectiveness.

The last piece of information shows where the Appraisers did not match the Standard.

The highlighted diagonal (Green Oval) shows the number of times the Appraisers agreed with the Standard for each defect category. All other cells indicate the mistakes made by Appraisers.

For instance, in the last row, the Appraisers response was Smudge, but 4 of those should have been Mottle, and one should have been No Defect.

MSA – Audits

The final measurement system to analyze is one where the data is pulled from a database – a very common situation for many Six Sigma projects. If these databases contain errors, then the data used for the project is wrong.

To determine the correctness of data in a database, an audit is required. The audit will not look at every record, because a task of this magnitude would be beyond the team's resources. Instead, check a sample of records for accuracy and completeness.

It is important to obtain a sample that represents the entire database if the audit is to be correct. Several methods are available to obtain an appropriate sample, these include random, stratified, and systematic sampling.

Random Samples

To create a random sample using SigmaXL, create a column that contains a list of all records. This can be a simple string of numbers from 1 to the last record. The number of records to be selected is dependent upon the resources available, to perform the audit.

If there are 500 records available and the team wants to randomly check 50, create a column in SigmaXL with the values from 1 to 500. Name the column '**Record No.**'

Record No.
1
2
3
4
5
6
7
8

To collect 50 random records from the 500, perform the following steps.

- Create a column (label it **Random**) of 500 random numbers. (In the column next to the Record No.)
- Sort worksheet by column **Random**.
- Choose the first 50 rows of Record No. for your sample.

Create Column of Random Numbers:

Menu command: ***SigmaXL > Data Manipulation > Random Data > Uniform (Integer)***

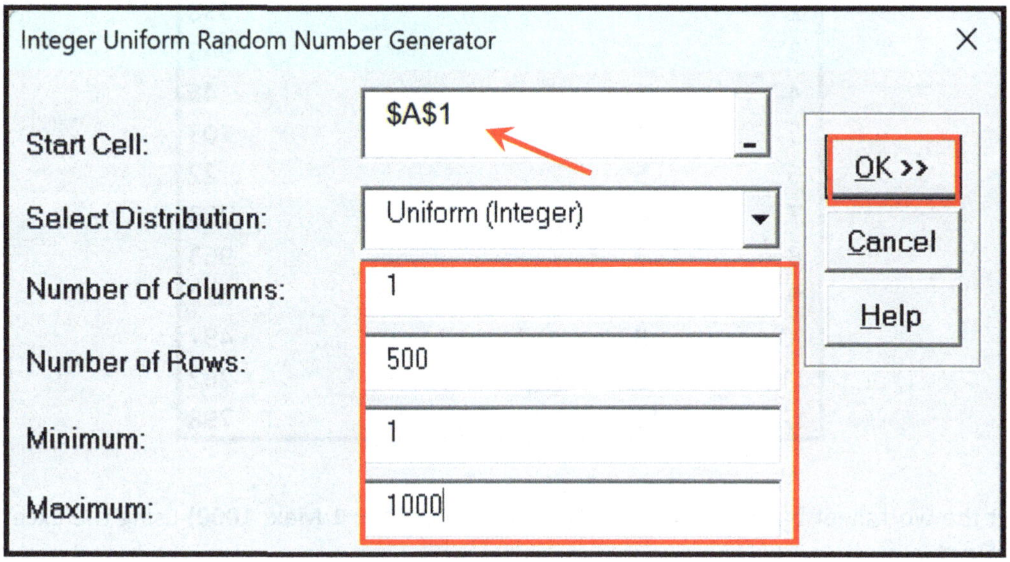

Select the Start Cell at A1. (The program automatically creates a new worksheet for the random numbers titled **SigmaXL Random Data (1)**.)

For **Number of Columns** type **1**. For **Number of Rows** choose **500.**

The **Minimum** is **1** and the **Maximum** is **1000**.

Click **OK**.

1. Uniform(Int.) Min: 1 Max: 1000
338
945
46
103
22
783
963
822
497
262

A column of 500 random numbers is created. Copy this column and paste next to the **Record No.** column.

	A	B
1	Record No.	**1. Uniform(Int.) Min: 1 Max: 1000**
2	1	338
3	2	945
4	3	46
5	4	103
6	5	22
7	6	783
8	7	963
9	8	822
10	9	497
11	10	262
12	11	798

Next, sort the worksheet based on column B (**Uniform(Int) Min: 1 Max: 1000**) using the Excel function: ***Data > Sort***.

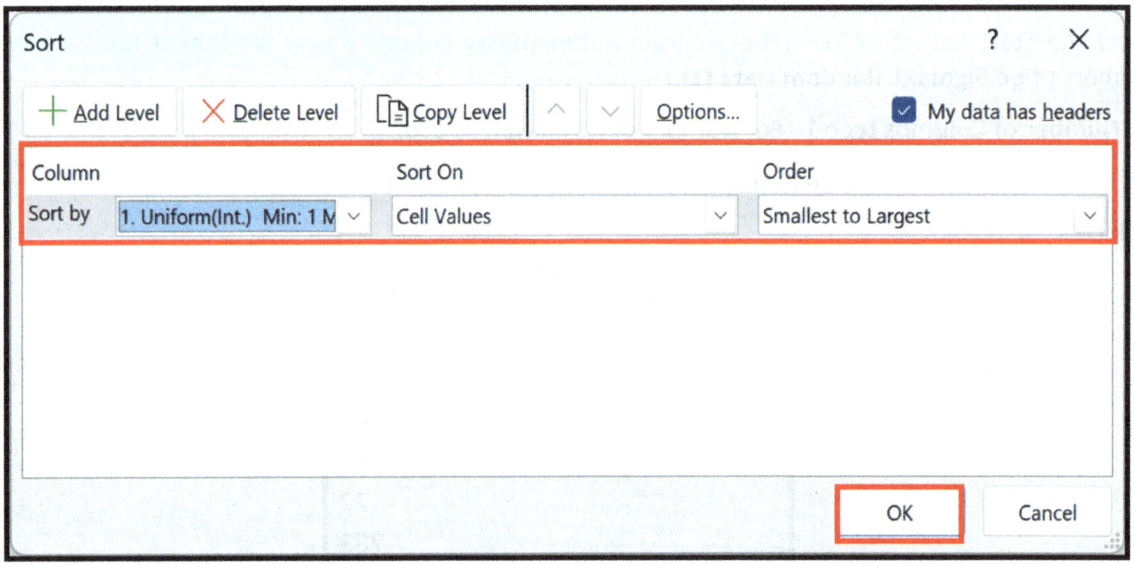

Sort by column **1.Uniform(Int) Min: 1 Max: 1000**.

Sort on **Cell Values**. Order: **Smallest to Largest**.

Click **OK**.

Sorted Worksheet:

	A	B
1	Record No.	**1. Uniform(Int.) Min: 1 Max: 1000**
2	216	1
3	475	2
4	61	5
5	143	8
6	361	11
7	247	17
8	183	18
9	435	19
10	5	22
11	31	23

Pick the **Record No.**'s in the first 50 rows for the sample.

The first 10 for this example would be records number 216, 475, 61, 143, 361, 247, 183, 435, 5, 31.

Stratified Samples

A stratified sample is used when there are specific criteria associated with the database of records and the team wants to see the sample represent the proportion of records that fall into each group.

Examples of such criteria might include gender; income; size of client; types of material purchased; health care procedures performed; size of loans; and the like.

To perform a stratified sample, begin with the desired sample size and then determine the percentage of each group in the final database. The sample size of each stratum corresponds to the percentage of the records they represent.

Example: The team is working with loans and they want to check the database for accuracy and completeness. There are three categories (strata) of loans: small (< $100,000), medium ($100,000 to $500,000), and jumbo (>$500,000). The approximate proportion of each category is 45%, 35% and 20% respectively.

The teams will use a sample size of 75 records, so according to the general proportions of different types of loans the sample should contain 33.75 records of small loans; 26.25 records of medium loans; and 15 records of jumbo loans.

(Collect 34 small loans, 26 medium and 15 jumbos.)

Use worksheet: **Loan**

Record No.	Loan Value
1	$54,519
2	$302,166
3	$326,474
4	$190,575
5	$4,522,418
6	$1,045,457
7	$91,674
8	$80,424
9	$100,453

To obtain the desired records label column C: **Loan Size**.

Next, use the following formula to determine the **Loan Size**: (See Excel help on creating formula for columns).

=IFS(B2 < 100000,"Small",B2 > 500000,"Jumbo",B2 <> 0, "Medium")

Record No.	Loan Value ($)	Loan Size
1	54,519.40	Small
2	302,165.81	Medium
3	326,474.01	Medium
4	190,574.91	Medium
5	4,522,417.81	Jumbo
6	1,045,456.72	Jumbo
7	91,674.02	Small
8	80,424.38	Small
9	100,452.98	Medium

Subset the worksheet based on **Loan Size.**

Menu command: ***SigmaXL > Data Manipulation > Category Subset***

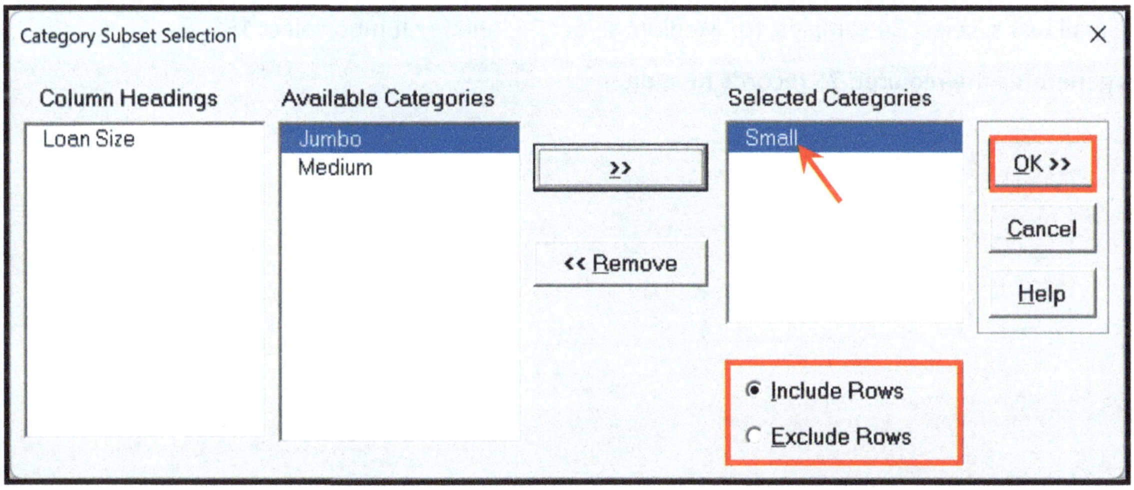

Select; **Loan Size** for the Column Headings. Choose; **Small** for the Selected Categories and keep the **Include Rows** option. Click **OK**.

The new sheet (**Category Subset (1)**) containing the rows for Small Loans.

	A	B	C
1	Record No.	Loan Value ($)	Loan Size
2	1	54,519.40	Small
3	7	91,674.02	Small
4	8	80,424.38	Small
5	10	82,000.03	Small
6	11	52,128.32	Small
7	15	14,915.82	Small
8	18	76,657.41	Small
9	21	60,162.57	Small
10	24	16,460.95	Small
11	26	13,696.13	Small

... **Category Subset (1)** Cate

Repeat this procedure on the worksheet **Loan** to create subsets for Medium and Jumbo loans.

Use the Category Subset worksheet to randomly select the desired number of records. Follow the procedure shown previously on randomly selecting records.

For Small loans, select 34 samples; for Medium select 26; and for Jumbo select 15.

This generates the required 75 records to audit.

Systematic Samples

Systematic samples are often used as a sampling method for the convenience of the team. In this type of sampling, items are selected based on a pre-determined system (every 10th item, every 20th item, etc.). This method will usually produce a good quality sample, but sometimes there is an issue with an unknown sequence that mimics the sampling system.

For instance, if the system calls for collecting every 10th item; but, based on the manufacturing and arrival patterns, every 10th item comes from the same source, then the entire sample will come from one source and not the other. This is certainly not a desirable condition. Issues of an unknown sequence mimicking the sampling system are relatively rare, but it is worth the effort to double check before proceeding with this type of sample.

To select the records for this type of sample, determine the percent of the records to audit and create a column containing numbers representing that percent. For instance, if 10% of the records are desired, use the numbers 1 to 10; if 20% of the records are required, use the values 1 to 5; and so on. To select 5% of the records, a column with the numbers 1 to 20 is required. Use SigmaXL to create this column.

Worksheet: ***Loan***

Label column D as **Reference**. Create the sequence of number from 1 to 20.

	A	B	C	D
1	Record No.	Loan Value ($)	Loan Size	Reference
2	1	54,519.40	Small	1
3	2	302,165.81	Medium	2
4	3	326,474.01	Medium	3
5	4	190,574.91	Medium	4
6	5	4,522,417.81	Jumbo	5
7	6	1,045,456.72	Jumbo	6
8	7	91,674.02	Small	7
9	8	80,424.38	Small	8
10	9	100,452.98	Medium	9
11	10	82,000.03	Small	10
12	11	52,128.32	Small	11
13	12	4,848,451.44	Jumbo	12
14	13	1,824,086.99	Jumbo	13
15	14	110,894.57	Medium	14
16	15	14,915.82	Small	15
17	16	4,525,134.91	Jumbo	16
18	17	1,747,066.65	Jumbo	17
19	18	76,657.41	Small	18
20	19	355,328.80	Medium	19
21	20	2,388,965.27	Jumbo	20

Next, in row 22, type; **=D2**.

19	18	76,657.41	Small	18
20	19	355,328.80	Medium	19
21	20	2,388,965.27	Jumbo	20
22	21	60,162.57	Small	=D2

Hit **Enter**.

19	18	76,657.41	Small	18
20	19	355,328.80	Medium	19
21	20	2,388,965.27	Jumbo	20
22	21	60,162.57	Small	1
23	22	420,217.69	Medium	
24	23	471,324.33	Medium	

The value from D2 is now copied into D22. To fill in the rest of the column, place the cursor in the lower

19	18	76,657.41	Small	18
20	19	355,328.80	Medium	19
21	20	2,388,965.27	Jumbo	20
22	21	60,162.57	Small	1

right corner of cell D2 and **Double-Click** (Left mouse button).

The sequence 1 – 20 repeats for the entire column.

Using the method shown previously, create a **Category Subset** of the worksheet using one of the values; 1 – 20.

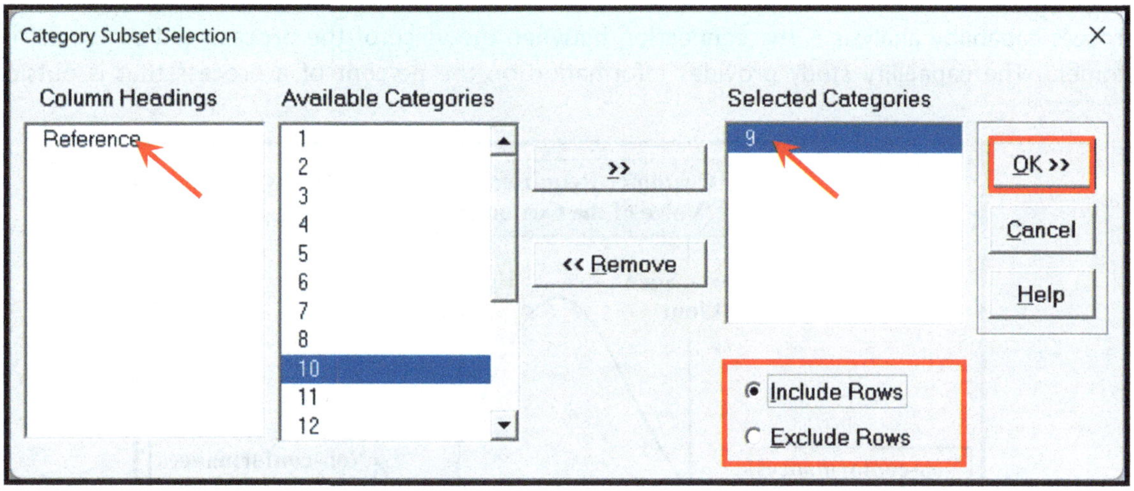

The new worksheet contains the records for the sample.

Record No.	Loan Value ($)
9	100,452.98
29	32,411.26
49	3,756,032.07
69	32,680.19
89	160,452.49
109	59,978.49
129	183,218.81
149	296,180.07
169	53,131.94
189	85,120.00
209	445,254.10
229	67,307.22
249	437,867.57
269	48,874.97
289	307,785.73
309	21,263.08

With this type of sampling, the size of the loan is not a consideration.

Determining Process Capability

A process capability analysis is the connection between the voice of the process and the voice of the customer. The capability study provides information on the percent of a process that is outside of

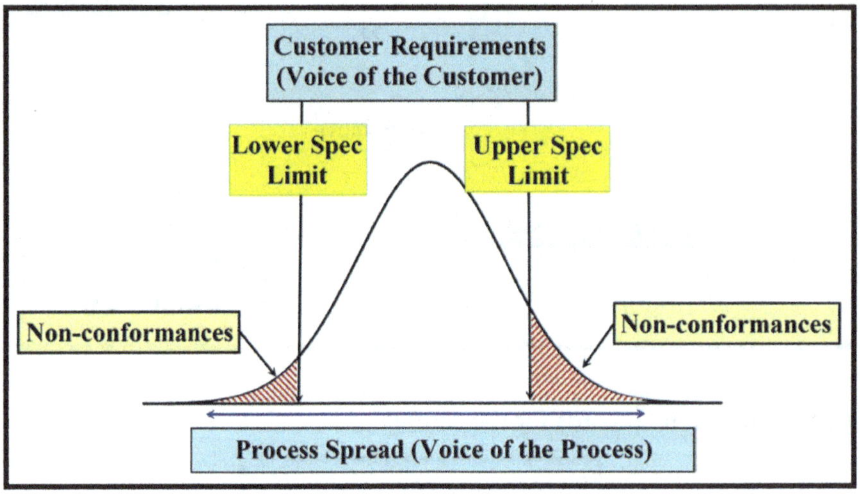

customer specifications, so without customer specifications the capability study is simply not possible.

The initial evaluation of process capability provides a baseline from which a goal is determined, and the amount of progress from the baseline to the goal determines the success of the project.

Process capability analysis requires an estimate of the process spread based on the sample information. Customer requirements are then overlaid, and the percent of the process outside these specifications is determined. This type of display makes it much easier to evaluate process spread vs. customer specs.

Metrics

Continuous Data

When a process is measured using a metric on a continuous scale, (weight, length, thickness, time, etc.) the Process Capability metrics help to compare unrelated processes. The values calculated allow process owners to determine the need for improvements. The formula used is as follows:

$$Cp = \frac{USL - LSL}{6 * s}$$

(Where **s**, is the standard deviation based on the subgroup size)

Cp:

- Compares the process specification window to the spread of the process represented by 6 standard deviations (or 99.73% of a normally distributed process).
- Calculations assume a process is centered within specifications, which means a Cp calculation offers no indication of whether the process is on target.
- It is possible that a process with a high Cp value could have a high percent of the process outside of the specifications.

Cpk: is the metric that looks at the process mean in relation to the specifications. It is the minimum of **Cpu** and **Cpl**, shown as follows:

$$\text{Cpu} = \frac{\text{USL} - \overline{\text{X}}}{3 * \text{s}}$$

$$\text{Cpl} = \frac{\overline{\text{X}} - \text{LSL}}{3 * \text{s}}$$

Cpk = Min(Cpu, Cpl)

SigmaXL uses two methods to estimate the standard deviation. For the Cp and Cpk, using a sample size of 1, SigmaXL will use, as an estimate of **σ**, the Average Moving Range divided by a correction factor based on the number of values used to calculate the moving range. The default is to use 2 values for the moving range. (This the method used in the Individuals & Moving Range Control Chart.)

With a moving range of size 2, the formula becomes:

$$\text{s} = \frac{\overline{\text{MR}}}{1.128}$$

For subgroup sizes greater than 1, SigmaXL allows for use of either the average Range, or the average Standard Deviation of the subgroups.

Pp and **Ppk** (the overall capability values) are calculated in the same manner as **Cp** and **Cpk** (the within or short term capability values, only the standard deviation is based on the overall standard deviation of the data, not a subgroup standard deviation. This is the same value as the standard deviation calculated using Descriptive Statistics.

SigmaXL > Statistical Tools > Descriptive Statistics, or any other method to obtain basic summary statistics.

By definition, a Six Sigma process has a Pp ≥ 2.0 and a Ppk ≥ 1.5; however, **Cpm** is the proper metric for use when the target value is not centered within the specifications. If a target value is provided, then the **Cpm** will be calculate. Otherwise, the output leaves this value blank.

Discrete Data

When a process is measured using counts of defects, or defective items, a go/no go metric, the values calculated relate to defects per unit, or defects per opportunity.

DPU

DPU (Defects per Unit) is calculated by taking the total number of defects in a sample and dividing by the number of units in that sample. It is assumed that a unit may have more than one defect.

DPMO

When the quality level of a process improves the DPU value decreases, often to a level where the DPU is a very small fraction that shows up as .000 on spreadsheets. To improve the discrimination of this metric, the DPMO (Defects per Million Opportunities) metric was developed. With DPMO, defects are measured in relation to defects that could potentially exist.

The formula for DPMO;

$$\text{DPMO} = \frac{(Defect\ Count) * 1{,}000{,}000}{\#\ \text{Units} * (\text{Opportunities/Unit})}$$

The **Opportunity** is defined as the number of chances of not meeting a customer's requirement on each unit examined.

Percent Defective

Describing an item as either good or bad is one way to determine if an item is defective, but this is not the same thing as identifying a specific defect because an item classified as bad may have one or more defects.

When measuring defectives, gather a sample of items and determine the percent of items that fall into the defective category. Calculate the percent of the total and post it as the percent defective. To properly measure the percent defective of a process, the sample size should have on average five defective items. This means as a process improves, the sample size required to properly measure defective rate increases.

Process Sigma Level

The important information regarding a process is; How often are we creating defective product. The metrics mentioned previously provides this information. However, as the process improves the percent defective, or Defects per Million Opportunities become small and it's often difficult for audience members to understand the quality level.

The metric; **Process Sigma**, provides a simple value with a goal of 6.0. This would indicate that the defects level is defined as 3.4 parts per million defectives. This, for most process, is a standard goal. (Certain metrics such as deaths by airline accidents would aim at a much lower value.)

To obtain the Process Sigma level, use SigmaXL's **Process Capability Templates**.

Capability Study

Continuous Data

SigmaXL's capability study are considered within capabilities and are used as an internal guide to how good a process could become; Pp and Ppk are considered overall capabilities and are what the customer sees with incoming material. As a first step, teams try to move the process from current (Pp and Ppk) levels to Cp and Cpk levels. If this does not satisfy the project goals, additional work is needed.

Continuous Data – Individual Readings

Worksheet: ***Capability***

Menu command:

SigmaXL > Process Capability > Capability Combination Report (Individuals)

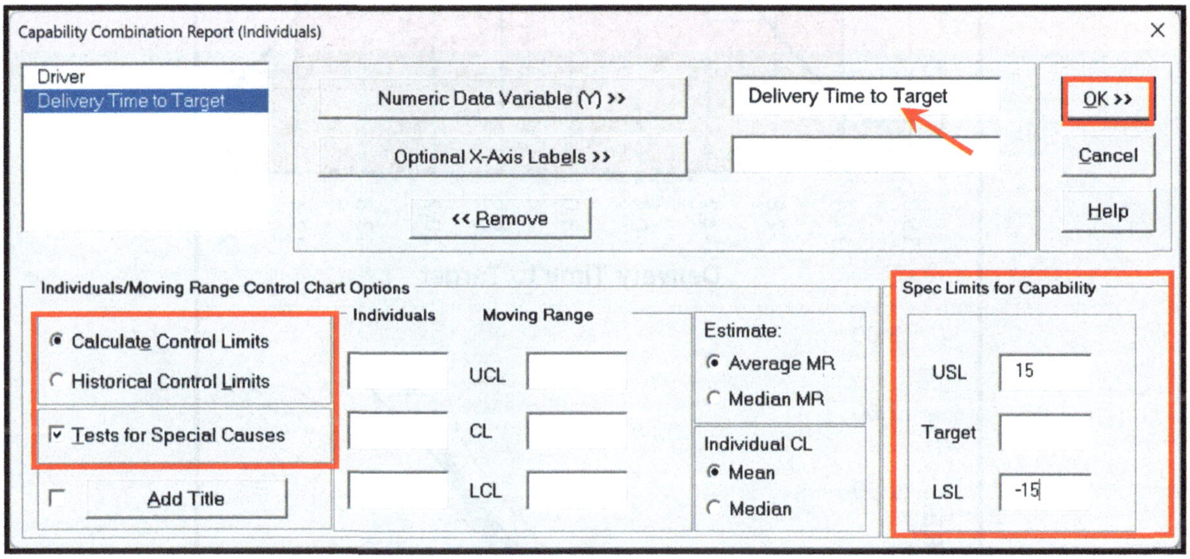

For Numeric Data Variable (Y): **Delivery Time to Target**.

Select; **Calculate Control Limits** and **Tests for Special Causes**.

Under Spec Limits for Capability, the **USL** (Upper spec Limit) is **15** and the **LSL** (Lower spec Limit) is **-15**.

Leave the other options at their default values.

Click **OK**.

The results are displayed in both graphical and analytical form.

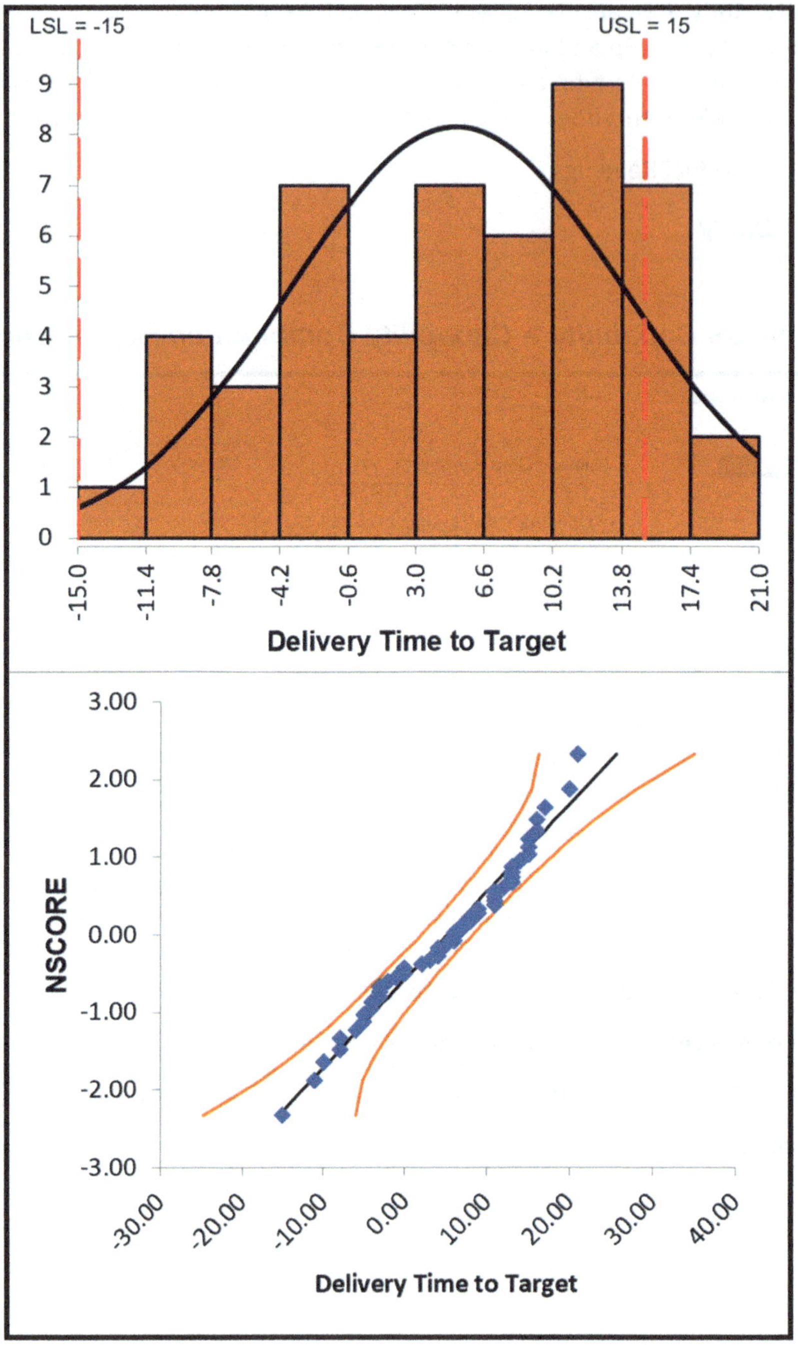

The initial graphical output shows a Histogram with the specification limits, along with a normal curve based on the sample data. The second graph is a Probability chart.

Analytical Output

The Process Capability Report shows the process information (Sample Size or Count, the Sample Mean along with the two types of calculated Standard Deviations, Overall and Within). The bottom portion shows the process specifications. Defects are shown as both PPM and % greater than and less than the specification limits. The AD test for normality is also presented. (This relates to the Probability chart.)

Process Capability Report: Delivery Time to Target	
Count	50
Mean	5.140
StDev (Overall, Long Term)	8.809
StDev (Within, Short Term)	8.449
USL	15
Target	
LSL	-15

The Capability and Potential Capability indices, based on the two methods of calculating the standard deviation, are listed. Remember the customer is receiving the quality level listed under the Pp and Ppk values.

Capability Indices using Overall StDev	
Pp	0.57
Ppu	0.37
Ppl	0.76
Ppk	0.37
Cpm	
Potential Capability Indices using Within StDev	
Cp	0.59
Cpu	0.39
Cpl	0.79
Cpk	0.39

Next, the defect levels, or performance levels, are shown as ppm (parts per million), and as a percent. Both are listed as they relate to the Upper and Lower Specifications. This is what the customer is receiving. The Actual (Empirical) Performance show the percentages above and below specification that occurred in the sample.

Expected Overall Performance	
ppm > USL	131494.4
ppm < LSL	11115.7
ppm Total	142610
% > USL	13.15%
% < LSL	1.11%
% Total	14.26%
Actual (Empirical) Performance	
% > USL	10.00%
% < LSL	
% Total	10.00%

The final information shows the Anderson-Darling Normality test information.

Anderson-Darling Normality Test	
A-Squared	0.522332
P-Value	0.1753

If the P-Value is low, the capability study based on the Normal distribution could produce erroneous results. In this case, refer to the end of the Control unit on how to calculate the capability based on non-normal populations.

Graphical Output

The final graph shows an Individuals and Moving Range chart. Use this chart to determine if there's any process stability issues. Having a stable process is one of the assumptions to run the capability study.

Processes that appear to be unstable show be investigated and have the cause of the instability removed before conducting the capability study.

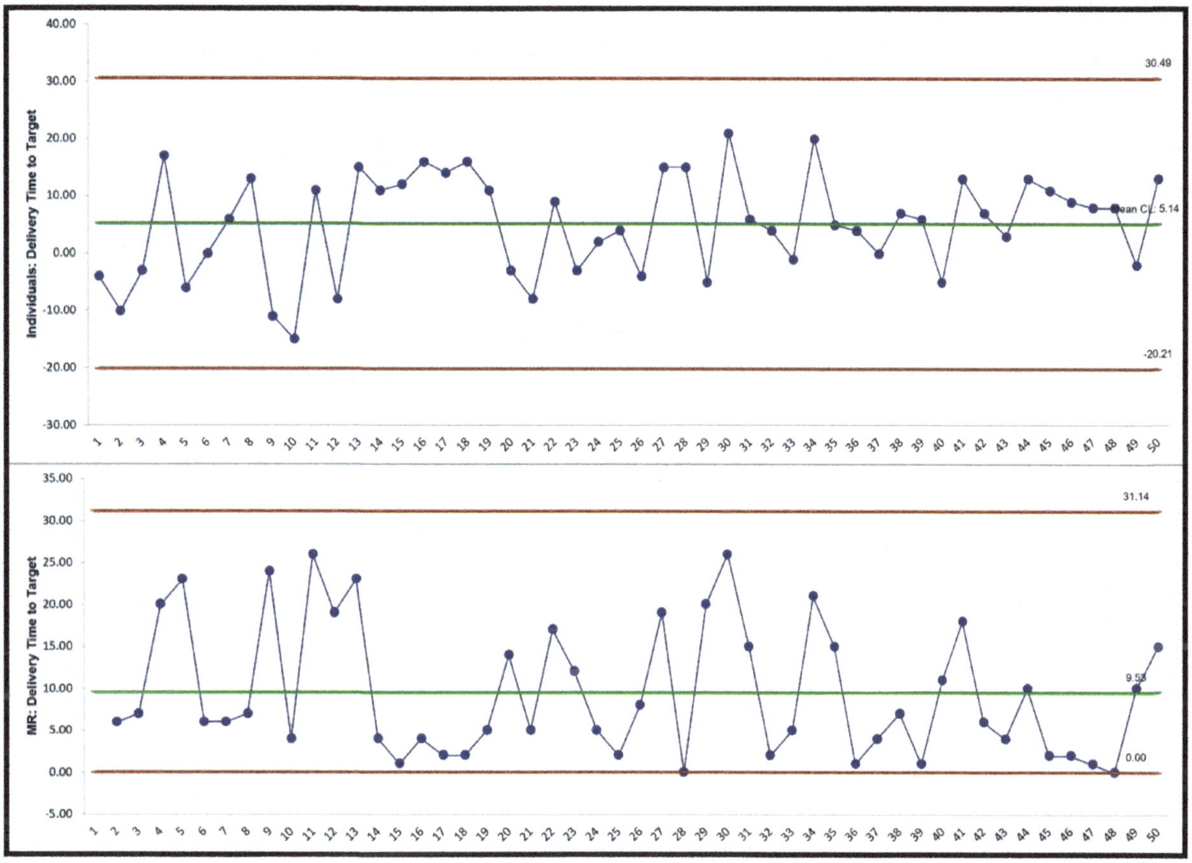

Continuous Data – Subgroups

Process's that use subgroups (measuring more than one item) provide similar information as shown with the Individual readings.

Worksheet: ***Capability***

Menu command:

SigmaXL > Process Capability > Capability Combination Report (Subgroups)

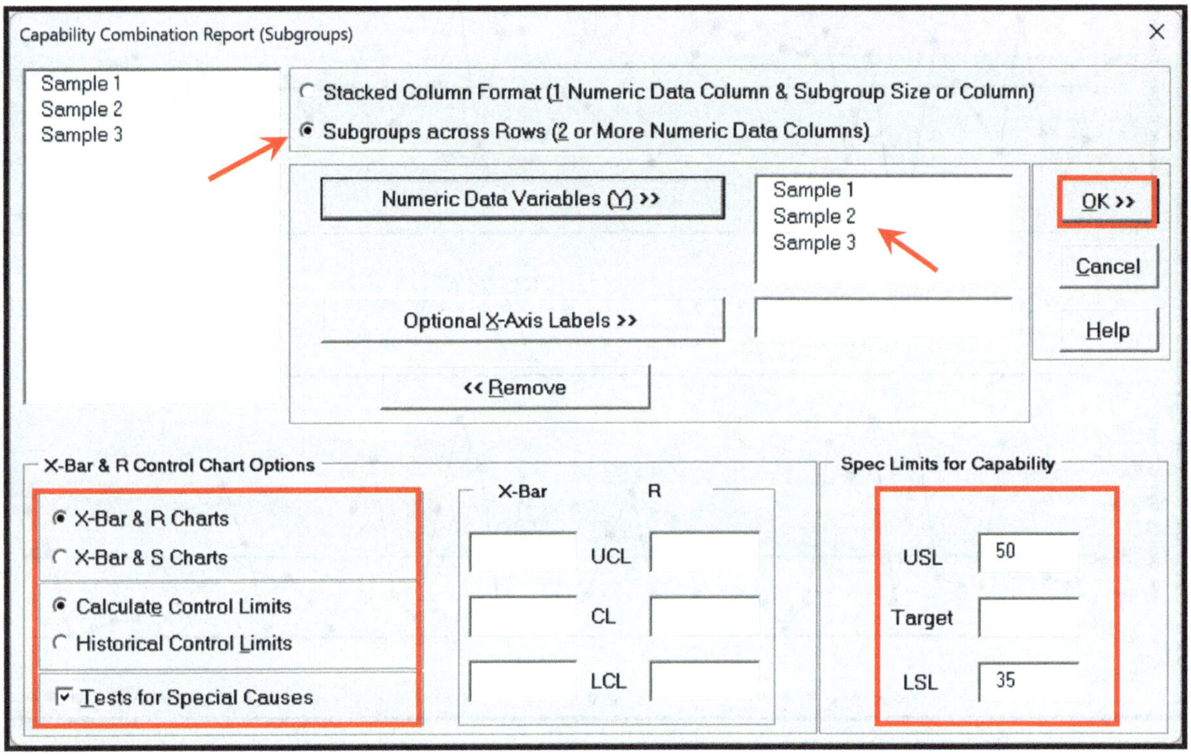

Select; **Subgroups across Rows**.

For the Numeric Data Variables (Y), choose **Sample 1**, **Sample 2** and **Sample 3**.

In the X-Bar & R Control Chart Options, select; **X-Bar & R Charts**, **Calculate Control Lim**its, and **Tests for Special Causes**.

The **Specification Limits for Capability** are: **USL = 50** and the **LSL = 35**.

Click **OK**.

Output

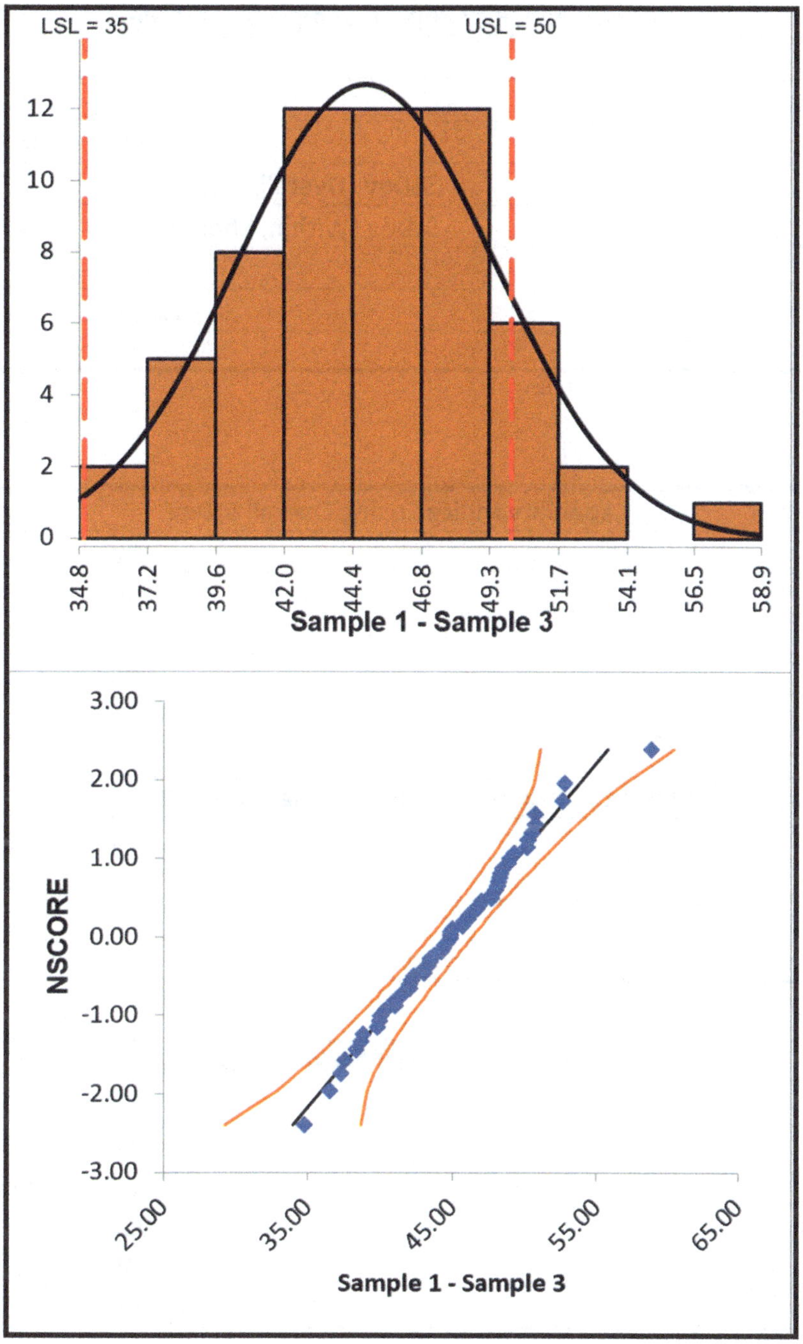

The graphs and output are the same as shown in the individual's example.

Process Capability Report: Sample 1 - Sample 3	
Count	60
Mean	44.896
StDev (Overall, Long Term)	4.552
StDev (Within, Short Term)	4.573
USL	50
Target	
LSL	35

Capability Indices using Overall StDev	
Pp	0.55
Ppu	0.37
Ppl	0.72
Ppk	0.37
Cpm	
Potential Capability Indices using Within StDev	
Cp	0.55
Cpu	0.37
Cpl	0.72
Cpk	0.37

Expected Overall Performance	
ppm > USL	131106.0
ppm < LSL	14862.8
ppm Total	145969
% > USL	13.11%
% < LSL	1.49%
% Total	14.60%
Actual (Empirical) Performance	
% > USL	13.33%
% < LSL	1.67%
% Total	15.00%

Anderson-Darling Normality Test	
A-Squared	0.150243
P-Value	0.9602

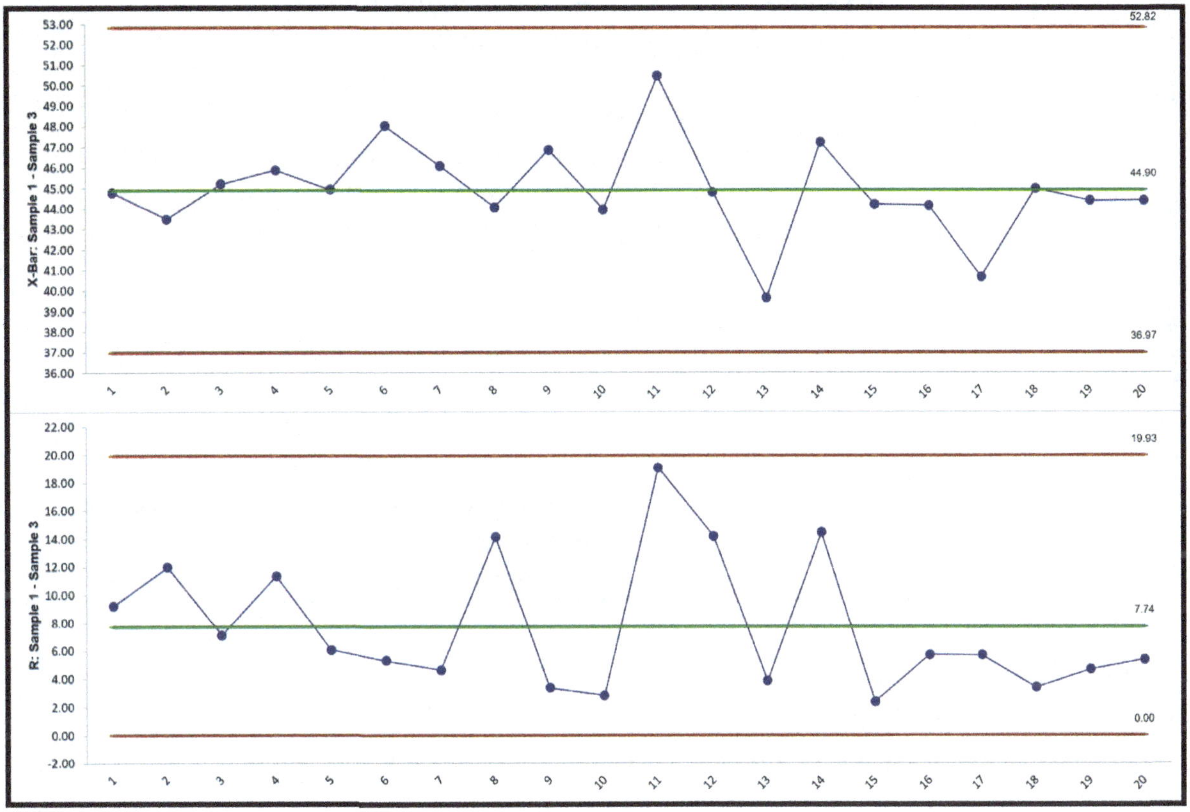

The only difference in the Control Chart from the previous example is that the Range occurs within the sample.

Process Sigma Level

Menu command:

SigmaXL > Process Capability > Basic Process Capability Templates > Process Sigma Level – Continuous

Using the Individuals example:

Process Sigma Level Calculator - Continuous Data (Assumes that data are normally distributed)		
Sample Data (user inputs):		
Mean	x-bar	5.14
Standard Deviation	s	8.809
Upper Specification Limit	USL	15
Lower Specification Limit	LSL	-15
Sigma Shift (typically +1.5)		1.5
Results:		
Expected ppm > USL		131504.0
Expected % > USL		13.15%
Expected ppm < LSL		11118.4
Expected % < LSL		1.11%
Expected ppm (overall)		142622.4
Expected yield (overall) %		85.74%
Process Sigma Level		2.569

Referring to the; Capability Combination Report (Individuals), obtain the values for the Mean, Standard Deviation (overall), and the specifications.

For this example, the Mean is 5.14, the Overall Standard Deviation is 8.809, and the specifications are 15 for the upper and -15 for the lower. Leave the Sigma Shift at 1.5, unless the company uses a different value. Click out of the input area and the results are updated.

The results show the expected defects (in ppm and percent units) above the upper specification limit (USL), and the expected defects below the lower specification limit (LSL).

The ppm values are added to produce the Expected ppm (overall).

The expected yield (overall) takes the percent values above and below the specifications, adds them together, then subtracts the sum from 100%. The final expected yield is 85.74%.

This level of defects produces a Process Sigma Level of 2.569.

Discrete Data

SigmaXL provides a template to assist in determining the DMO and Yield % for discrete data.

Menu command: ***SigmaXL > Process Capability > Basic Process Capability Templates > Process Sigma Level – Discrete***

Process Sigma Level Calculator - Discrete Data		
Sample Data (user inputs):		
Number of units	n	500
Total number of defects observed	d	5
Number of defect opportunities per unit	o	1
Sigma Shift (typically +1.5)		1.5
Results:		
Defects per Unit	dpu	0.01
Defects per Million Opportunities	dpmo	10,000.0
Defects per Opportunity	dpo%	1.00%
Yield	yield%	99.00%
Process Sigma Level	sigma	3.826

Input the Number of units (n) inspected, the Total number of defects observed (d), and the Number of defect opportunities per unit (o). The typical sigma shift is 1.5. Unless the company has determined to use a different value, leave it as is. Click out of the input area and the results are updated.

The results show the standard values of **dpu**, **dpmo**, **dpo%**, **yield%** and the **Process Sigma Level**.

Reference the SigmaXL online workbook for information regarding other templates.

(This page left intentionally blank)

Analyze Phase

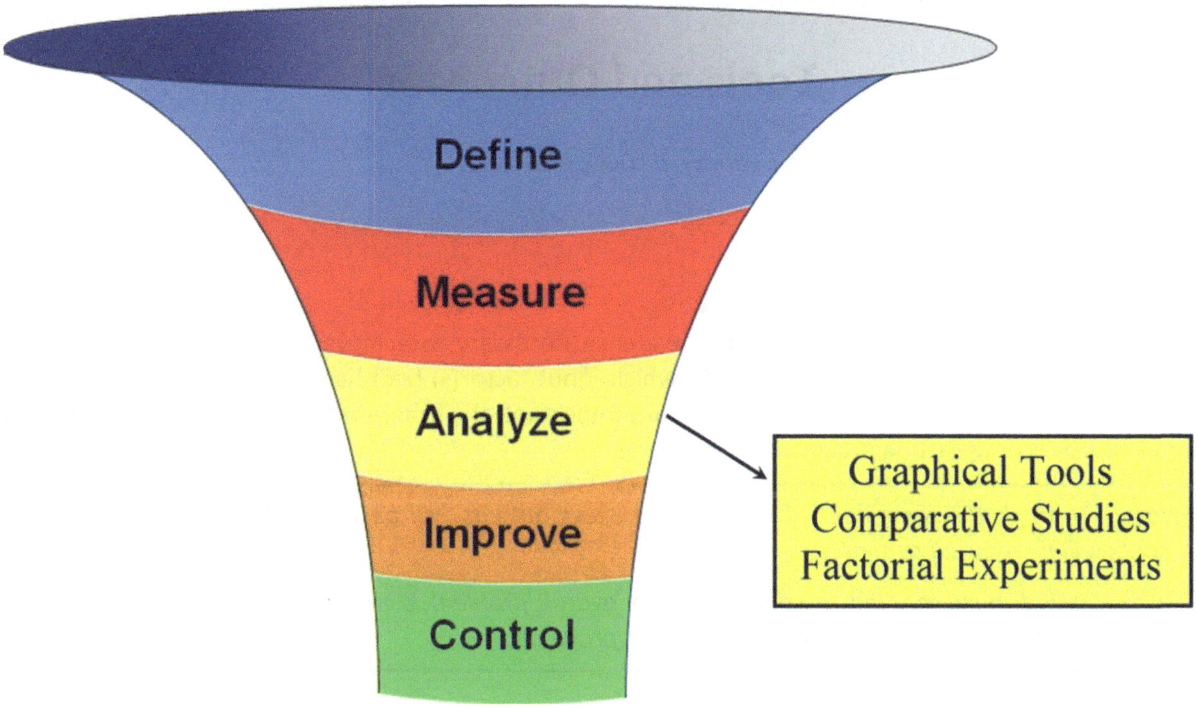

Analyze Phase

The Analyze phase, of a Six Sigma process, focuses on investigation and examination of potential critical inputs (X's) as identified in the Measure phase.

Statistical analysis and graphs become the primary focus of teams during this phase, as they attempt to identify links between inputs (X's) and critical outputs (Y's). What's more, **SigmaXL** becomes an increasingly critical instrument because it provides users with the computing power necessary to definitively show those links and relationships.

Tools and Outcomes

During the Analyze phase teams use a variety of tools, including:

- Graphical Tools
- Comparative Studies
- Factorial Experiments

These tools help teams generate the clear evidence necessary to achieve the major outcome of this phase; that is, they can clearly demonstrate which input factor(s) (X's) have the greatest effect on the critical outputs (Y's). Knowing which factors are important and where they have influence is the first step toward creating lasting process improvements.

> ***Note:*** *Through the remainder of this book, process outputs will be referred to simply as Y's, and inputs will be referred to simply as X's.*
>
> *Keep in mind, however, that a solution to the overall problem is not expected in this phase; that occurs during the final part of the process, the Improve phase.*

Graphical Tools

In the Measure phase, detailed analysis is performed on critical Y's to make an initial assessment of their stability, normality and capability. In the Analyze phase, attention turns to determining whether any X's under investigation do indeed have an effect on those Y's. A common method of making this determination is through the use of analytical tests.

Before launching into analytical tests, teams must first take a look at the data collected to see if there are any obvious relationships or issues of concern.

The following graphs are used to make this determination:

- Probability Plot
- Interval Plot
- Multi-Vari Chart

Probability Plot

Tool Use: Use a Probability Plot to determine if a data set was obtained from a population with a specific distribution, usually the normal distribution.

Data Type: The Probability Plot requires numeric data.

Worksheet: ***Check in Time***

Many analytical tools used for data analysis assume a normal distribution of data. SigmaXL includes a Normality Test function to check this assumption.

Menu command: ***SigmaXL > Graphical Tools > Normality Probability Plots***

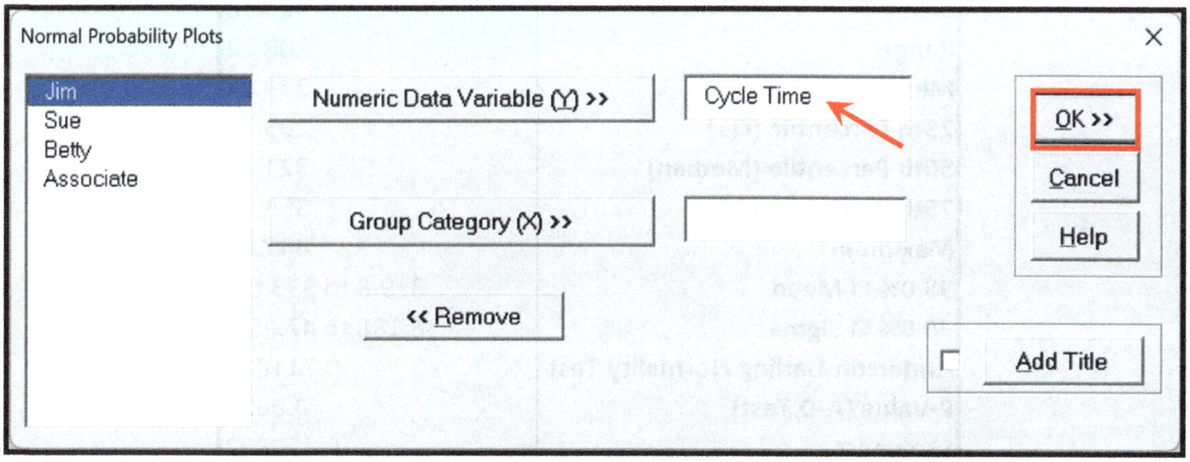

Select **Cycle Time** as the Numeric Data Variable (Y). Click **OK**.

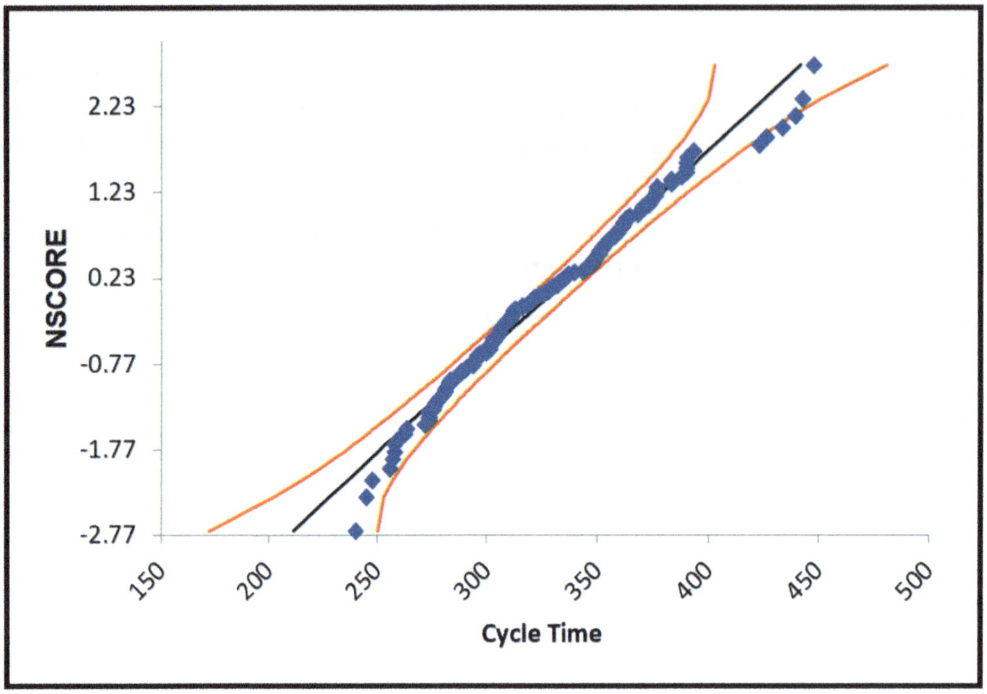

Summary information: (Use DESCRIPTIVE STATISTICS or HISTOGRAM AND SUMMARY INFO for the A-D TEST for normality).

Descriptive Statistics	Cycle Time
Count	150
Mean	326.66
StDev	42.516
Range	208.02
Minimum	239.84
25th Percentile (Q1)	295.79
50th Percentile (Median)	321.21
75th Percentile (Q3)	355.06
Maximum	447.85
95.0% CI Mean	319.8 to 333.52
95.0% CI Sigma	38.188 to 47.959
Anderson-Darling Normality Test	0.711828
P-Value (A-D Test)	0.0620
Skewness	0.452807
P-Value (Skewness)	0.0244
Kurtosis	0.081116788
P-Value (Kurtosis)	0.7096

Mean, Standard Deviation (StDev), Sample size (N), Anderson-Darling test for normality (AD) and the associated p-value.

Hypothesis testing associated with the Anderson-Darling criteria is discussed later in this unit. For now, simply stated, if the p-value is greater than .05 there's no evidence that the sample did not originate from a population with a normal distribution. In the example above, the P-Value (A-D Test) for Cycle Time is; p-value = 0.0620, which cannot reject the assumption of a population with a normal distribution.

Other Distributions

SigmaXL can also perform a test for distributions other than the normal. To run a test to see whether the Cycle Time data originated from a 2 Parameter Weibull distribution, select:

Menu command: ***SigmaXL > Process Capability > Nonnormal > Distribution Fitting***

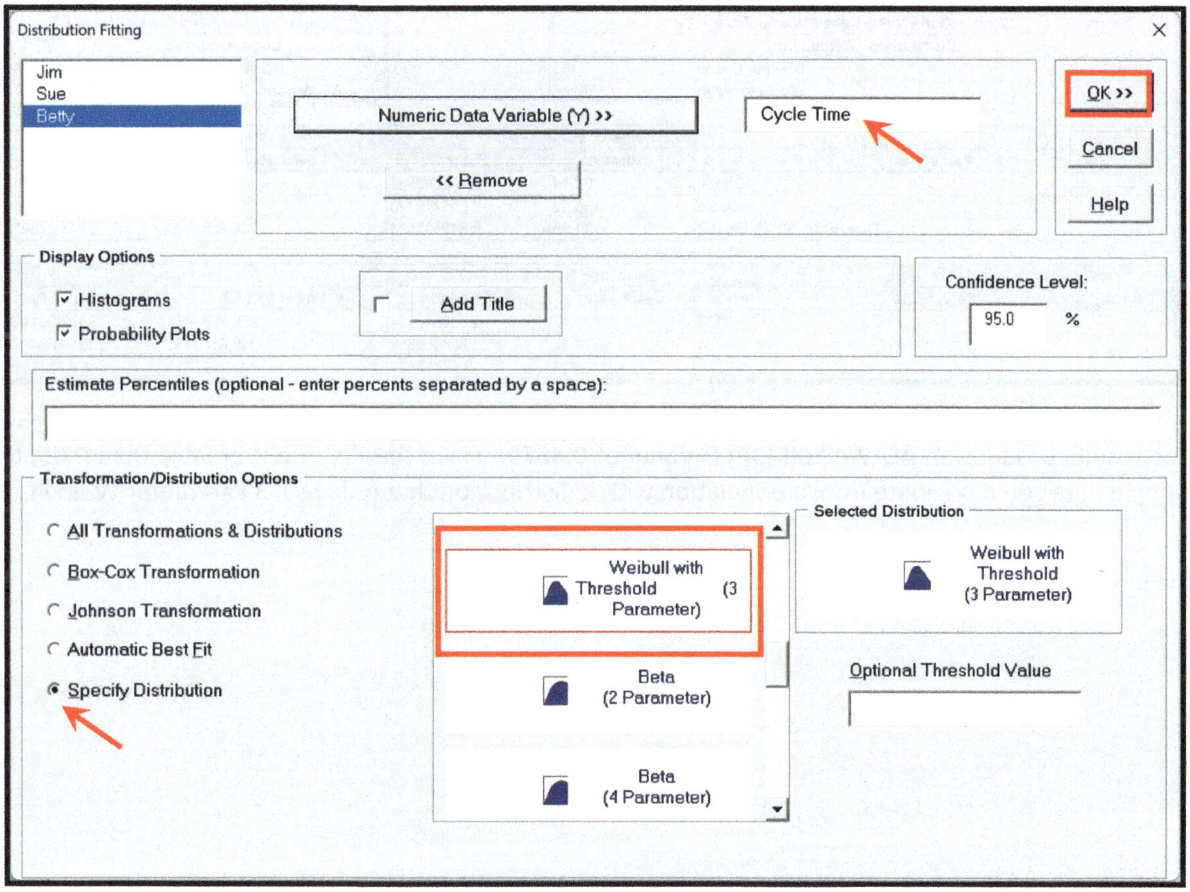

Choose **Cycle Time** as the Numeric Data Variable (Y). Click **Specify Distribution**. The available distributions selection area opens. Choose **Weibull with Threshold (3 Parameter)**. Click **OK**.

Output:

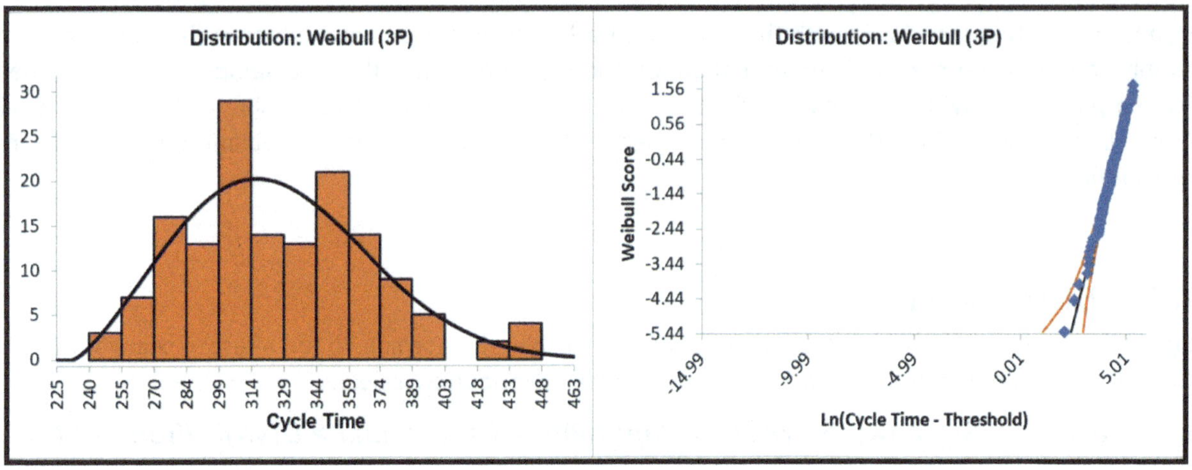

Distribution Fitting Report: Cycle Time	
Distribution: Weibull (3P)	
Sample Count	150
Sample Mean	326.66

Model Summary and Goodness-of-Fit	
Log-Likelihood	-771.136
AD Weibull (3P)	0.351316
AD Weibull (3P)P-Value	0.4679

Parameter Estimates				
Parameter	Estimate	SE Estimate	Lower 95.0 CI	Upper 95.0 CI
Shape	2.374	0.252742832	1.926900673	2.92483953
Scale	106.92	8.653778123	91.23306936	125.2977157
Threshold (ML Estimate)	231.85	6.849711934	218.4285786	245.278956

Percentile Report				
Percentage	Cycle Time	SE Percentile	Lower 95.0 CI	Upper 95.0 CI
0.135	238.47	4.960643284	228.9393677	248.3901199
50	323.48	3.828465858	316.0582331	331.0668895
99.865	468.7052814	13.63855827	442.7221719	496.2133247

The results produce an **AD Weibull (3P) P-Value** of **0.4679**. Since the P-Value is greater than 0.05, the sample data could originate from a population with a distribution that follows a 3 Parameter Weibull.

Comparing groups with Graphs

The most informative method to compare different groups is a combination of graphs and statistical summary information.

Worksheet: ***Check in Time***

Menu command: ***SigmaXL > Graphical Tools > Histogram & Descriptive Statistics***

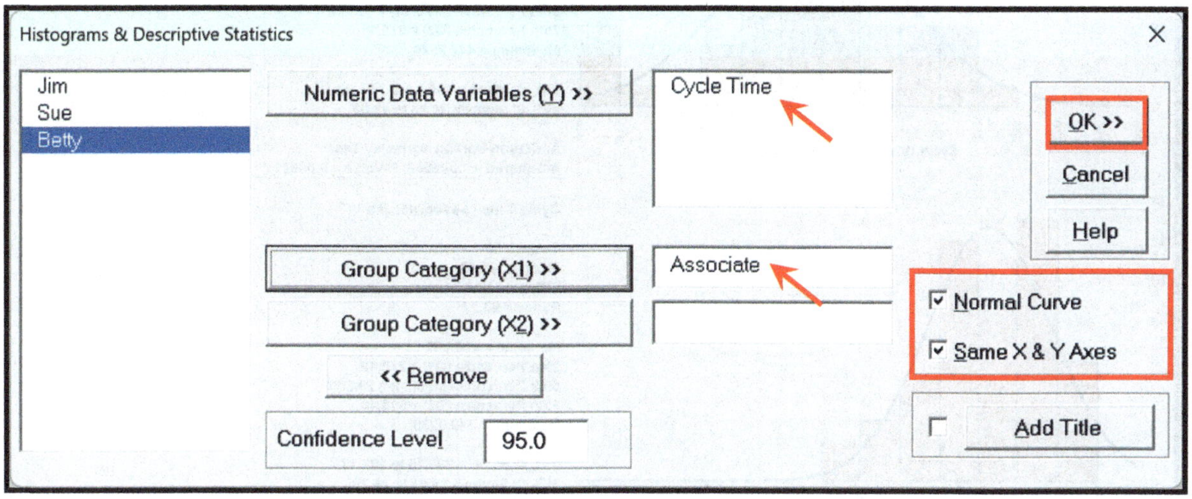

Input **Cycle Time** for the Numeric Data Variables (Y).

Select **Associate** for the Group Category (X1).

Choose both Normal Curve and Same X & Y Axes.

Click **OK**.

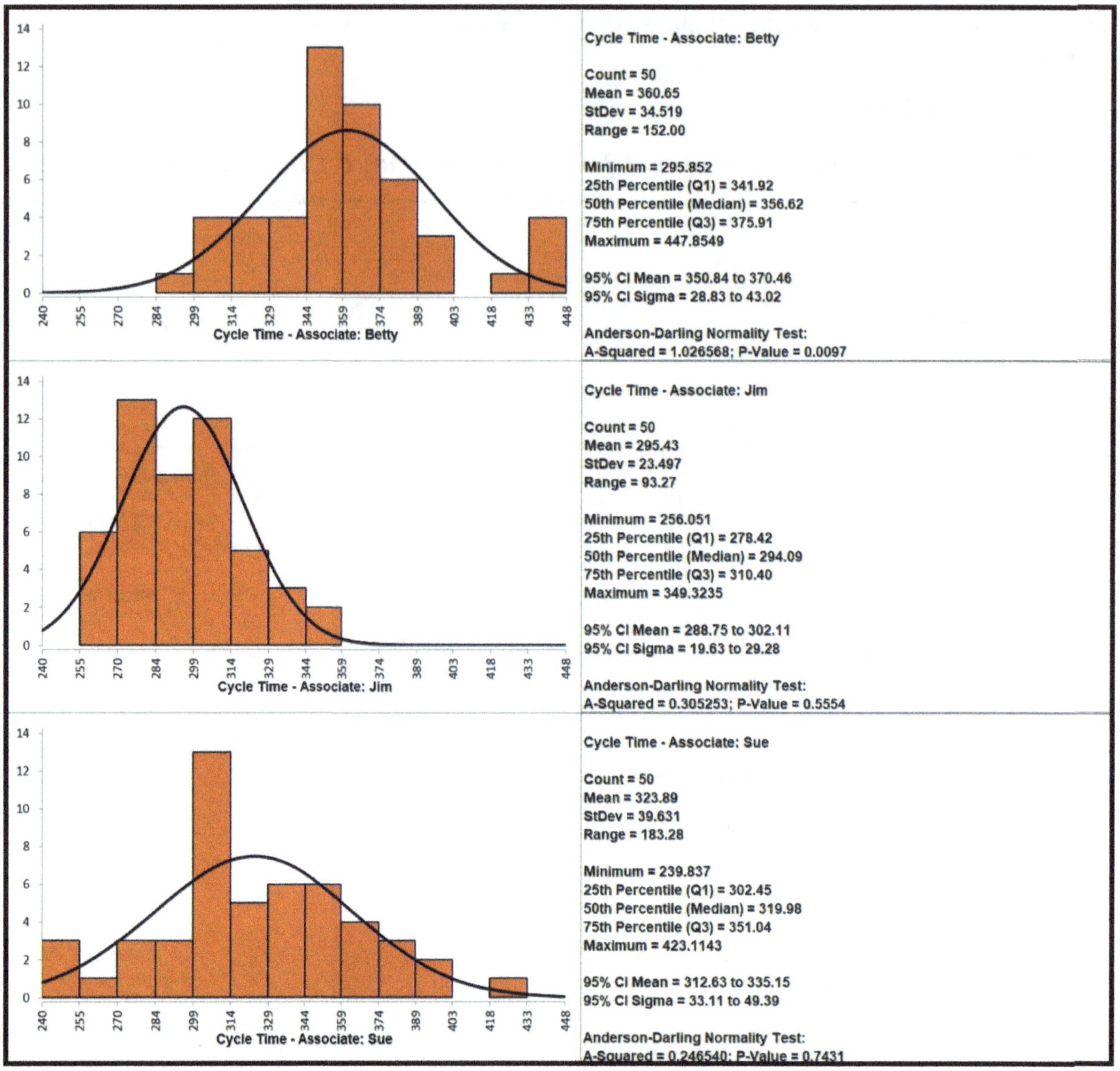

Having the X & Y axes the same for all Associates makes it easy to compare the Histograms.

The Anderson – Darling statistics along with their p-values are shown to the right of the graphs.

Hint: *The Histogram portion of the output is a great visual for presentations. The summary data on the right is not. Crop off the Summary Output and only show the Histograms. For simplicity, use a separate slide with only the statistics pertinent to the discussion.*

Anderson – Darling Test

The Anderson – Darling Test checks to see if a sample of data could have been selected from a parent population with a specific distribution. The typical distribution is the Normal, but any distribution can be used.

Hypotheses for the test:

H_o: Sample originates from the specified distribution.

H_a: Sample does not originate from the specified distribution.

> **Note:** ***A high p-value does not prove the sample originated from the specified distribution, it only indicates there's not enough evidence to reject that distribution. When testing a sample verses many distributions, there will be several that the sample could have as their parent distribution. It is up to the team to decide which distribution makes the most sense, based on process knowledge and past experience.***

Results: Low p-values – reject H_o in favor of H_a.

Multi-Vari Chart

Tool Use: Use a Multi-Vari Chart to visualize the variation within a nested study.

> ***Note:*** *Nested studies are discussed later in this chapter.*

Data Type: The response requires numeric data; factors may be either numeric or attribute.

Worksheet: ***Carpet***

Data originates from a test of carpet crushability. Five samples were measured from each of two locations per roll. The samples are nested within location and the location is nested within the roll. Seven rolls were used in the study.

Visual representation of the nested design.

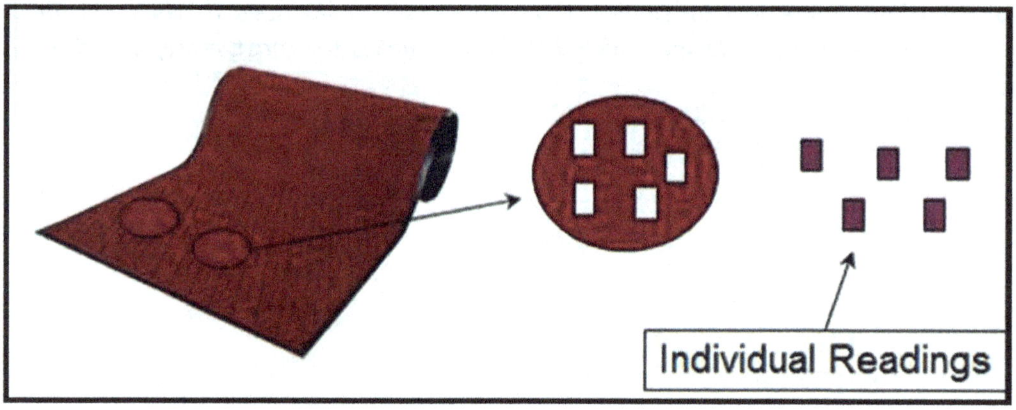

Menu command: ***SigmaXL > Graphical Tools > Multi-Vari Options***

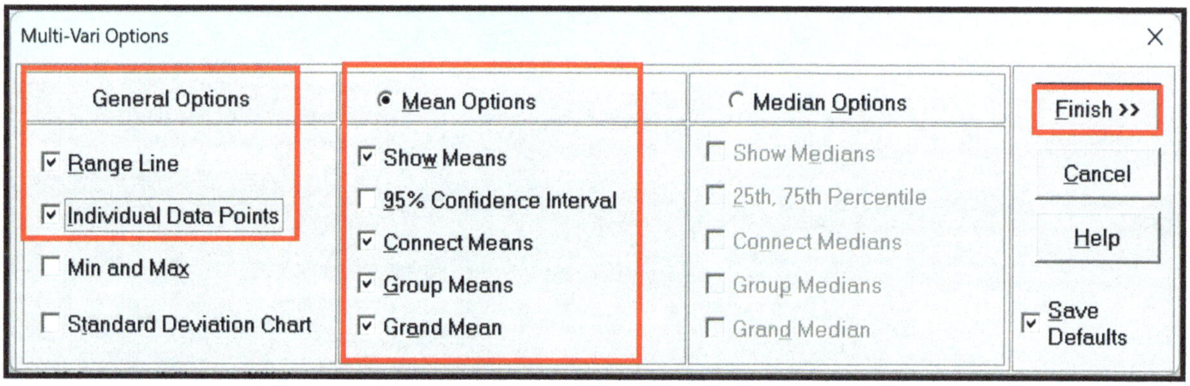

For the General Options select **Range Line** and **Individual Data Points**.

For Mean Options, choose Show Means, Connect Means, Group Means and Grand Mean.

Click **Finish**, then choose entire table. The Multi-Vari Charts dialog box appears.

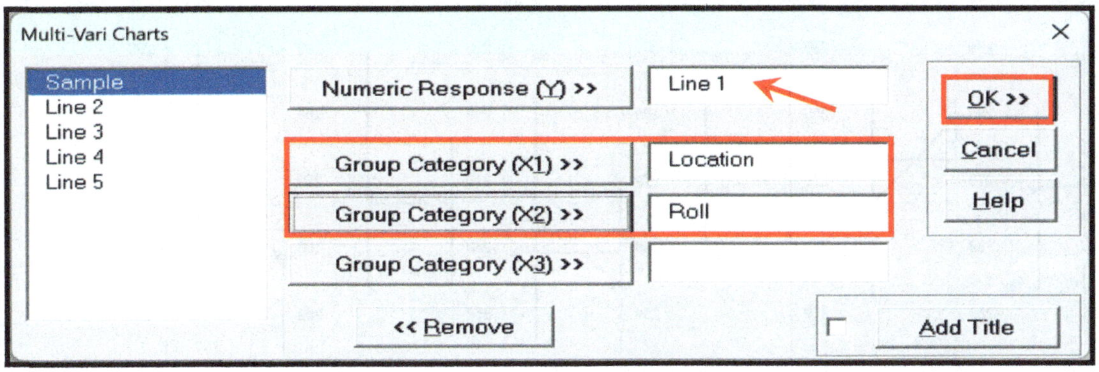

Select **Line 1** as the Numeric Response (Y). Select **Location** for Group Category (X1) and **Roll** for Group Category (X2). Click **OK**.

The sequence for factors is important to obtain a usable chart. Start with the lowest level of nesting; in this case, it is the **Location**. Move up from there until the top item **Roll** is reached.

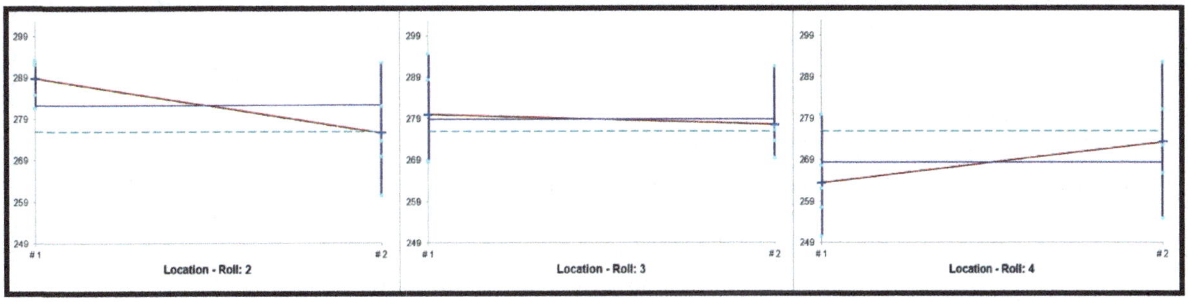

There are 7 graphs, one for each Roll. The Multi-Vari graph tries to visualize where the greatest source of variation exists. With the graphs so spread out, it's hard to make that determination. To aid in the analysis, reduce the width of the columns to 15. Highlight the columns, then right-click and select Column Widths. Input **15** for the column width.

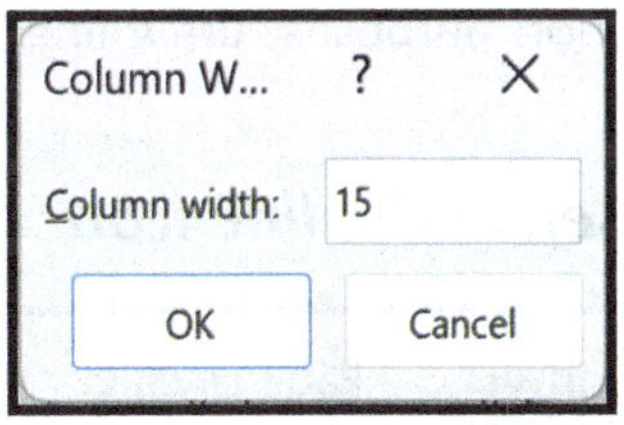

Click **OK**.

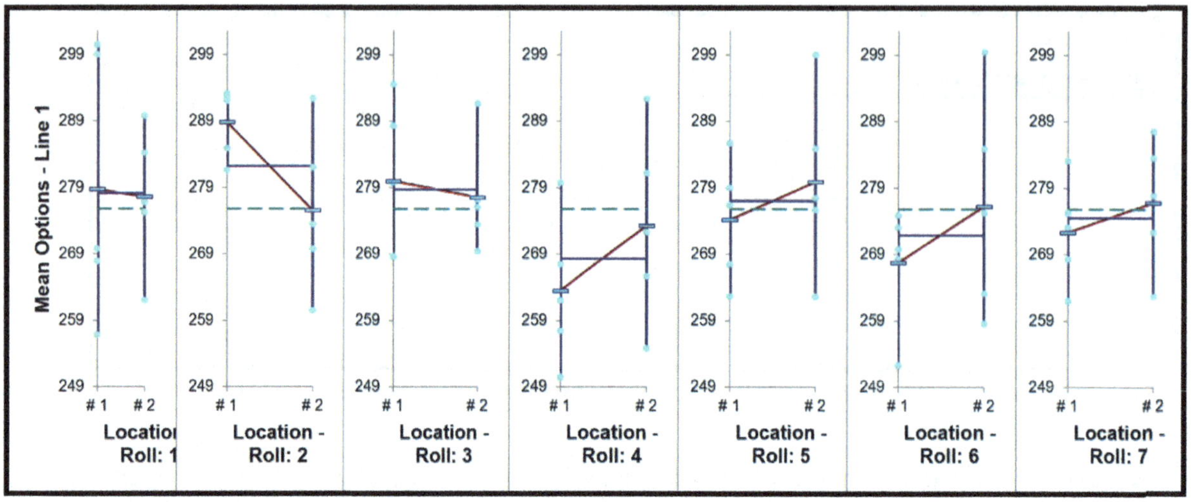

To improve on the visual for Roll 1, delete the Y-axis Title. Click on the Title and delete.

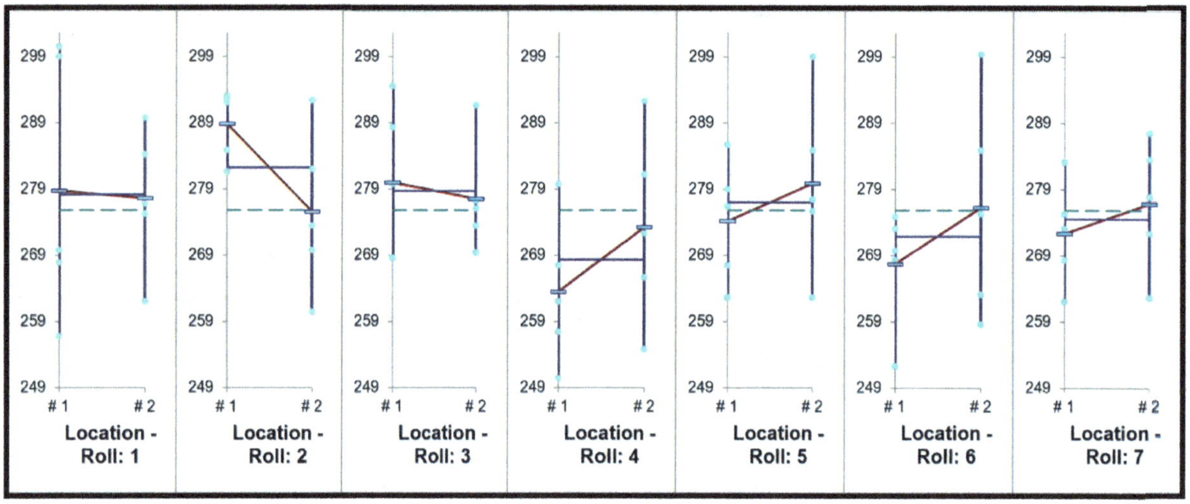

One final modification. For presentation purposes, draw lines that connect the overall mean of each Roll.

Select: ***Insert > Shapes > then select the line icon***.

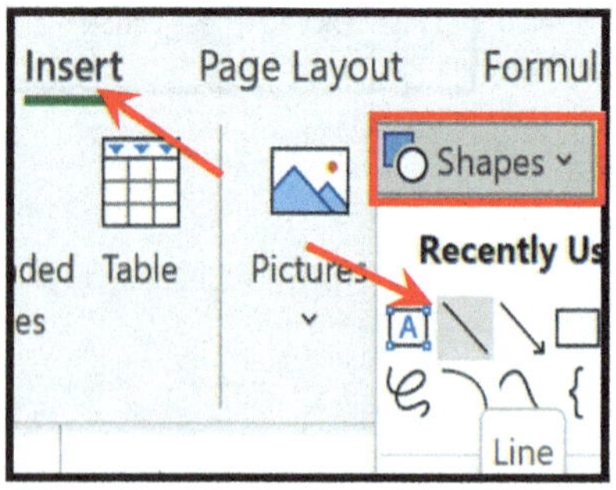

Format the line and connect the Mean value of each Roll. The mean is the midpoint for each location within the Roll.

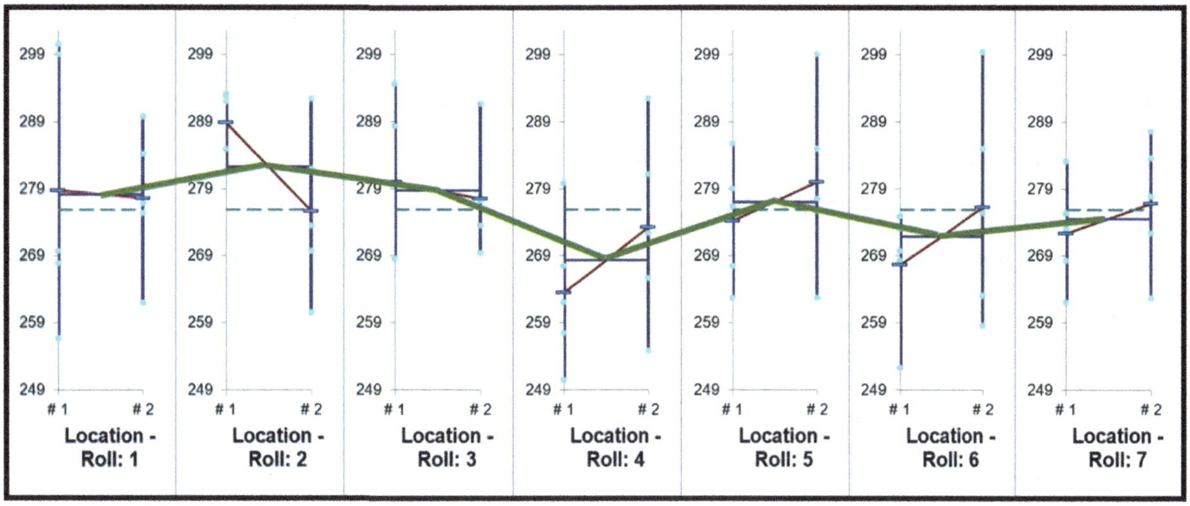

Finished graph for presentation.

Notice that the spread within the locations for each Roll is higher than the differences in the mean of the locations within the Roll and compared to the Roll-to-Roll average (Green Line). The largest sources of variation in this situation are the individual samples.

Repeating this process with Line 3 shows the largest source of variation to be Roll-to-Roll.

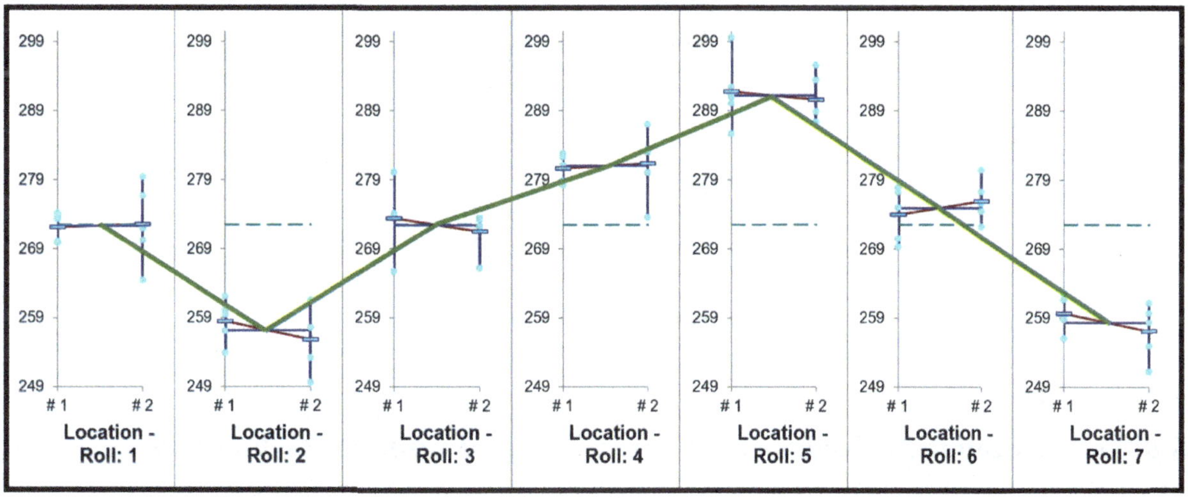

For Line 3 the Roll averages have a large variation compared to the Location means within the Roll or the individual readings within the Locations.

Confidence Intervals

The team will often be concerned with estimating a population parameter such as the mean (μ) or standard deviation (σ). However, since the calculations use sample information, the estimates are not exact. This uncertainty requires an interval, within which the population value resides.

SigmaXL offers several methods to create confidence intervals.

For the population **Mean** use:

1 Sample t-Test and Confidence Intervals

Descriptive Statistics

Histograms and Descriptive Statistics

For the Population **Median** use:

For the Standard Deviation use:

Create a column of data in a SigmaXL worksheet as shown.

	A
1	Output
2	45
3	52
4	68
5	49
6	52
7	66
8	73
9	47
10	66
11	54

Menu command:

SigmaXL > Statistical Tools > 1 Sample t-Test and Confidence Intervals

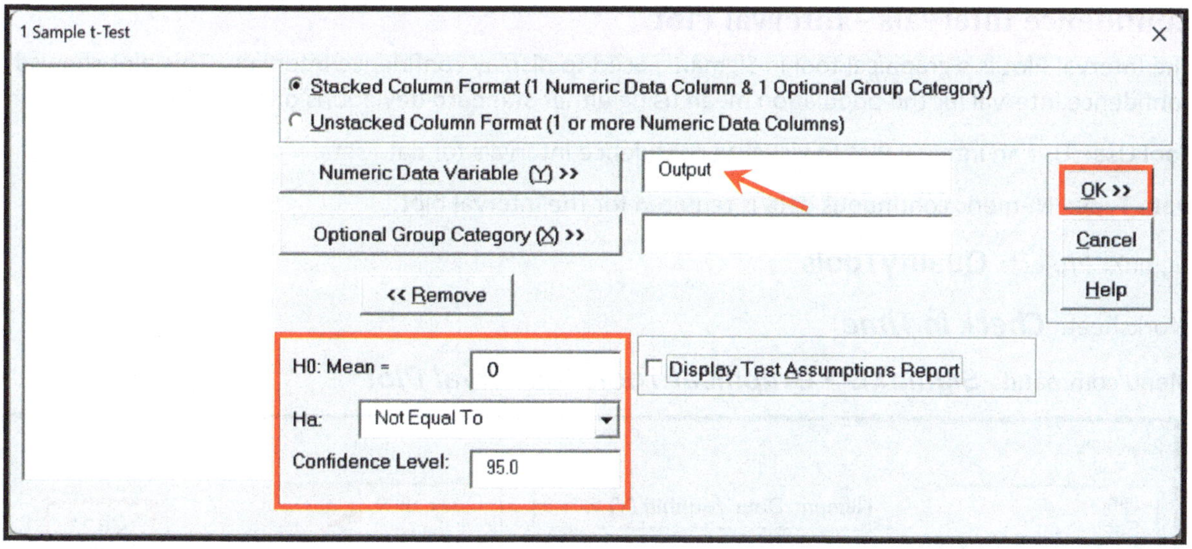

Input **Output** as the Numeric Data Variable (Y): Set the H0 Mean to zero. For Ha: use the pull-down menu and select **Not Equal To**. Decide on the proper Confidence Level, then click **OK**.

Summary Report:

1 Sample t-Test	
Test Information	
H_0: Mean (Mu) = 0	
H_a: Mean (Mu) Not Equal To 0	
Results:	**Output**
Count	10
Mean	57.200
StDev	10.03106287
SE Mean	3.172
t	18.032
P-Value (2-sided)	0.0000
UC (2-sided, 95%)	64.376
LC (2-sided, 95%)	50.024

Based on sample data supplied, the population mean is between **50.024** and **64.376**

Confidence Intervals – Interval Plot

The Interval Plot is a graphical tool in SigmaXL, used to display confidence intervals. This plot shows the confidence interval for the population mean using either standard deviations or % confidence.

Tool Use: Use an Interval Plot to visualize confidence intervals for data sets.

Data Type: Numeric continuous data is required for the interval plot.

SigmaXL Project: **QualityTools**

Worksheet: ***Check in Time***

Menu command: ***SigmaXL > Graphical Tools > Interval Plot***

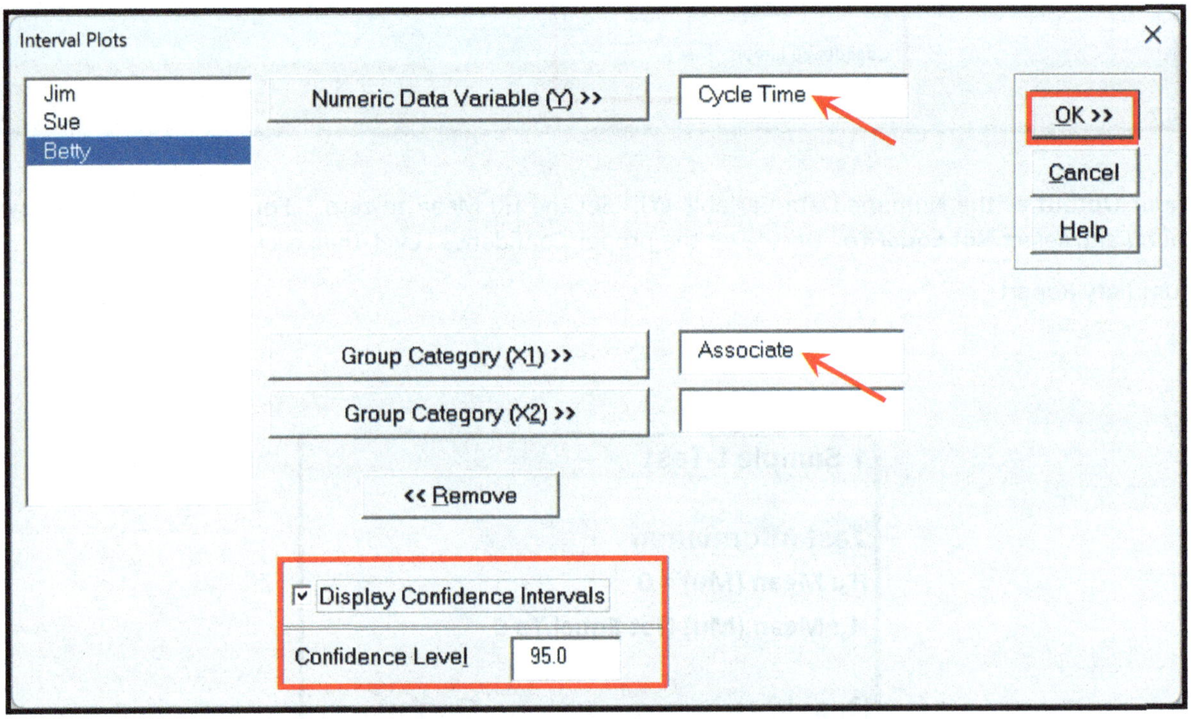

Input **Cycle Time** as the Graph variables. Use **Associate** for Group Category (X1).

Click **OK**.

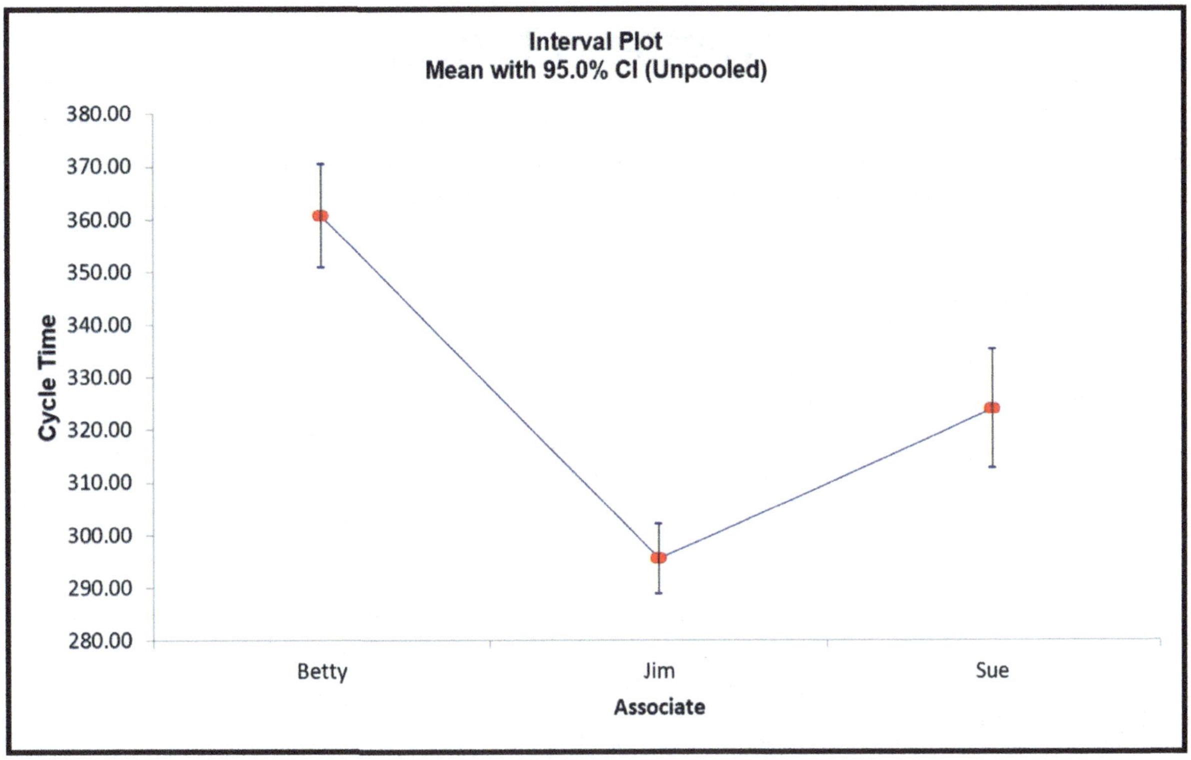

The circle is the sample average ($\bar{X}$), the point estimate for the population's mean (**μ**).

The bars indicate the 95% confidence interval (**CI**) for each associates population mean.

The Standard Error is based on the sample standard deviation divided by the square root of the sample

$$\left(s/\sqrt{n}\right)$$

size.

The Confidence Interval is equal to (**1-α**).

Select the Multiples of the desired type of interval.

Decide on the type of interval; the choices are upper one-sided, lower one-sided and two-sided.

Click **OK**.

> **Hint:** *At first glance, it may not be obvious what type of confidence interval is displayed, so verify what the interval represents before making any decisions.*

The confidence interval for the population mean can also be accessed using the Descriptive Statistics option under ***SigmaXL > Statistical Tools > Descriptive Statistics***.

Results are listed as **95% CI Mean**.

Hypothesis Testing

In the Analyze phase, use data obtained in the Measure phase and begin to dig into it. The goal is to determine if differences exist between groups and whether there are significant relationships between X's and critical Y's. The technique used to make this determination is called hypothesis testing.

The steps in hypothesis testing are as follows:

1) Write the Alternative Hypothesis (H_a)
2) Write the Null Hypothesis (H_o)
3) Select a critical p-value
4) Choose the type of test to run
5) Plan and run the test (SigmaXL will calculate a **Test Statistic** based on the type of test performed. It will then calculate a p-value based on that Test Statistic.)
6) Based on the test results' p-value, reject H_o or fail to reject H_o and draw conclusions

Step 1: Write the Alternative Hypothesis

Experiments are performed with the intent of demonstrating a relationship (correlation) between factors, or a difference between the population parameter values of different groups. The Alternative Hypothesis is the statement used to explain which differences are being tested.

For example, suppose the team wishes to show that the input factor (Training) makes a difference in the number of errors produced in the invoice process. The team is investigating two different training methods – online training and classroom training.

If the team wishes to show only that there's a difference between the two methods and are not concerned about which one has the lower error rate, then the Alternative Hypothesis is:

The mean error rate of online training is **not equal** to the mean error rate of classroom training.

This is written as:

$$H_a: \mu_{\text{Error Online}} \neq \mu_{\text{Error Classroom}}$$

Step 2: Write the Null Hypothesis

The Null Hypothesis comprises all other options not included in the Alternative Hypothesis. For the example above, the Null Hypothesis is:

The mean error rate for online training is **equal** to the mean error rate of classroom training.

This is written as:

$$H_o: \mu_{\text{Error Online}} = \mu_{\text{Error Classroom}}$$

After performing the experiment, if evidence shows the alternative is correct then the team can make the statement:

The training method makes a difference in the mean number of errors for the invoice process.

If the evidence does not support this then the team can make the statement:

There is not enough evidence to show a difference in the mean number of errors based on the training method.

In some other situations, the team might expect the difference to favor one group over another. For example, suppose a drug company claims their diet pill (Mega Diet) produces greater weight loss compared to a rival diet pill (Mini Diet).

The proper Alternative Hypothesis is:

$$H_a: \mu_{\text{Weight loss Mega Diet}} > \mu_{\text{Weight loss Mini Diet}}$$

The Null Hypothesis is:

$$H_o: \mu_{\text{Weight loss Mega Diet}} \leq \mu_{\text{Weight loss Mini Diet}}$$

SigmaXL allows the team to select which type of Alternative Hypothesis to run. The team then runs and analyzes the experiment. The results determine if there is enough evidence to support the claim for the Mega Diet pill or if there is not enough evidence to support the claim for the Mega Diet pill.

Step 3: Select a p-value

Definition of p-value:

The probability of obtaining the Test Statistic's value, or something larger, if the Null Hypothesis is correct.

The key to this statement is the IF statement. If the Null Hypothesis is not true, the p-value is meaningless.

Errors in Hypothesis Testing

The p-value indicates the risk the team is willing to accept in making a Type I error.

When running a test of hypothesis, there are four possible outcomes as shown in the following table:

	Your Decision	
The Truth	Do not reject H_o	Reject H_o
H_o is true	Correct decision	Type I Error (α Risk)
H_o is false	Type II Error (β Risk)	Correct decision

The table shows the true condition as **The Truth**; this is what the experiment is trying to determine. The Truth may never actually be known. An experiment can be created that minimizes the two types of error, thus improving the chance of making a **Correct Decision**.

Two of the boxes show the situations where a correct decision is made:

1. Do not reject the Null Hypothesis (H_o) when it is in fact true.
2. Reject H_o when it is in fact false.

There are also two boxes demonstrating potential errors:

1. **H_0** is the true condition, but the decision is to reject H_0. (This is called a Type I error, also referred to as the Alpha (α) risk.)

2. Based on the data, the decision is to not reject H_0 when it is in fact false. (This is called a Type II error or the Beta (β) risk.)

The critical p-value is that value below which the decision is to reject the Null Hypothesis in favor of the Alternative Hypothesis. (The p-value is calculated by SigmaXL during the analysis.)

So, what is the correct critical p-value to use? The answer depends on the seriousness of making a Type I error.

Typically, if a Type I error is not serious, a p-value of **.1** is used; if a Type I error is moderately serious a **.05** value is used; and if a Type I error is very serious a p-value of **.01** or less is used.

Step 4: Choose the type of test to run

Testing the hypothesis may involve several different statistical tests. These tests depend upon the data type of the inputs and the output. The following table is designed to help determine the best statistical test based on the type of data. Use it as follows:

1. Determine the input data type, discrete for count data, and continuous for variables data.
2. Determine the output data type.
3. Find the intersection of the two data types to determine the correct statistical analysis to perform.

		X Data	
		Discrete	**Continuous**
Y Data	**Discrete**	**Chi-Square**	**Logistic Regression**
	Continuous	**t-Test / ANOVA**	**Correlation & Regression**

Below are some examples of how this works.

EXAMPLE #1

Input (X data): Associate (discrete data).

Output (Y data): Thickness of paint (a continuous factor).

Test: t-Test or ANOVA.

EXAMPLE #2

Input (X data): Gender (Female/Male) – Discrete

Output (Y data): Job Offer (Yes / No) – Discrete

Test: Chi-Square

EXAMPLE #3

Input (X data): Hours of overtime – Continuous

Output (Y data): Hours missed for illness – Continuous

Test: Regression

EXAMPLE #4A

Input (X data): Weight of Truck – Continuous

Output (Y data): Severity of Injury in accident (Mild, Moderate or Severe) – Discrete

Test: Logistic Regression

EXAMPLE #4B

An alternative for this example is to classify the trucks into groups (Light Duty, Medium Duty and Heavy Duty). In that situation, the results are as follows:

Input (X data): Truck Group – Discrete

Output (Y data): Severity of Injury in accident (Mild, Moderate or Severe) – Discrete

Test: Chi-Square

There are several hypotheses for each test. The following table shows the commonly used hypotheses.

Test	Null Hypothesis	Alternative Hypothesis
One Sample t-Test:	μ = Specified value The population mean is (specify value) $\mu \leq$ Specified value The population mean is less than or equal to (specify value) $\mu \geq$ Specified value The population mean is greater than or equal to (specify value)	$\mu \neq$ Specified value The population mean is not (specify value) $\mu >$ Specified value The population mean is greater than (specify value) $\mu <$ Specified value The population mean is less than (specify value)
Two Sample t-Test	$\mu_1 = \mu_2$ The mean of population 1 is equal to the mean of population 2 $\mu_1 \leq \mu_2$ The mean of population 1 is less than or equal to the mean of population 2 $\mu_1 \geq \mu_2$ The mean of population 1 is greater than or equal to the mean of population 2	$\mu_1 \neq \mu_2$ The mean of population 1 is not equal to the mean of population 2 $\mu_1 > \mu_2$ The mean of population 1 is greater than the mean of population 2 $\mu_1 < \mu_2$ The mean of population 1 is less than the mean of population 2
ANOVA	$\mu_1 = \mu_2 = \mu_3 ......= \mu_n$ The population mean of all groups are equal	At least one $\mu_i \neq \mu_j$ At least one of the population means is not equal to another population mean
Regression	β (coefficient) = 0 The factor's coefficient is equal to zero. (Factor X does not have an effect on the output.)	β (coefficient) $\neq$ 0 The factor's coefficient is not equal to zero. (Factor X does have an effect on the output.)
Logistic Regression	Model coefficient $\beta = 0$ Coefficient for model is equal to zero. (Factor X in model does not have an effect on output.)	$\beta \neq 0$ Coefficient for model is not equal to zero. (Factor X does have an effect on output.)
Chi-Square	Factors are Independent The factors are statistically independent.	Factors are dependent The factors are statistically dependent.

Comparative Studies

Chi–Square Test

Tool Use: Use the Chi-Square analysis to determine if there is a relationship between two factors.

Data Types: Input – Discrete; Output – Discrete

Null Hypothesis H_o: The factors are independent

Alternative Hypothesis H_a: The factors are not independent

Worksheet: ***Delivery***

Service	Delivery Results
Quick Delivery	On Time
Fast Delivery	Late
Quick Delivery	On Time
Fast Delivery	Late
Fast Delivery	Early
Quick Delivery	Early
Fast Delivery	Early
Fast Delivery	On Time
Quick Delivery	Early
Fast Delivery	Early
Quick Delivery	On Time
Quick Delivery	On Time
Quick Delivery	On Time
Friendly Delivery	Early

A delivery service wanted to see if there was a relation (Dependency) between the delivery results and the service selected.

There are 3 choices; Quick, Friendly, and Fast. The deliveries were either Early, On Time, or Late.

The data presented itself in a 'Raw' platform. Over a period of time, as a service was selected, it was tracked and the delivery results recorded.

SigmaXL will perform the analysis in either the data's raw form, or as a summarized table.

Raw Data Analysis

Open worksheet ***Delivery.***

Menu command: ***SigmaXL > Statistical Tools > Chi-Square Tests > Chi-Square Test and Association***

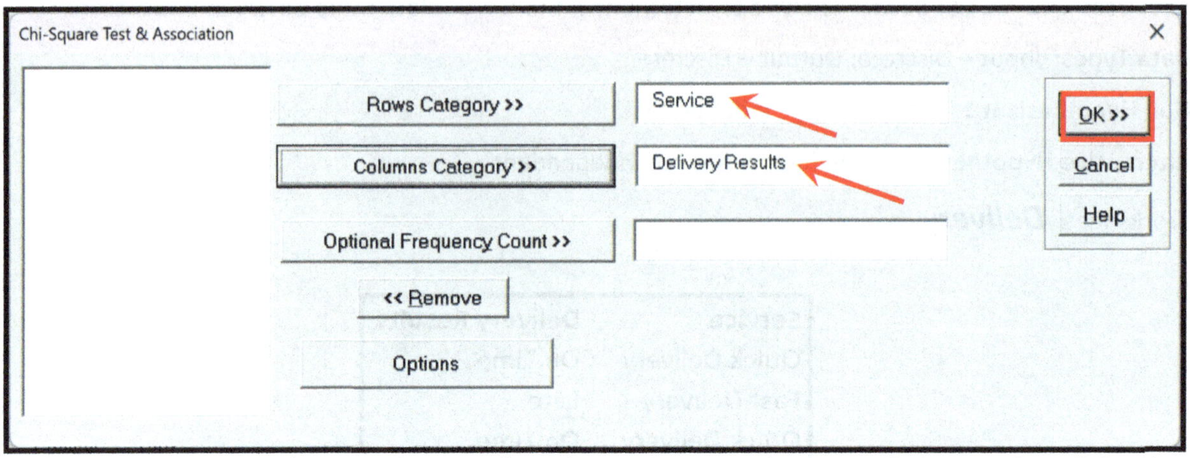

For the Rows Category, select; **Service**. For the Columns Category choose; **Delivery Results**. Click **OK**.

Chi-Square Test			
Service - Delivery Results			
Observed Counts	**Early**	**Late**	**On Time**
Fast Delivery	7	13	5
Friendly Delivery	9	5	22
Quick Delivery	14	2	23
Expected Counts	**Early**	**Late**	**On Time**
Fast Delivery	7.500	5	12.500
Friendly Delivery	10.800	7.200	18
Quick Delivery	11.700	7.800	19.500
Std. Residuals	**Early**	**Late**	**On Time**
Fast Delivery	-0.182574	3.578	-2.121
Friendly Delivery	-0.547723	-0.819892	0.942809
Quick Delivery	0.672411	-2.077	0.792594
Chi-Square	24.588		
DF	4		
P-Value	0.0001		

The **Observed Counts** portion shows the raw data, summarized in a **Two-Way table**.

The **Expected Counts** portion shows the counts for each cell, **IF** the Null Hypothesis is true.

The **Standardized Residuals** (Std. Residuals) portion shows the difference between the Observed and Expected columns. Large values indicate large differences.

The bottom portion shows the results of the Hypothesis Test. The Chi-Square value is compared to a Chi-Square distribution. The P-Value indicates the probability of obtaining the Observed Counts, **IF** the Null is true.

Each cell in the table will have a Chi-Square value calculated using the following formula:

$$\chi^2 = \left| \frac{(f_o - f_e)^2}{f_e} \right|$$

- f_o is the observed count in each cell of the table. This comes from observations or existing data.
- f_e is the expected count in each cell of the table, assuming H_o is true. This value is calculated by SigmaXL.
- The statistic will increase when there are large differences between observed and expected counts. (Chi-Sq)

The total Chi-Square value is 24.588. This corresponds to a P-Value of .0001. With this low P-Value, the Null hypothesis can be rejected. The idea that the Service and Delivery Results are independent can be rejected.

Graphical Analysis

A very convenient graph to indicate the dependency would be the Pareto Chart.

Use the worksheet **Delivery**.

Menu command: ***SigmaXL > Graphical Tools > Advanced Pareto Charts***

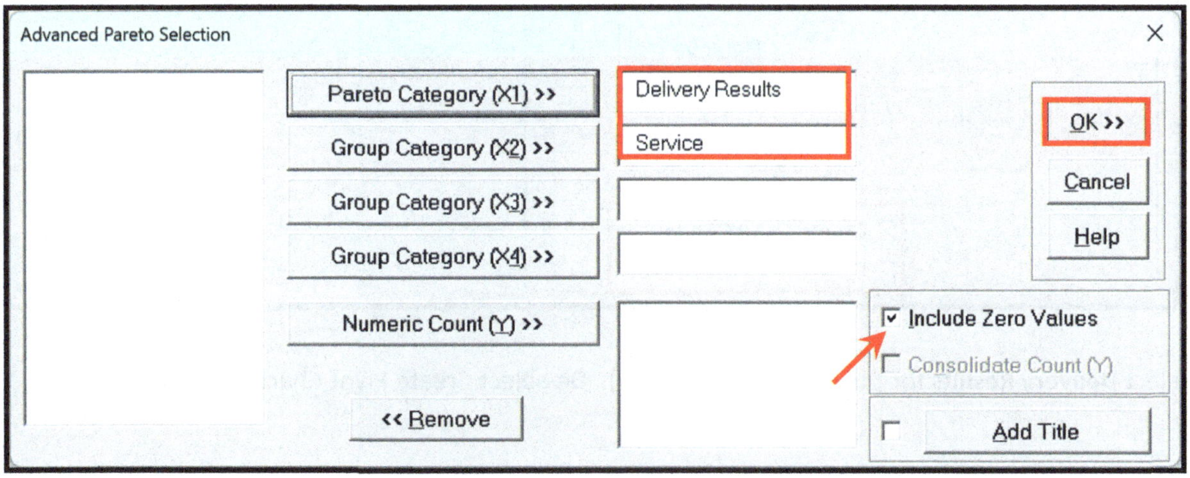

Select **Delivery Results** as the Pareto Category (X1). For the Group Category (X2), input **Service**.

Be sure to check the box for **Include Zero Values**. Click **OK**.

Chi-Square Results:

The graph shows a difference in the pattern (bar heights) for the Delivery results based on the type of Service requested. For the Friendly and Quick the bars have a similar pattern. Lowest is Late, then Early and the highest bar is Quick Delivery. For the Fast service, the high bar is for Late, the Early and the lowest bar is the On Time result. Since the pattern of the bars depends on the Service, reject the Null.

Two-Way Table summary Analysis.

SigmaXL has a tool to easily create Pivot Tables.

Menu Command: ***SigmaXL > Graphical Tools > EZ Pivot/Pivot Charts***

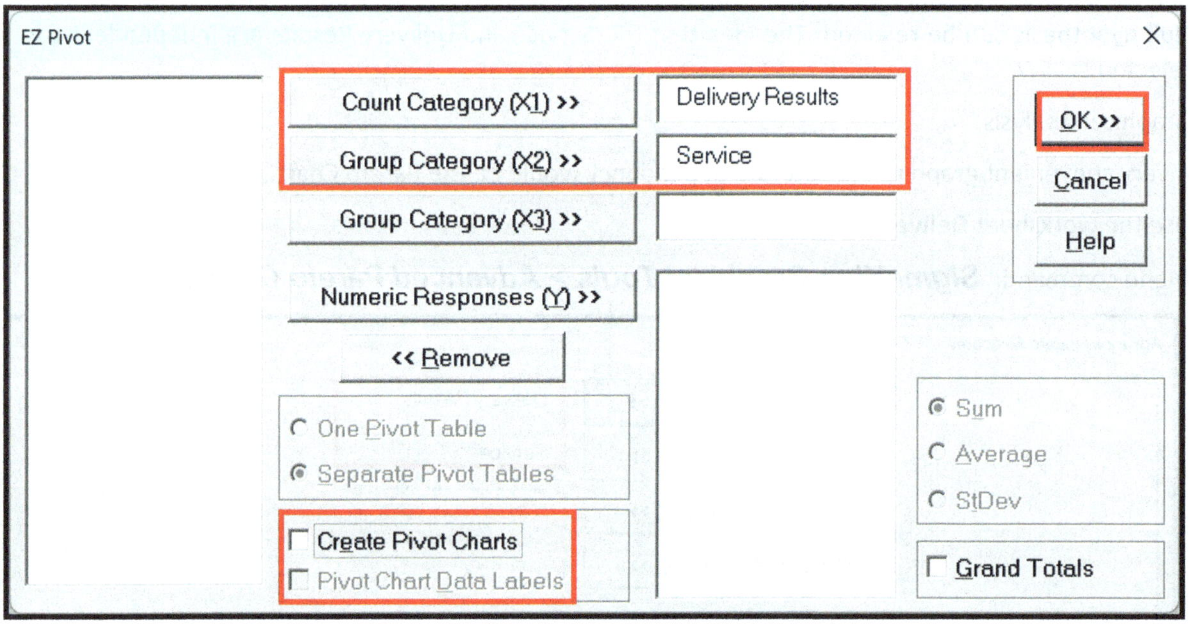

Select **Delivery Results** for the Count Category (X1). De-select Create Pivot Charts. Click **OK**.

The Pivot Table is automatically created.

Count of Delivery Results	Service		
Delivery Results	Fast Delivery	Friendly Delivery	Quick Delivery
Early	7	9	14
Late	13	5	2
On Time	5	22	23

To analyze the data in this format, use the Menu command:

SigmaXL > Statistical Tools > Chi-Square Tests > Chi-Square Tests & Association - Two-Way Table Data

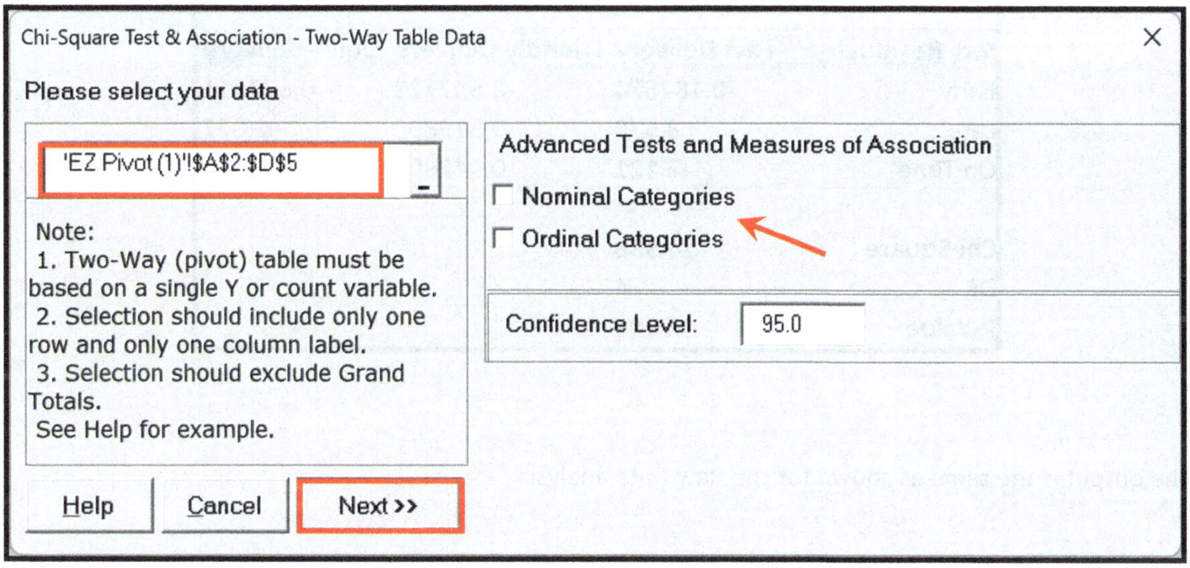

Highlight the table, (Cells A2 to D5).j Do not include the first row (Count of Delivery Results and Service).

De-select both options under Advanced Tests and Measures of Association. Click Next.

Results:

Chi-Square Two-Way Table Statistics			
Observed Counts	**Fast Delivery**	**Friendly Delivery**	**Quick Delivery**
Early	7	9	14
Late	13	5	2
On Time	5	22	23
Expected Counts	**Fast Delivery**	**Friendly Delivery**	**Quick Delivery**
Early	7.500	10.800	11.700
Late	5	7.200	7.800
On Time	12.500	18	19.500
Std. Residuals	**Fast Delivery**	**Friendly Delivery**	**Quick Delivery**
Early	-0.182574	-0.547723	0.672411
Late	3.578	-0.819892	-2.077
On Time	-2.121	0.942809	0.792594
Chi-Square	24.588		
DF	4		
P-Value	0.0001		

The output is the same as shown for the Raw Data analysis.

One Sample t-Test

Tool Use: Use a One Sample t-Test to determine if a sample originated from a population with a specified mean, or to create a confidence interval for the population mean.

Data Type: Input - Discrete (1 group); Output – Continuous

Sue
24.2
25.4
24
26
25
25.4
23
25.3

Worksheet: ***One Sample t-Test***

This worksheet contains paint thickness data from a single operator (Sue). Her manager wants to determine if Sue's population mean for paint thickness is not equal to 25 mils.

Null Hypothesis: $\mu_{Sue} = 25$ mils Alternative Hypothesis: $\mu_{Sue} \neq 25$ mils

Menu command: ***SigmaXL > Statistical Tools > 1 Sample t-Test & Confidence Intervals***

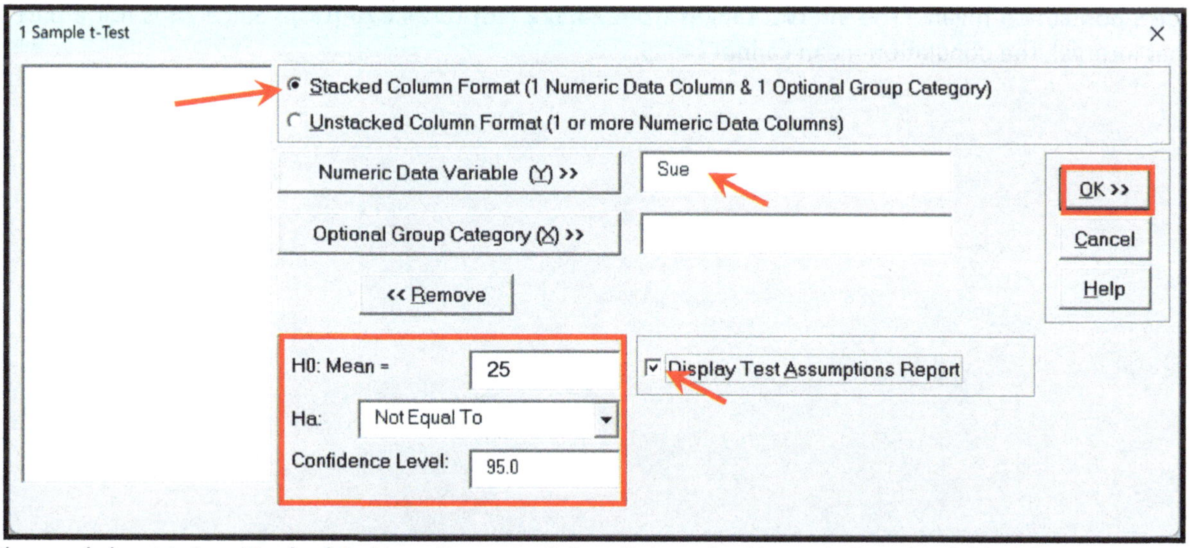

The worksheet is in a **Stacked Column Format**. Select **Sue** as the Numeric Data Variable (Y).

Choose; Display Test Assumption Report.

The Null Hypothesis is; The Population mean is equal to **25**.

The alternative is that the population mean is **Not Equal To** (25).

Use a **95%** confidence level for this test. Click **OK**.

Output:

1 Sample t-Test	
Test Information	
H_0: Mean (Mu) = 25	
H_a: Mean (Mu) Not Equal To 25	
Results:	Sue
Count	50
Mean	24.596
StDev	0.962768
SE Mean	0.136156
t	-2.967
P-Value (2-sided)	0.0046
UC (2-sided, 95%)	24.870
LC (2-sided, 95%)	24.322

The top portion shows the hypothesis test information.

Results: The first four rows summarize the sample. The last four rows show the results of the **t-Test**; the **t**-value and the corresponding **P-Value**. The last 2 lines show the **95% confidence interval** (CI) for Sue's population mean. The interval ranges from **24.322** (LC) to **24.870** (UC). Since 25 is not a part of that interval, the population mean cannot be 25.

The bottom portion of the output shows the Assumptions Report. The report is color coded. **Green** indicates that portion is a Go. **Yellow** means there's an issue that needs to be investigated. And **Red** means there's been a violation.

The assumptions are:

Normality: Process data originates from a population with a normal distribution.

Robustness: If the sample data does not originate from a normal distribution, is the sample size large enough to compensate?

Outliers: If outliers are present, based on the criteria for the Box Plots, does removing them allow Populations have equal variances (not applicable for a single sample test).

Randomness: Looking at run rules violations. Indicates independence of values.

1 Sample t-Test Assumptions Report	
Normality:	Anderson Darling P-Value = 0.154. Fail to reject null hypothesis: "data are sampled from a normal distribution," so conclude that the assumption of normality is not violated.
Robustness:	Not applicable for normal data.
Outliers (Boxplot Rules):	No outliers found.
Randomness (Independence):	Nonparametric Runs Test (Exact) P-Value = 0.116. Fail to reject null hypothesis: "data are random," so conclude that the assumption of randomness (independence) is not violated.

Since all areas are Green, there's no issues with the assumptions.

As a final check the user might want to perform is to investigate the sample using an **Individuals and Moving Range** control chart for the stability of the process.

Two Sample t-Test

Tool Use: Use the Two Sample t-Test to determine if two samples originated from populations with equal mean values or from populations with mean values that are not equal.

The Two Sample t-Test can be performed with or without the assumption of equal variances between the populations.

Data Type: Input - Discrete (2 groups); Output – Continuous

Worksheet: ***Two Samples***

Data was collected from two associates to determine if it is reasonable to believe their population means are not equal.

Null Hypothesis: $\mu_{Sue} = \mu_{Fred}$ Alternative Hypothesis: $\mu_{Sue} \neq \mu_{Fred}$

Menu command: ***SigmaXL > Statistical Tools > 2 Sample t-Test***

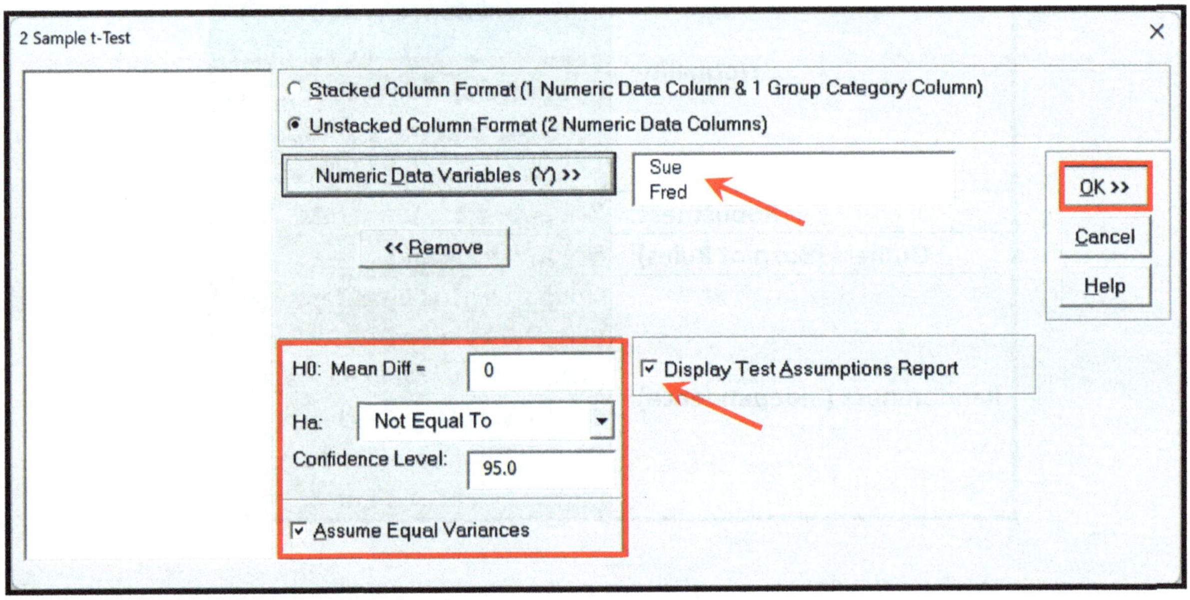

The data is arranged in an **Unstacked** condition.

For the Numeric Data Variables (Y) select both associates, **Sue** and **Fred**.

The null hypothesis has the two population means equal, so the Mean Diff = **0**.

The alternative hypothesis is **Not Equal To**.

Keep the confidence level at **95%**, and **Assume Equal Variances**.

Choose to display the **Test Assumptions Report**. Click **OK**.

The Results appear in the tab; **2-Sample t-Test (1)**.

Assumptions for the Two-Sample t-Test are:

Processes are **stable**, originating from populations with a **normal distribution**, and **equal variances**.

Test Assumption Report

2 Sample t-Test Assumptions Report		
Normality:	**Anderson Darling P-Value = 0.154. Fail to reject null hypothesis: "data are sampled from a normal distribution," so conclude that the assumption of normality is not violated.**	**Anderson Darling P-Value = 0.531. Fail to reject null hypothesis: "data are sampled from a normal distribution," so conclude that the assumption of normality is not violated.**
Robustness:	**Not applicable for normal data.**	
Outliers (Boxplot Rules):	**No outliers found.**	**No outliers found.**
Randomness (Independence):	**Nonparametric Runs Test (Exact) P-Value = 0.116. Fail to reject null hypothesis: "data are random," so conclude that the assumption of randomness (serial independence) is not violated.**	**Nonparametric Runs Test (Exact) P-Value = 0.116. Fail to reject null hypothesis: "data are random," so conclude that the assumption of randomness (serial independence) is not violated.**
Equal Variance:	**F-test for Equal Variances P-Value = 0.161. Fail to reject null hypothesis: "variances are equal," so conclude that the assumption of equal variances (or standard deviations) is not violated.**	

All assumptions are Green, indicating there are no issues. The Two-Sample t-Test results are valid.

Analytical Results:

2 Sample t-Test		
Test Information		
H_0: Mean Difference = 0		
H_a: Mean Difference Not Equal To 0		
Assume Equal Variance		
Results:	**Sue**	**Fred**
Count	50	50
Mean	24.596	26.954
Standard Deviation	0.962768	1.178
Mean Difference	-2.358	
Std Error Difference	0.215182	
DF	98	
t	-10.958	
P-Value (2-sided)	0.0000	
UC (2-sided, 95%)	-1.931	
LC (2-sided, 95%)	-2.785	

Test Information:

Null Hypothesis: $\mu_{Sue} = \mu_{Fred}$ (Mean Difference = 0)

Alternative Hypothesis: $\mu_{Sue} \neq \mu_{Fred}$ (Mean Difference Not Equal To 0.)

The Two Sample t-Test is run assuming equal variances.

Results:

The Output shows the results of the Two-Sample t-Test analysis.

The low **P-Value** (0.000) indicates the data supports a finding of two populations with different mean values. (Reject the Null Hypothesis in favor of the Alternative Hypothesis.)

The true difference between population means in the **UC** (Upper Confidence) and **LC** (Lower Confidence) rows. Notice that the interval, (-1.931 to -2.785) does not contain the value zero. This indicates, that at the 95% confidence, the two populations do not have equal means, ($\mu_{Sue} \neq \mu_{Fred}$).

Note: An advantage of the Two Sample t-Test is that it allows for an assumption of equal variances. If the Test Assumption Report indicates there's a difference between population variances, simply leave the **Assume equal variances** box unchecked.

ANOVA Test

Tool Use: Use the ANOVA technique to test two (or more) levels of a factor.

Data Type: Input - Discrete (2 or more groups); Output – Continuous

Worksheet: ***3LevelANOVA***

Sue	Fred	Jerry
24.2	26.4	24.3
25.4	26.9	24.8
24	25.5	26.2
26	26.5	25.3
25	26.1	26.7
25.4	24.6	24.9
23	27.7	23.6
25.3	29.2	24.4
25.3	27	24.6
25.6	26.5	25
27.3	27.7	24.9

Compare the abilities of three operators: Sue, Fred and Jerry.

Assumptions for the ANOVA analysis is an extension of the Two Sample t-Test. Check stability and normality of each group (the three operators), then check for equal variance.

ANOVA Analysis

Null Hypothesis: H_o: $\mu_{Sue} = \mu_{Fred} = \mu_{Jerry}$

Alternative Hypothesis: H_a: At least one $\mu_i \neq \mu_j$

Menu command: ***SigmaXL > Statistical Tools > One-Way ANOVA and Means Matrix***

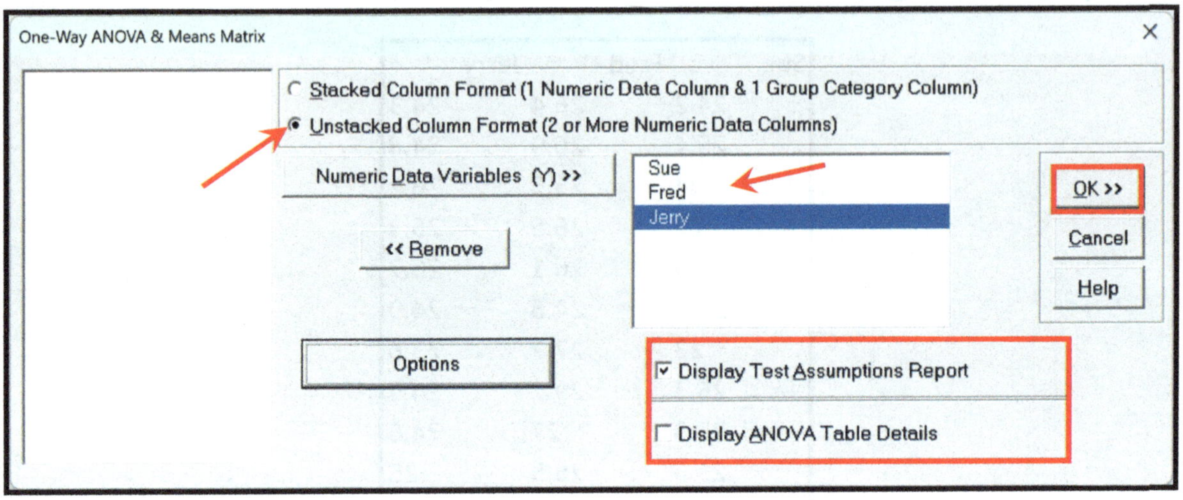

Select **Unstacked Column Format**. Choose **Sue**, **Fred**, and **Jerry** as the Numeric Data Variables (Y).

Choose Display Test Assumptions Report. Click OK.

Output: (Tab: One-Way ANOVA (1))

An **Interval Plot** is generated. The graph is located to the right of the Analytical output.

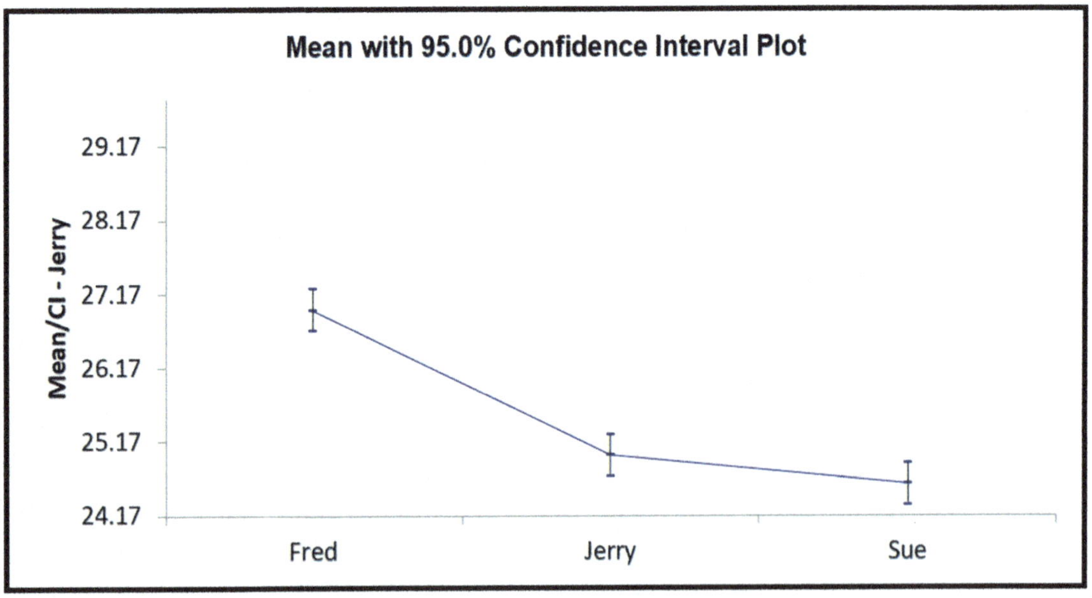

This graph shows the 95% confidence interval for each operator's population mean. If the intervals do not overlap, it suggests that the population mean for those groups are not equal.

The Interval plot shows that Fred's population mean is not equal to Jerry's or Sue's. Jerry and Sue's confidence intervals show an overlap, so their population means could be equal.

Analytical Output:

	Fred	Jerry	Sue		
Count	50	50	50		
Mean	26.954	24.980	24.596		
Standard Deviation	1.178	0.853803	0.962768		
UC (2-sided, 95.0%, pooled)	27.236	25.262	24.878		
LC (2-sided, 95.0%, pooled)	26.672	24.698	24.314		
Pooled Standard Deviation =	1.0073			R-Sq =	51.76%
F =	78.875			R-Sq adj. =	51.11%
P-Value =	0.0000				
DF =	147				

The top portion of the output shows each associates Mean, Standard Deviation and 95% Confidence Interval for their respective population mean. The lower portion shows the results of the Hypothesis Test.

- Null Hypothesis: Population Means for all groups are equal.
- Alt. Hypothesis: At least one of the population's mean values is not equal to another population mean value.

With the low P-Value, reject the null hypothesis. Refer to the Confidence Intervals and the Interval Plot to determine which group's population means are not equal.

Test Assumptions Report:

The Test Assumptions Report does not show any violations, so the One-Way ANOVA assuming equal

One-Way ANOVA Assumptions Report			
Normality:	Anderson Darling P-Value = 0.531. Fail to reject null hypothesis: "data are sampled from a normal distribution," so conclude that the assumption of normality is not violated.	Anderson Darling P-Value = 0.188. Fail to reject null hypothesis: "data are sampled from a normal distribution," so conclude that the assumption of normality is not violated.	Anderson Darling P-Value = 0.154. Fail to reject null hypothesis: "data are sampled from a normal distribution," so conclude that the assumption of normality is not violated.
Robustness:	Not applicable for normal data.		
Outliers (Boxplot Rules):	No outliers found.	No outliers found.	No outliers found.
Randomness (Independence):	Nonparametric Runs Test (Exact) P-Value = 0.116. Fail to reject null hypothesis: "data are random," so conclude that the assumption of randomness (serial independence) is not violated.	Nonparametric Runs Test (Exact) P-Value = 0.670. Fail to reject null hypothesis: "data are random," so conclude that the assumption of randomness (serial independence) is not violated.	Nonparametric Runs Test (Exact) P-Value = 0.116. Fail to reject null hypothesis: "data are random," so conclude that the assumption of randomness (serial independence) is not violated.
Equal Variance:	Bartlett's test for Equal Variances P-Value = 0.073. Fail to reject null hypothesis: "variances are equal," so conclude that the assumption of equal variances (or standard deviations) is not violated.		

variance is the correct analysis.

Additional Analytical Output:

For additional output information, return to the input dialog box and select the **Options** tab.

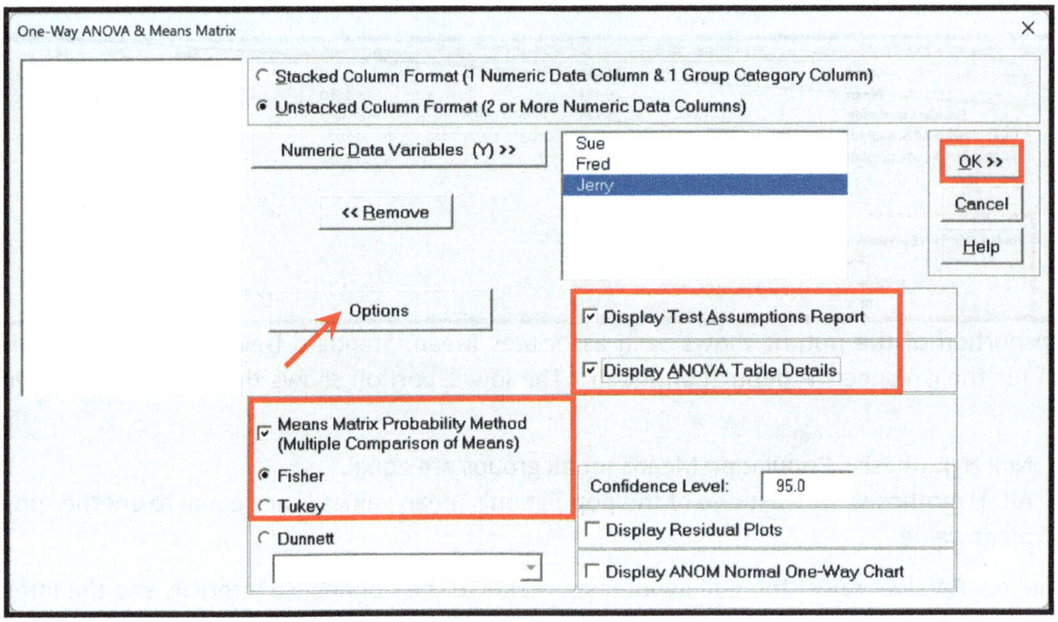

Add; **Display ANOVA Table Details** to the dialog box, then click the tab **Options**. The lower portion of the dialog box appears. Click the **Means Matrix Probability Method**, then select **Fisher**. Click **OK**.

The Interval plot remains to the right of the analytical output.

The Associate information output remains the same. But the ANOVA table is now expanded to show information for the Between, Within, and Overall sources of variation.

ANOVA Table					
Source	SS	DF	MS	F	P-Value
Between	160.0716	2.0000	80.0358	78.875	0.0000
Within	149.1634	147.0000	1.0147		
Total	309.2350	149.0000			
Pooled Standard Deviation =	1.0073		R-Sq =	51.76%	
			R-Sq adj. =	51.11%	

Information for the source **Between** references the associates. This source has a low P-Value indicating there's a difference between associates.

The final portion of the output shows the results of the multiple comparisons.

Pairwise Mean Difference (row - column)	Fred	Jerry	Sue
Fred	0	1.974	2.358
Jerry		0	0.384000
Sue			0

Fisher Pairwise Probabilities	Fred	Jerry	Sue
Fred		0.0000	0.0000
Jerry			0.0586
Sue			

The top portion indicates the Pairwise Mean Differences. The red values indicate those comparisons that fall outside the 95% limits for the normal reference distribution. This table indicates; Fred's population mean is not the same as Jerry's or Sue's. For the Jerry and Sue comparison, the P-Value is slightly above the 0.05 value indicating their population means could be equal.

Paired t-Test

Tool Use: Use the Paired t-Test to determine if a difference exists between the population means of two groups where a natural pairing of information exists. Examples of natural pairings include the measure of a student's before and after scores for a class or standardized test, and matching the two associates' output when working on the same items.

Null Hypothesis: (H_o): $d_i = 0$

The difference between population means of the two groups is zero.

Alternative Hypothesis: (H_a): $d_i \neq 0$

The difference between population means of the two groups is not zero. (Could also use **Greater Than**, or **Less Than** as an alternative hypothesis.)

Data Type: Input – Discrete; Output – Continuous.

A pre-test was administered to a group of students at the beginning of a unit. Students were then given a post-test after the unit was completed. Question: are post-test scores higher (on average) than pre-test scores?

Worksheet: ***Paired Data***

Menu command: ***SigmaXL > Statistical Tools > Paired t-Test***

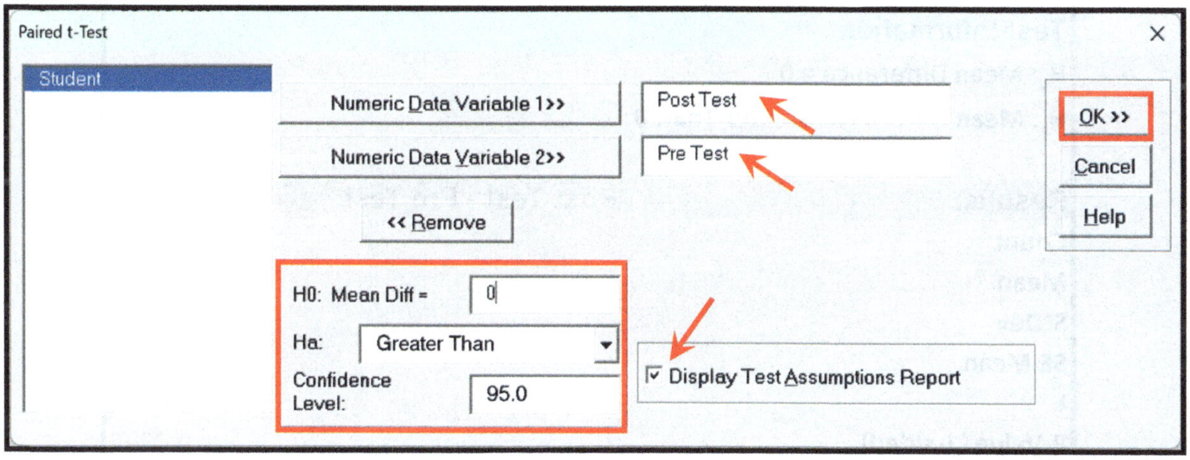

Select **Post Test** as the Numeric Data Variable 1. For Numeric Data Variable 2, choose **Pre Test**.

Click Display Test Assumptions Report.

For the Mean Diff =, input **0**. Post-test scores are expected to be higher than pre-test stores, so the alternative hypothesis is **Greater Than**.

Leave the Confidence Level at **95.0**. Click **OK**. Results are in tab: **Paired t-Test (1)**.

Output

Assumptions Report:

Paired t-Test Assumptions Report	
Normality:	Anderson Darling P-Value = 0.209. Fail to reject null hypothesis: "data are sampled from a normal distribution," so conclude that the assumption of normality is not violated.
Robustness:	Not applicable for normal data.
Outliers (Boxplot Rules):	No outliers found.
Randomness (Independence):	Nonparametric Runs Test (Exact) P-Value = 1.000. Fail to reject null hypothesis: "data are random," so conclude that the assumption of randomness (independence) is not violated.

The assumptions report does not indicate any issues with the data.

Paired t-Test	
Test Information	
H_0: Mean Difference = 0	
H_a: Mean Difference Greater Than 0	
Results:	**Post Test - Pre Test**
Count	10
Mean	3.500
StDev	3.598
SE Mean	1.138
t	3.076
P-Value (1-sided)	0.0066
LC (1-sided, 95%)	1.414

The analytical output shows a P-Value of 0.0066. This allows the experimenter to reject the null hypothesis. The average difference between the Post and Pre-tests is not zero. Since the Pre-test was subtracted from the Post test, the **LC** or **Lower Confidence** interval indicates the difference is at least 1.414.

Two-Way ANOVA

Tool Use: Use the Two-Way ANOVA to determine the effect of two factors. The worksheet must have an equal number of readings for each unique factor combination.

Null Hypothesis: (H_o): $\mu_i = \mu_j$ (for each factor and interaction)

Alternative Hypothesis: (H_a): At least one $\mu_i \neq \mu_j$ (for each level within each factor or interaction)

Data Type: Input – Discrete; Output – Continuous

Worksheet: ***2-Way ANOVA***

Menu command: ***SigmaXL > Statistical Tools > Two-Way ANOVA***

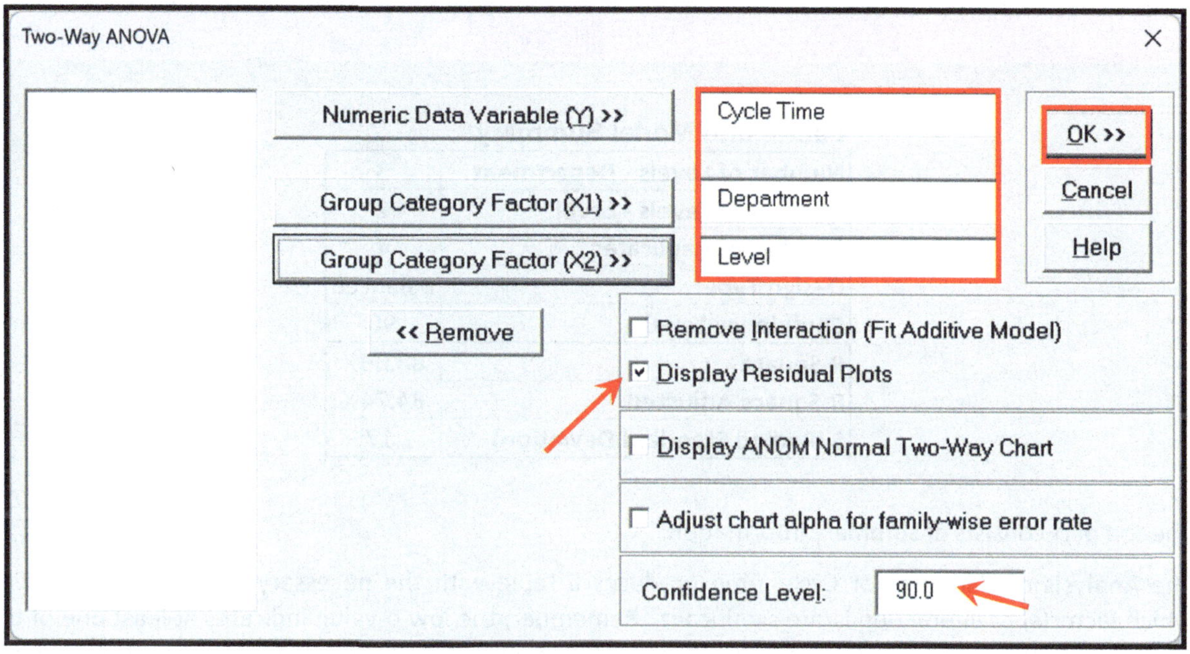

Input **Cycle Time** as the Numeric Data Variable (Y).

Use **Department** and **Level** for the Group Category Factor (X1 & X2).

Choose to **Display Residual Plots**. Since there's no option for the Assumptions Report, it's a good idea to take a look at the Residuals.

Set the Confidence Level. For this example, use **90.0**.

Click **OK**. The output tabs are: Two-Way ANOVA (1), and Two-Way Residuals (1)

Output:

Two-Way ANOVA: Cycle Time

H0 (Factor Department): Mean 1 = Mean 2 = ... = Mean k
Ha (Factor Department): At least one pair Mean i ≠ Mean j

H0 (Factor Level): Mean 1 = Mean 2 = ... = Mean k
Ha (Factor Level): At least one pair Mean i ≠ Mean j

H0 (Interaction): There is no interaction between factors X1 and X2
Ha (Interaction): There is an interaction between factors X1 and X2

Factor and Model Summary:

Number of Levels - Department	3
Number of Levels - Level	2
Number of Replicates	4
Design Type:	Balanced
Confidence Level	90
R-Square	88.06%
R-Square Adjusted	84.74%
S (Pooled Standard Deviation)	2.176

The top part consists of summary information.

The **Analysis of Variance** for Cycle Time produces a table with the necessary information to decide which factor(s) or interaction is/are significant. Remember, the low p-value indicates at least one of the factor level's population mean, is not equal to at least one other level's population mean. The R-sq and R-sq (adj) values are discussed in the Multiple Regression unit.

Analysis of Variance:

Source	DF	SS	MS	F	P
Department	2	105.58	52.792	11.147	0.0007
Level	1	513.38	513.38	108.40	0.0000
Interaction	2	9.750	4.875	1.029325513	0.3773
Error	18	85.250	4.736		
Total	23	713.96	31.042		

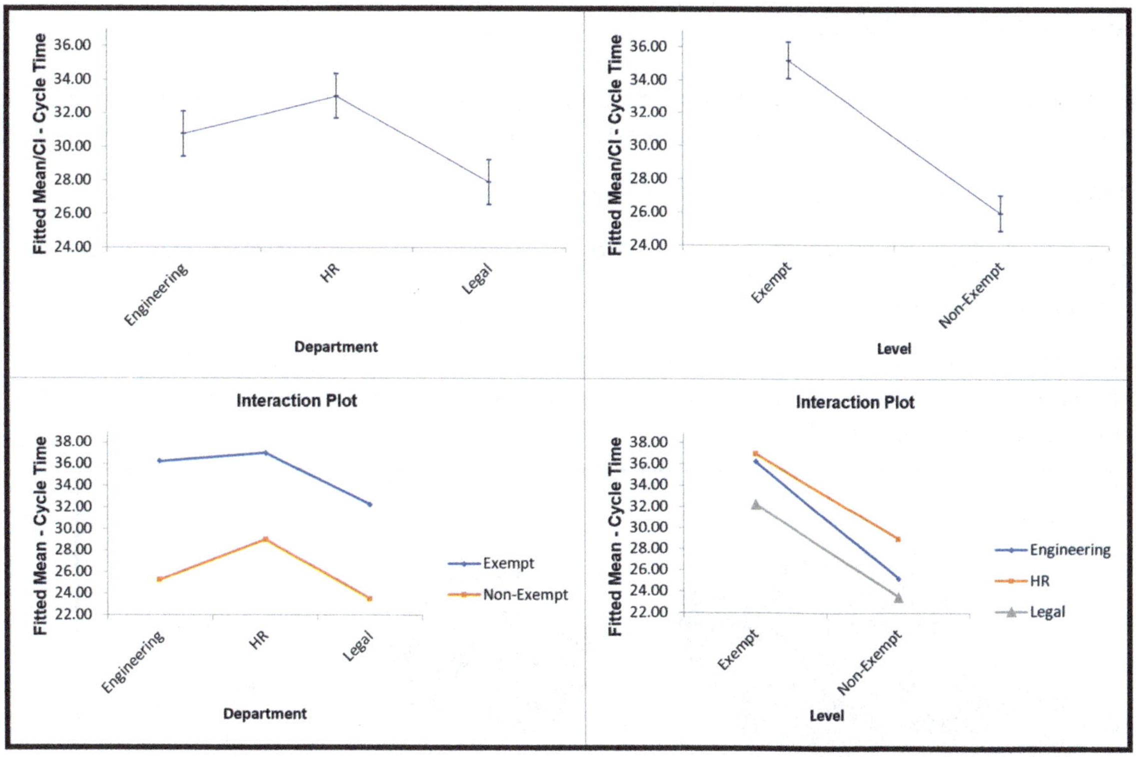

The top portion shows the Main Effects plots. The bottom is the interaction between the Department and the Level. Non-parallel lines indicate an interaction exists.

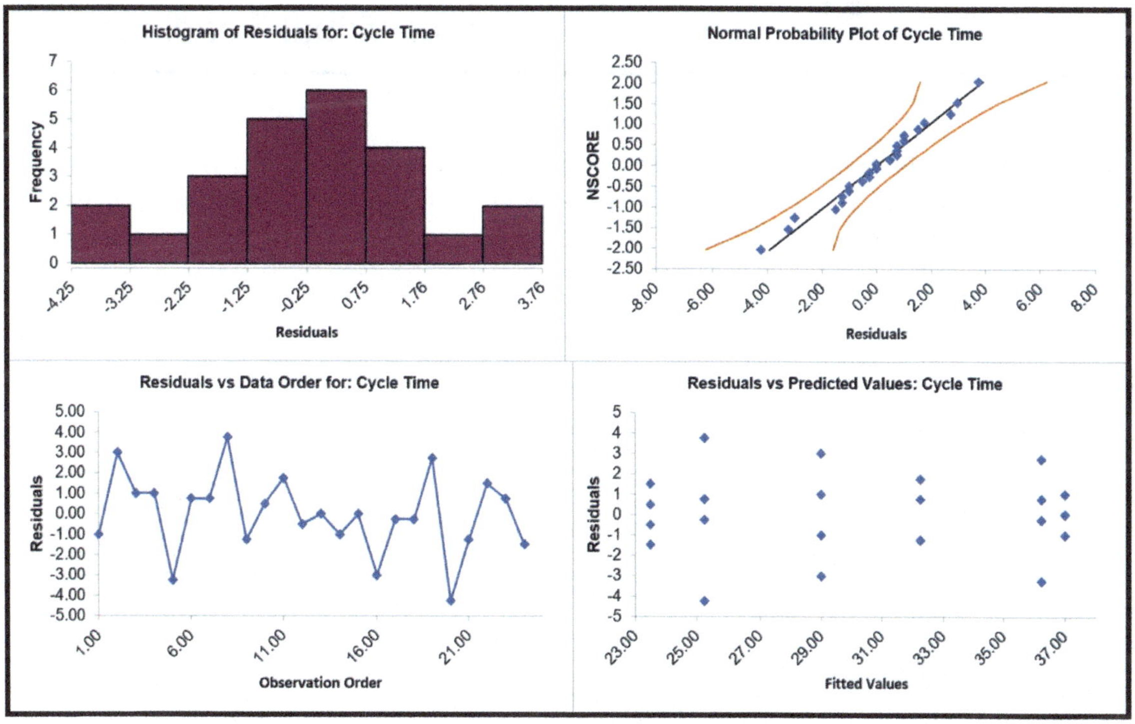

The residual plots don't show any abnormal conditions.

Fully Nested ANOVA

Tool Use: Use the Fully Nested ANOVA to determine the effect of two or more factors in a situation where one or more factors are **Nested** within other factors.

Null Hypothesis: (H_o): $\mu_i = \mu_j$ (for each factor and interaction)

Alternative Hypothesis: (H_a): At least one $\mu_i \neq \mu_j$ (for each level within each factor or interaction)

Data Type: Input – Discrete; Output - Continuous

Data originates from a test of carpet crushability. Five samples were measured from each of two locations per roll. The samples are nested within location and the location is nested within the roll. Seven rolls were used in the study.

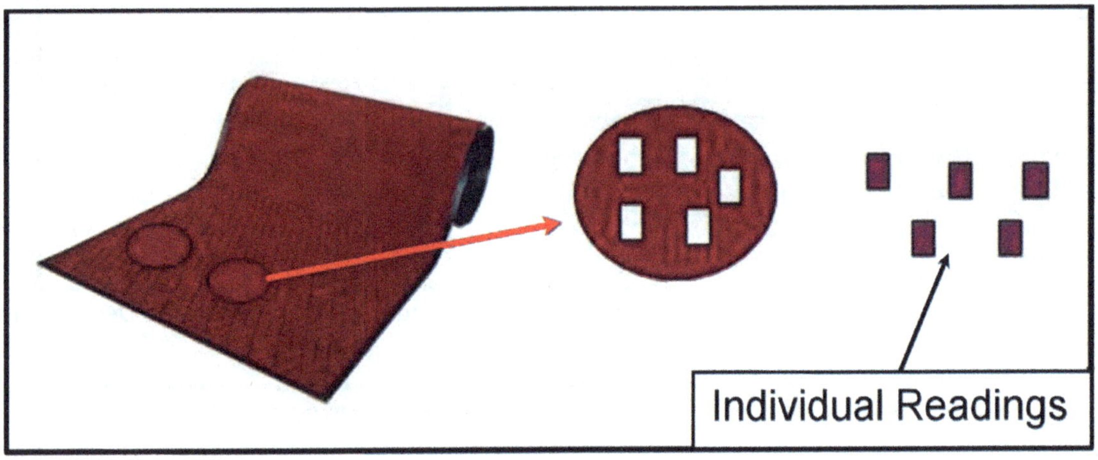

The nesting occurs because the five readings in location 1 are not the same as the five readings in location 2. Also, location 1 in roll 1 is not the same as location 1 in roll 2. Therefore, the samples are nested in location, the location is nested in rolls.

Worksheet: ***Carpet***

Menu command: ***SigmaXL > Statistical Tools > General Linear Model > Fit General Lineal Model***

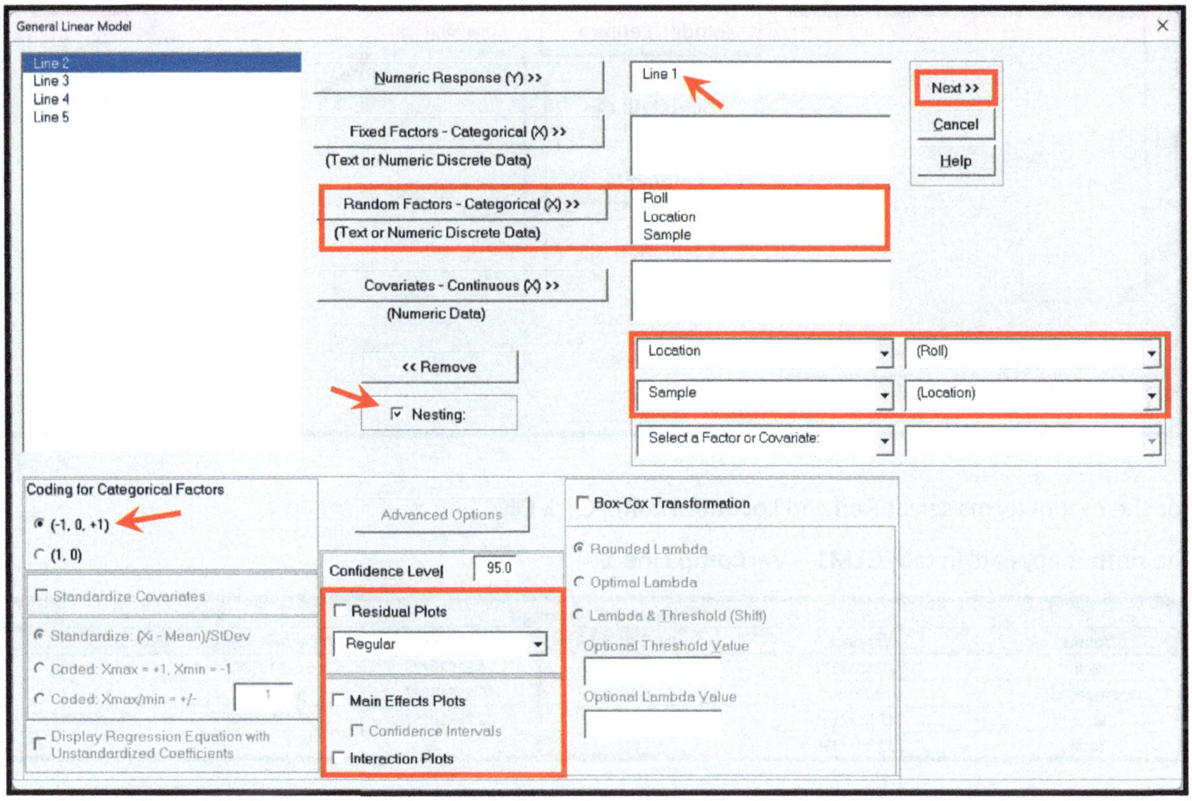

Input **Line 1** for the Numeric Response (Y). For the Random Factors – Categorical (X) select **Roll**, **Location** and **Sample**. (Factors must be input as Random to create a Variance Component Report.)

Click the **Nesting** option. Set up the nesting structure; Location is nested in Roll. Sample is nested in Location. Follow the image above.

For Coding for Categorical Factors select the **(-1, 0, +1)** option. Deselect the **Residuals Plots**, **Main Effects Plots** and the **Interaction Plots**.

Click **Next**.

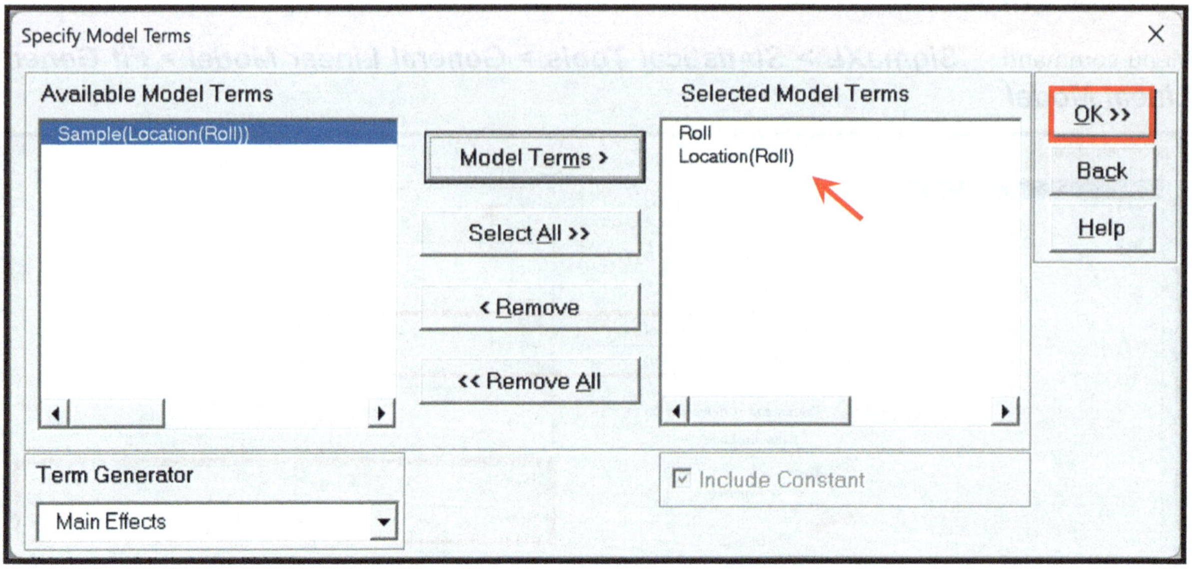

For the model terms select **Roll** and **Location(Roll)**. Click **OK**.

The output appears in tab: **GLM1 – VarComp Line 1**

Variance Components					
Source	**Variance**	**Var % of Total**	**SE Var for CI**	**Var Lower 95% CI**	**Var Upper 95% CI**
Roll	7.024009524	4.71%	14.61029775	0.119135861	414.121403
Location(Roll)	0.5805	0.39%	16.35313547	6.09E-25	5.53E+23
Error	141.6382143	94.90%	26.76710652	97.79540992	205.136251
Total	149.2427238				

The critical information is found in the column **Var % of Total** (Percent of Total Variation).

The results indicate that the Error (Sample information) accounts for 94.9% of the Total Variation. To improve this process, the team must investigate and solve the variation with the samples. At this level, the issue might be the Measurement System. Perform an MSA before proceeding.

Repeating this analysis for Line 3 produces the following results.

Variance Components					
Source	**Variance**	**Var % of Total**	**SE Var for CI**	**Var Lower 95% CI**	**Var Upper 95% CI**
Roll	142.462981	90.05%	82.74545006	45.19847145	445.0131999
Location(Roll)	-1.438742857	0.00%			
Error	15.74971429	9.95%	2.685436348	10.51375937	21.25927879
Total	158.2126952				

For Line 3, the Roll-to-Roll variation is the largest. For this situation the team should investigate differences between the Roll's setup, machine functionality, issues reports, recent adjustments, etc.

Using the Multi-Vari Graph along with the GLM (General Linear Model) information.

Variance Components					
Source	Variance	Var % of Total	SE Var for CI	Var Lower 95% CI	Var Upper 95% CI
Roll	7.024009524	4.71%	14.61029775	0.119135861	414.121403
Location(Roll)	0.5805	0.39%	16.35313547	6.09E-25	5.53E+23
Error	141.6382143	94.90%	26.76710652	97.79540992	205.136251
Total	149.2427238				

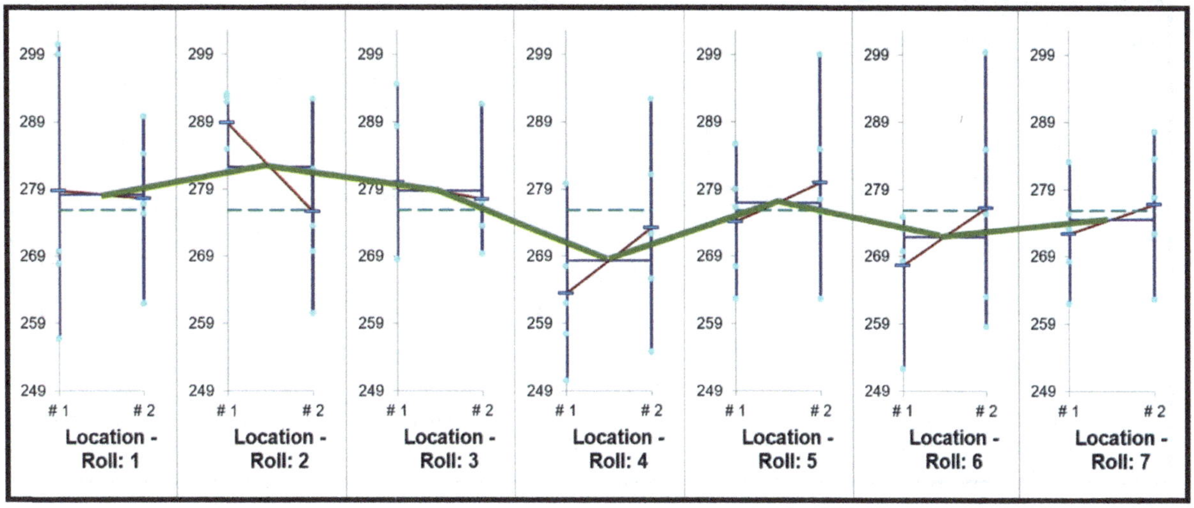

Line 1

Variance Components					
Source	Variance	Var % of Total	SE Var for CI	Var Lower 95% CI	Var Upper 95% CI
Roll	142.462981	90.05%	82.74545006	45.19847145	445.0131999
Location(Roll)	-1.438742857	0.00%			
Error	15.74971429	9.95%	2.685436348	10.51375937	21.25927879
Total	158.2126952				

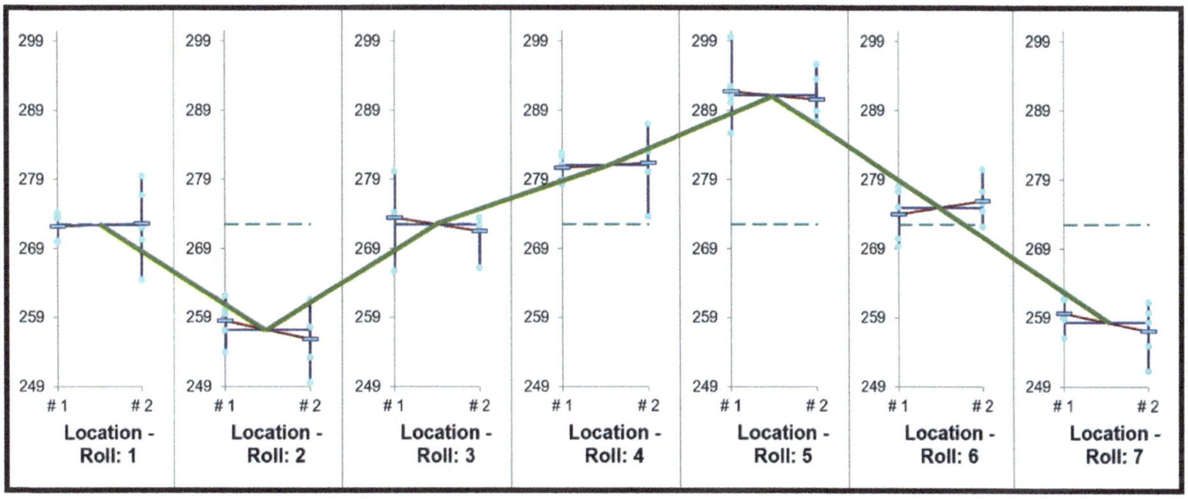

Line 3

Results for Line 4:

Variance Components					
Source	Variance	Var % of Total	SE Var for CI	Var Lower 95% CI	Var Upper 95% CI
Roll	-124.3666238	0.00%			
Location(Roll)	253.7363286	84.13%	58.27747491	61.06265522	316.1230759
Error	47.85521429	15.87%	9.04378577	33.04207397	69.30925776
Total	301.5915429				

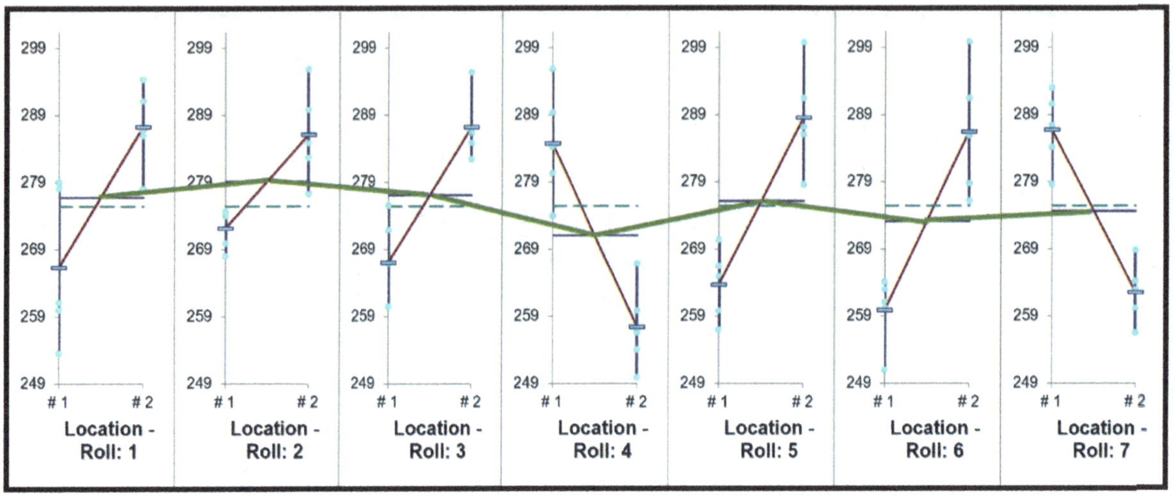

Line 4

For Line 4 the largest variation occurs with the Location to Location within the Roll.

Hint: For presentations, show the Multi-Vari plot, not the Variance Component table. Pictures are worth a thousand words. Explain where the largest source of variation exists. But, always have the Variance Component information somewhere that it can be reference quickly. Then if a question arises as to the analysis, the presenter can provide the numbers.

Correlation

Tool Use: Use Correlation analysis to describe the degree of linear relationship between two factors. The Pearson product-moment coefficient measures the degree of this relationship.

The Correlation Coefficient (r)

Values lie between -1 and +1

A value of -1 depicts complete inverse (negative) dependence

A value of 0 depicts complete independence

A value of +1 depicts complete direct (positive) dependence

General Rules

Correlation Coefficient (r) > .75 or < -.75 is strong

Correlation Coefficient (r) between -.50 and .50 is not strong.

Data Type: All factors (inputs and outputs) are **Continuous**

Null Hypothesis (H_o): Correlation coefficient (r) = 0

Alternative Hypothesis (H_a): Correlation coefficient (r) ≠ 0

Worksheet: ***Correlation***

The Correlation analysis will create a graph showing the data values.

To run the Correlation, select:

Menu command: ***SigmaXL > Statistical Tools > Correlation Matrix***

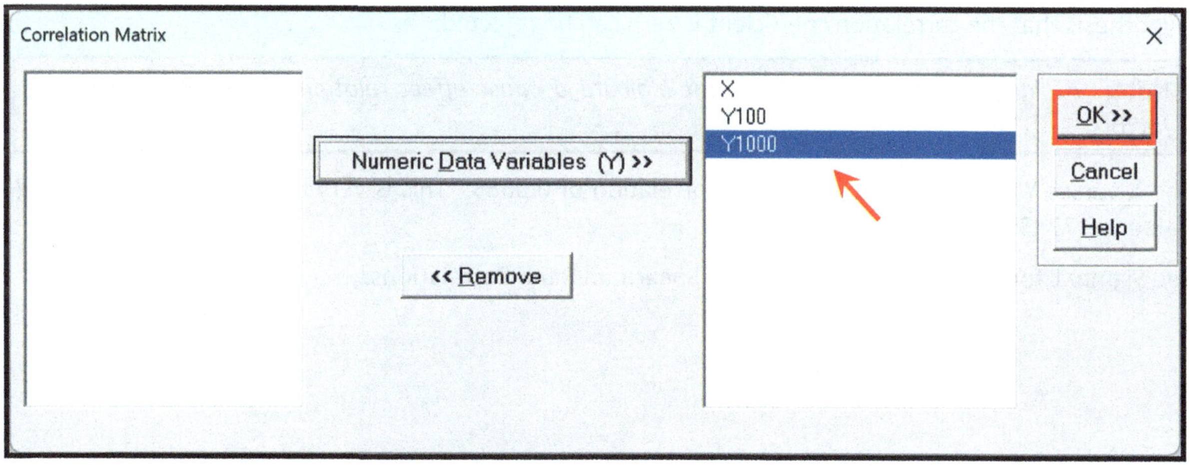

Select the factors **X** and **Y100** and **Y1000**. Click **OK**.

Results appear in the **Correlation Matrix (1)** tab.

Pearson Correlations	X	Y100	Y1000
X	1	0.9807	0.0688
Y100		1	0.0636
Y1000			1
Pearson Probabilities	**X**	**Y100**	**Y1000**
X		0.0000	0.7733
Y100			0.7900
Y1000			
Spearman Rank Correlations	**X**	**Y100**	**Y1000**
X	1	0.9624	0.0008
Y100		1	0.0684
Y1000			1
Spearman Rank Probabilities	**X**	**Y100**	**Y1000**
X		0.0000	0.9975
Y100			0.7743
Y1000			

The **Pearson Correlations** values show the pairwise correlations. The **Pearson Probabilities** produce the P-Values. For X verses Y100 the correlation coefficient 0.9807. The P-Value is 0.0000 so the Null Hypothesis that the correlation coefficient is zero can be rejected.

Note: *A significant correlation does not indicate a cause-effect relationship between the two factors.*

The X verses Y1000 produces a Pearson Correlation of 0.0688. This is very low. The corresponding P-Value is 0.7733

See SigmaXL for information regarding the Spearman Rank Correlations.

Graphical representation of Correlations:

Worksheet: ***Correlation***

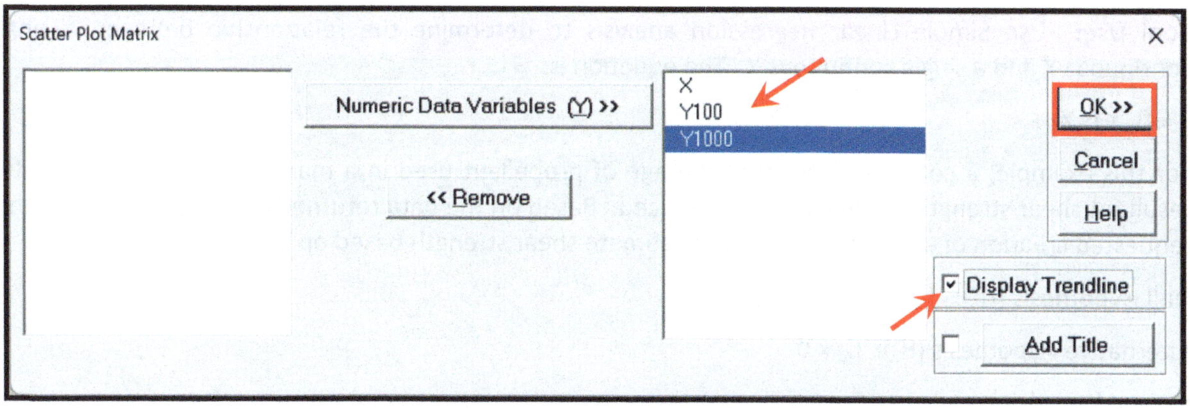

Menu Command: ***SigmaXL > Graphical Tools > Scatter Plot Matrix***

Select all three inputs; **X**, **Y100**, and **Y1000**. Select the **Display Trendline** option, then click **OK**.

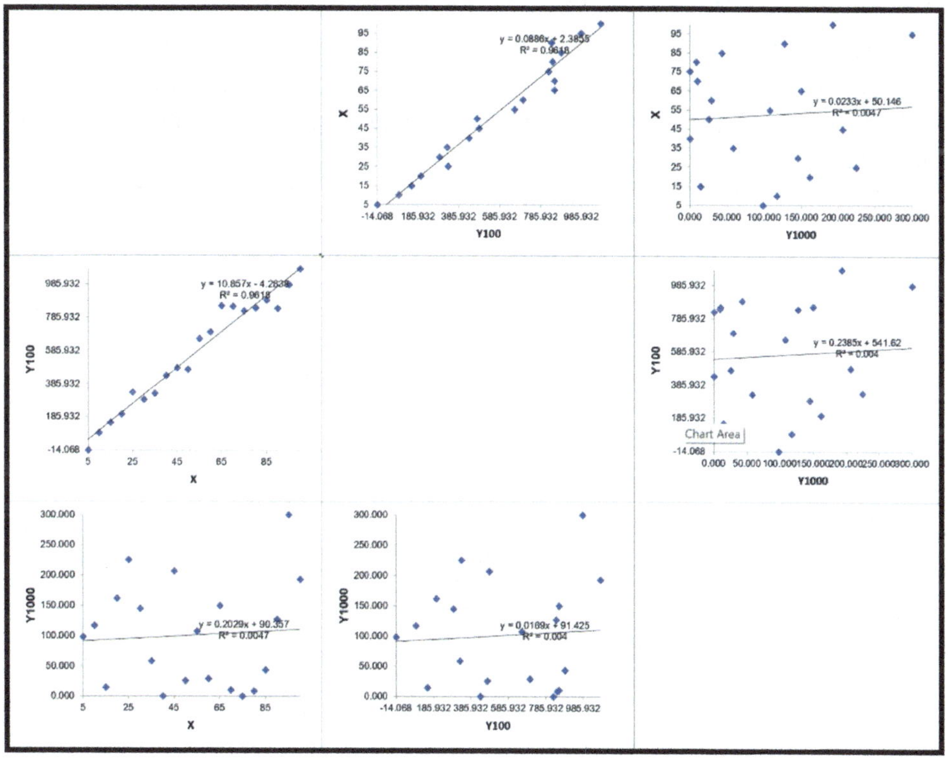

The Trendlines for each combination of factors is a visual of the correlation. Steep slopes are strong correlations, while shallow slopes are weak correlations.

Regression Models

Simple Linear Regression Analysis

Tool Use: Use Simple Linear Regression analysis to determine the relationship between a single continuous X and a single continuous Y. The equation is:

$Y = \beta_0 + \beta_1 X_1 + \varepsilon$

For this example, a company compared the age of propellant used in a manufacturing process to the resultant shear strength of the material produced. Based on the data returned, the organization further requested creation of a predictive model to estimate shear strength based on age of the propellant.

Null Hypothesis (H_0): $\beta_0 = 0$

Alternative Hypothesis (H_a): $\beta_0 \neq 0$

Second hypothesis:

Null Hypothesis (H_0): $\beta_1 = 0$

Alternative Hypothesis (H_a): $\beta_1 \neq 0$

Data Type: Input – Continuous; Output - Continuous

Worksheet: ***Propellant***

> Note: *This example is taken from* ***Introduction to Linear Regression Analysis*** *by* **Montgomery and Peck ©1992 p. 10.**

Menu command: ***SigmaXL > Statistical Tools > Regression > Multiple Regression***

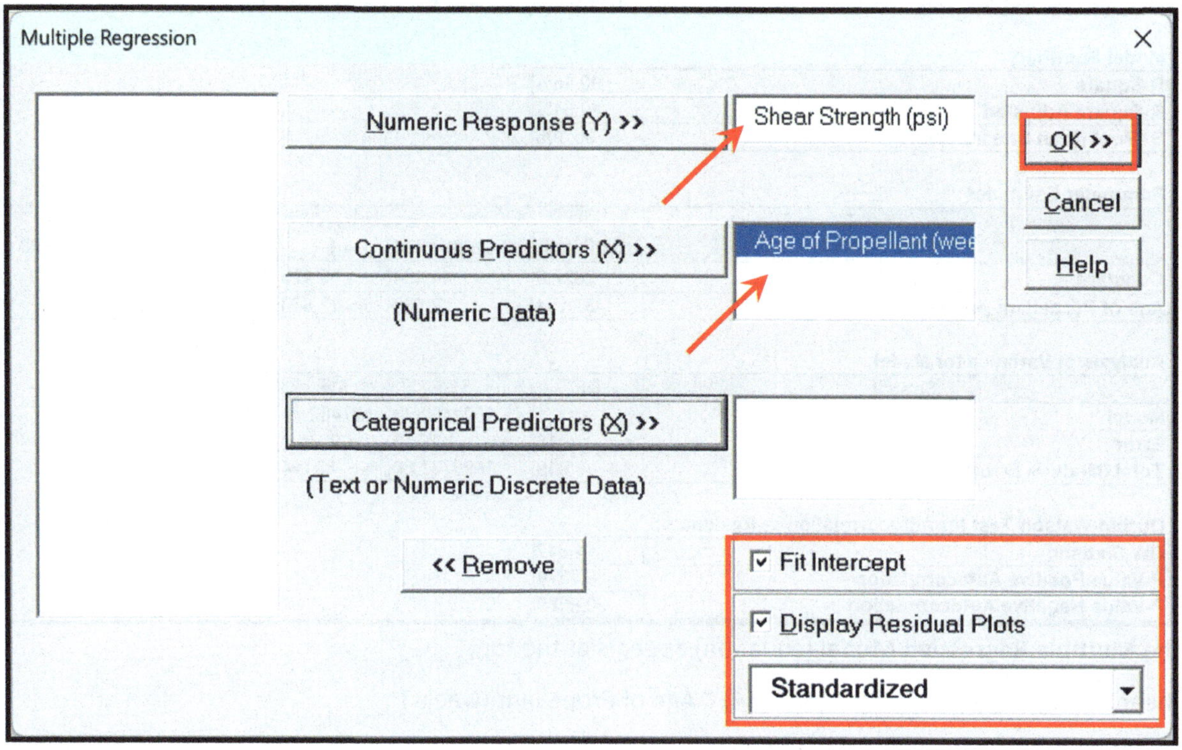

Input **Shear Strength (psi)** as the Numeric Response (Y):

Input **Age of Propellant (weeks)** as the Continuous Predictors (X):

Choose **Fit Intercept** and **Display Residuals**. For the type of Residuals, select **Standardize**. Click **OK**.

The output appears in two tabs; Multiple Regression and Mult Reg Residuals (1).

Multiple Regression tab contains:

Multiple Regression Model

Model Summary

Parameter Estimates

Analysis of Variance for Model

Durbin-Watson Test for Autocorrelation in Residuals

Predicted Response Calculator

Mult Reg Residuals (1) tab contains:

Graphical analysis of Residuals

Multiple Regression Analysis

Multiple Regression Model: Shear Strength (psi) = (2627.8) + (-37.154) * Age of Propellant (weeks)

Model Summary:

R-Square	90.18%
R-Square Adjusted	89.64%
S (Root Mean Square Error)	96.106

Parameter Estimates:

Predictor Term	Coefficient	SE Coefficient	T	P	VIF	Tolerance
Constant	2627.8	44.184	59.475	0.0000		
Age of Propellant (weeks)	-37.154	2.889	-12.860	0.0000	1.00000	1

Analysis of Variance for Model:

Source	DF	SS	MS	F	P
Model	1	1527482.74	1527482.74	165.38	0.0000
Error	18	166255	9236.4		
Total (Model + Error)	19	1693737.60	89144		

Durbin-Watson Test for Autocorrelation in Residuals:

DW Statistic	1.842
P-Value Positive Autocorrelation	0.3874
P-Value Negative Autocorrelation	0.6689

The **Multiple Regression Model** (equation) appears at the top:

Shear Strength (psi) = 2627.8 + (-37.154) * Age of Propellant (weeks)

The Model Summary shows the R-Square (90.18%), the R Square Adjusted (89.64%) and the S (Root Mean Square Error) (96.106).

R-Sq indicates the percent of variation explained by the equation; in this example, R-Sq is 90.18%. Therefore, the equation above explains 90.18% of the variation observed in the Shear Strength.

R-Sq (adj) is explained in the Multiple Regression section.

S (Root Mean Square Error) is the standard deviation of the model's error term.

The **Parameter Estimates** shows the results of the hypothesis test for the **Constant** and the Coefficient for the **Age of Propellant (weeks)**. Both factors have low P-values (0.0000), so their values cannot be zero.

The **Analysis of Variance for Model** shows the breakdown for the degrees of freedom (**DF**), the Sum of Squares (**SS**), the Mean Square values (**MS**) along with the **F** and **P** values.

The **Analysis of Variance** table tests the regression equation to determine if at least one of the coefficients is not equal to zero. Since there are two predictors (one for the Constant and one for the Coefficient of the Predictor Factor (Age of Propellant (weeks))), the low p-value indicates that either the Constant, or the Coefficient for that predictor, or both are not zero.

The **Durbin-Watson Test for Autocorrelation in Residuals**. This shows the **DW Statistic** (1.842), and the two P-Values for the **Positive** and **Negative Autocorrelation** (0.3874 and 0.6689 respectively). Autocorrelation in the residuals could be caused by external bias factor affecting your process over time. This should be investigated. Ho issues with autocorrelation exist with this data.

The **Predicted Response Calculator** allows for predictions of the output based on the input value of the predictor. The Predictor values should be within the range of values used for the analysis.

Predicted Response Calculator:						
Predictors	**Enter Settings:**	**Predicted Response**	**Lower 95% CI**	**Upper 95% CI**	**Lower 95% PI**	**Upper 95% PI**
Age of Propellant (weeks)						

Example:

Input 9 for Age of Propellant.

Predicted Response Calculator:						
Predictors	**Enter Settings:**	**Predicted Response**	**Lower 95% CI**	**Upper 95% CI**	**Lower 95% PI**	**Upper 95% PI**
Age of Propellant (weeks)	9	2293.44004	2241.099119	2345.780962	2084.854833	2502.025248

The **Predicted Response**, based on the Regression equation is: 2293.44. (Values are rounded.)

The **Lower 95% CI** (Confidence Interval) is 2241.10. The **Upper 95% CI** is 2345.78.

The **Lower 95% PI** (Predictive Interval) is 2084.86 and the **Upper 95% PI** is 2502.03.

The Confidence Interval is an estimate of the population mean, while the Predictive Interval is the range of values for individual readings.

Note: Use these results to **interpolate** between sample values for the Age of Propellant, but do not **extrapolate** beyond these values. In other words, do not extend the equation beyond the upper and lower X values (Age of Propellant) used to determine the equation.

Residual Analysis (Go to tab: Mult Reg Residuals (1))

The residuals demonstrate the appropriateness of the model. The residual equals the fitted (or predicted) value minus the actual value. Residuals may be positive or negative.

With the Lease Squares analysis, an adequate model is demonstrated by residuals with the following characteristics:

- Residuals originate from a population with a normal distribution.
- The process is stable.
- Residuals are independent.
- Residuals have a constant variance.
- Residuals have a mean value equal to zero.

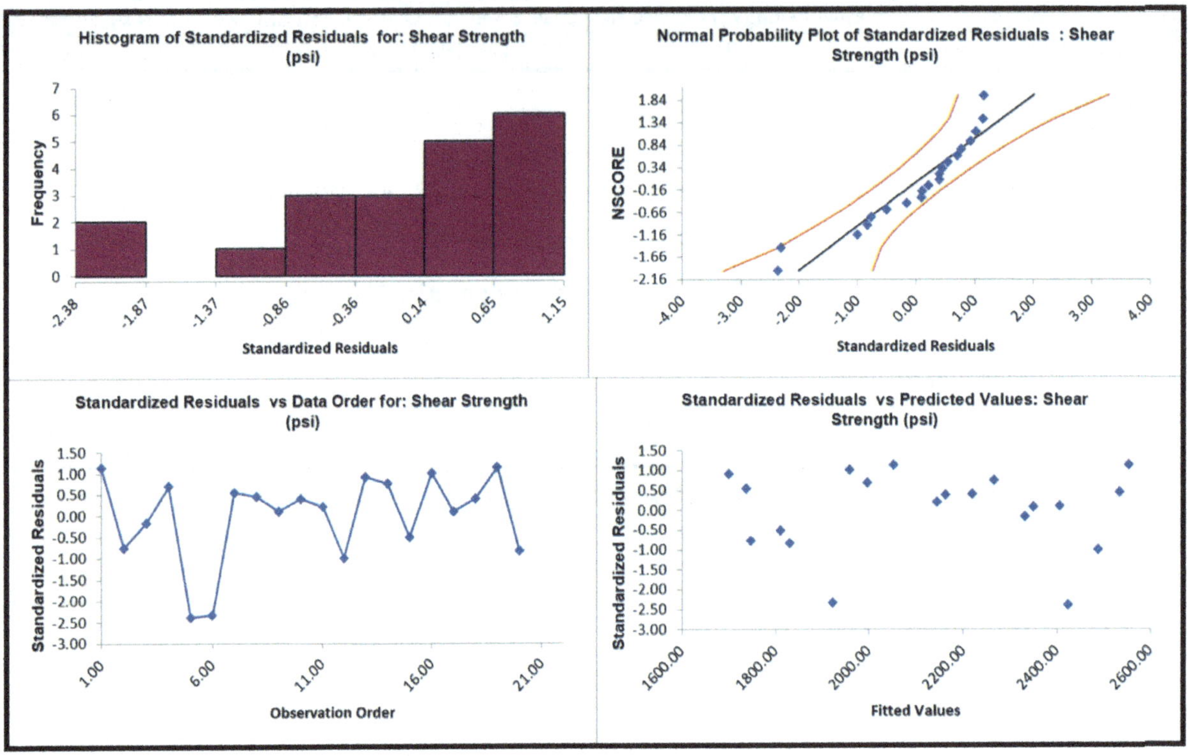

> **Hint:** If there's a question regarding the Normality assumption, go to column **D** (Residuals) of this tab and run a Normality Test using the Descriptive Statistics tool. (This will also test the assumption that the Residuals have a mean value of zero.

The top two graphs represent the distribution of Residuals. The Normality Plot is on the right.

The lower two graphs are used to determine the independence and equal variance assumptions. No trends or shifts occur in the lower left graph, so the process appears to be stable. The lower right graph represents the equal variance assumption. The spread of values along the fitted values, should be approximately equal. There might be an issue with the lowest 2 points. This should be investigated.

The final graph shows the Residuals vs. the Input Factor (Age of Propellant) values. This should also show an approximate equal spread. Again, the same 2 points appear to be an issue.

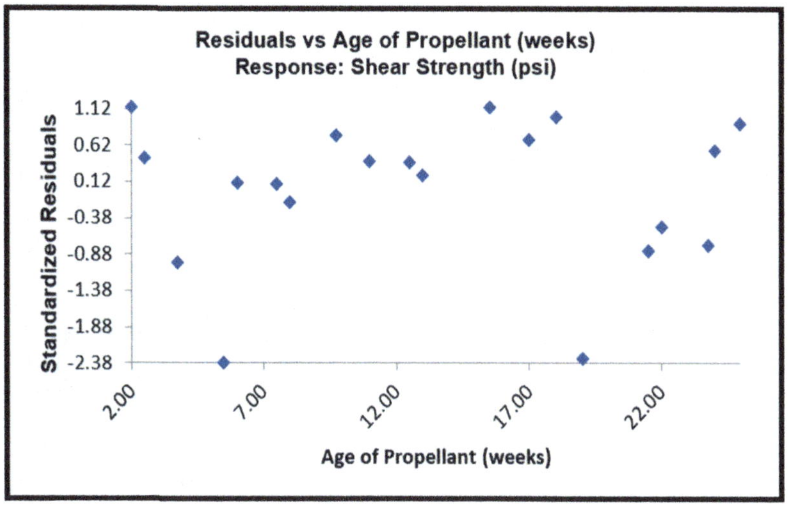

Graphical Representation of Model:

Create a Scatter Plot with a fitted Regression line to demonstrate the Regression Model.

Return to the Propellant tab.

Menu Command: ***SigmaXL > Graphical Tools > Scatter Plots***

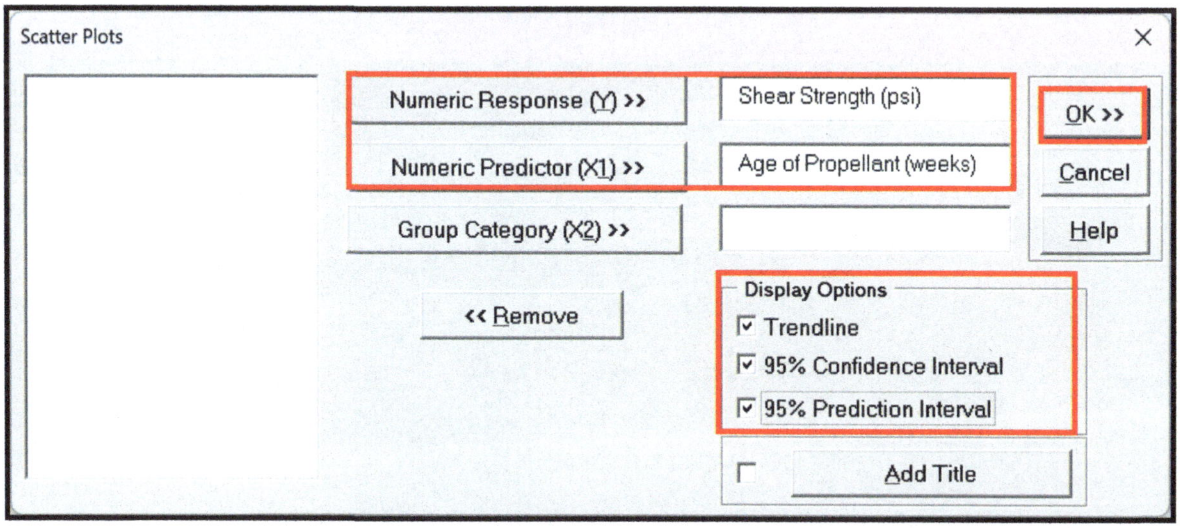

Input **Shear Strength (psi)** for the Numeric Response (Y). Choose **Age of Propellant (weeks)** for the Numeric Predictor (X1). For the **Display Options** choose all three. Click **OK**.

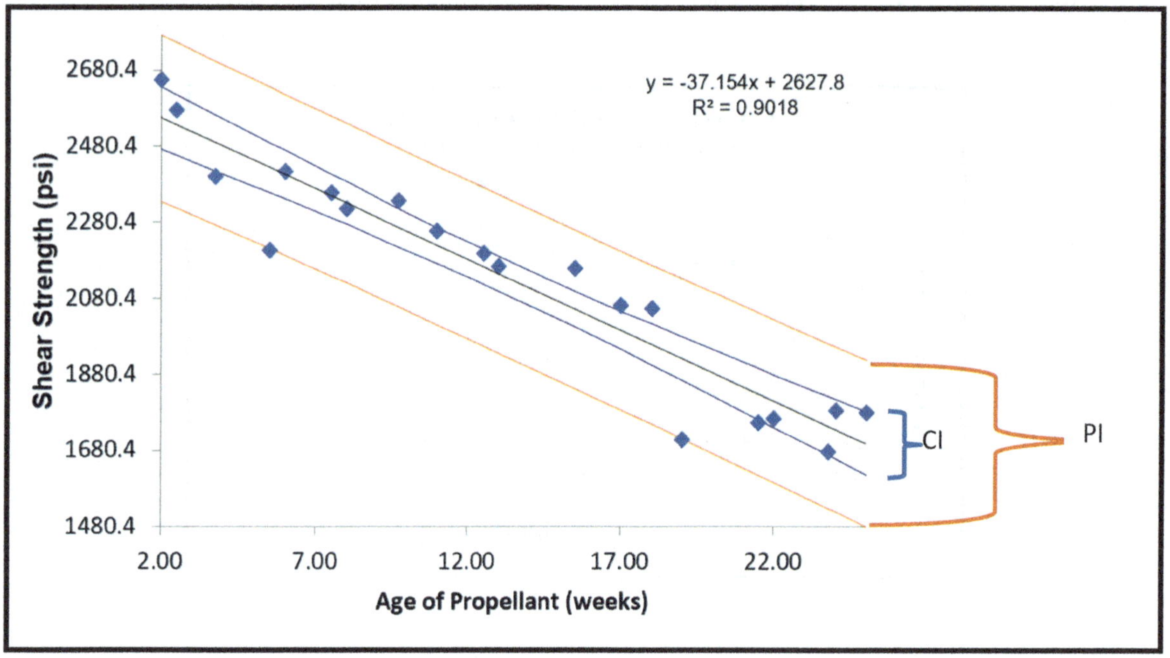

The outer lines represent the Predictive Interval while the inner (Blue) lines represent the Confidence Interval.

Residuals versus Fits

The Residuals versus Fits plot checks the constant variance assumption and looks for patterns in the residuals. If the scatter of points shows a constant spread throughout the range of Fitted values, the assumption of constant variance is upheld. Abnormal patterns may demonstrate the need for either a transformation or higher order terms.

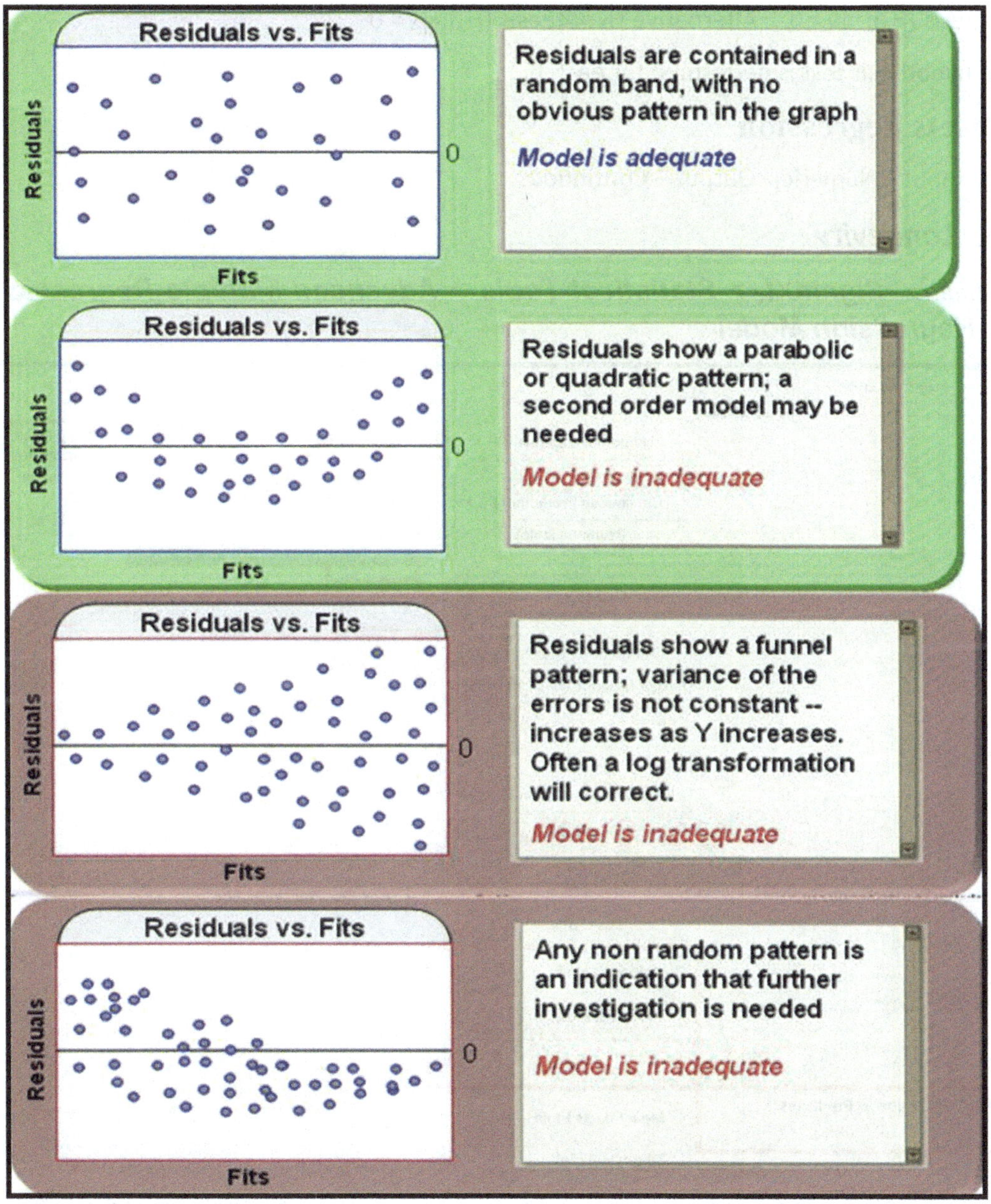

Multiple Regression

Tool Use: Use the SigmaXL Regression analysis to determine the relationship between several continuous inputs and a single continuous output variable. This creates the following equation:

$Y = \beta_0 + \beta_1 X_1 + \beta_2 X_2 + \beta_3 X_3 + \ldots + \beta_n X_n + \varepsilon$

Null Hypothesis (H_o): $\beta_i = 0$ Alternative Hypothesis (H_a): $\beta_i \neq 0$

A separate hypothesis test is performed for each β_i .

Best Subsets Regression

Data Type: Input – Numeric; Output – Continuous.

Worksheet: ***Longevity***

Menu command: ***SigmaXL > Statistical Tools > Advanced Multiple Regression > Fit Multiple Regression Model***

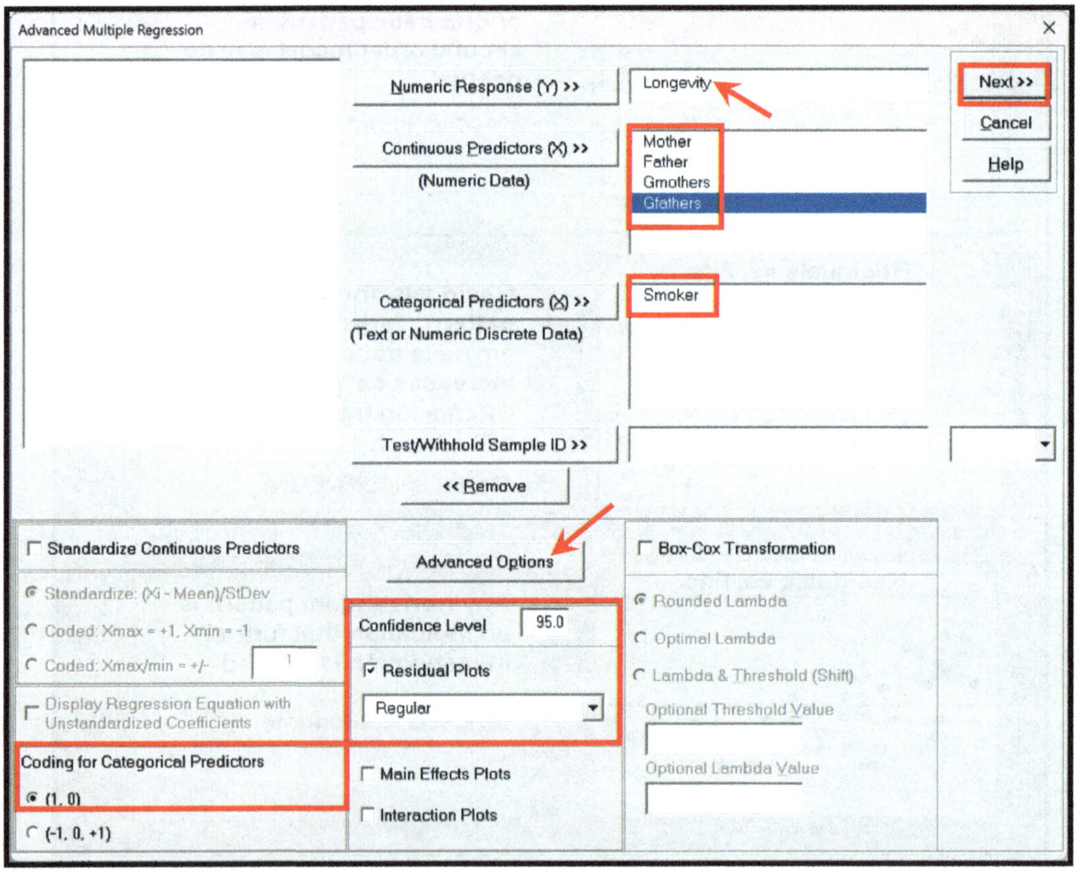

Input **Longevity** as the Numeric Response (Y). Choose **Mother**, **Father**, **Gmothers**, and **Gfathers** for the Continuous Predictors (X). **Smoker** is the Categorical Predictor (X).

Select the option **(1,0)** for the Coding for Categorical Predictors. Leave the Confidence Level at 95.0. Check the Residuals Plots option. For the type of residual, choose **Regular**. Click **Advanced Options**.

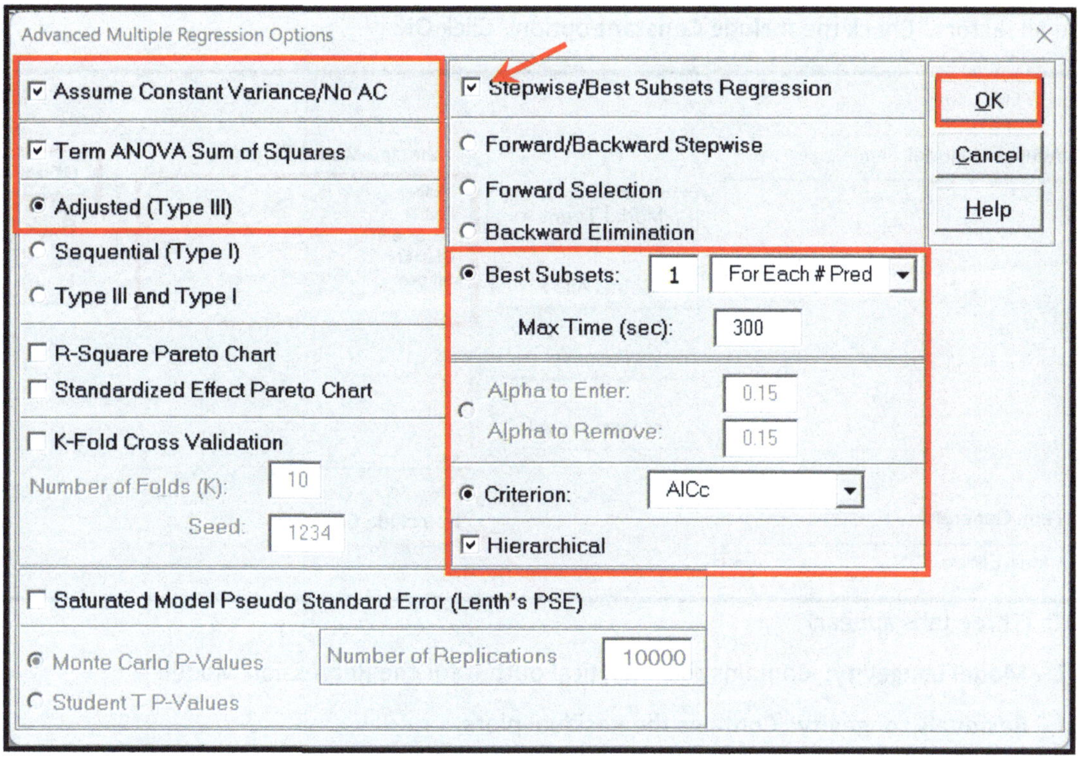

Select; Assume Constant Variance/No AC. Check the Term ANOVA Sum of Squares then choose the Adjusted (Type III) option.

For the **Stepwise/Best Subset Regression** choose **Best Subsets:** fill in the information as shown.

For **Criterion:** use **AICc**. Check the **Hierarchical** option.

Click **OK**. This will return to the **Advanced Multiple Regression** dialog box.

Click **Next**.

Choose all factors. Check the **Include Constant** option. Click **OK**.

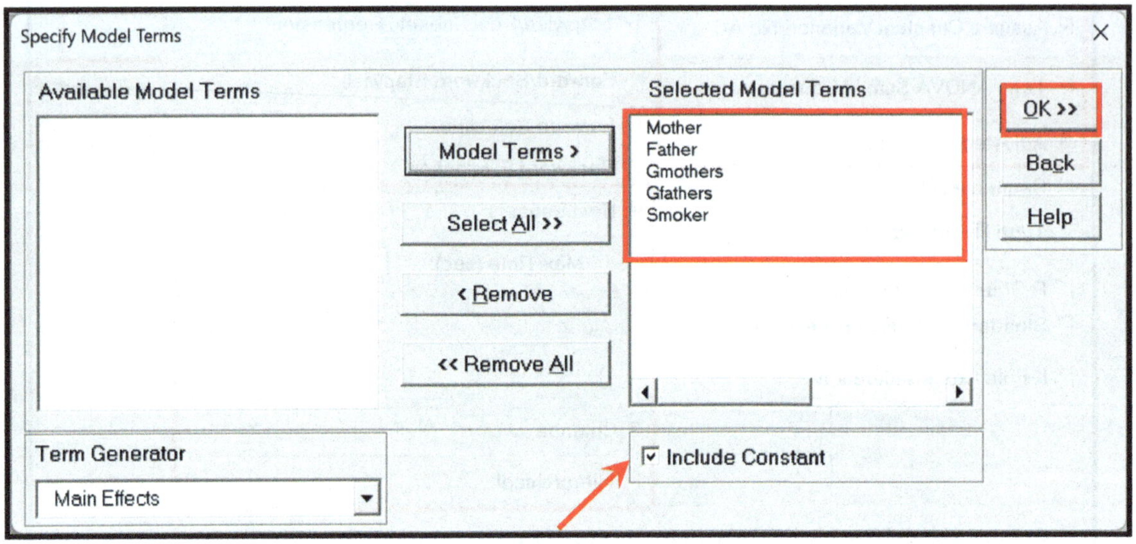

Output: (Three tabs appear)

MReg1 – Model Longevity: Contains the analytical output for the Regression Model.

MReg1 – Residuals Longevity: Contains the Residual plots

MReg1 – Report Longevity: Contains the Best Subset Report

Tab: MReg1 – Model Longevity

This tab contains a multitude of information. Some of the common outputs are;

Model Summary	
R-Square	80.12%
R-Square Adjusted	79.50%
R-Square Predicted	78.32%
S (Root Mean Square Error)	2.3220

Model Summary with the R-Square values.

The R-Square values are near 80%. While these values are not good for the laboratory physical sciences, it is good for healthcare.

Parameter Estimates						
Predictor Term	**Coefficient**	**SE Coefficient**	**T**	**P**	**VIF**	**Tolerance**
Constant	27.22780108	5.096036449	5.3429	0.0000		
Mother	0.334439938	0.047466048	7.0459	0.0000	1.5240	0.6562
Father	0.323757591	0.044831287	7.2217	0.0000	1.3359	0.7486
Smoker_Yes	-3.73771495	0.667316264	-5.6011	0.0000	1.8790	0.5322

The Parameter Estimates all have low P values, indicating they have an effect on the output.

The VIF (Variance Inflation Factor) is an indication of multi-collinearity between inputs; values less than 5 are considered acceptable. Multi-collinearity indicates inputs are correlated, which can lead to erroneous results.

Analysis of Variance for Model					
Source	**DF**	**SS**	**MS**	**F**	**P**
Model	3	2086.156396	695.3854652	128.9732	0.0000
Error	96	517.6036044	5.391704213		
Error: Lack-of-Fit	87	487.9369377	5.608470549	1.7014	0.1961
Error: Pure Error	9	29.66666667	3.296296296		
Total (Model + Error)	99	2603.76	26.30060606		

The Analysis of Variance for Model has the Lack-of-Fit error with a high p-Value (0.1961), so there's no concern at this time for the fitted model.

Analysis of Variance for Predictors (Adjusted Type III)							
Predictor Term	**DF**	**SS**	**MS**	**F**	**P**	**R-Square**	**Std. Effect (T)**
Mother	1	267.6678259	267.6678259	49.6444	0.0000	10.28%	7.0459
Father	1	281.1923917	281.1923917	52.1528	0.0000	10.80%	7.2217
Smoker	1	169.1511657	169.1511657	31.3725	0.0000	6.50%	5.6011

The Analysis of Variance for the Predictors shows all three are significant.

Durbin-Watson Test for Autocorrelation in Residuals	
DW Statistic	1.9853
P-Value Positive Autocorrelation	0.4674
P-Value Negative Autocorrelation	0.5263

The Durbin-Watson Test for Autocorrelation shows high P-Values. This test was discussed previously.

Breusch-Pagan Test for Constant Variance (Normal)			
H0: Variance is constant; Ha: Variance is not constant.			
Predictor Term	**Chi-Square**	**DF**	**P-Value**
All Terms	0.25796	3	0.9677
Mother	0.00626688	1	0.9369
Father	0.232652	1	0.6296
Smoker	0.0114188	1	0.9149

The tests for equal variance show high P-Values. Therefore, no issues exist.

Information Criteria and Validation	
AICc	458.8300
BIC	471.2175
R-Square 10-Fold	N/A
S 10-Fold	N/A

The AICc and BIC criteria are listed. These are also found in the tab: **MReg1-Report Longevity**

Predicted Response Calculator							
Predictors	Enter Settings:	Predicted Response	SE	Lower 95% CI	Upper 95% CI	Lower 95% PI	Upper 95% PI
Mother	87	77.85395547	0.575114542	76.71236213	78.99554882	73.10554234	82.60236861
Father	66.5						
Smoker	No						
Goal:	Target						
Target:							

For the Predicted Response Calculator, inputting 87 for the Mother and 66.5 for the Father along with No Smoker, predicts a lifespan of 77.85 years. The Confidence and Predictive Intervals are shown.

Tab: MReg1 – Residuals Longevity

Output:

Columns A – L:

Data for factors in the model (Mother, Father, Smoker) plus the Response

Predicted (Fitted) Values

Residuals:

Regular

Standardized

Standardize (Delete t)

Cook's Distance (Influence)

Leverage

DFITS

Seven graphs:

Histogram of Standardized Residuals,

Normal Probability Plot

Residuals vs Data Order

Residuals vs Predicted Values

Residuals vs Factors

Mother

Father

Smoker

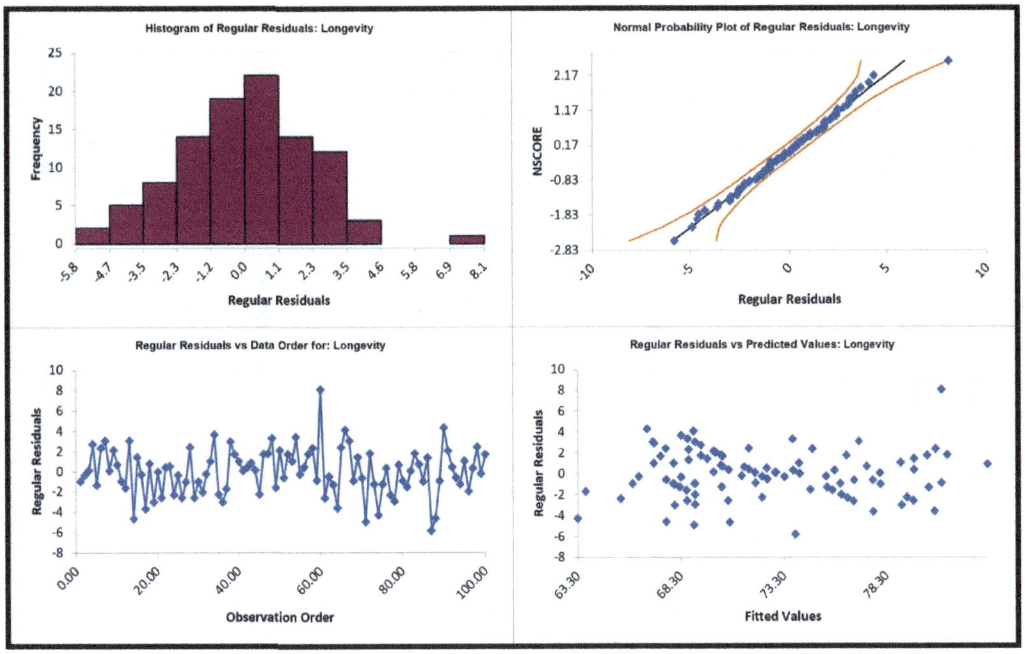

The Histogram and the Probability Plot are used to determine whether the residuals could originate from a population with a normal distribution.

The lower left graph is used for checking the stability of the residuals, and the lower right is used to

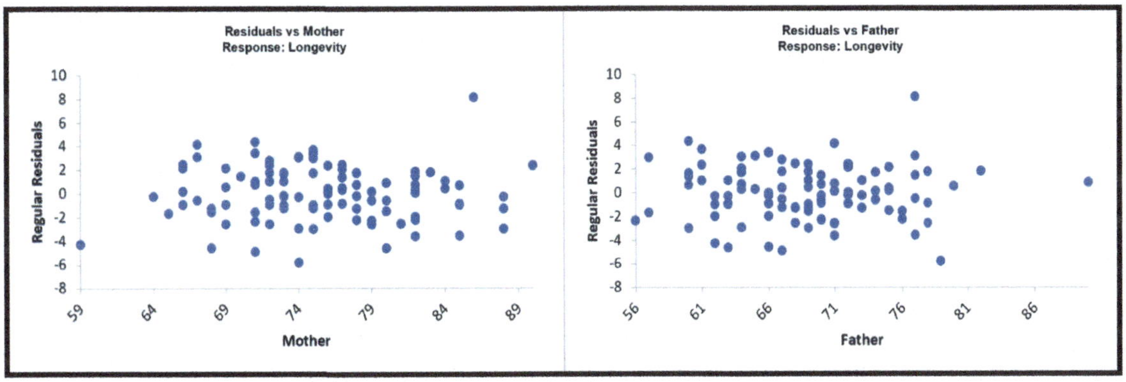

check for equal variance or spread across the Fitted values.

The final graphs are checks to see if the residuals have an equal spread across the values of each factor.

The first two show the results for the factors Mother and Father.

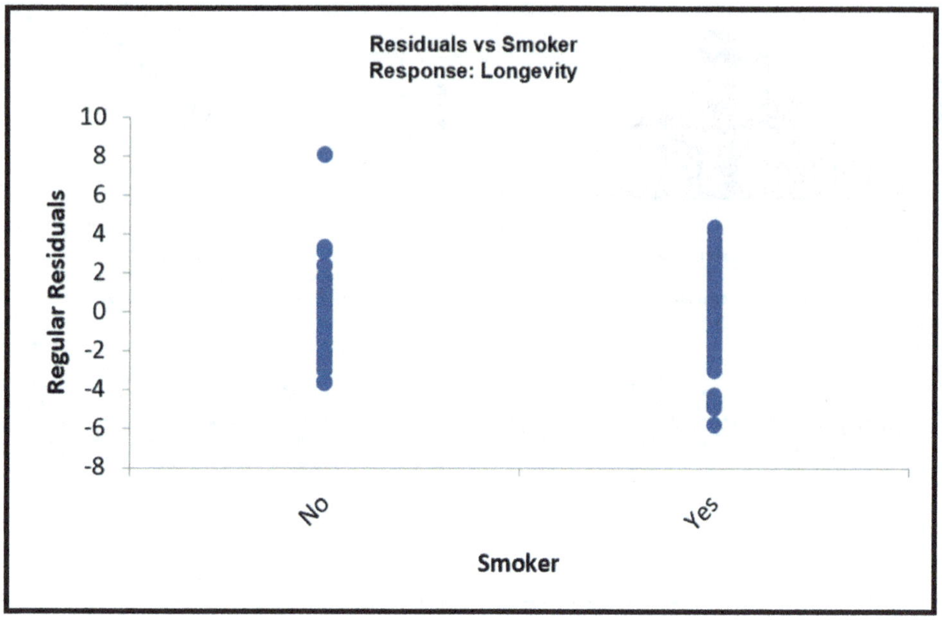

The final graph shows the residuals verses the factor, Smoker.

None of the factor graphs show any issues.

If there are questions regarding the normality of the Probability Plot graph, run the **Descriptive Statistics** tool to display the A-D Normality Test and p-Value on column **G** (Residuals).

Tab: **MReg1-Report Longevity**

Model	# Predictors	# Model Terms	S	R-Sq	R-Sq(Adj)	R-Sq(Pred)	PRESS	** AICc **	BIC	Mallows' Cp	Condition #	Mother	Father	Gmothers	Gfathers	Smoker
1	1	2	3.2787	59.54%	59.13%	57.81%	1098.4886	525.5062	533.0717	99.1443	1.0000	0	0	0	0	1
2	2	3	2.6608	73.62%	73.08%	71.93%	730.9826	484.8895	494.8891	33.2127	1.7647	1	1	0	0	0
3	** 3	4	2.3220	80.12%	79.50%	78.32%	564.5674	458.8300	471.2175	3.8796	5.4625	1	1	0	0	1
4	4	5	2.3149	80.45%	79.63%	78.28%	565.4376	459.4335	474.1613	4.2998	6.6669	1	1	0	1	1
5	5	6	2.3235	80.51%	79.47%	78.00%	572.7135	461.4292	478.4480	6.0000	8.5561	1	1	1	1	1

This report shows the best 1, 2, 3, 4 and 5 factor models. The best model is highlighted, based on the AICc criteria. For more information on this metric see the SigmaXL help information.

For the other metrics;

Look for the model with a high R-sq, a high R-sq (adj), a high R-sq (pred), low S, and a Mallows Cp close to the number of predictors (factors) plus one (for the constant term).

The **R-sq** value indicates the percent of variation explained by the model. Higher values of R-Sq are preferred; however, the R-Sq value will increase by adding factors whether they are significant or not.

The **R-sq (adj)** metric is the R-sq value adjusted for the number of factors. If factors are added to the model and they don't improve understanding of the variation, the R-sq (adj) value will begin to decrease.

The **R-sq (pred)** shows how well the model will predict the value for a new observation.

Mallows Cp is another method of determining how well the model fits the data. Typically look for values equal to the number of factors in the model plus.1. So, for a model with 3 factors, a Mallow Cp value of 4 is sought.

S is the standard deviation of the model's error. Smaller values are desired.

Different software packages present different metrics for the model assessment.

If the AICc metric is not available, then:

When comparing models with an equal number of parameters, use the one with the highest **R-Sq** value. For models that differ in the number of factors, look for the highest **R-Sq (adj)** and a **Mallow's Cp** equal to 1 more than the number of factors. Finally, if everything else is equal, look for the model with the smallest **S** value.

Based on the desired outcome for each criterion, the three variables model is the best option; the factors should be **Mother**, **Father** and **Smoker**. Although there might be a slight improvement in values going to the 4-factor model, the amount of improvement does not justify the increased model complexity.

In the example above, the three-factor model is selected because overall it provides the best values with the fewest number of factors.

Regression Equation

Longevity = (27.2278) + (0.33444)*Mother + (0.323758)*Father + (-3.73771)*(Smoke)

Notice the effect of smoking. A smoker (Smoker = 0 is a non-smoker. Smoker = 1 is a smoker), will have their longevity reduced by 3.738 years. Notice the effect of smoking. A smoker (Smoker = 0 is a non-smoker. Smoker = 1 is a smoker), will have their longevity reduced by 3.738 years.

Stepwise Regression

Another option to determine which factors should be in the Regression model would be to use the Stepwise Regression.

Return to the Longevity worksheet.

Menu command:

SigmaXL > Statistical Tools > Advanced Multiple Regression > Fit Multiple Regression Model

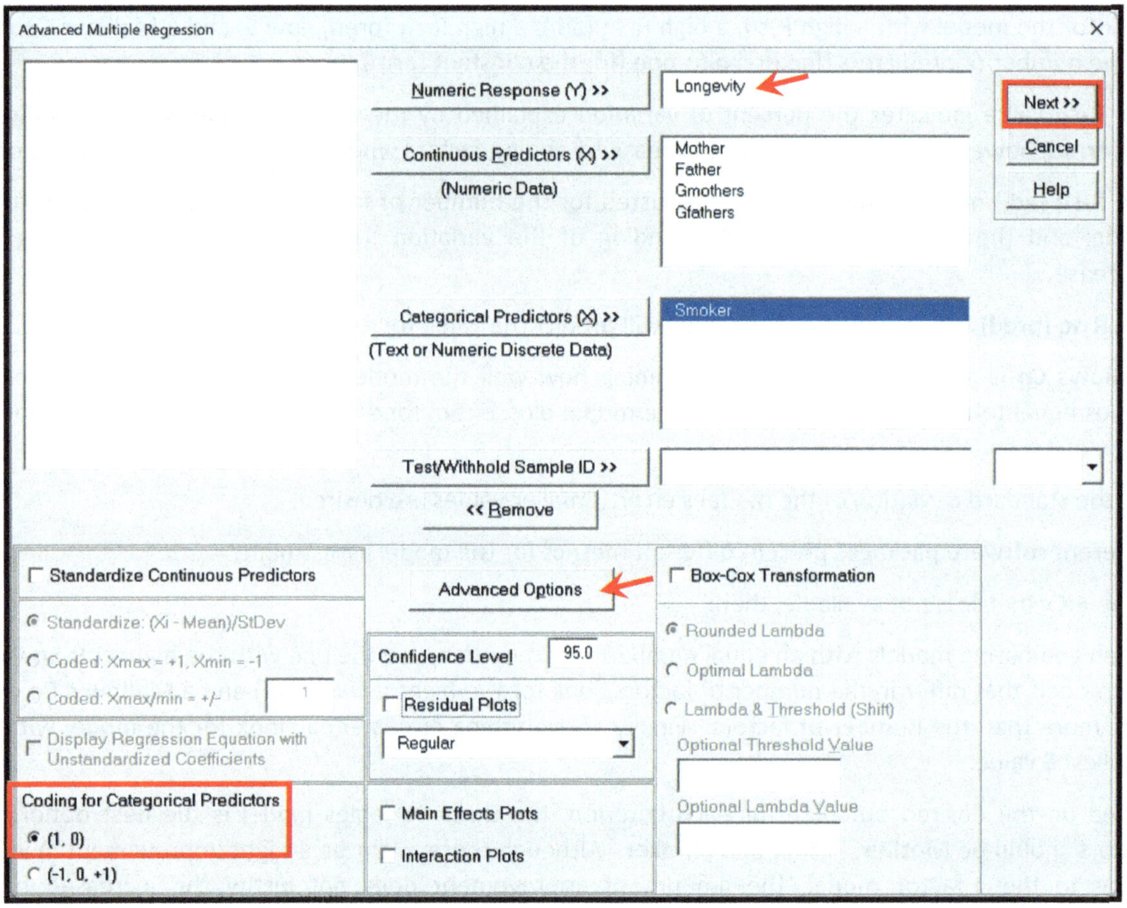

For the Numeric Response (Y), select **Longevity.**

For Continuous Predictors (X), select **Mother**, **Father**, **Gmothers**, **Gfathers**.

For the Categorical Predictor (X) select **Smoker**. Use the **(1, 0)** coding.

Click Advanced Options.

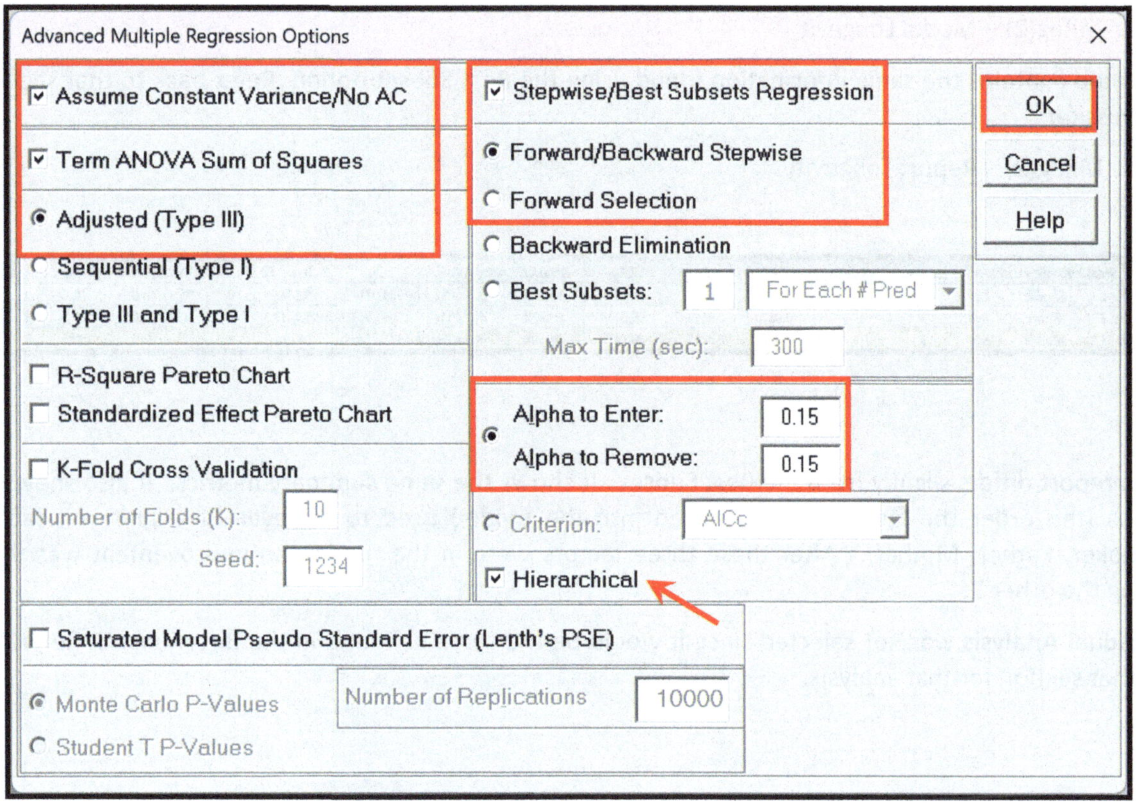

Select; Assume Constant Variance/No AC. Check the Term ANOVA Sum of Squares then choose the Adjusted (Type III) option.

For the Stepwise/Best Subset Regression choose Forward/Backward Stepwise.

Click the **Alpha to Enter** option. Input **0.15** for both **Enter** and **Remove**.

Check the **Hierarchical** option.

Click **OK**. This will return to the **Advanced Multiple Regression** dialog box. Click **Next**.

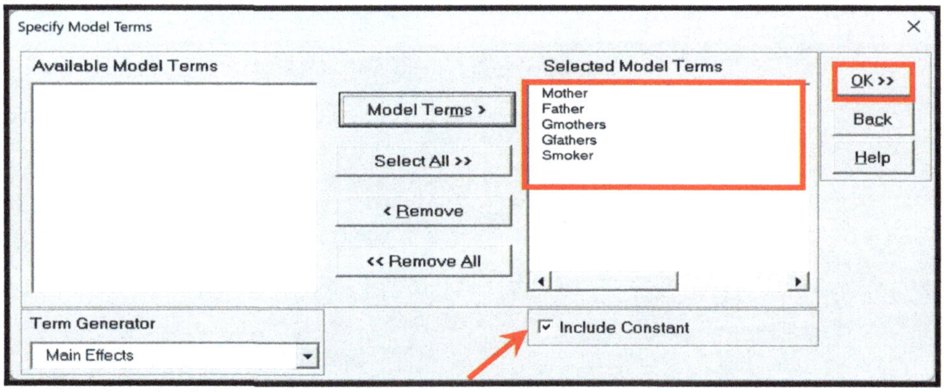

Use all factors for the Model Terms. Click **OK**.

Two tabs are created (the Residuals were not requested).

Tab: MReg(2) – Model Longevit

This tab contains the same information found using the Best Subset option. Refer back to that section's discussion.

Tab: MReg(2) – Report Longevity

Step	Predictor Term	Mode	# Predictors	# Model Terms	** P **	S	R-Sq	R-Sq(Adj)	AICc	BIC	Mallows' Cp	Mother	Father	Gmothers	Gfathers	Smoker
1	Smoker	Add	1	2	0.0000	3.2787	59.54%	59.13%	525.5062	533.0717	99.1443	0	0	0	0	1
2	Father	Add	2	3	0.0000	2.8453	69.84%	69.22%	498.2947	508.2943	51.4617	0	1	0	0	1
3	Mother	Add	3	4	0.0000	2.3220	80.12%	79.50%	458.8300	471.2175	3.8796	1	1	0	0	1

This report differs slightly from the Best Subset. It shows the same summary metrics. It also shows the steps (the order the factors were inserted into the model) used to discover the significant factors. (Smoker, Father, Mother). After these three factors were in the model, no improvement was found using the other 2.

Residual Analysis was not selected since it would be the same as found in the Best Subset. Refer back to that section for that analysis.

GLM (General Linear Model)

Extends Advanced Multiple Regression to include:

- Fixed and Random Factors
- Nested Factors
- Covariates (can be Nested)
- For Random or Mixed Random/Fixed Factors with a balanced design, the ANOVA and
- Variance Components (VC) report is given based on Expected Mean Squares. VC confidence
- intervals using Restricted Maximum Likelihood (REML) are included.
- If the design is unbalanced or model is non-hierarchical, REML is used to compute the VC
- values and confidence intervals. Fixed Effects Tests are based on Satterthwaite
- approximation degrees of freedom.
- Main Effects with Confidence Intervals and Interaction Plots of Fitted Means for Non-Nested
- Fixed Factors
- Tukey and Fisher Pairwise Comparison of Means for Non-Nested Fixed Factors
- Predicted Response Calculator

Tool Use: Use the GLM tool to determine the effect of two or more X's on the Y's. The worksheet for the GLM does not require an equal number of readings for each unique factor combination. (A balanced worksheet is not required for the **GLM** procedure.)

Model: $Y = B_0 + B_1X_1 + B_2X_2 + \ldots\ldots\ldots + B_nX_n + \varepsilon$

Null Hypothesis: (H_o): $B_i = 0$

Alternative Hypothesis: (H_a): At least one $B_i \neq 0$

Data Type: Input – Discrete or Continuous; Output – Continuous

Worksheet: ***GLM***

Data shows the error rate for coders per 10,000 lines. A new training program was implemented. Two options were available, online and classroom training. The manager wanted to know if there's a difference between the training methods based on the associates Degree status, and experience level. Participants were randomly assigned to either the Classroom or Online training.

Menu command:

SigmaXL > Statistical Tools > General Linear Model > Fit General Linear Model

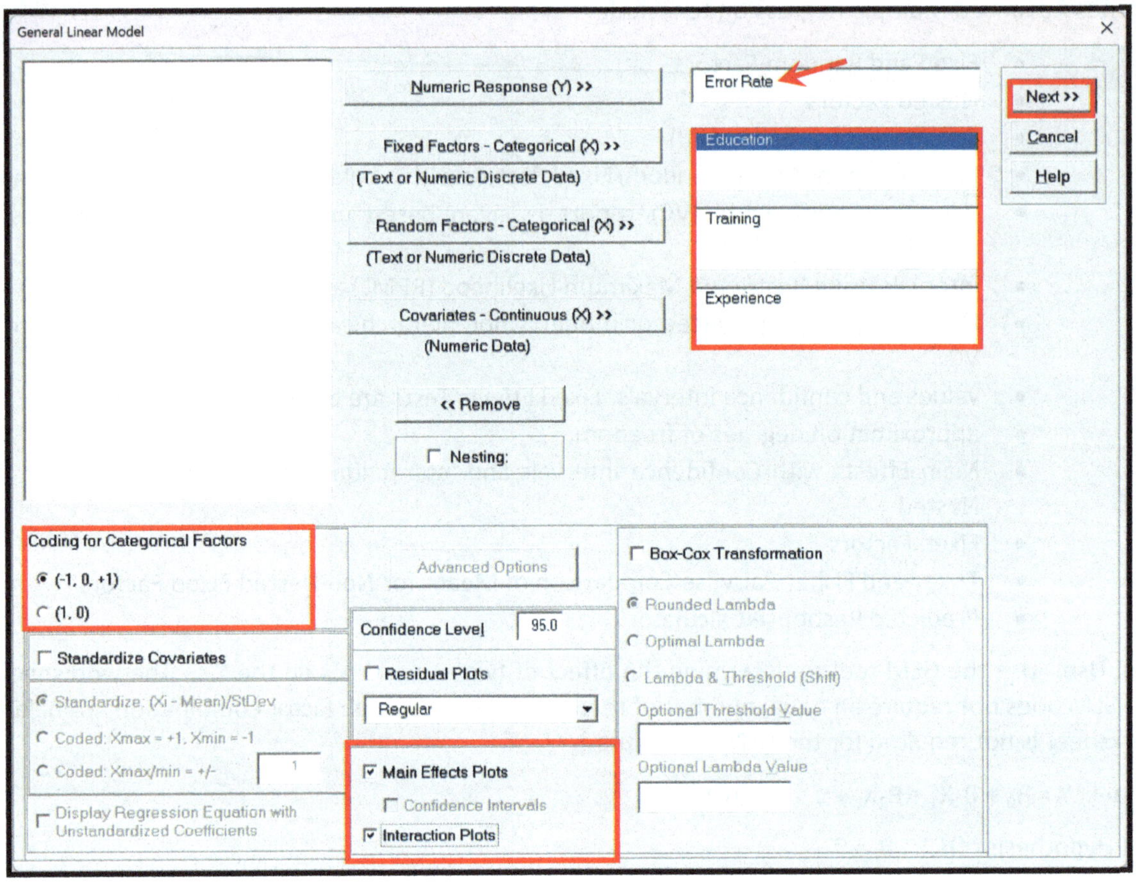

Input **Error Rate** for the Numeric Response (Y). For Fixed Factors - Categorical, select; **Education.** For Random Factors select **Training**. The Covariate – Continuous (X) is **Experience**.

For Coding for Categorical Factors, use the; **(-1, 0 1)** option. Keep the Confidence Level at **95.0.** Click **Main Effects Plots** and **Interaction Plots**. Click **Next**.

Specify Model Terms

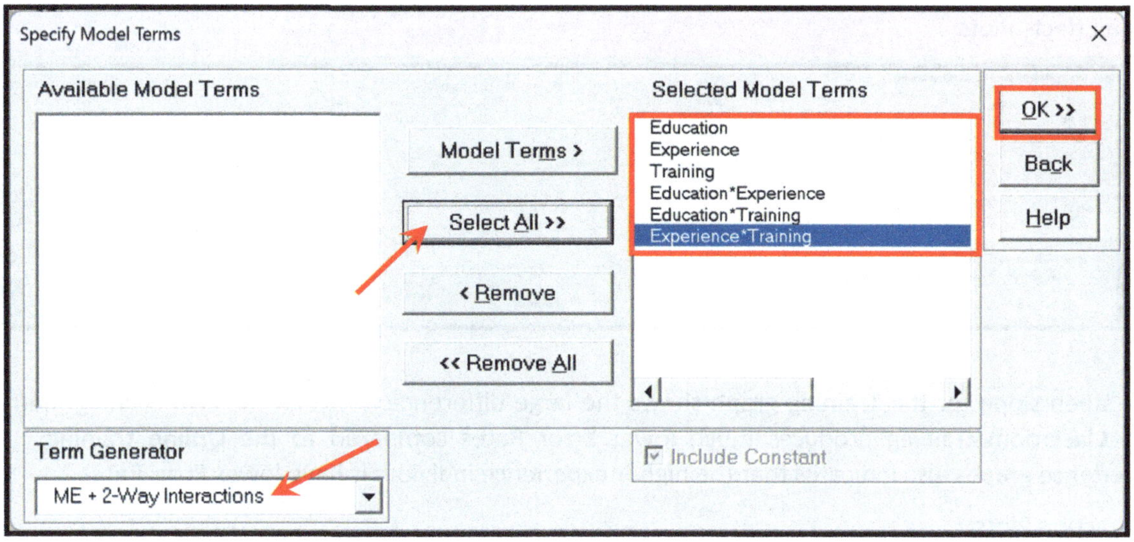

For the Term Generator, use the pull-down menu and select **ME + 2-Way Interactions**.

Choose **Select All** for the Model Terms. Click **OK**.

Output:

Tab: **GLM1 - Model Error Ra**

Much of the output has been shown previously so only the critical information will be shown.

Parameter Estimates						
Predictor Term	Coefficient	SE Coefficient	T	P	VIF	Tolerance
Constant	33.27864962	1.054597672	31.5558	0.0000		
Experience	-0.486288932	0.185983387	-2.6147	0.0204	1.3106	0.7630
Education_Degree	1.310572769	1.017244127	1.2884	0.2185	3.1378	0.3187
Training_Classroom	-4.37034185	1.039884526	-4.2027	0.0009	3.2791	0.3050
Experience*Education_Degree	-0.142673562	0.175125815	-0.8147	0.4289	3.3941	0.2946
Experience*Training_Classroom	-0.049662632	0.183967529	-0.2700	0.7911	3.7286	0.2682
Education_Degree*Training_Classroom	0.631344989	0.583593373	1.0818	0.2976	1.0328	0.9683

The factors P-Values highlighted in Red are below the .05 level. (**Experience**, and **Training**.)

Durbin-Watson Test for Autocorrelation in Residuals	
DW Statistic	2.4990
P-Value Positive Autocorrelation	0.8548
P-Value Negative Autocorrelation	0.0719

The Durbin Watson Test shows a low P-Value for the Negative Autocorrelation. But, with the low VIF values above, the issue is not serious.

Tab: **GLM1 – Plots Error Rate**

Main Effects Plots

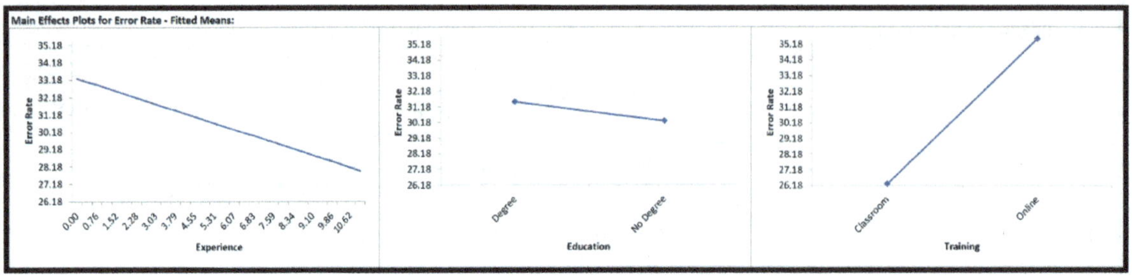

The steep slope for the **Training** graph shows the large difference between the two training methods. The **Classroom** training produces much lower Error Rates compared to the **Online** training. The Experience graphs also indicates that the higher experience individuals have lower Error Rates.

Interaction Plots:

Since none of the interactions were significant, the graph will be skipped.

Tab: VarComp Error Ra

Variance Components							
Source	Variance	Var % of Total	SE Var for CI	Var Lower 95% CI	Var Upper 95% CI	Z	P
Training	38.19697768	77.98%	55.53097075	2.210790747	659.9489826	0.6878	0.2458
Experience*Training	0	0.00%					
Education*Training	0.424106589	0.87%	2.290968101	1.07E-05	16809.46826	0.1851	0.4266
Error	6.477027373	13.22%	2.290529014	3.238603132	12.95369697	2.827742994	0.0023
Total	48.98522979						

Training was considered a Random Factor, so a Variance Component table was created looking at the Main Effect of Training along with the two interactions of Training and Experience, plus Training and Education. Training takes up 77.98% of the total variation. So, even though the P-Value for this situation is large, based on the % of Total variation and the graphical evidence for Training, this is a factor to further investigate.

Rerun the analysis using only Experience and Training as Main Factors.

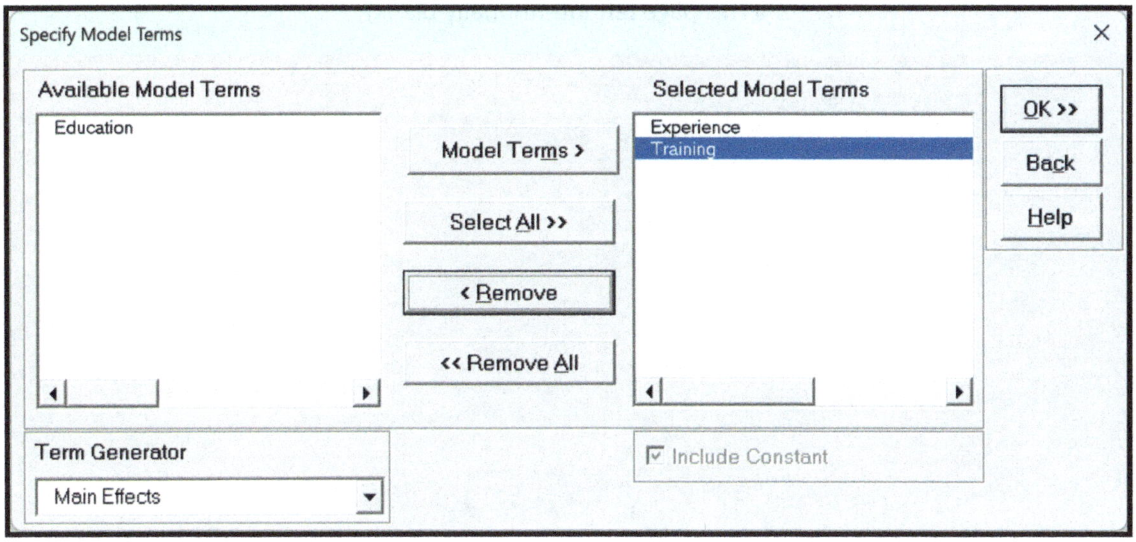

Parameter Estimates						
Predictor Term	Coefficient	SE Coefficient	T	P	VIF	Tolerance
Constant	33.16490701	0.960430935	34.5313	0.0000		
Experience	-0.456579499	0.159339179	-2.8655	0.0103	1.0068	0.9932
Training_Classroom	-4.564641309	0.563246632	-8.1042	0.0000	1.0068	0.9932

Select just the two Main Effects (**Experience** and **Training**). Click **OK**.

Here the **Constant**, **Experience** and **Training** are significant.

Final Main Effects Graphs:

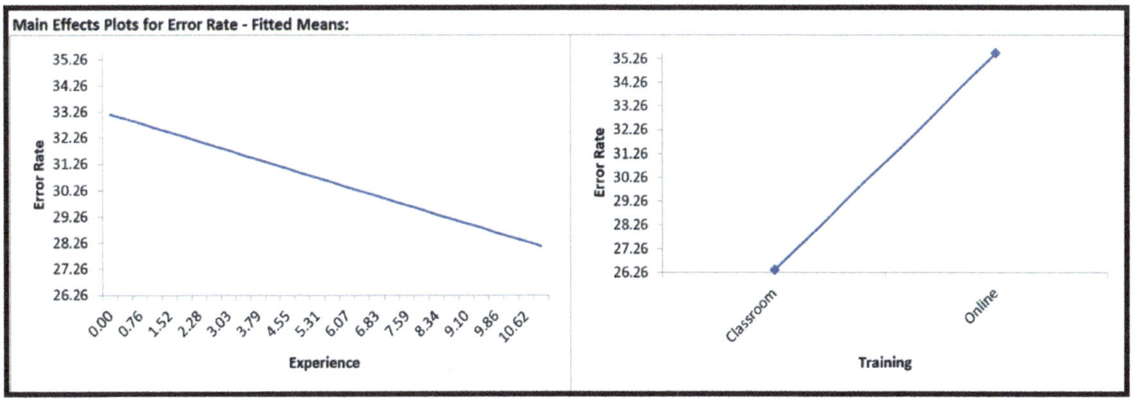

(This page left intentionally blank)

Improve Phase

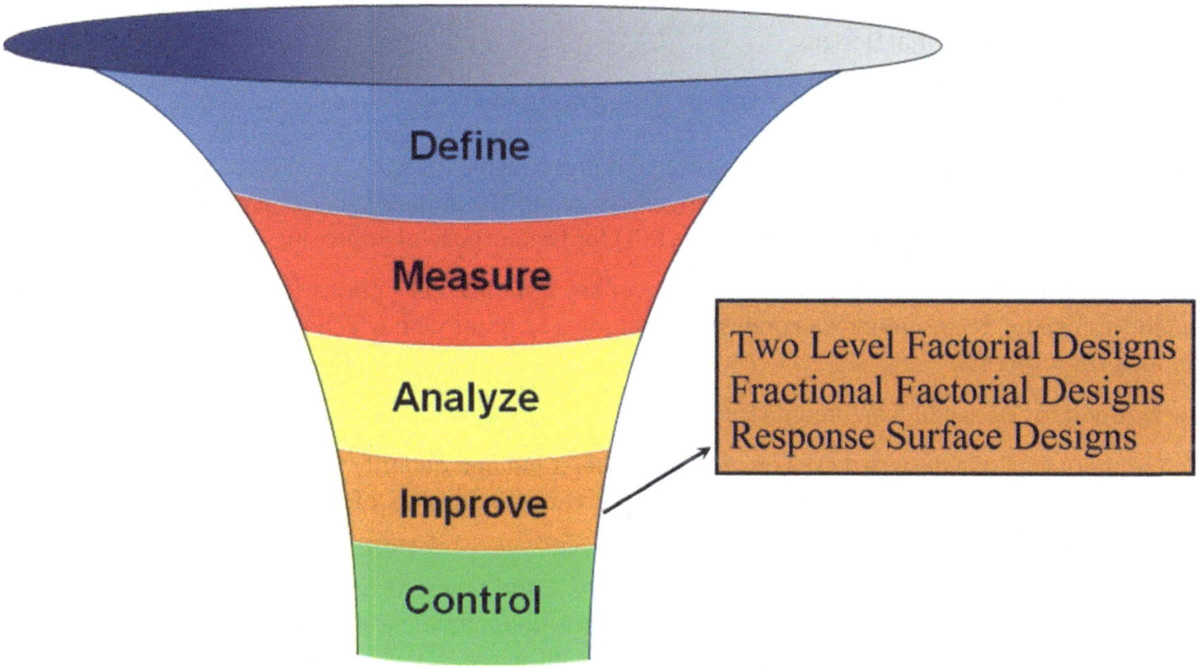

Improve Phase

The Improve phase of a Six Sigma process builds on previous phases, focusing on investigation and examination of which factors (X's) have the largest effect on critical Y's. By the end of this phase, teams have clearly identified and quantified the relationship between critical inputs and critical outputs.

Tools and Outcomes

During the Improve phase teams use a variety of tools, including:

- Two Level Factorial Designs
- Fractional Factorial Designs
- Response Surface Designs

These tools help teams come to a clear understanding of which factors are critical to the output, and then use this information to create an improvement plan. The primary goal of an improvement plan is to determine the best way(s) to control inputs (X's) for the purpose of improving critical outputs (Y's).

It is not unusual for the Improve phase to uncover several different options for creating improvement; when this occurs, teams generally conduct pilot studies to determine which option has the best chance for long term success.

Background for Design of Experiments (DOE)

The primary goal of a designed experiment is to understand and quantify the relationship of inputs (X's) with critical outputs (Y's). A good DOE explores the relationship of individual factors and factor interactions, creating quantifiable results.

Keep in mind that experimentation, while both efficient and powerful, is an iterative process. In other words, no single experiment will result in a complete understanding of a situation; many times, the results of an experiment produce more questions than answers.

Teams control the amount of variation in X's during an experiment by changing inputs in a purposeful manner. If too much change occurs, the effect of a single factor may overshadow all other factors; if too little change occurs, the effect of a single factor may not be seen. Because of this, a critical part of every Designed Experiment is planning which factors will be manipulated and at what levels those manipulations will occur.

The Interactive Nature of Experimentation

The experimental process begins with a conjecture, which may or may not be the result of previous experiments. Based on this conjecture, teams specify a design, conduct the experiment, and analyze the results. Results of analysis may or may not support the original conjecture, which often leads to additional questions. When this occurs, the experimental process is repeated (perhaps several times) until a truer conjecture and associated answers emerge.

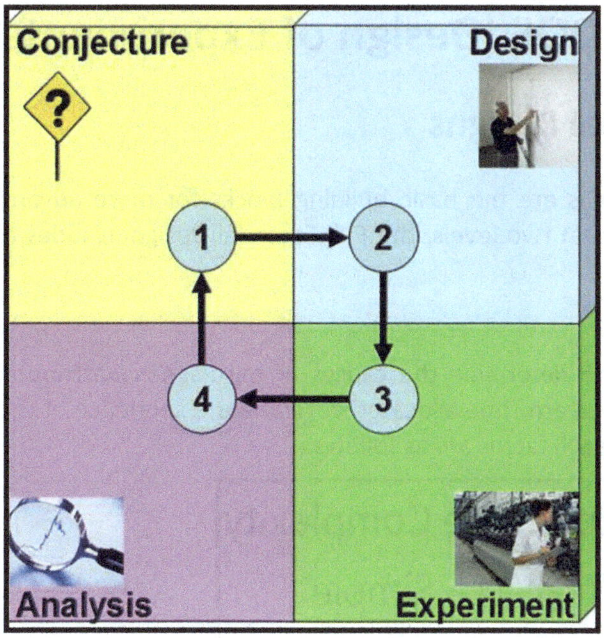

This chapter will discuss the benefits of designed experiments and show how to construct, run and analyze those experiments using SigmaXL.

DOE (Design of Experiments)

Two Level Factorial Designs

Two Level Factorial Designs are the basic building blocks for more advanced designs. As the name implies, each factor is run at two levels; the Full Factorial Design includes all possible combinations of the factors' two levels.

Example:

A medical school wants to determine the causes of misdiagnosis attributable to Physician Assistants (PAs). Factors to be studied are Time allocated per Patient; Experience of the PA; and Complexity of the Diagnosis. The levels for each factor are as follows:

Time/Patient	Experience	Complexity
5 Minutes	1 Year	Simple
15 Minutes	5 Years	Complex

At this point some definitions are required regarding the important terminology associated with Two Level Factorial Designs.

Factorial Points

Factorial points are the experimental runs consisting of either a high or low condition of each factor. Looking at the medical school example, the eight unique factorial points are as follows:

Time/Patient	Experience	Complexity
5 Minutes	1 Year	Simple
15 Minutes	1 Year	Simple
5 Minutes	5 Years	Simple
15 Minutes	5 Years	Simple
5 Minutes	1 Year	Complex
15 Minutes	1 Year	Complex
5 Minutes	5 Years	Complex
15 Minutes	5 Years	Complex

Replicates

The eight runs identified constitute a replicate of the experiment; these eight runs can be repeated if a second replicate is desired. Teams use replicates to improve the precision of the error term.

Randomization

Experiments should be run in random order to prevent unknown factors from affecting output. If experiments are run in blocks, runs within each block should run in random order.

Creating Two Level Factorial Designs

Tool Use: Use designed experiments to determine relationships between input factors (X's) and response(s) (Y's). If an experiment uses qualitative X's, use a coding system to solve the response equation. For instance, if the experiment included three factors it will determine coefficients for the following equation:

$Y = \beta_0 + \beta_1 X_1 + \beta_2 X_2 + \beta_3 X_3 + \beta_{12} X_1 X_2 + \beta_{13} X_1 X_3 + \beta_{23} X_2 X_3 + \beta_{123} X_1 X_2 X_3$

Each coefficient (β) is tested using a Test of Hypothesis. Therefore, designed experiments will test multiple hypotheses, one for each coefficient. For each coefficient, the hypotheses tested are:

Null Hypothesis: (H_o): $\beta_i = 0$

Alternative Hypothesis: (H_a): $\beta_i \neq 0$

Data Type: Input – Discrete or Continuous; Output - Numeric

The following steps will create an experiment in SigmaXL using the above example.

Menu command: ***SigmaXL > Design of Experiments > 2 Level Factorial/Screening > 2 Level Factorial/Screening Design***

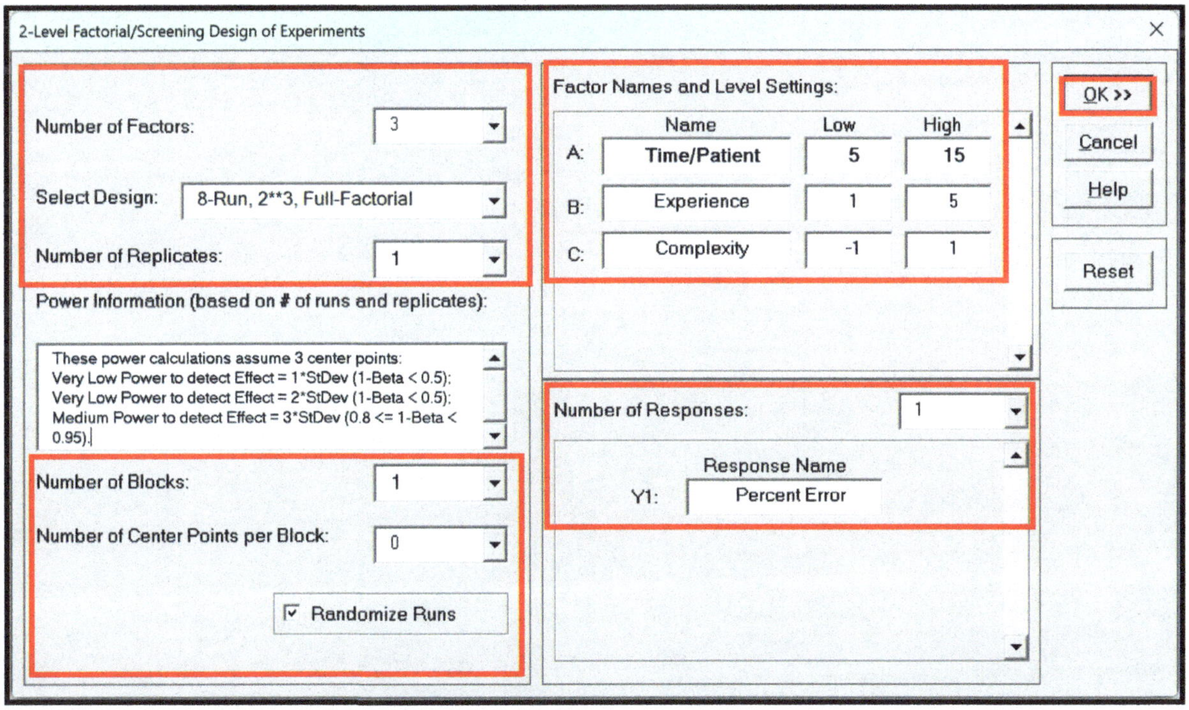

Using the pull-downs select;

3 for the Number of Factors.

8-Run, 2**3, Full-Factorial as the Selected Design:

1 for Number of Blocks; and

0 for Number of Center Points per Block.

Check the Randomized Runs option, then Input the Factor Names and Level Settings as shown.

For number of Responses; select **1**.

There's one Response. The Response is **Percent Error**.

Click **OK**.

> **Note:** Notice that the Complexity values are -1 and 1, even though the actual values are Simple and Complex. SigmaXL does not accept Text for the Input Levels. The -1 refers to Simple, and the 1 refers to Complex.

SigmaXL creates the experimental design in a new worksheet.

The design is listed in a random order (Run Order).

Design of Experiments Worksheet

Title:	
Date:	
Name of Experimenter:	
Notes:	

Design Type:	3 Factor, 8-Run, 2**3, Full-Factorial
Number of Replicates:	1
Number of Blocks:	1
Number of Center Points per Block:	0
Number of Responses:	1

Run Order	Std. Order	Center Points	Blocks	A: Time/Patient	B: Experience	C: Complexity	Percent Error
1	4	1	1	15	5	-1	
2	8	1	1	15	5	1	
3	6	1	1	15	1	1	
4	7	1	1	5	5	1	
5	3	1	1	5	5	-1	
6	5	1	1	5	1	1	
7	1	1	1	5	1	-1	
8	2	1	1	15	1	-1	

A warning appears below the design;

Do not add or delete rows or sort this worksheet.

Aliasing of Effects:
None (Full Factorial Design)

Changing the rows in any manner will corrupt the worksheet. Follow the instructions.

DO NOT: Add, Delete, or Sort the rows.

Additional information appears regarding the Aliasing of the Factors. In a Full-Factorial design, there are no alias conditions.

The experiment's worksheet with the result column (Percent Errors) is found in the following SigmaXL worksheet.

Worksheet: ***Patient Diagnosis***

Run Order	Std. Order	Center Points	Blocks	A: Time/Patient	B: Experience	C: Complexity	Percent Error
1	2	1	1	15	1	-1	6
2	8	1	1	15	5	1	3
3	6	1	1	15	1	1	3
4	5	1	1	5	1	1	6
5	7	1	1	5	5	1	5
6	4	1	1	15	5	-1	8
7	3	1	1	5	5	-1	18
8	1	1	1	5	1	-1	19

Analysis of the Two-Level Factorial Experiment

Analysis of the Full Factorial Experiment proceeds as follows:

1. Create the Full Model (all factors and interactions)
2. Determine significant factors based on a predetermined alpha level
3. Run Factorial Plots to visualize significant factors
4. Run a new model with significant factors; this is called the Reduced Model
5. Check the model using ANOVA and Coefficients Outputs
6. Check the final model using residual analysis (graphs).

Menu command: ***SigmaXL > Design of Experiments > 2 Level Factorial/Screening > Analyze 2 Level Factorial/Screening Design***

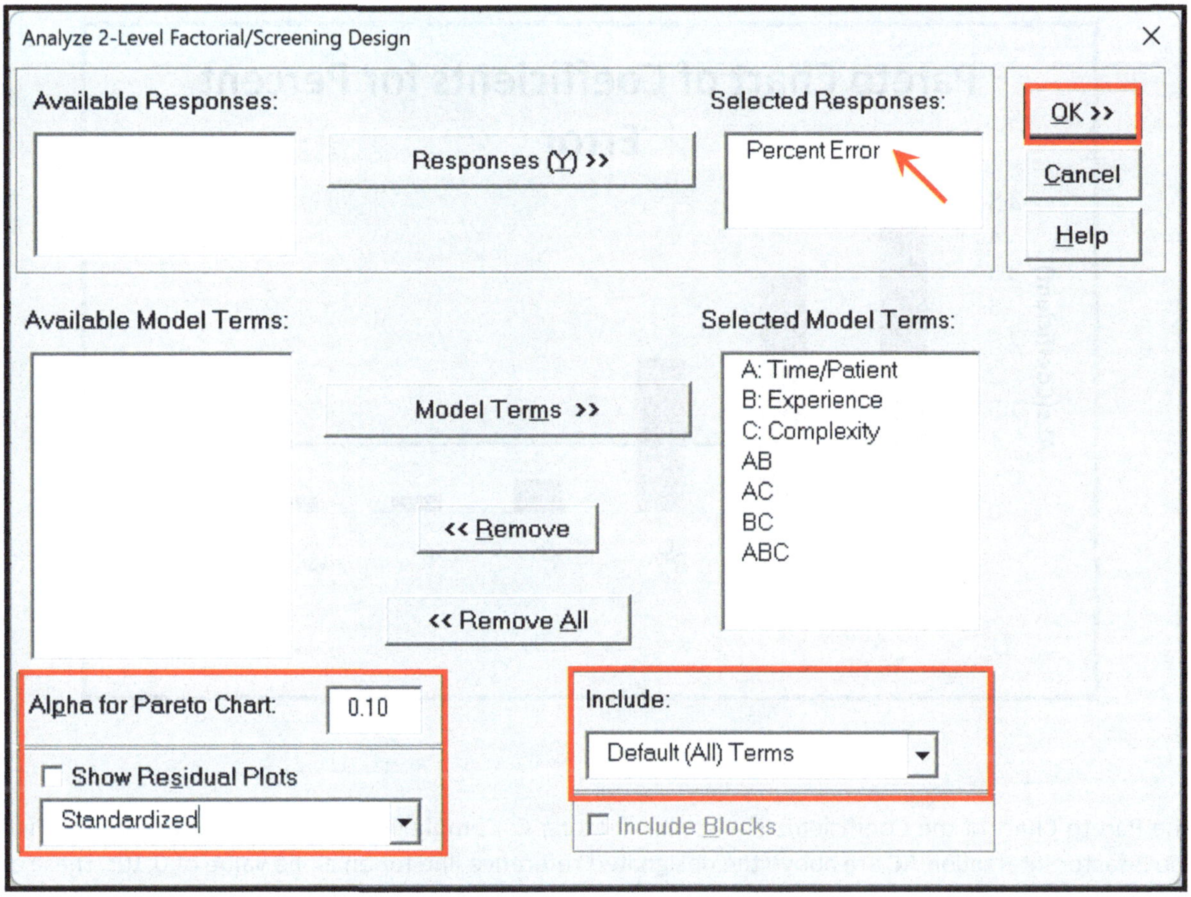

Input **Percent Errors** as the Selected Responses:

Under, Include: use the pull-down menu and select **Default (All) Terms**.

Set the Alpha for Pareto Chart to **0.10**, and de-select the Show Residual Plots.

Click **OK**.

> **Note:** The Residual plot will be shown with the final model. This is a check to see the strength of the model.

The output appears in the tab: **Analyze – 3 Factor DOE**

Pareto Chart of Coefficients

In the Pareto Chart the significant factors are those factors with bars extending above the reference line.

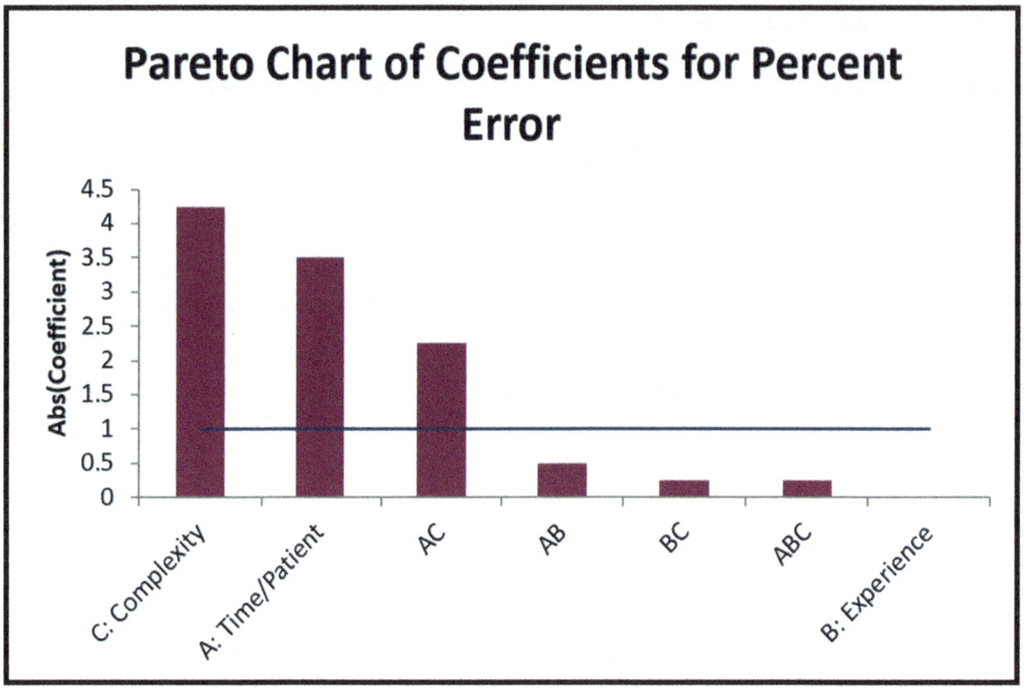

The Pareto Chart of the Coefficients shows that factors; **C: Complexity** and **A: Time/Patient** along with the 2-factor interaction **AC** are above the designated reference line for an alpha value of 0.10. These are the factors that should be use for the **Reduced Model**.

Parameter Estimates

The Parameter Estimates are shown for the Coded Units. P-values below the designated alpha level will appear in red, indicating these factors are statistically significant.

Parameter Estimates (Coded Units):	Note SE, T, and P are derived from Lenth's Pseudo Standard Error					
Term	**Coefficient**	**SE Coefficient**	**T**	**P**	**VIF**	**Tolerance**
Constant	8.5					
A: Time/Patient	-3.5	0.375	-9.333	0.0067	1	1
B: Experience	0	0.375	0	1.0000	1	1
C: Complexity	-4.25	0.375	-11.333	0.0043	1	1
AB	0.5	0.375	1.333	0.2977	1	1
AC	2.25	0.375	6	0.0183	1	1
BC	-0.25	0.375	-0.666667	0.5649	1	1
ABC	-0.25	0.375	-0.666667	0.5649	1	1

As expected, this analysis corresponds to the Pareto Chart of Coefficients.

The remaining portions of the Output (Model Summary, Analysis of Variance for Model, and the DOE Multiple Regression Model), will be explained with the **Reduced Model**.

Factorial Plots

A series of Factorial Plots are available to display the calculated effects. The first is for Main Effects; it shows changes in output that occur as each factor is moved from the low to high condition.

The Interaction Plot displays all possible two factor interactions. If an interaction is present, visualize it first (before the Main Effects). This is important, because if the interaction is strong enough it could produce an insignificant result in one of the Main Effects terms.

Return to the complete experiment worksheet (Patient Diagnosis)

Menu command: ***SigmaXL > Design of Experiments > 2 Level Factorial/Screening > Main Effects & Interaction Plots***

The Plots are created automatically.

Interaction Plots

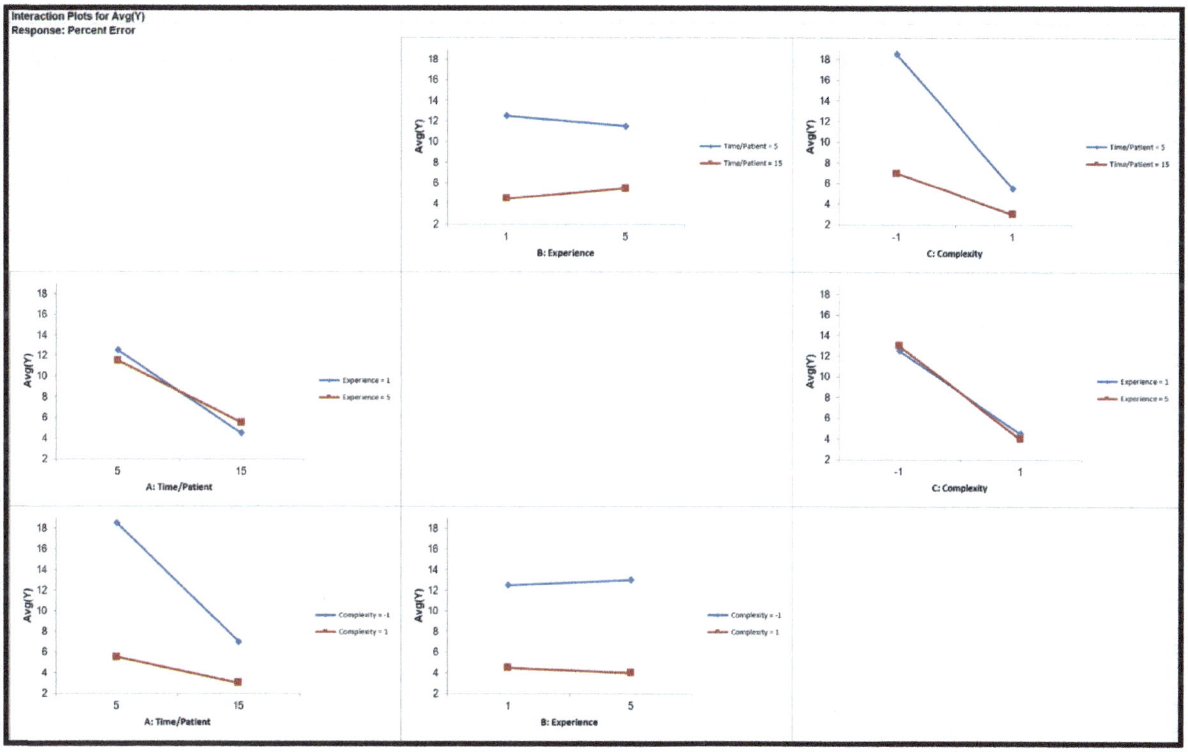

The Interaction Plots appear as a matrix. Running a diagonal line from the upper left corner to the lower right creates the upper and lower matrix. The upper matrix has a corresponding graph in the lower matrix. The Y axis in all cases is the output. Each graph has 2 inputs, one of the inputs is on the x-axis, and the other is referenced in the graph. The graph in the middle of the first row (2nd column) has the x-axis as Experience and the Y axis as Avg(Y).

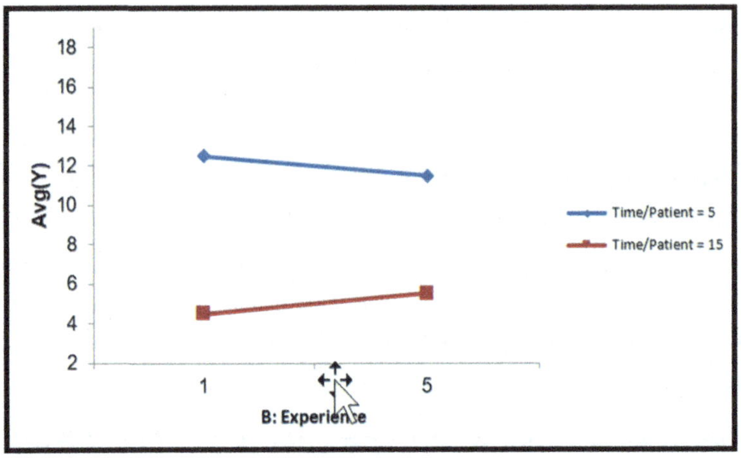

The x-axis is Experience, the two lines represent the values for the second factor, Time/Patient. If the lines are parallel to one another, then there's no interaction. The further away from parallel, the stronger the interaction. The outputs analytical portion provides a p-value to determine if the

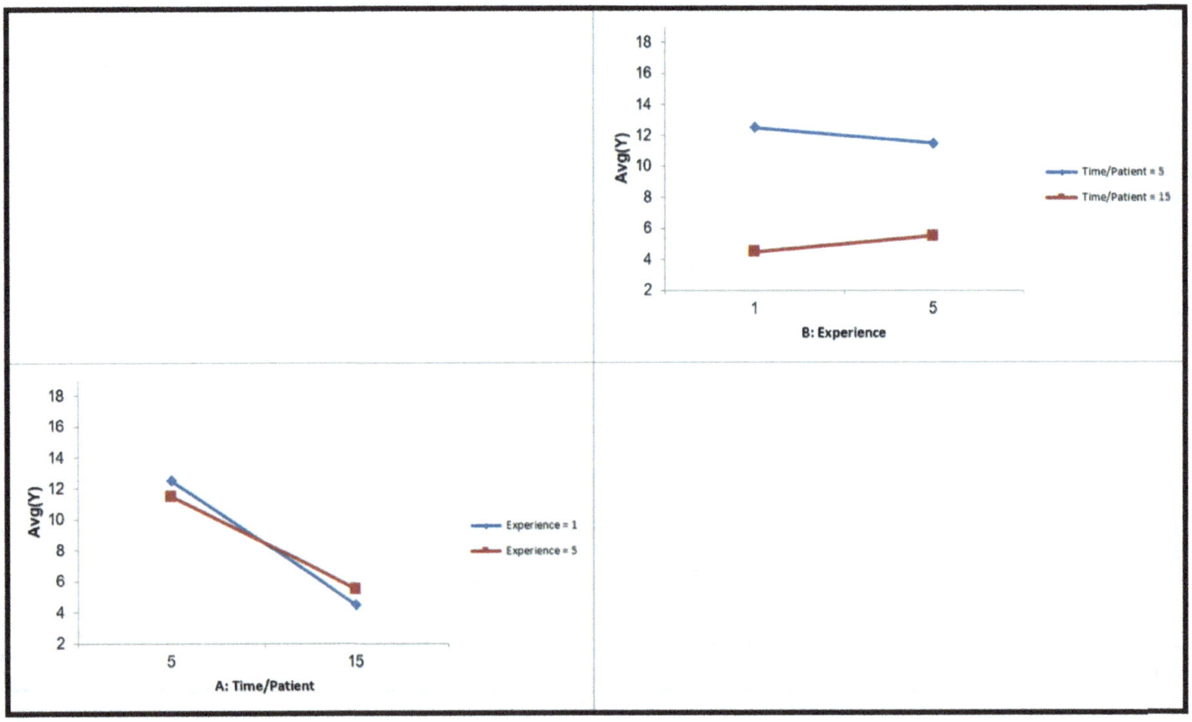

interaction is statistically significant.

The corresponding graph has the x-axis as Time/Patient, and the two lines representing the Experience

> Hint: For presentation purposes, use the graph that is easiest to explain. The full matrix is presented so the user can decide which factor to put on the x-axis to explain the interaction.

levels.

Main Effects Plot

The Main Effects plots appear above the interactions.

The Main Effects plot shows the Time/Patient Percent Errors decreases as the time per patient increases. This is called a negative effect. (Negative in the fact that it is referring to the slope of the line.) The factor Experience has no effect (horizontal line), and the Complexity follows the Time/Patient pattern.

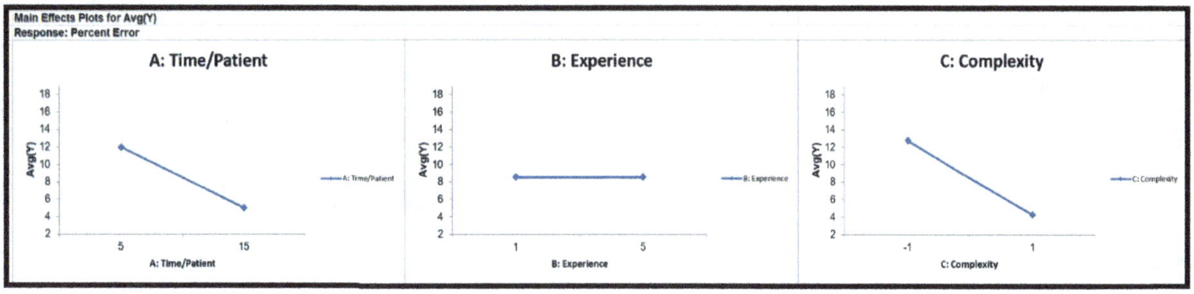

Reduced Model

After reviewing Effects Plots, Output, and Factorial Plots, it is evident that factors A, C, and the AC interaction are important terms to use in a final model.

Re-run the analysis using these three terms and analyze the residuals. Remember, a residual is calculated as the difference between expected and actual values. Analysis of the residuals, demonstrate the appropriateness of the model. If the model is adequate, residuals will have the following characteristics:

- They have a normal distribution
- They have a mean value of zero
- They are independent
- They demonstrate a constant variance along the range of fitted values.

For more detailed discussion of residuals, review the Regression section in the Analysis chapter.

Return to the **Patient Diagnosis** worksheet.

Menu command: ***SigmaXL > Design of Experiments > 2 Level Factorial/Screening > Analyze 2 Level Factorial/Screening Design***

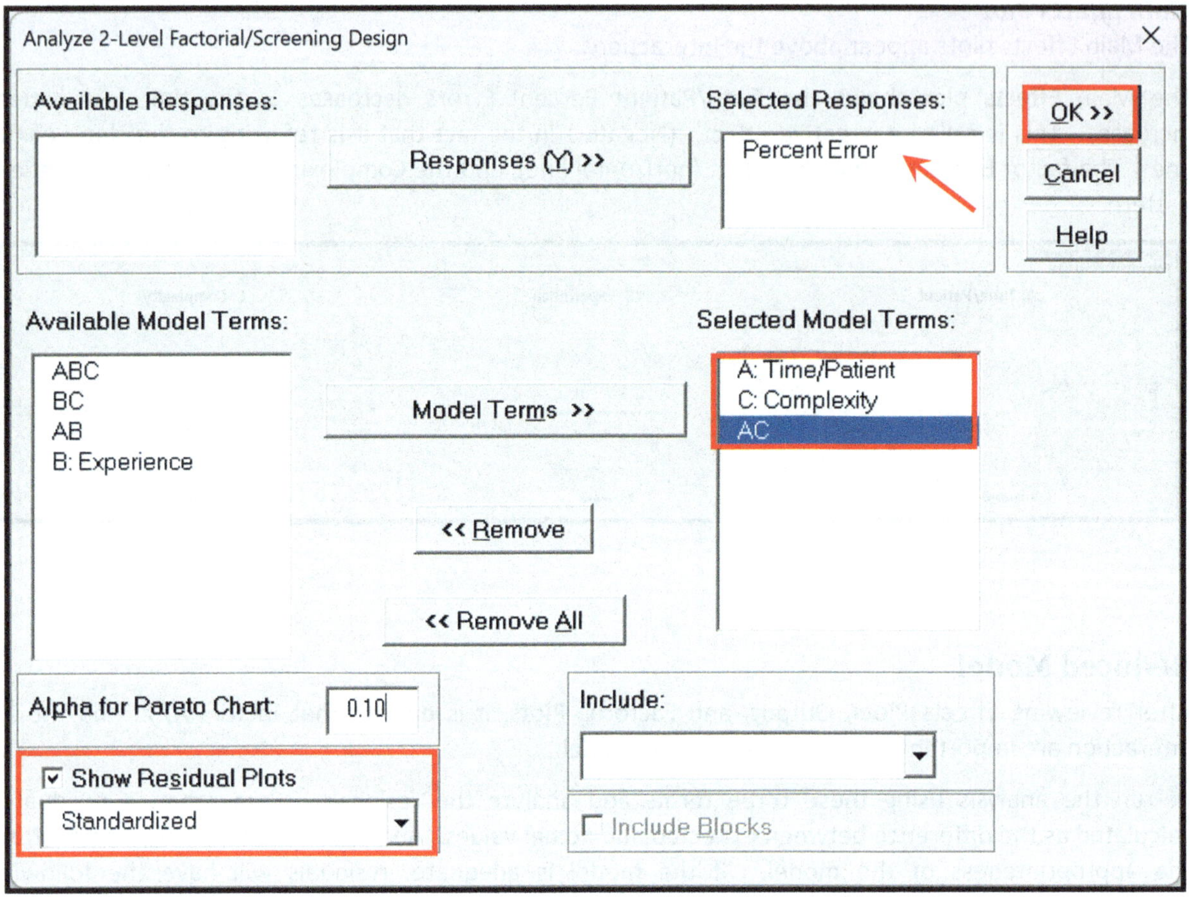

The Selected Response is **Percent Error**. Select **A**, **C** and the **AC** interaction as the Selected Model Terms. Click the **Show Residual Plots** option and use the pull-down to select **Standardized**.

Click **OK**.

Output:

The Pareto Chart of the Coefficients shows all factors in the model to be significant.

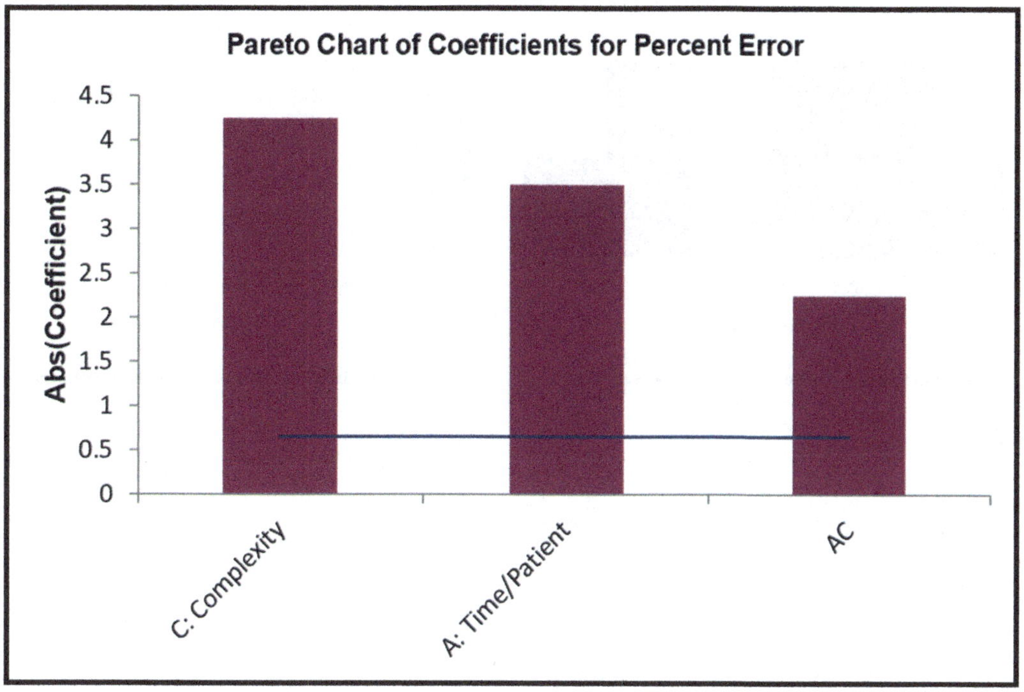

Parameter Estimates (Coded Units):						
Term	Coefficient	SE Coefficient	T	P	VIF	Tolerance
Constant	8.5	0.306186218	27.761	0.0000		
A: Time/Patient	-3.5	0.306186218	-11.431	0.0003	1	1
C: Complexity	-4.25	0.306186218	-13.880	0.0002	1	1
AC	2.25	0.306186218	7.348	0.0018	1	1

The Parameter Estimates confirms the Pareto information with p-values for the coefficients.

The **Analysis of Variance**, along with the **Model Summary**, shows that by using the two main factors of Time/Patient, and Complexity along with the interaction of these two factors, 98.15% of the variation in the output can be explained. The high R-sq (pred) indicates that the model does a good job of predicting the response of new observations.

Model Summary:	
R-Square	98.95%
R-Square Adjusted	98.16%
S (Root Mean Square Error)	0.866025

Analysis of Variance for Model:					
Source	DF	SS	MS	F	P
Model	3	283	94.333	125.78	0.0002
Error	4	3	0.750000		
Pure Error	4	3	0.750000		
Total (Model + Error)	7	286	40.857		

Residual Analysis

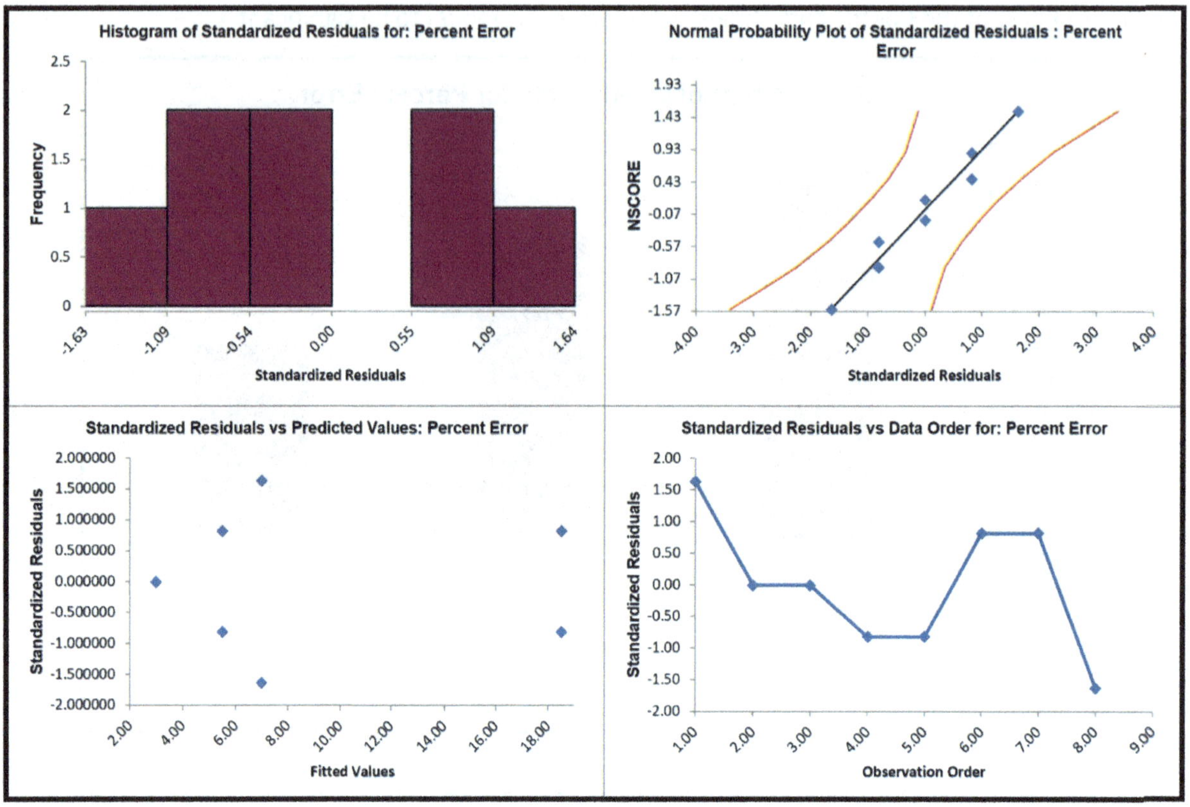

The upper right histogram along with the Normal Probability plot checks the assumption of Normality.

The lower left graph looks at equal variation throughout the fitted values. The lower right graph looks for randomness in the residuals.

Residual Report

A: Time/Patient	B: Experience	C: Complexity	Percent Errc	Predicted (Fitted) Values	Residuals	Standardized Residuals	Studentized (Deleted t)	Cook's Distance (Influence)	Leverage	DFITS
15	5	-1	8	7.000	1	1.633	2.449	0.666667	0.500000	2.449
15	5	1	3	3.000	4.44089E-16	7.25195E-16	6.28E-16	0	0.500000	6.28037E-16
15	1	1	3	3.000	4.44089E-16	7.25195E-16	6.28E-16	0	0.500000	6.28037E-16
5	5	1	5	5.500	-0.500000	-0.816497	-0.774597	0.166667	0.500000	-0.774597
5	5	-1	18	18.500	-0.500000	-0.816497	-0.774597	0.166667	0.500000	-0.774597
5	1	1	6	5.500	0.500000	0.816497	0.774597	0.166667	0.500000	0.774597
5	1	-1	19	18.500	0.500000	0.816497	0.774597	0.166667	0.500000	0.774597
15	1	-1	6	7.000	-1.00000	-1.633	-2.449	0.666667	0.500000	-2.449

The **Residual Report** will highlight issues. In this report, nothing abnormal appears.

Regression Model

The Regression equation:

Percent Error = (8.5) + (-3.5) * A: Time/Patient + (-4.25) * C: Complexity + (2.25) * AC

Predicted Response Calculator:

Predicted Response Calculator:							
Predictors	Enter Actual Settings:	Coded Settings	Predicted Response	Lower 95% CI	Upper 95% CI	Lower 95% PI	Upper 95% PI
A:							
C:							

Note:
1. Enter settings for predictors. If the predictors are block terms, specify a 0 or 1 for each level.
2. Do not insert or delete rows or columns in this worksheet.

The Predicted Response Calculator uses the Regression equation. To run the Predicted Response Calculator, input the actual values for Predictors A and C. For this example, use 12 for Predictor A and +1 for Complexity. (Remember that Complexity was a text input, Simple and Hard. It was decided that +1 would represent the Hard condition.)

Predicted Response Calculator:							
Predictors	Enter Actual Settings:	Coded Settings	Predicted Response	Lower 95% CI	Upper 95% CI	Lower 95% PI	Upper 95% PI
A:	12	0.4	3.75	2.455152204	5.044847796	1.019044786	6.480955214
C:	1	1					

Results:

The Predictor provides a Point, or Predicted Response (3.75) and two Confidence Intervals. The **CI** represents a confidence interval on the Mean, and the **PI**, or Predictive Interval is the possible range for any single run at these conditions.

Create Factorial Experiments with Center Points and Blocks

Scenario:

A company wants to reduce the number of man hours required to assemble a product. It decides to study the effects of three variables on Man-Hours per Unit assembly time. The factors along with the levels are;

- Number of Items per order; (5, 15)
- Number of Subassemblies available; (30, 60)
- Number of Associates on a team; (2, 6)

The Average Cycle Time per unit is calculated on a per shift basis.

Center Points

Continuous factors have the ability to create a center value (the value midway between the high and low values in a two level design). A Center Point exists when **all** continuous factors are run at their center or middle condition simultaneously. Here are the Center Points for the example above.

Items per Order	# Subassemblies	#Associates
10	45	4

Hint: When using Center Points, select the factor settings so the Center Point is a whole number, or a fraction that can be run.

The Center Point has several purposes:

1) ***Verify the assumption of a linear response***. If the response between the high and low condition of an X factor is linear, the center point falls on the line connecting the response at the high and low conditions.

Note: *The Center Point indicates if curvature exists, but does not indicate which factor or factors cause the curvature.*

2) ***Estimate the pure error of an experiment.*** When there are multiple Center Points, the variation of results is an estimate of the experiment's pure error.

3) ***Show process stability over time, when multiple Center Points are spaced throughout the experiment.*** A stable process is required for reliable experimental results. An experiment run on an unstable process could produce results based on the effect of special cause variation, not the effect of factor(s) under consideration.

Blocks

Running experiments in blocks allows for proper distribution of runs to account for potential factors that are not part of the current experiment. These factors are called Noise factors.

For instance, if for logistical purposes the experiment must be split between two days, day is a Noise variable. Simply dividing the random runs into two groups and running one group on day 1 and the other group on day 2 may not result in an even distribution of all factor settings. Running the experiment in two blocks, however, assures an equal number of high and low conditions for each factor in each block.

This type of situation is used for the experiment example.

Menu command: ***SigmaXL > Design of Experiment > 2-Level Factorial/Screening > 2-Lever Factorial/Screening Designs***

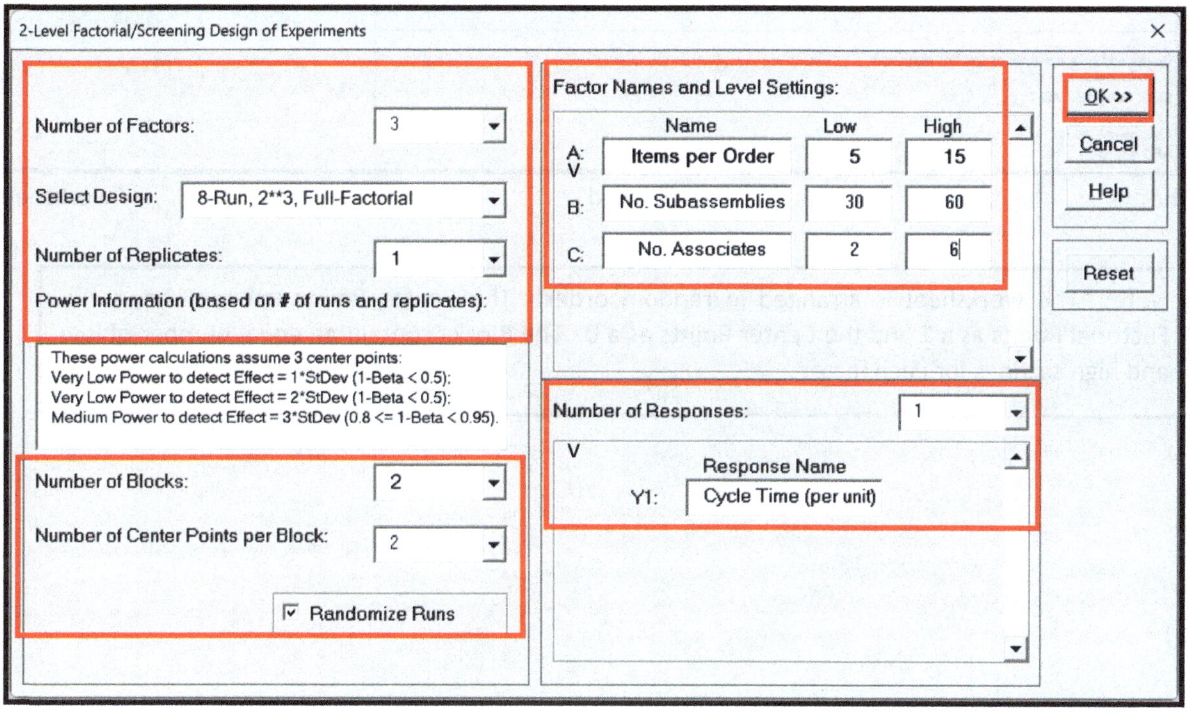

Fill in the information as shown, then click **OK**.

Design of Experiments Worksheet

Title:	
Date:	
Name of Experimenter:	
Notes:	

Design Type:	3 Factor, 8-Run, 2**3, Full-Factorial
Number of Replicates:	1
Number of Blocks:	2
Number of Center Points per Block:	2
Number of Responses:	1

Run Order	Std. Order	Center Points	Blocks	A: Items per Order	B: No. Subassemblies	C: No. Associates	Cycle Time (per unit)
1	2	1	1	15	60	2	
2	1	1	1	5	30	2	
3	4	1	1	5	60	6	
4	5	0	1	10	45	4	
5	6	0	1	10	45	4	
6	3	1	1	15	30	6	
7	8	1	2	5	60	2	
8	9	1	2	5	30	6	
9	10	1	2	15	60	6	
10	12	0	2	10	45	4	
11	7	1	2	15	30	2	
12	11	0	2	10	45	4	

Do not add or delete rows or sort this worksheet.

Block Generator: ABC

Aliasing of Effects:
ABC = Block

The finished worksheet.

Note: The worksheet is arranged in random order. The Center Points column shows the Factorial Points as a 1 and the Center Points as a 0. The Blocks contain an equal number of low and high settings for each factor.

For the analysis, open the following worksheet:

Worksheet: ***Unit Cycle Time***

Run Order	Std. Order	Center Points	Blocks	A: Items per Order	B: No. Subassemblies	C: No. Associates	Cycle Time (per unit)
1	2	1	1	15	60	2	18
2	1	1	1	5	30	2	10
3	6	0	1	10	45	4	9
4	5	0	1	10	45	4	6
5	4	1	1	5	60	6	7
6	3	1	1	15	30	6	1
7	10	1	2	15	60	6	2
8	7	1	2	15	30	2	15
9	11	0	2	10	45	4	8
10	8	1	2	5	60	2	12
11	9	1	2	5	30	6	6
12	12	0	2	10	45	4	10

This is the experiment just created, with the output in column Cycle Time (per unit).

Analyze Factorial Experiments with Center Points and Blocks

Analysis of the Full Factorial design with Center Points and Blocks proceeds as follows:

1. Create the Full Model (all factors and interactions)
2. Determine significant factors based on a predetermined alpha level
3. Determine if the Center Points and or Blocks are significant
4. Run Factorial Plots to visualize significant factors
5. Run a new model with significant factors (the Reduced Model)
6. Check the model using ANOVA and Coefficients Outputs
7. Check the model using residual analysis (graphs)

Menu command: ***SigmaXL > Design of Experiments > 2-Level Factorial/Screening > Analyze 2-Level Factorial/Screening Design***

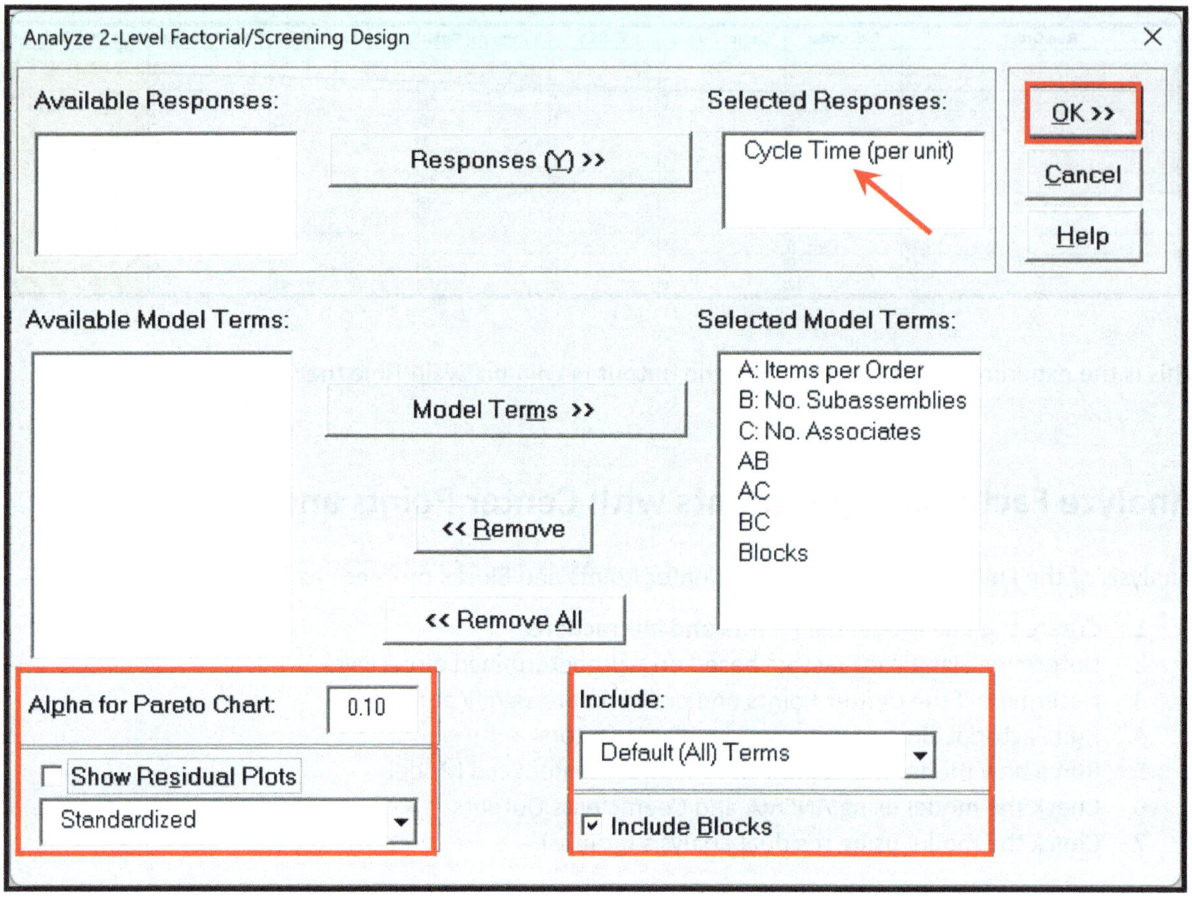

Select **Cycle Time (per unit)** as the Selected Responses:

For Include: use the pull-down and choose **Default (All) Terms** to create the Full Model Use the value **0.10** for Alpha for Pareto Chart. De-select the **Show Residual Plots** option.

Click **OK**.

Output:

Pareto Chart of Coefficients.

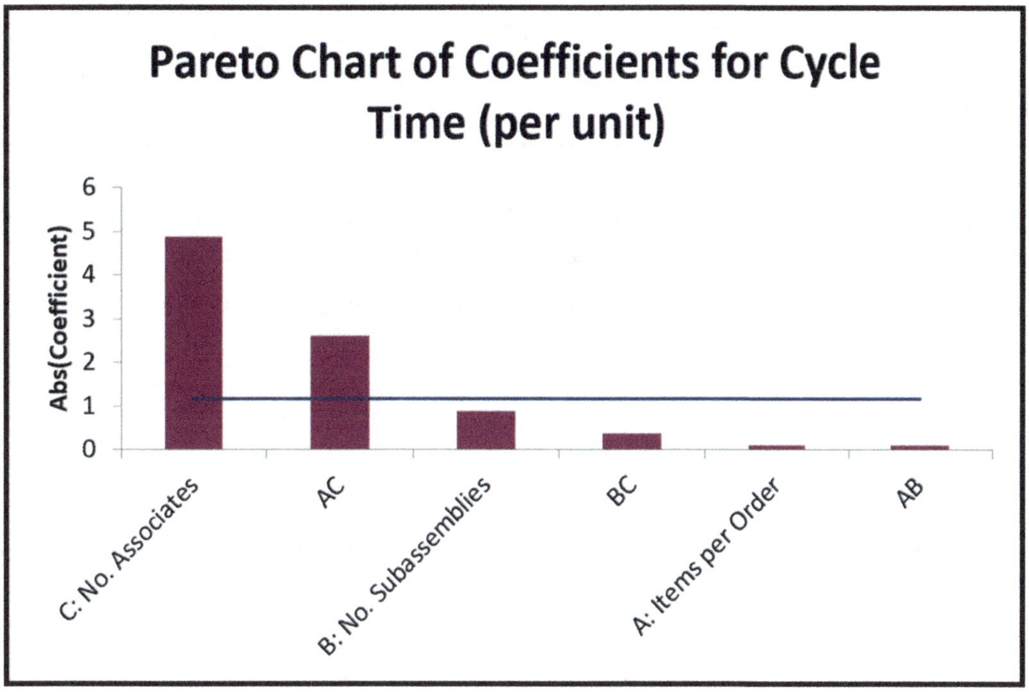

Factors **C (No. Associates)** and the **AC** interaction (**Items per Order * No. Associates** interaction) are shown to be significant.

The Parameter Estimates (Coded Units) shows factor C and the AC interaction to be significant.

Parameter Estimates (Coded Units):						
Term	**Coefficient**	**SE Coefficient**	**T**	**P**	**VIF**	**Tolerance**
Constant	8.5	0.631906287	13.451	0.0002		
A: Items per Order	0.125	0.547246897	0.228416	0.8305	1	1
B: No. Subassemblies	0.875	0.547246897	1.599	0.1851	1	1
C: No. Associates	-4.875	0.547246897	-8.908	0.0009	1	1
AB	0.125	0.547246897	0.228416	0.8305	1	1
AC	-2.625	0.547246897	-4.797	0.0087	1	1
BC	-0.375	0.547246897	-0.685248	0.5308	1	1
Blocks_2	0.333333333	0.893650441	0.373002	0.7281	1	1

Notice that the Blocks_2 factor is not significant, so in the reduced model, the blocking factor can be removed.

Analysis of Variance for Model:

Analysis of Variance for Model:					
Source	**DF**	**SS**	**MS**	**F**	**P**
Blocks	1	0.333333	0.333333	0.139130	0.7281
Model	6	252.75	42.125	17.583	0.0076
Error	4	9.583	2.396		
Curvature	1	1.041666667	1.04166667	0.365854	0.5880
Lack of Fit	1	2.042	2.042	0.628205	0.5111
Pure Error	2	6.500	3.250		

In the Analysis of Variance for Model output, under Error, the Curvature row has a high p-value (0.5880). This indicates there's no curvature in the response that needs to be investigated.

For the Reduced Model, neither the curvature nor the blocks need to be considered.

Factorial Plots:

Create and analyze the Factorial plots as shown previously.

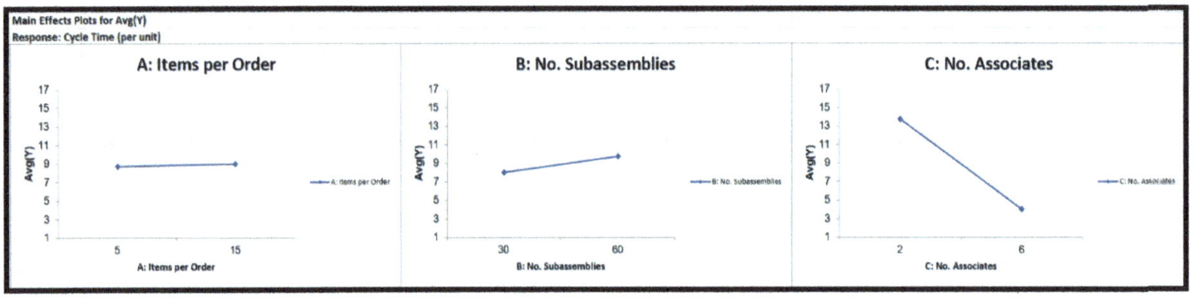

Main Effects Plots:

Interactions Plots:

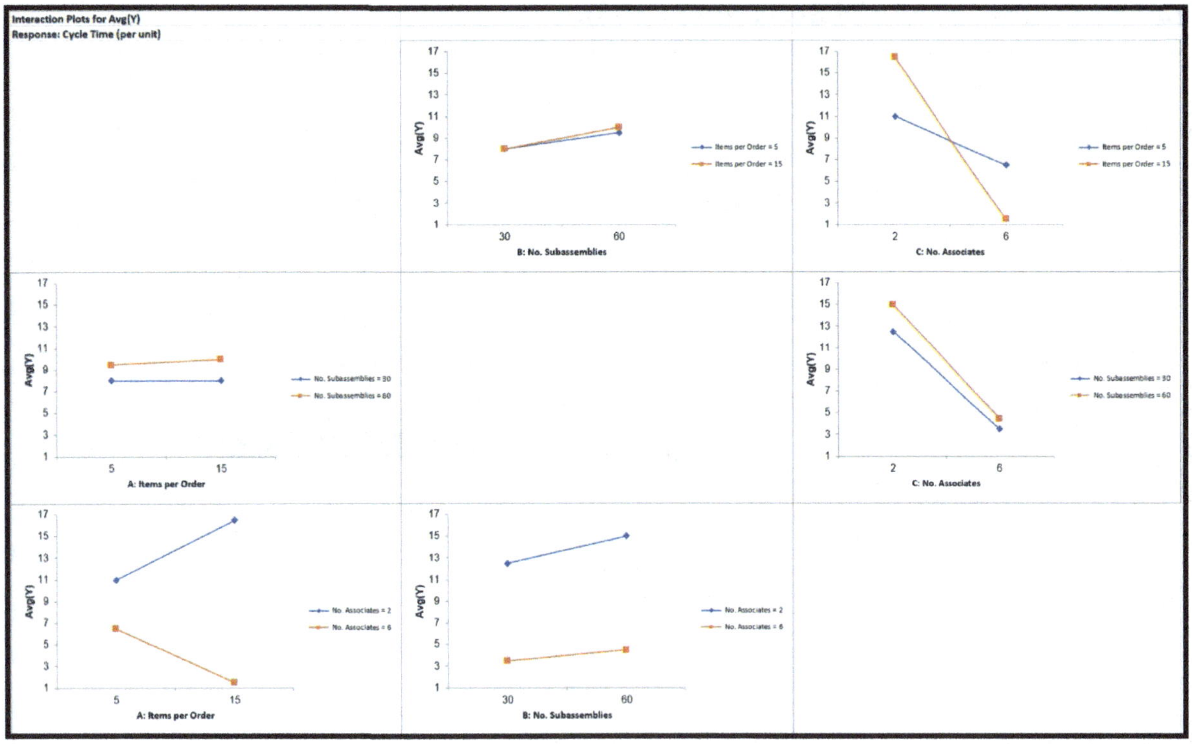

Create the Reduced Model

As shown before, the Reduced Model is created and analyzed using the significant factors. Re-run the analysis using the following factors:

- No. Associates
- Items per Order
- Items per Order * No. Associates

> ***Note:*** *Items per Order is not significant, but it must be included in the model because it is a factor of the AC interaction.*

Menu command: ***SigmaXL > Design of Experiments > 2-Level Factorial/Screening > Analyze 2-Level Factorial/Screening Design***

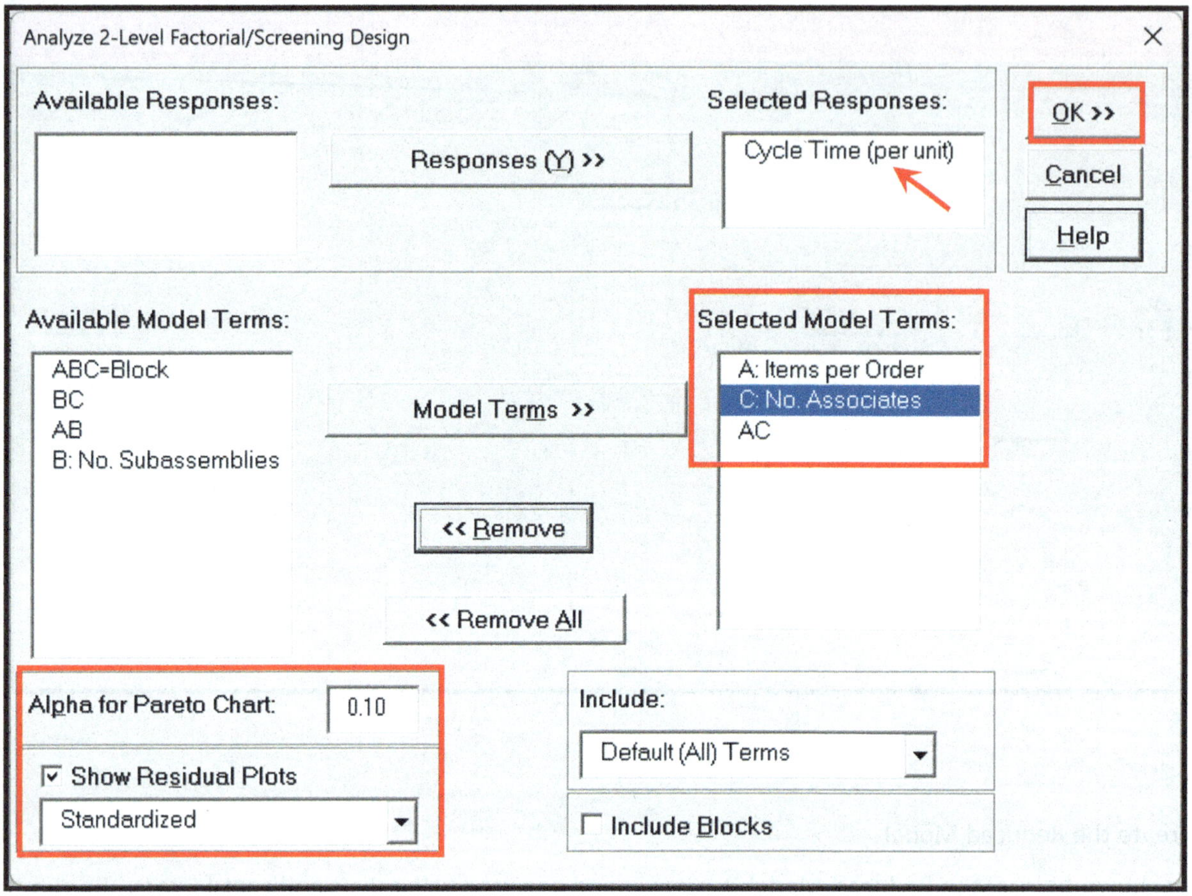

Choose the output; **Cycle Time (per unit)**.

Select the significant terms. (**A**, **C,** and **AC**).

De-select the; **Include Blocks** options.

Use the alpha of **0.10**, and click the **Show Residuals Plots** option. Use the **Standardized** residuals. Click **OK**.

Note: SigmaXL offers 3 types of Residuals, **Regular, Standardized**, and **Studentized (Deleted t)**. The **Standardized** residual is the residual, divided by an estimate of its standard deviation. This makes it easier to detect outliers. Standardized residuals greater than 3 and less than -3 are considered large (these outliers are highlighted in red). **Studentized (Deleted t)** residuals are computed in the same way that standardized residuals are computed, except that the ith observation is removed before performing the regression fit. This prevents the ith observation from influencing the regression model, resulting in unusual observations being more likely to stand out.

Residual plots were discussed in the Simple Linear Regression section of the Analyze chapter.

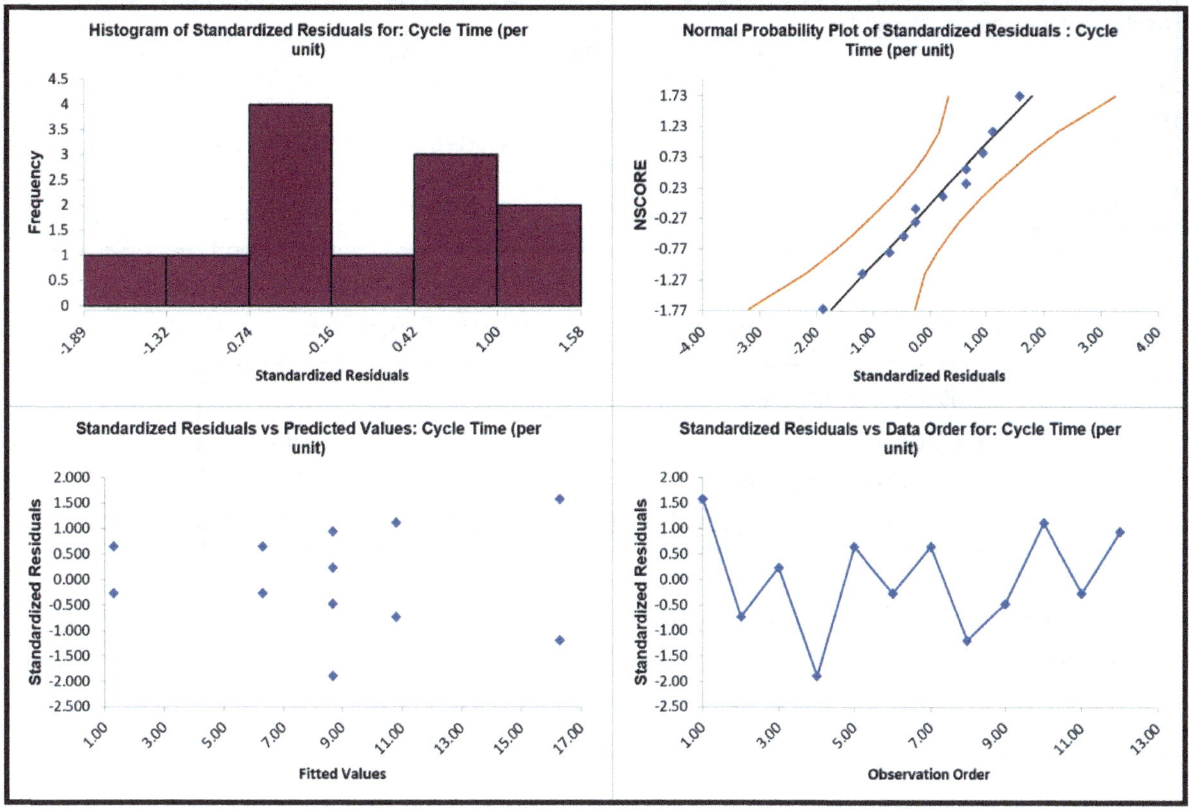

Normal Probability Plot

Observing the Normal Probability Plot, indicates the normality assumption is upheld.

Histogram

The Histogram shows nothing abnormal regarding the normality assumption. This is a visual display showing the general shape of distribution.

Residuals versus Fitted Values

The Residuals versus Fitted Values plot shows the general width of residuals. No evidence exists to reject the constant variance assumption.

Residuals versus Observation Order

No patterns exist in the Residual versus Run Order plot. The pattern appears to resemble a stable process.

Output: (Outputs were explained previously.)

Analysis of Variance for Model:					
Source	DF	SS	MS	F	P
Model	3	245.38	81.792	37.841	0.0000
Error	8	17.292	2.161		
Curvature	1	1.041666667	1.04166667	0.448718	0.5244
Lack of Fit	0				
Pure Error	7	16.250	2.321		
Total (Model + Error)	11	262.67	23.879		

One additional metric is the R-Sq (adj) value. This is related to the R-Sq value.

Model Summary:	
R-Square	93.42%
R-Square Adjusted	90.95%
S (Root Mean Square Error)	1.470

The **R-Sq (93.42%)** value indicates the percent of variation of output explained by the model. The **R-Sq (adj) (90.95%)** value displays the percent of variation explained by the model, adjusted for the number of terms in the model. Both values are at or above 90%.

The model for Cycle Time is developed using the coefficients for the uncoded units.

The DOE Multiple Regression Model is:

Cycle Time (per unit) = (8.666666667) + (0.125) * A: Items per Order + (-4.875) * C: No. Associates + (-2.625) * AC

Predicted Response Calculator:

Predicted Response Calculator:							
Predictors	Enter Actual Settings:	Coded Settings	Predicted Response	Lower 95% CI	Upper 95% CI	Lower 95% PI	Upper 95% PI
A:	12	0.4	5.754166667	4.487535126	7.020798208	2.135016859	9.373316474
C:	5	0.5					
			Note: 1. Enter settings for predictors. If the predictors are block terms, specify a 0 or 1 for each level. 2. Do not insert or delete rows or columns in this worksheet.				

Using the value 12 for Factor A, and 5 for Factor C produces an estimate of 5.75, with a Confidence range of 4.49 – 7.02 and a Predictive Interval of 2.14 – 9.37. Blocks were shown to be insignificant, so there's no term for Blocks in the final Model.

Fractional Factorial Designs

Tool Use: Use a Fractional Factorial Design in the same way as a Full Factorial when resources are a concern. With this approach the number of runs is reduced by deciding beforehand which interaction coefficients are not important.

The equation for a Fractional Factorial depends upon the degree of fractionation.

The hypothesis is the same - determining if the coefficients are zero or not equal to zero.

Understanding the compromises made with Fractional Factorial designs is assumed throughout this section.

Null Hypothesis: (H_o): $\beta_i = 0$

Alternative Hypothesis: (H_a): $\beta_i \neq 0$

Data Type: Input – Discrete or Continuous; Output – Numeric

Creating a Fractional Factorial Design

Menu command: ***SigmaXL > Design of Experiment > 2-Level Factorial/Screening > 2-Lever Factorial/Screening Designs***

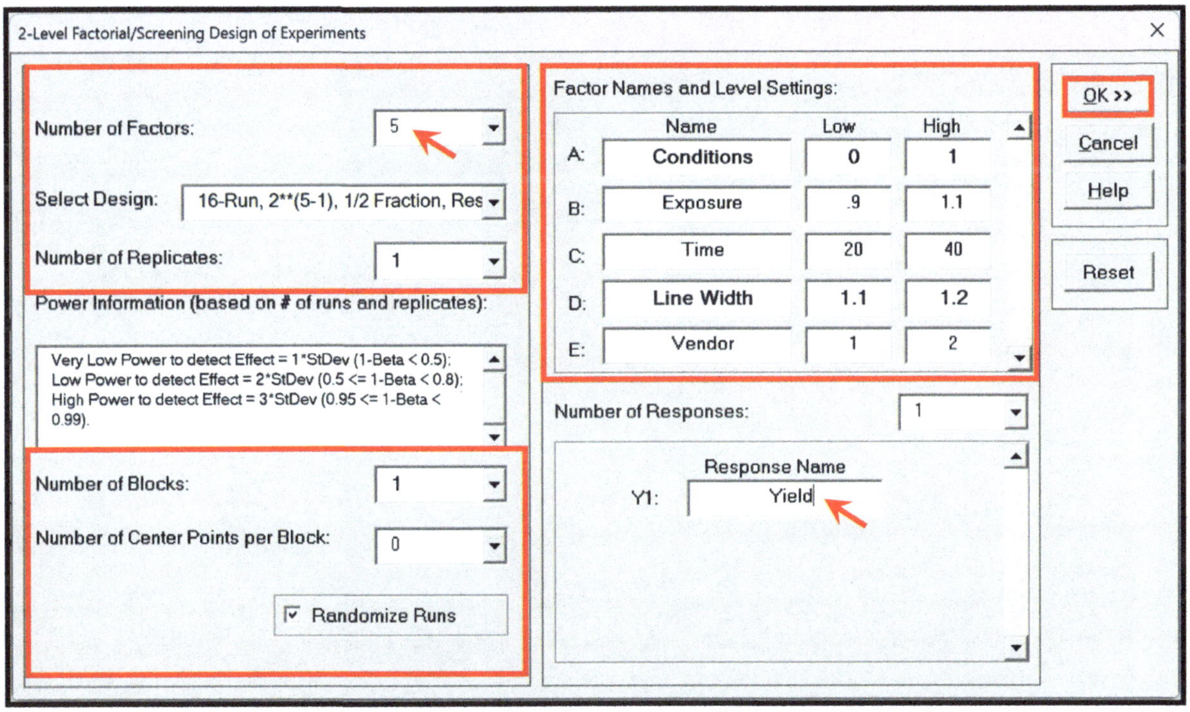

Select **5** factors, then choose the 16-Run, ½ Fraction design. Fill in the Name of the factors and their levels as shown. Use 1 Replicate, 1 Block and zero Center Points. The Response is **Yield**. Click **OK**.

The Experimental worksheet is shown below. The Alias Structure is **E=ABCD**.

Run Order	Std. Order	Center Points	Blocks	A: Conditions	B: Exposure	C: Time	D: Line Width	E: Vendor	Yield
1	3	1	1	0	1.1	20	1.1	1	
2	4	1	1	1	1.1	20	1.1	2	
3	15	1	1	0	1.1	40	1.2	1	
4	6	1	1	1	0.9	40	1.1	2	
5	11	1	1	0	1.1	20	1.2	2	
6	2	1	1	1	0.9	20	1.1	1	
7	14	1	1	1	0.9	40	1.2	1	
8	5	1	1	0	0.9	40	1.1	1	
9	1	1	1	0	0.9	20	1.1	2	
10	8	1	1	1	1.1	40	1.1	1	
11	12	1	1	1	1.1	20	1.2	1	
12	16	1	1	1	1.1	40	1.2	2	
13	7	1	1	0	1.1	40	1.1	2	
14	9	1	1	0	0.9	20	1.2	1	
15	13	1	1	0	0.9	40	1.2	2	
16	10	1	1	1	0.9	20	1.2	2	

Aliasing of Effects (to Order 2): None (Resolution V design).

Analyze Fractional Factorial Designs

Run Order	Std. Order	Center Points	Blocks	A: Conditions	B: Exposure	C: Time	D: Line Width	E: Vendor	Yield
1	3	1	1	0	1.1	20	1.1	1	34
2	4	1	1	1	1.1	20	1.1	2	42
3	15	1	1	0	1.1	40	1.2	1	44
4	6	1	1	1	0.9	40	1.1	2	22
5	11	1	1	0	1.1	20	1.2	2	30
6	2	1	1	1	0.9	20	1.1	1	9
7	14	1	1	1	0.9	40	1.2	1	21
8	5	1	1	0	0.9	40	1.1	1	16
9	1	1	1	0	0.9	20	1.1	2	8
10	8	1	1	1	1.1	40	1.1	1	50
11	12	1	1	1	1.1	20	1.2	1	40
12	16	1	1	1	1.1	40	1.2	2	53
13	7	1	1	0	1.1	40	1.1	2	45
14	9	1	1	0	0.9	20	1.2	1	6
15	13	1	1	0	0.9	40	1.2	2	15
16	10	1	1	1	0.9	20	1.2	2	10

To analyze the experiment, go to worksheet: ***Fractional Factorial***

Menu command: ***SigmaXL > Design of Experiments > 2-Level Factorial/Screening > Analyze 2-Level Factorial/Screening Design***

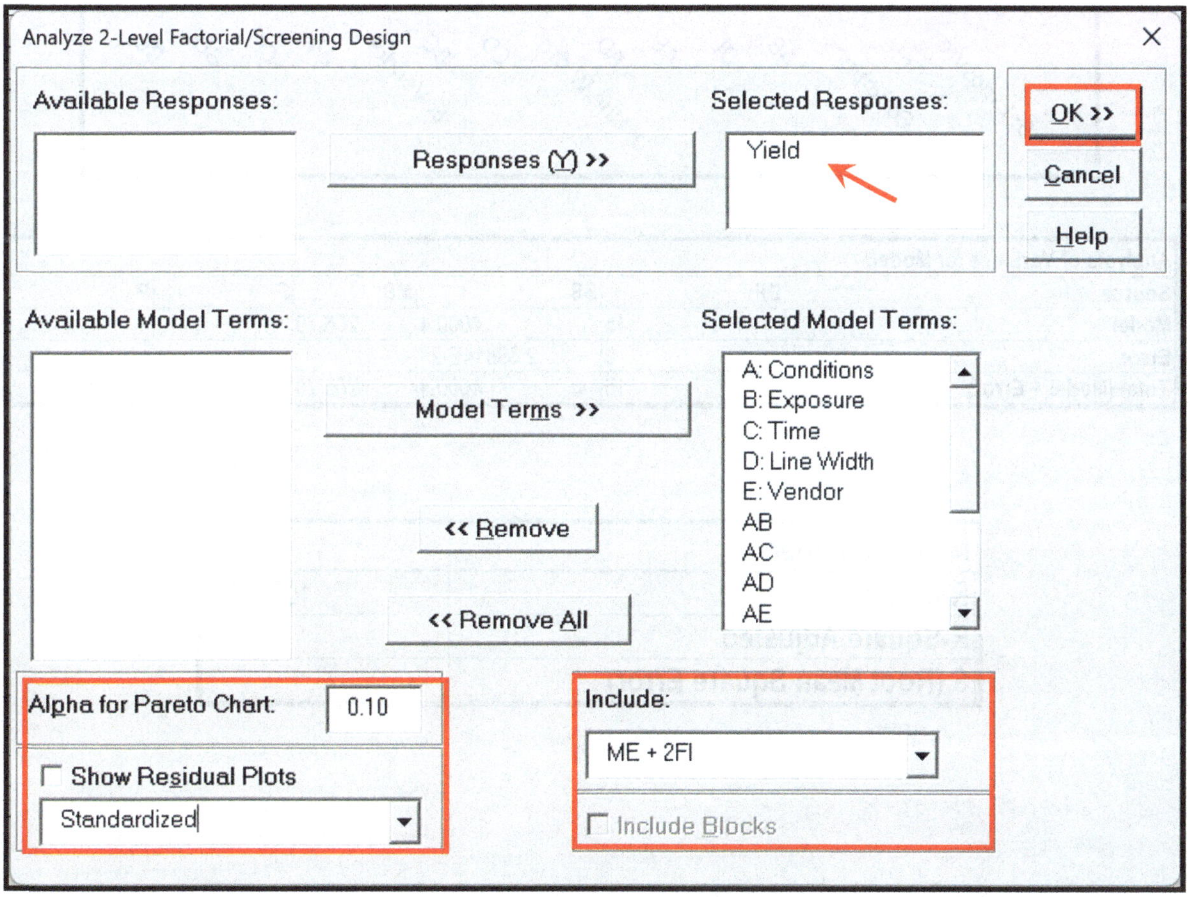

Input **Yield** for the Selected Responses, use an alpha of 0.10, then de-select Show Residual Plots. Include ME (Main Effects) + 2FI (2 factor interactions). Click **OK**.

The analysis is carried out in the same manner found in the Full Factorial design.

The Pareto plot show factors A, B, and C are significant.

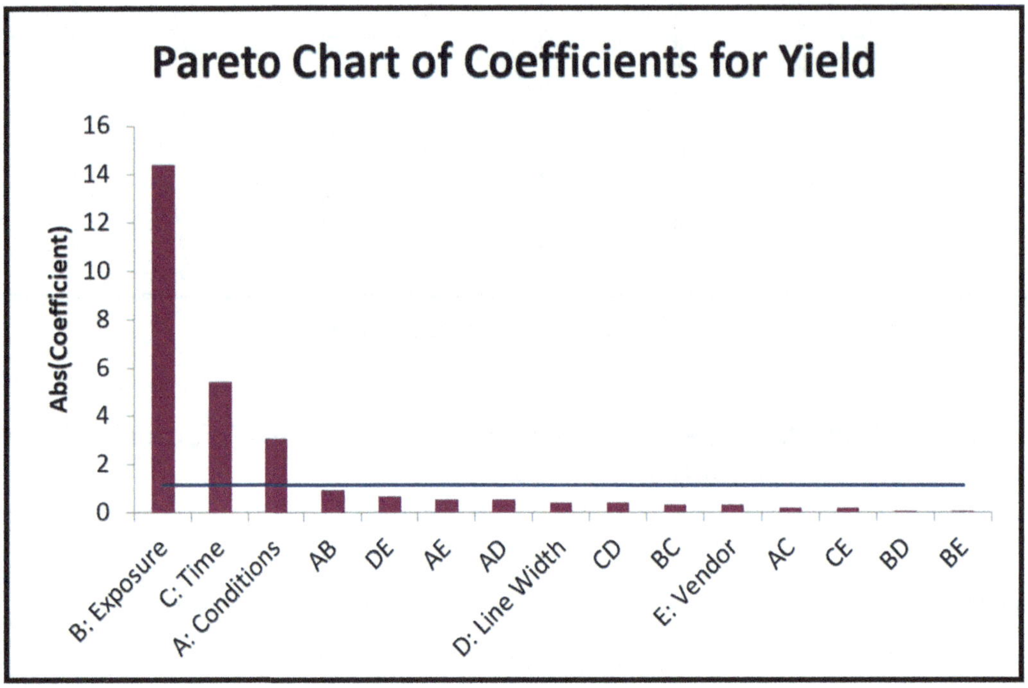

Analysis of Variance for Model:					
Source	DF	SS	MS	F	P
Model	15	4000.4	266.70		
Error	0	2.39814E-28			
Total (Model + Error)	15	4000.4	266.70		

Model Summary:	
R-Square	100.00%
R-Square Adjusted	N/A
S (Root Mean Square Error)	

Parameter Estimates (Coded Units):	Note SE, T, and P are derived from Lenth's Pseudo Standard Error			
Term	**Coefficient**	**SE Coefficient**	**T**	**P**
Constant	27.8125			
A: Conditions	3.0625	0.5625	5.444	**0.0028**
B: Exposure	14.4375	0.5625	25.667	**0.0000**
C: Time	5.4375	0.5625	9.667	**0.0002**
D: Line Width	-0.4375	0.5625	-0.777778	0.4719
E: Vendor	0.3125	0.5625	0.555556	0.6025
AB	0.9375	0.5625	1.667	0.1565
AC	0.1875	0.5625	0.333333	0.7524
AD	0.5625	0.5625	1.00000	0.3632
AE	0.5625	0.5625	1.00000	0.3632
BC	0.3125	0.5625	0.555556	0.6025
BD	-0.0625	0.5625	-0.111111	0.9159
BE	-0.0625	0.5625	-0.111111	0.9159
CD	0.4375	0.5625	0.777778	0.4719
CE	0.1875	0.5625	0.333333	0.7524
DE	-0.6875	0.5625	-1.222	0.2761

Note: *Follow previous examples to view Main Effects and Interaction Plots.*

Next, create the **reduced model**.

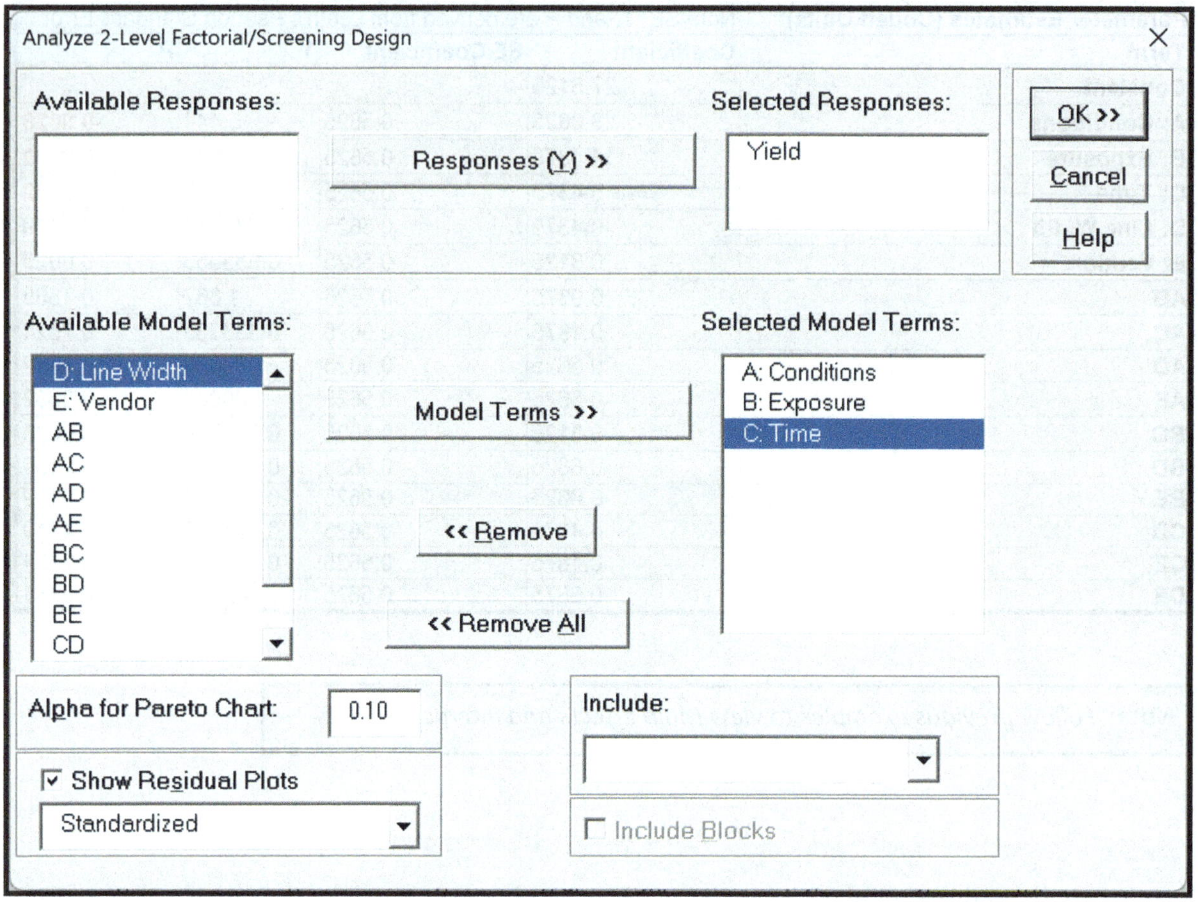

In the **Terms** window, select **A**, **B**, and **C**.

Model Summary:	
R-Square	98.94%
R-Square Adjusted	98.68%
S (Root Mean Square Error)	1.876

Click **OK**.

Analysis of Variance for Model:					
Source	DF	SS	MS	F	P
Model	3	3958.2	1319.4	374.74	0.0000
Error	12	42.250	3.521		
Lack of Fit	4	23.750	5.938	2.568	0.1194
Pure Error	8	18.500	2.313		
Total (Model + Error)	15	4000.4	266.70		

Parameter Estimates (Coded Units):				
Term	**Coefficient**	**SE Coefficient**	**T**	**P**
Constant	27.8125	0.469097094	59.289	0.0000
A: Conditions	3.0625	0.469097094	6.528	0.0000
B: Exposure	14.4375	0.469097094	30.777	0.0000
C: Time	5.4375	0.469097094	11.591	0.0000

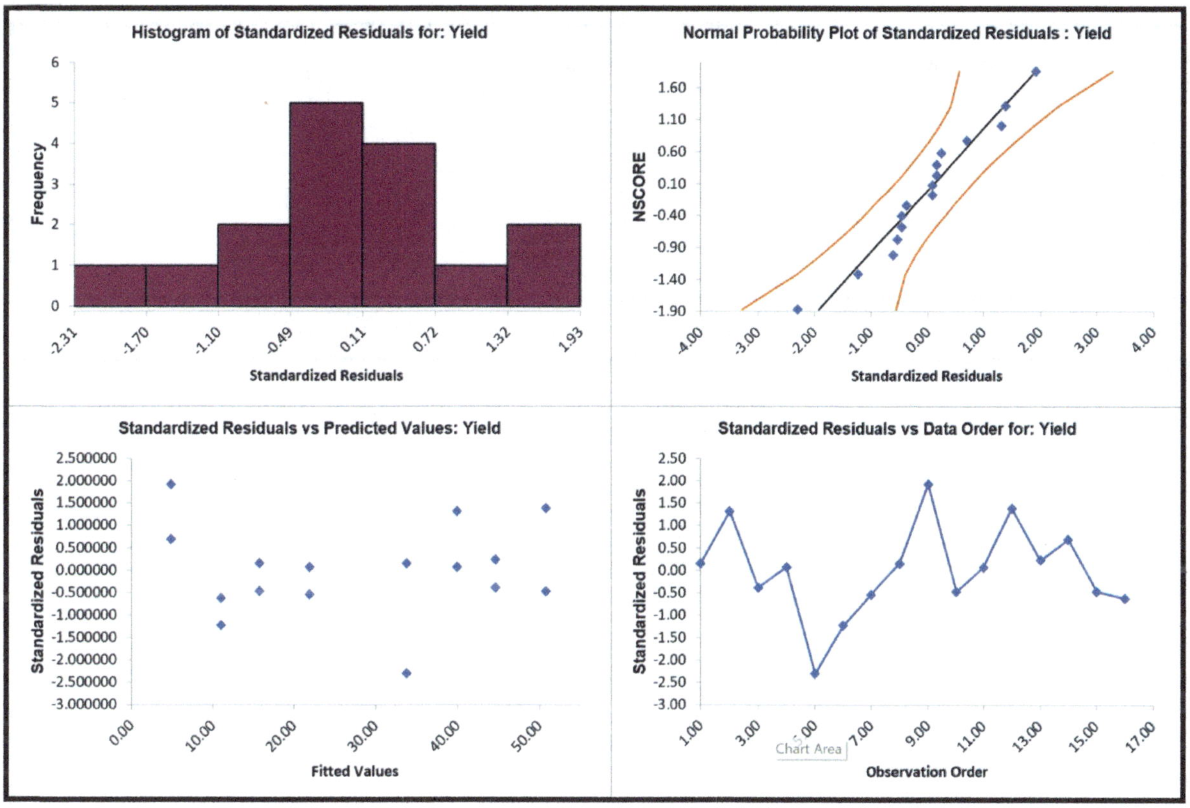

There's no need for Effects Plots since the factors selected were deemed significant.

Analysis of the Reduced Model for the Fractional Factorial experiment proceeds along the line of the Full Factorial.

Residual plots were explained previously; in this example, no issues exist with residuals.

Create the Factorial Plots to visualize results; (create them in the same manner as in the Full Factorial analysis).

No interactions were significant so the Interaction Graphs are not displayed.

Output:

The R-Sq and R-Sq (adj) and R-sq (pred) values are all in the high 90% range.

All three factors show significance.

Remember, the **Condition** will be either a **-1** (for Condition 1), or a **1** (for Condition B).

The unusual observation should be checked and if found to be in error, corrected.

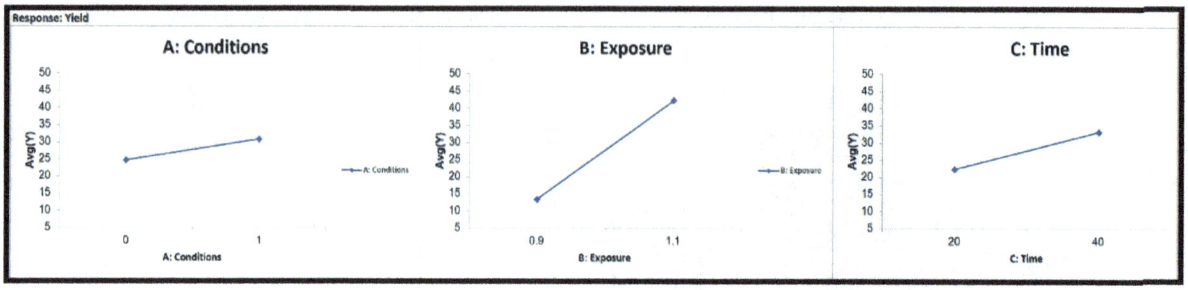

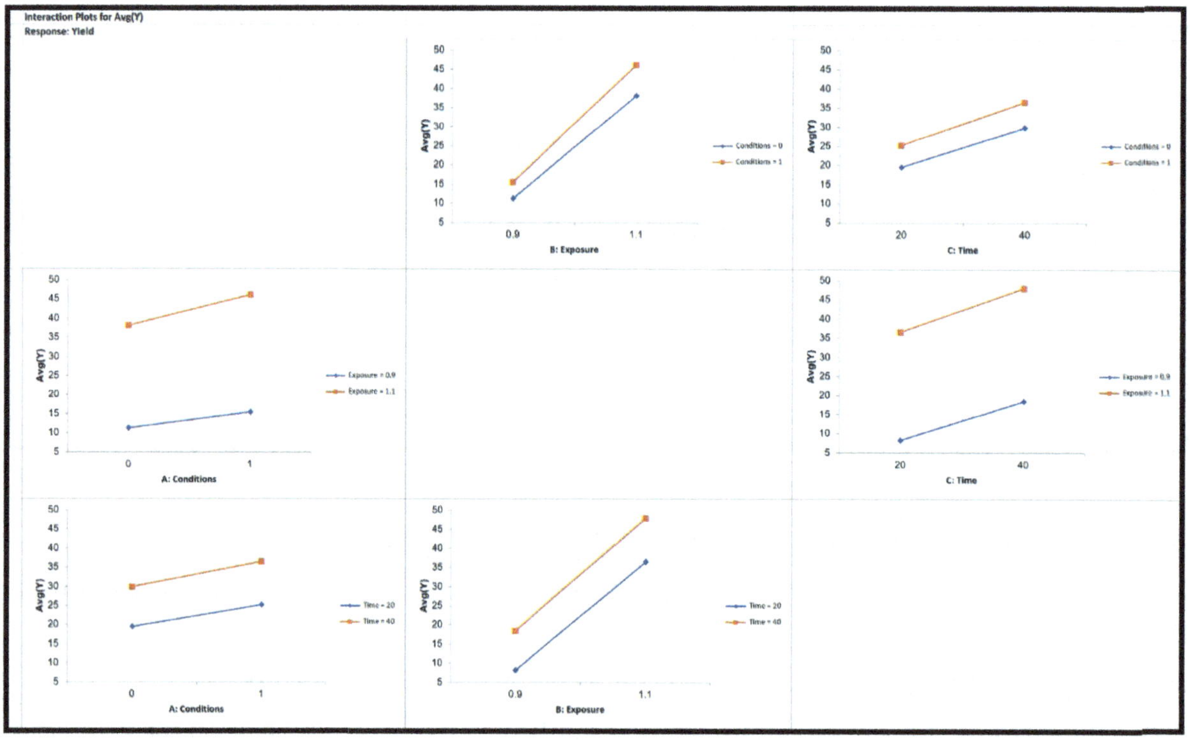

To display this value on the Four in one plot, return to the Residual graph.

Right click inside the graph window and select **Brush Points**.

With the Brush option on, point at and click the sixth observation in the Versus Order graph.

All points corresponding to the sixth point will be highlighted.

Only the Histogram will not have a highlighted point.

Response Surface Designs

Tool Use: Use a Response Surface Design in the same way as a Full Factorial to model a nonlinear response. This approach creates a model with quadratic terms.

The equation for a two factor Response Surface design:

$Y = \beta_0 + \beta_1 X_1 + \beta_2 X_2 + \beta_{11} X_1^2 + \beta_{22} X_2^2 + \beta_{12} X_1 X_2$

The hypothesis is the same - determining if the coefficients are zero or not equal to zero.

Null Hypothesis: (H_o): $\beta_i = 0$. Alternative Hypothesis: (H_a): $\beta_i \neq 0$.

Data Type: Input – Continuous; Output - Numeric

Creating the Response Surface Design

A three factor Central Composite design will be created. This experiment is set up to determine the best settings for minimum **% Clumping** of candy while maintaining a desired **Taste** level (as measured on a 1 – 10 scale).

Menu command:

SigmaXL > Design of Experiments > Response Surface > Response Surface Designs

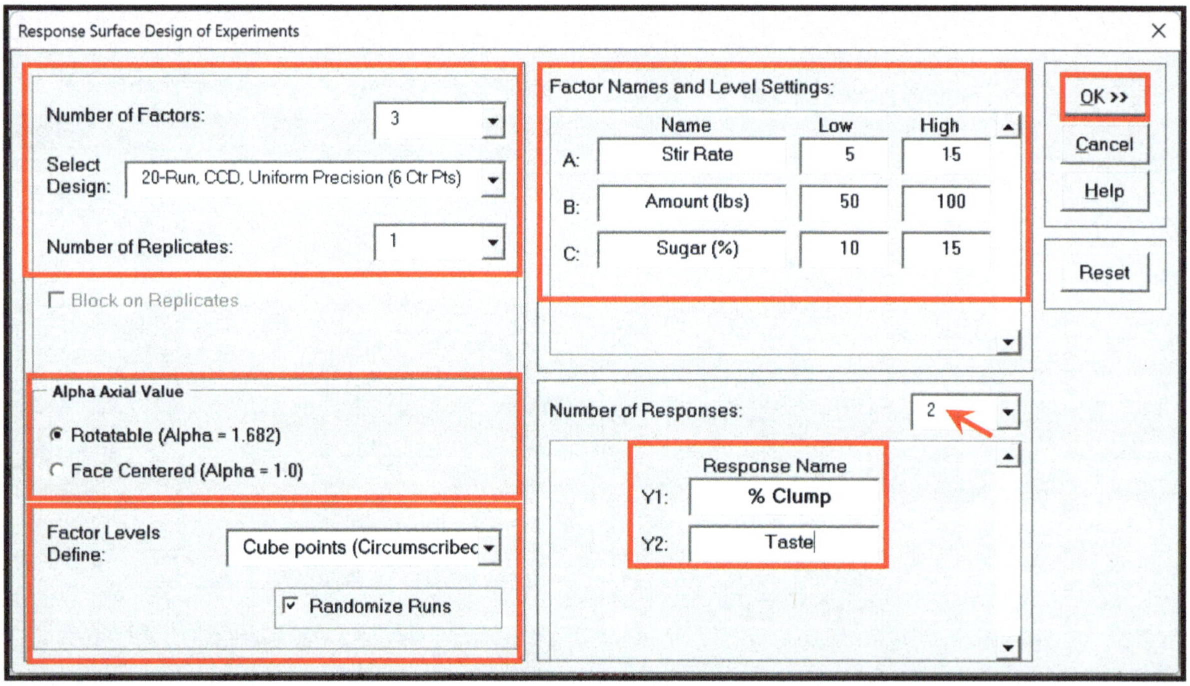

The Number of Factors is 3. For, Selected Design, choose; 20-run, CCD, Uniform Precision (6 Ctr Pts). The number of Replicates is **1**. Under Alpha Axial Value, click Rotatable (Alpha = 1.682). The Factor Levels Defined are; Cube points (Circumscribed).

For the Factor Names and Level Settings input the values as shown. There are 2 Responses **% Clump** and **Taste**. Click **OK**.

Run Order	Std. Order	Center Points	Blocks	A: Stir Rate	B: Amount (lbs)	C: Sugar (%)	% Clump	Taste
1	3	1	1	5	100	10		
2	14	1	1	10	75	16.704482		
3	7	1	1	5	100	15		
4	19	0	1	10	75	12.5		
5	4	1	1	15	100	10		
6	15	0	1	10	75	12.5		
7	16	0	1	10	75	12.5		
8	9	1	1	1.5910358	75	12.5		
9	13	1	1	10	75	8.2955179		
10	5	1	1	5	50	15		
11	20	0	1	10	75	12.5		
12	17	0	1	10	75	12.5		
13	12	1	1	10	117.0448208	12.5		
14	1	1	1	5	50	10		
15	10	1	1	18.408964	75	12.5		
16	8	1	1	15	100	15		
17	2	1	1	15	50	10		
18	18	0	1	10	75	12.5		
19	11	1	1	10	32.95517924	12.5		
20	6	1	1	15	50	15		

The experimental worksheet, (in random order) is shown.

The completed experiment is listed in the Worksheet: ***Candy***

Run Order	Std. Order	Center Points	Blocks	A: Stir Rate	B: Amount (lbs)	C: Sugar (%)	% Clump	Taste
1	3	1	1	5	100	10	18	5
2	14	1	1	10	75	16.704482	13	6
3	7	1	1	5	100	15	16	9
4	19	0	1	10	75	12.5	8	7
5	4	1	1	15	100	10	12	5
6	15	0	1	10	75	12.5	6	7
7	16	0	1	10	75	12.5	5	7
8	9	1	1	1.5910358	75	12.5	33	8
9	13	1	1	10	75	8.2955179	10	3
10	5	1	1	5	50	15	23	9
11	20	0	1	10	75	12.5	6	7
12	17	0	1	10	75	12.5	5	8
13	12	1	1	10	117.0448208	12.5	11	8
14	1	1	1	5	50	10	21	6
15	10	1	1	18.408964	75	12.5	12	8
16	8	1	1	15	100	15	12	8
17	2	1	1	15	50	10	15	5
18	18	0	1	10	75	12.5	4	7
19	11	1	1	10	32.95517924	12.5	9	7
20	6	1	1	15	50	15	14	8

Analyze Response Surface Designs

Menu command:

SigmaXL > Design of Experiments > Response Surface > Analyze Response Surface Design

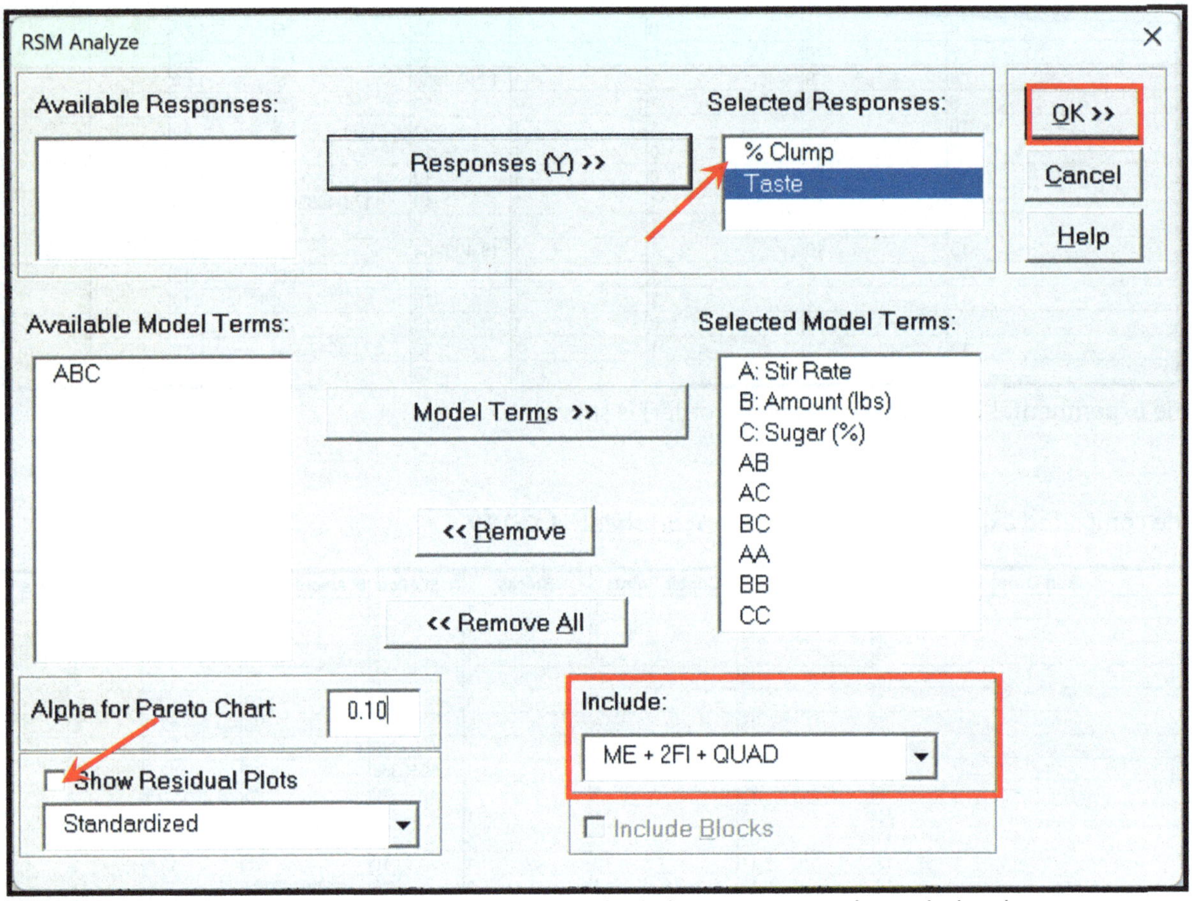

Select both Responses, then de-select the Show Residual Plots option. Under Include; choose; **ME+2FI+ QUAD** (Main Effects, 2 Factor Interactions, Quadratic terms). Click **OK**.

Two tabs are created; **Analyze - 3 Factor RSM** and **Analyze – 3 Factor RSM (1)**. One for each response.

Interpret Output in the same manner as for the Full and Fractional Factorial experiments. The important output for this step is to determine the significant factors.

For **% Clump** the following are significant factors:

- Stir Rate (A)
- Stir Rate*Stir Rate (A*A)
- Amount*Amount (B*B)

Parameter Estimates (Coded Units):						
Term	Coefficient	SE Coefficient	T	P	VIF	Tolerance
Constant	5.629134517	1.099171665	5.121	0.0004		
A: Stir Rate	-4.416657624	0.729275364	-6.056	0.0001	1	1
B: Amount (lbs)	-0.852056713	0.729275364	-1.168	0.2698	1	1
C: Sugar (%)	0.296215982	0.729275364	0.406179	0.6932	1	1
AB	0.625	0.952844181	0.655931	0.5267	1	1
AC	-0.125	0.952844181	-0.131186	0.8982	1	1
BC	-0.375	0.952844181	-0.393559	0.7022	1	1
AA	6.19677471	0.709929858	8.729	0.0000	1.018265261	0.982062374
BB	1.777357327	0.709929858	2.504	0.0313	1.018265261	0.982062374
CC	2.307687413	0.709929858	3.251	0.0087	1.018265261	0.982062374

- Sugar %*Sugar % (C*C)

For **Taste**, (using a P-value of less than 0.10), the significant factors are:

- Stir Rate*Stir Rate (A*A)
- Sugar % (C)
- Sugar %*Sugar % (CC)

Parameter Estimates (Coded Units):						
Term	Coefficient	SE Coefficient	T	P	VIF	Tolerance
Constant	7.158960529	0.2572382	27.830	0.0000		
A: Stir Rate	-0.219669914	0.170671686	-1.287	0.2271	1	1
B: Amount (lbs)	0.049923124	0.170671686	0.292510	0.7759	1	1
C: Sugar (%)	1.321342248	0.170671686	7.742	0.0000	1	1
AB	0.125	0.222993304	0.560555	0.5874	1	1
AC	-0.125	0.222993304	-0.560555	0.5874	1	1
BC	0.125	0.222993304	0.560555	0.5874	1	1
AA	0.344991549	0.166144274	2.076	0.0646	1.018265261	0.982062374
BB	0.168214854	0.166144274	1.01246254	0.3352	1.018265261	0.982062374
CC	-0.892445318	0.166144274	-5.372	0.0003	1.018265261	0.982062374

Next: Run Reduced Model.

Reduced Models:

Rerun the analysis on the outputs separately.

Use the significant factors found in the initial analysis, and include Residuals.

Reduced Model for % Clump

Menu command:

SigmaXL > Design of Experiments > Response Surface > Analyze Response Surface Design

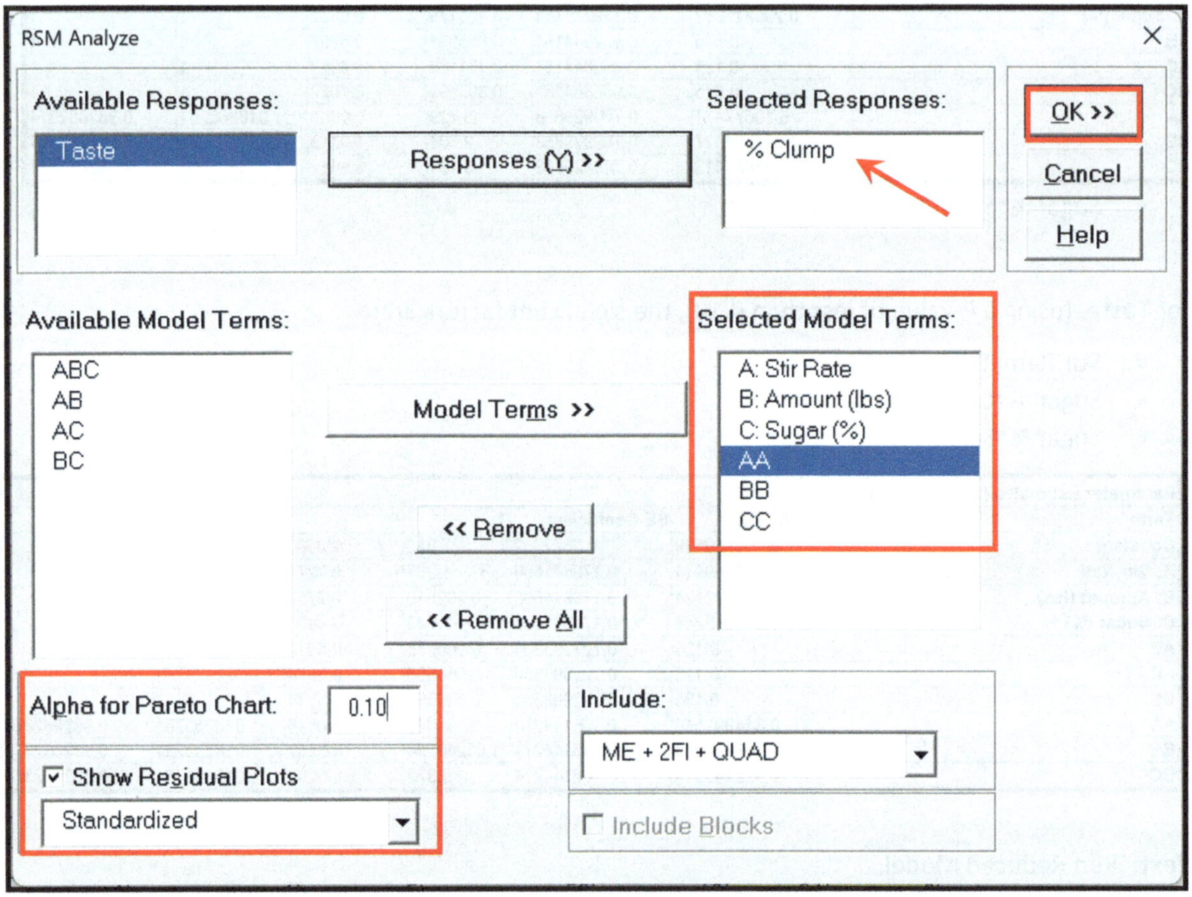

Note: If a quadratic or interaction term appears, the corresponding linear term must also appear; therefore B:Amount (lbs) is selected as well as C:Sugar %.

% Clump Output:

Regression equation:

% Clump = (5.629134517) + (-4.416657624) * A: Stir Rate + (-0.852056713) * B: Amount (lbs) + (0.296215982) * C: Sugar (%) + (6.19677471) * AA + (1.777357327) * BB + (2.307687413) * CC

Model Summary

Model Summary:	
R-Square	92.02%
R-Square Adjusted	88.33%
S (Root Mean Square Error)	2.434

The model summary shows good values for **R-Square** and **R-Square Adjusted**.

Analysis of Variance for Model:

Analysis of Variance for Model:					
Source	DF	SS	MS	F	P
Model	6	887.54	147.92	24.972	0.0000
Error	13	77.008	5.924		
Lack of Fit	8	67.675	8.459	4.532	0.0564
Pure Error	5	9.333	1.867		
Total (Model + Error)	19	964.55	50.766		

For the Model analysis, the Lack of Fit has a P-value that is low, but with all of the other metrics being sound it may not be an issue. To check, run several confirmation runs using the **Predicted Response Calculator** function. If the runs are not withing the Predicted Confidence Interval (PI), then further investigation is required.

Residual Analysis

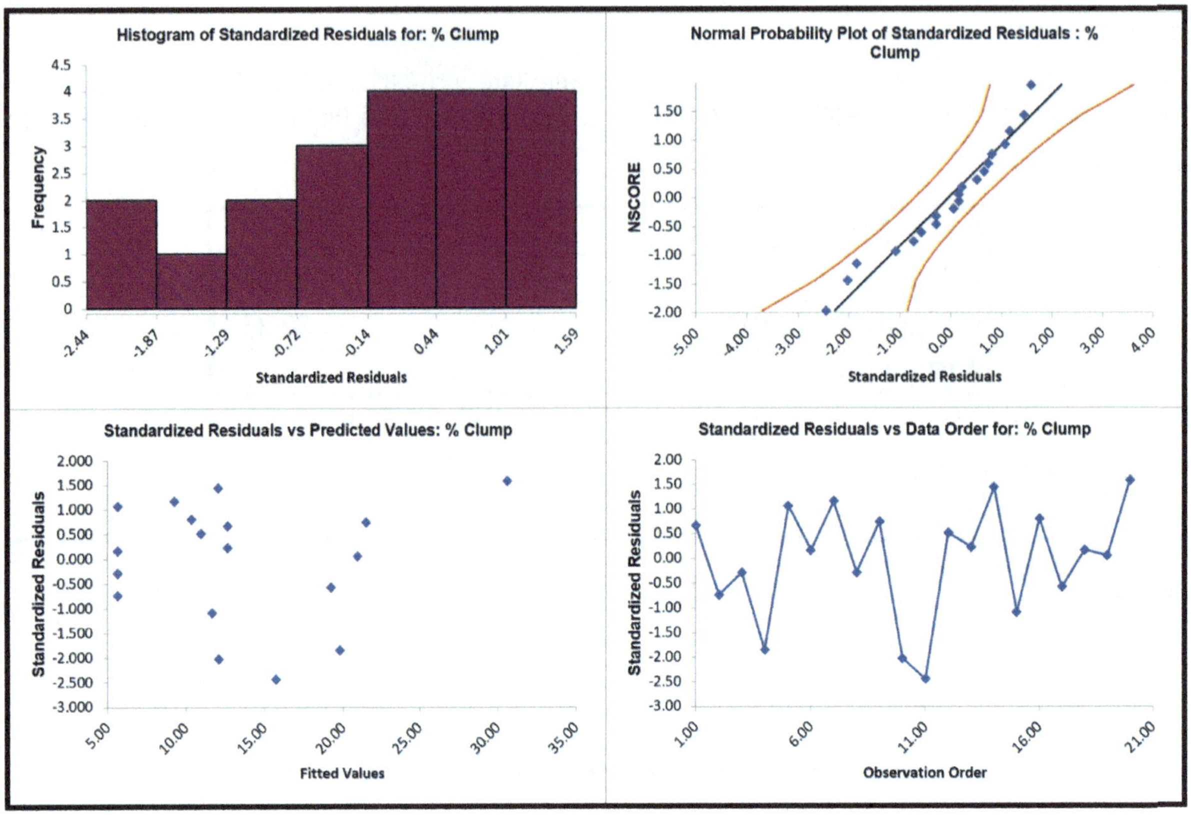

The residuals, while not perfect, don't show any extreme deviations from the assumptions.

Using this model is appropriate.

The rest of the outputs just support the reduced model as being correct.

Reduced Model for Taste

For **Taste** the significant factors are:

- Sugar%
- Sugar%*Sugar%
- Stir Rate * Stir Rate

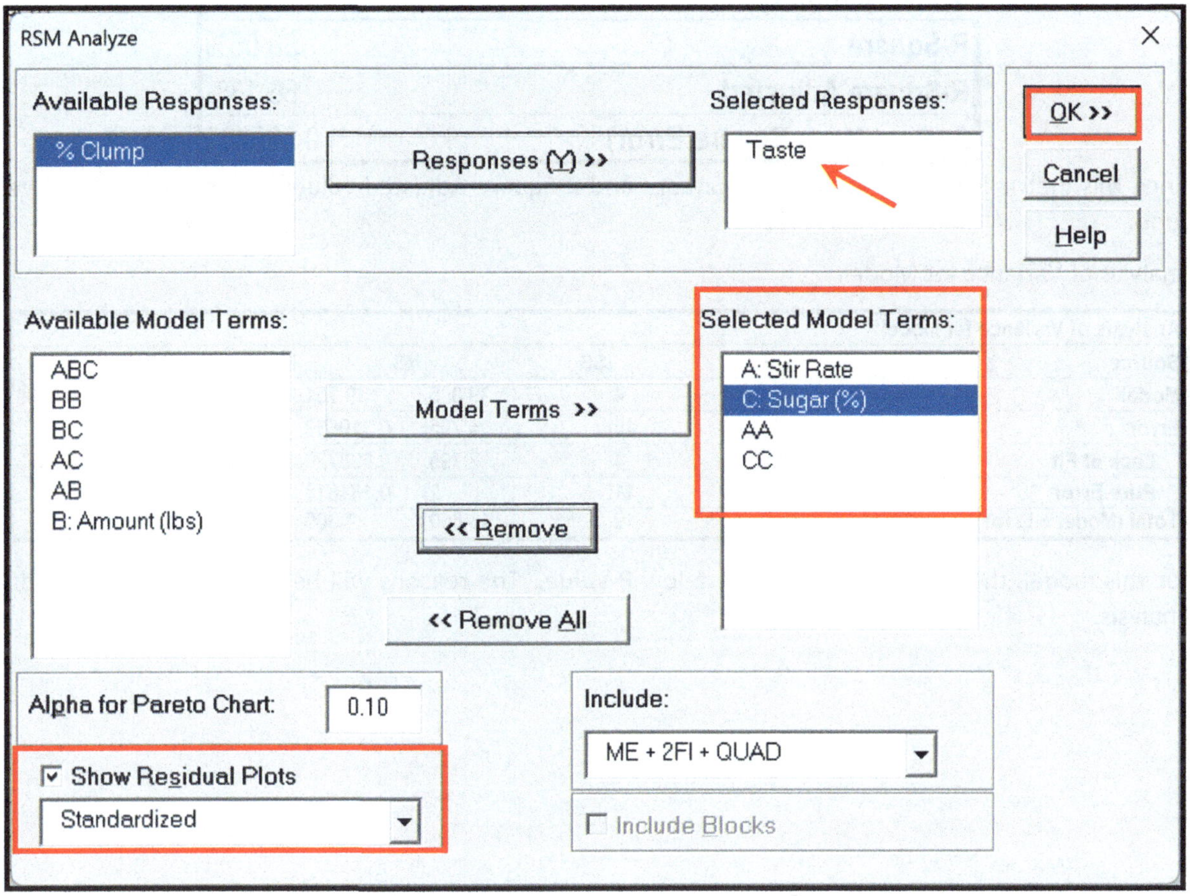

The Response is **Taste**. Select the terms as shown, and include the Residual plots.

Click **OK**.

Regression Equation:

Taste = (7.296635563) + (-0.219669914) * A: Stir Rate + (1.321342248) * C: Sugar (%) + (0.328288767) * AA + (-0.9091481) * CC

Model Summary:

Model Summary:	
R-Square	89.05%
R-Square Adjusted	86.13%
S (Root Mean Square Error)	0.565385

Since this metric is subjective, having R-Square and R-Square Adjusted values in the upper 80's is very good.

Analysis of Variance for Model:

Analysis of Variance for Model:					
Source	DF	SS	MS	F	P
Model	4	39.005	9.751	30.505	0.0000
Error	15	4.795	0.319660		
Lack of Fit	4	2.795	0.698726	3.843	0.0343
Pure Error	11	2	0.181818		
Total (Model + Error)	19	43.800	2.305		

For this model, the Lack of Fit does have a low P-Value. The reasons will be shown using the Residual Analysis.

Residual Analysis:

Residual analysis is the same as presented previously.

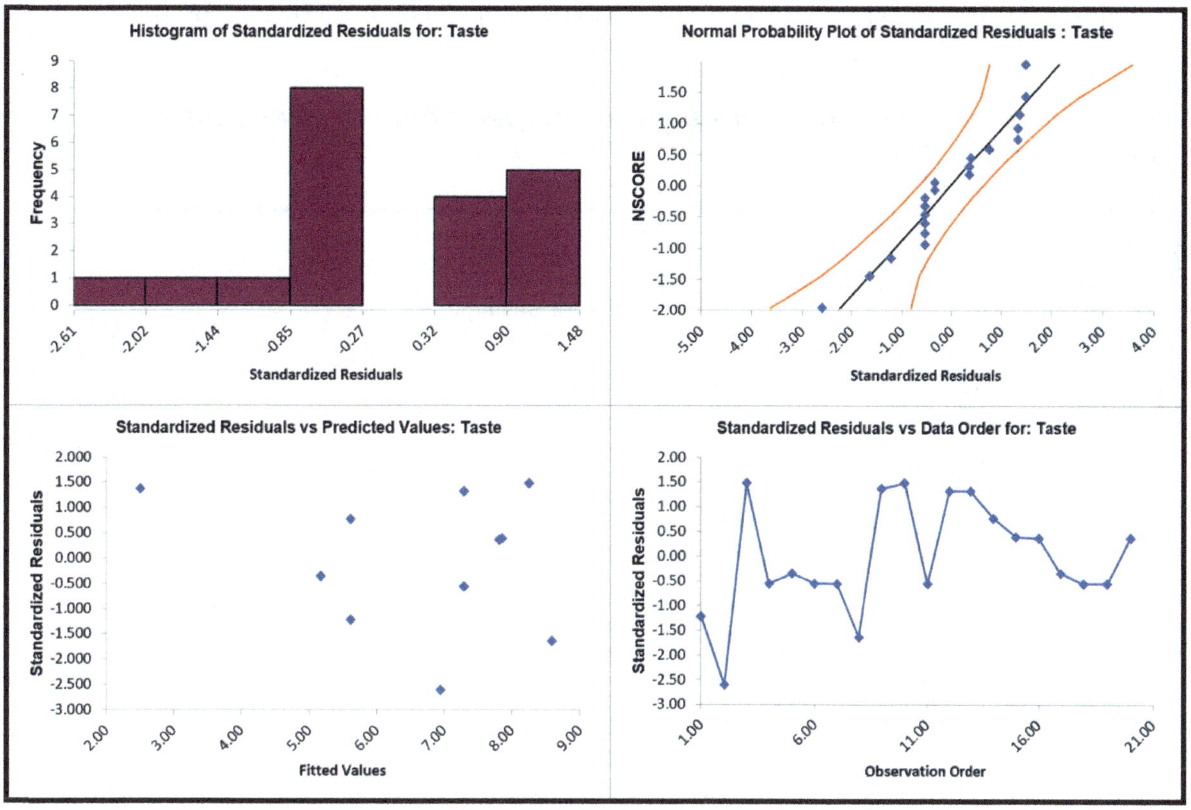

There's one residual with a high negative Standardized value. This should be investigated.

A: Stir Rate	B: Amount (lbs)	C: Sugar (%)	Taste	Predicted (Fitted) Values	Residuals	Standardized Residuals
5	100	10	5	5.614	-0.614104	-1.223
10	75	16.70448208	6	6.947	-0.947400	-2.608
5	100	15	9	8.257	0.743212	1.480
10	75	12.5	7	7.297	-0.296636	-0.559246

Taste is very subjective, so not having residuals that perfectly match the assumptions is not too surprising.

Graphical Display

The Contour/Surface plots are used to display results.

The Contour and Surface plots are generated through using the **Analysis – 3 Factor RSM** sheets.

Return to the sheet for Taste.

Menu command: ***SigmaXL > Design of Experiments > Response Surface > Contour/Surface Plots***

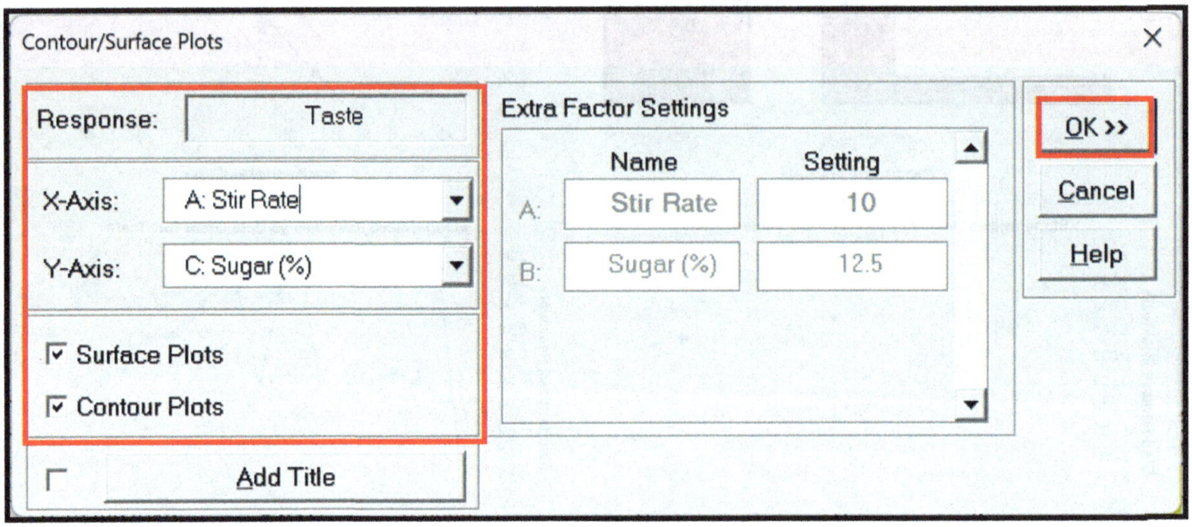

For the X-Axis select; **Stir Rate**. For the Y-Axis select **Sugar %**. While there are 3 factors, the model for **Taste** only contains **Stir Rate** and **Sugar %**. Therefore, no **Extra Factor Settings** are required.

Select the **Surface** and **Contour Plots** options. Click **OK**.

The plots show a high **Taste** score at the low Stir Rate and a Sugar % around 15.

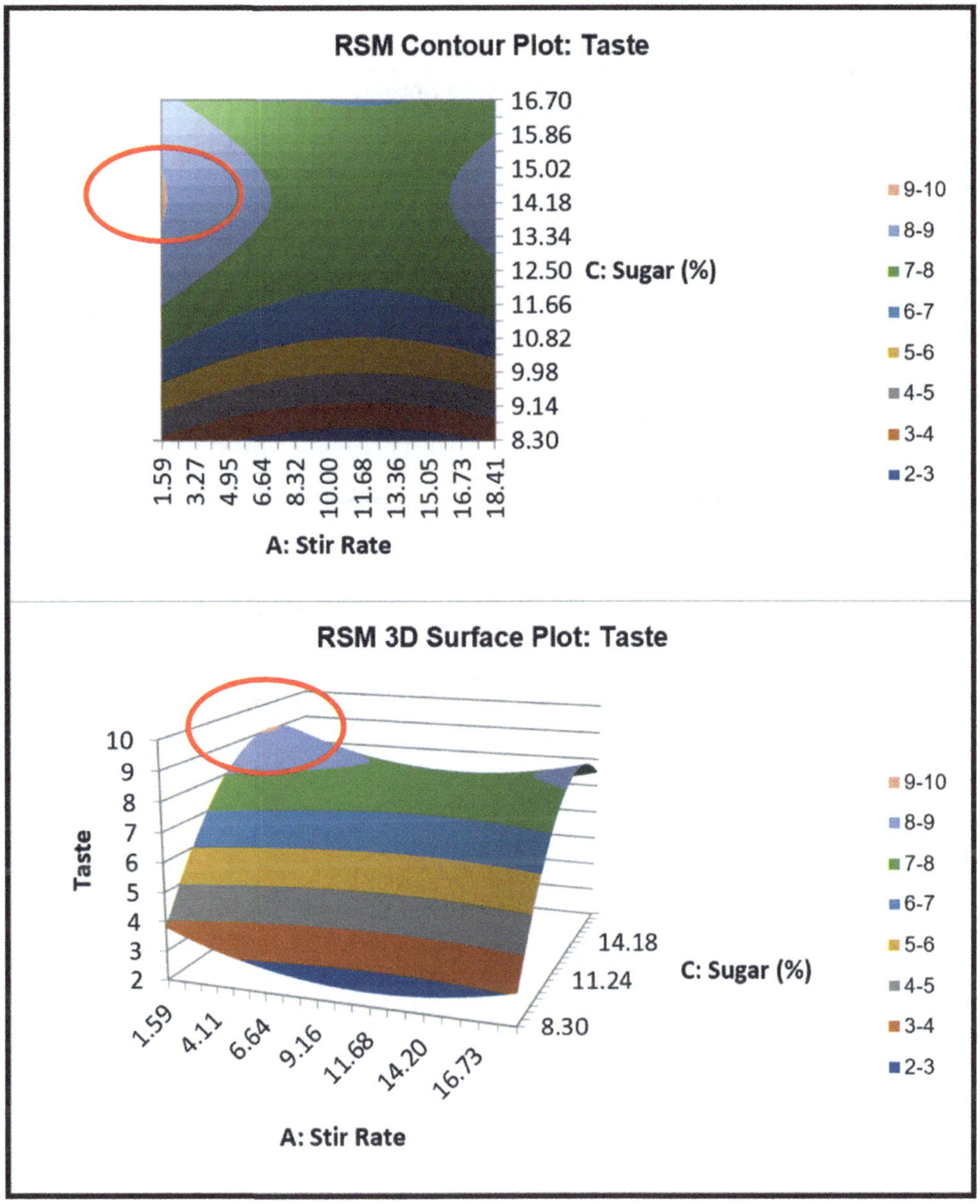

Repeat the procedure using the sheet for **% Clump**.

Contour/Surface Plots for % Clump

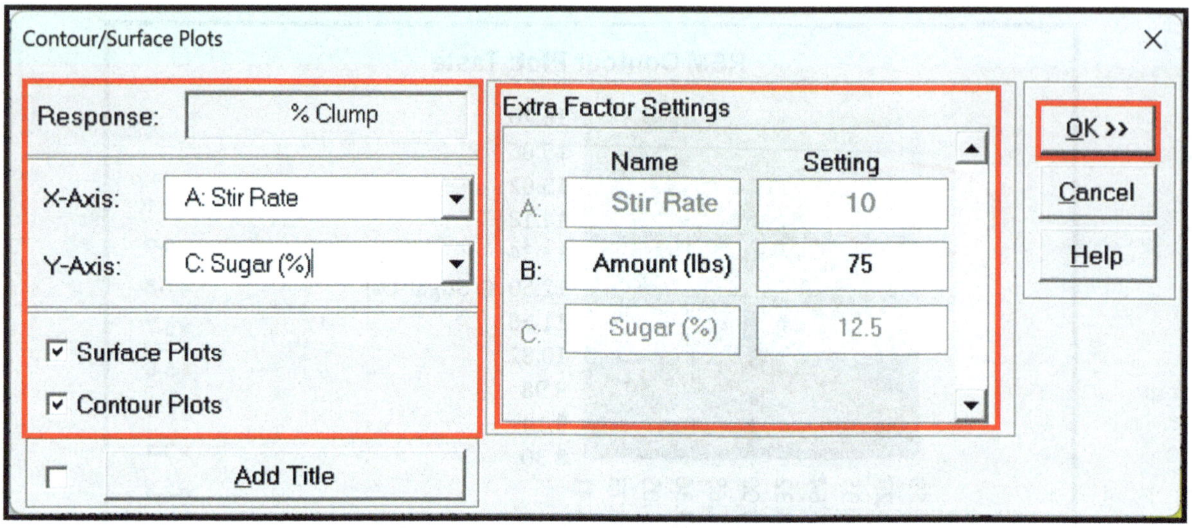

In this situation, the equation for % Clump uses all 3 factors. The Plots use only 2 factors. The operator has a choice as to which 2 factor to plot. The 3rd factor needs a set value for the equation. Choose a value within the experimental range. For this situation, multiple graphs can be created.

In this case, the two inputs are Stir Rate and Sugar %. The third factor, Amount (lbs) is set to 75.

Choose the options shown above, then click **OK**.

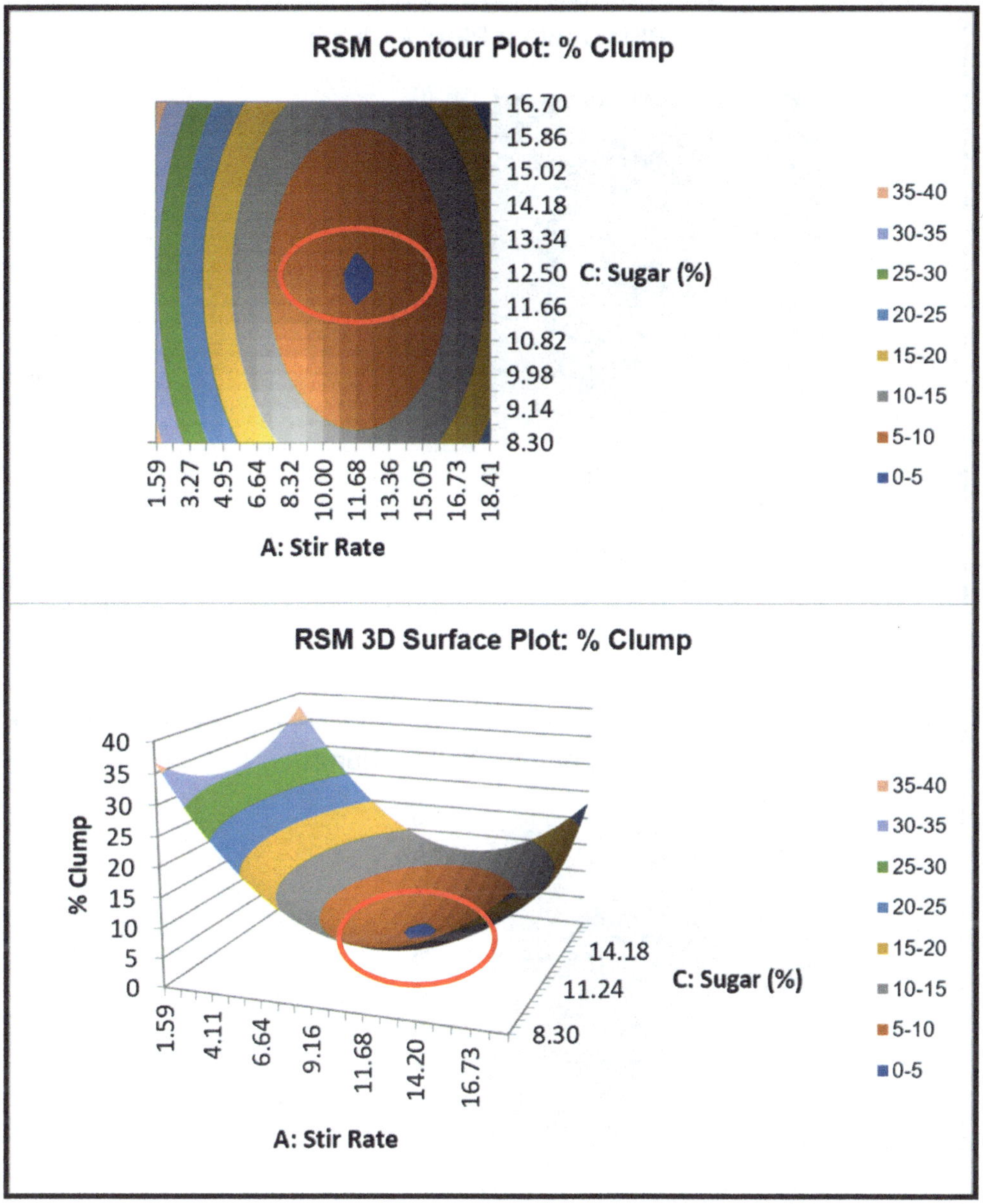

The graphs display shape referred to as a **Basin**. Less clumping is desirable, do run the settings at a Stir Rate of 11.5 and use a Sugar % of 12.5. These values are approximations.

What about other values of Amount (lbs)? Remember these graphs have this set to 75. Would the same graph occur at other values of Amount (lbs)?

Two additional graphs are shown, one with the Amount (lbs) set to 100, and the other with this value set to 50.

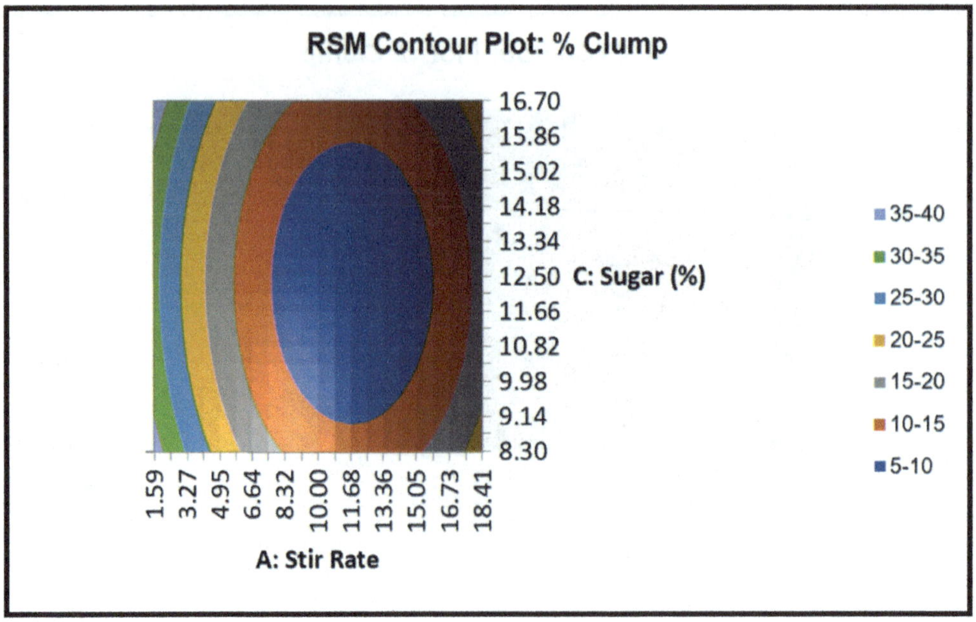

Amount (lbs) = 100

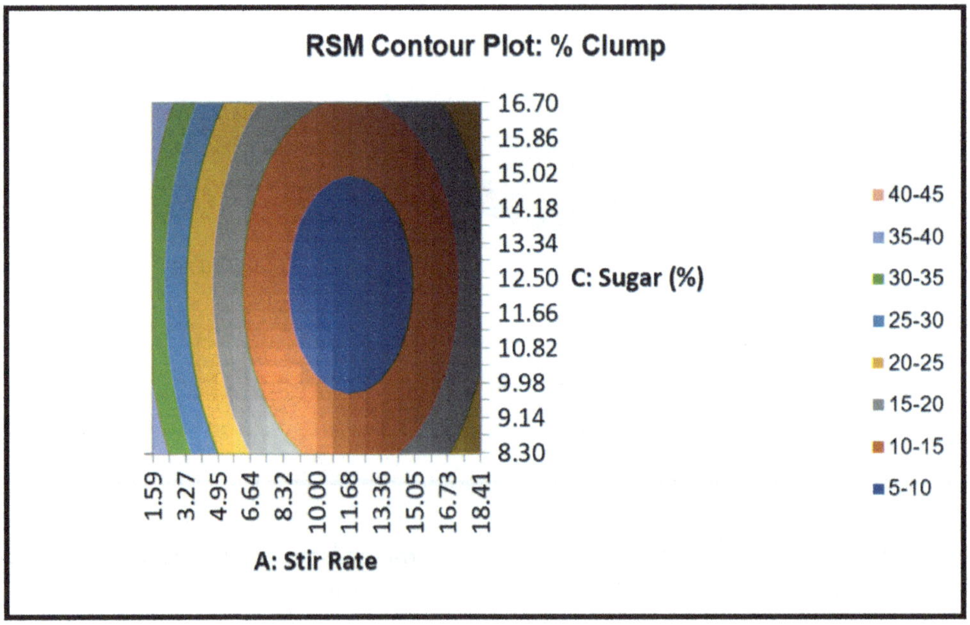

Amount (lbs) = 50

These two graphs are almost identical. The advantage they have over the first graph is the size of the Blue area. This is the area with the least % Clump.

Issue with Two Responses

For improvement in Taste, a lower Stir Rate is required, but this will increase the % Clump. Running at a Stir Rate around 11.5 will decrease Taste. So, what should be the Stir Rate? This is a Multiple Response issue.

SigmaXL's Multiple Response Optimizer will determine the parameter settings to obtain the best output for both responses. The procedure uses the Multiple Regressing function. The steps are;

Run the desired models for both outputs. (These are the reduced models from the DOE.)

Using the Multiple Regression results, activate the Multiple Response Optimizer.

Run verification runs to determine if the results are adequate.

Multiple Response Optimization

Tool Use: Use the Multiple Response Optimization tool in SigmaXL to obtain an estimate of the inputs that will produce the best value for all outputs. It is especially useful with multiple outputs (Y's), when trying to optimize one output may cause another to degrade.

Data Type: Input – Discrete or Continuous; Output – Numeric

Hint: *Before using the Multiple Response Optimization function in SigmaXL, it requires the use of the Fit Multiple Regression Model tool.*

SigmaXL Worksheet: ***Candy***

Create Regression Models

Menu command: ***SigmaXL > Statistical Tools > Advanced Multiple Regression > Fit Multiple Regression Model***

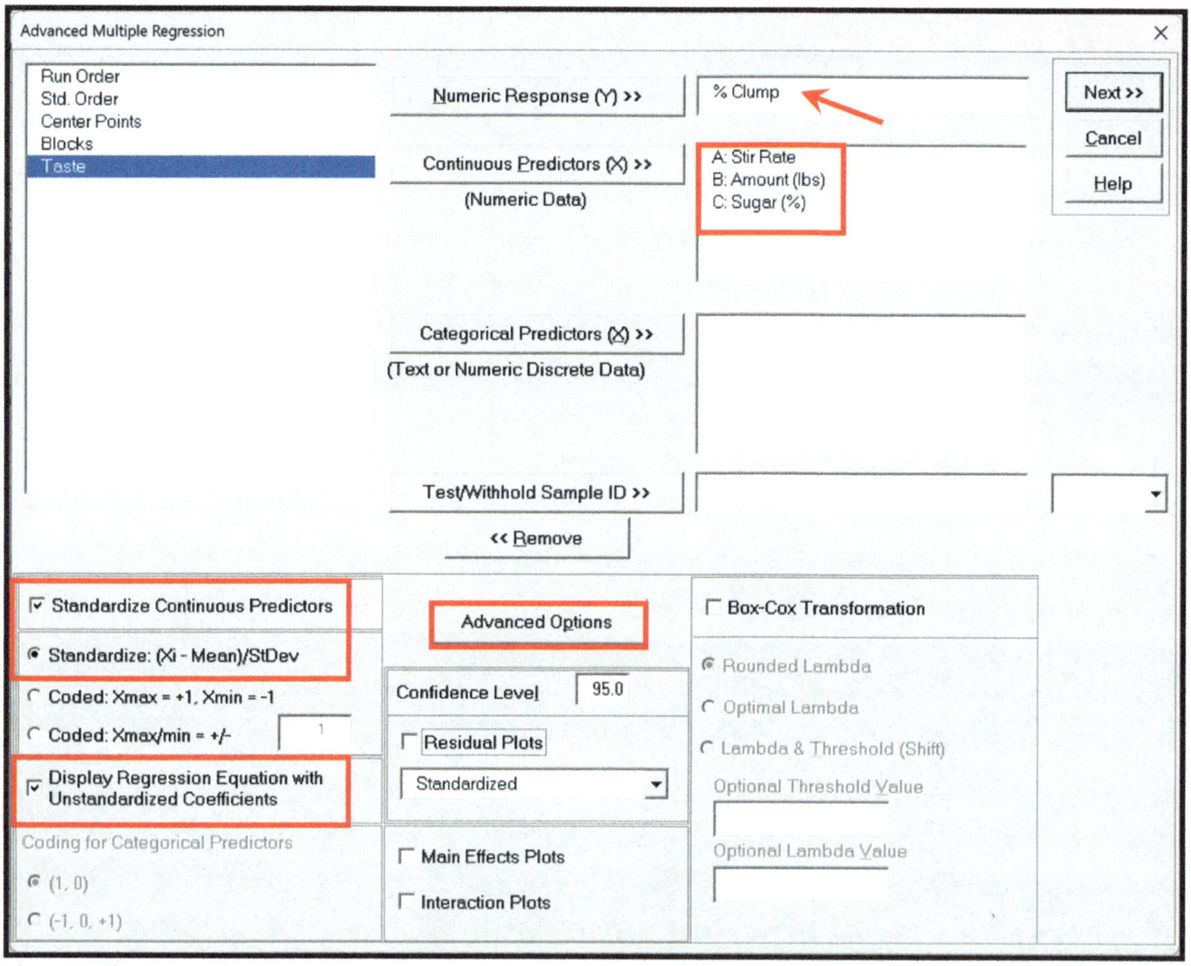

Select **% Clump** as the Numeric Response (Y). Choose the three main factors for Continuous Predictors (X). Check **Standardize Continuous Predictors** then choose **Standardize**. Check the **Display Regression Equation with Unstandardized Coefficients** option. Click **Advanced Options**.

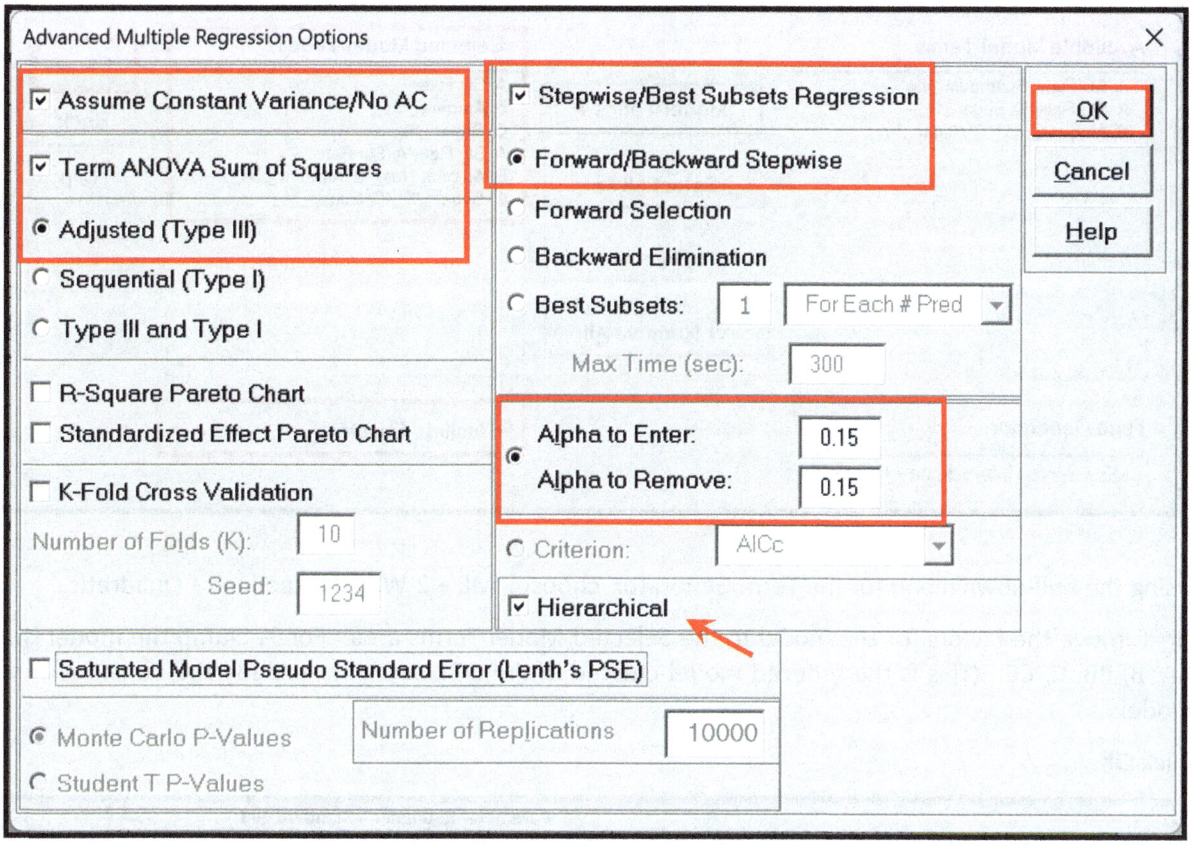

Select the options as shown;

Assume Constant Variance/No AC: Term ANOVA Sum of Squares: Adjusted (Type III).

Check Stepwise/Best Subsets Regression: Forward/Backward Stepwise.

Use a value of 0.15 for Alpha to Enter and Remove. Check the **Hierarchical** option.

De-select all other options. Click **OK**.

This will return the user to the Advanced Multiple Regression dialog box. Click **Next**.

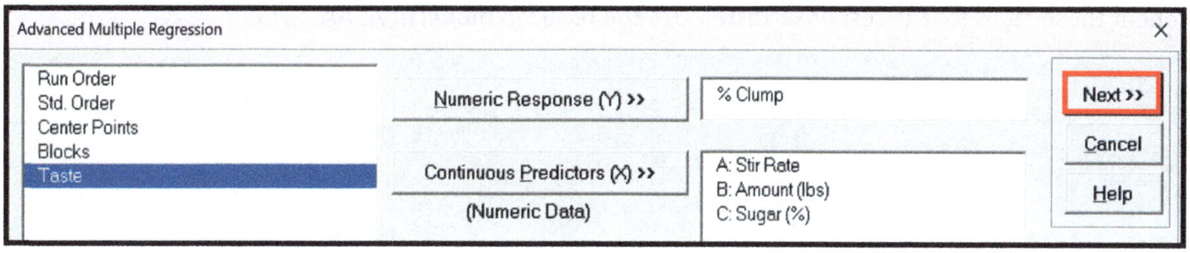

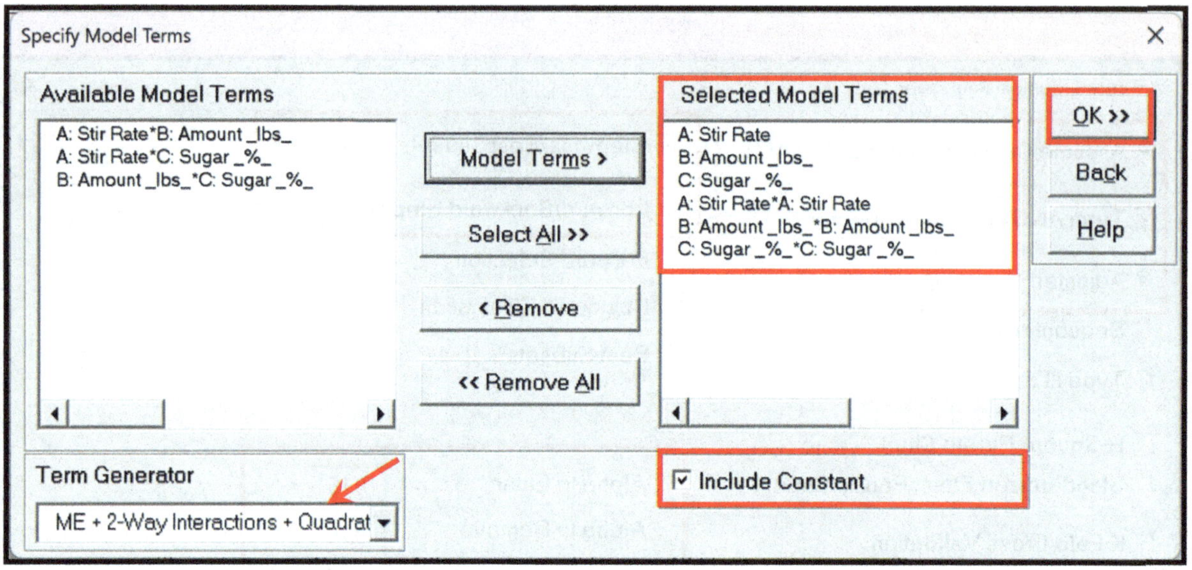

Using the pull-down menu for the Term Generator, choose; ME + 2-Way Interactions + Quadratic.

Next, move the factors for the model to the Selected Model Terms area. For % Clump the model is; A, AA, B, BB, C, CC. (This is the reduced model created in the DOE section). Include the Constant in the model.

Click **OK**.

Parameter Estimates - Standardized				
Predictor Term	**Coefficient**	**SE Coefficient**	**T**	**P**
Constant	5.629134517	0.992646888	5.6708	**0.0001**
A_ Stir Rate	-3.744486517	0.558366482	-6.7061	**0.0000**
B_ Amount _lbs_	-0.722382205	0.558366482	-1.2937	0.2183
C_ Sugar _%_	0.251134873	0.558366482	0.4498	0.6603
A_ Stir Rate*A_ Stir Rate	4.454128896	0.460831096	9.6654	**0.0000**
B_ Amount _lbs_*B_ Amount _lbs_	1.277532104	0.460831096	2.7722	**0.0158**
C_ Sugar _%_*C_ Sugar _%_	1.658723719	0.460831096	3.5994	**0.0032**

The results are the same as those found in the DOE analysis. This is the worksheet that will be used for the % Clump portion of the Multiple Response Optimization.

Return to the Candy worksheet.

Repeat these steps for the response Taste. Use the reduced model of A, AA, C, CC.

Multiple Response Optimizer tool:

Menu command: ***SigmaXL > Statistical Tools > Advanced Multiple Regression > Multiple Response Optimization***

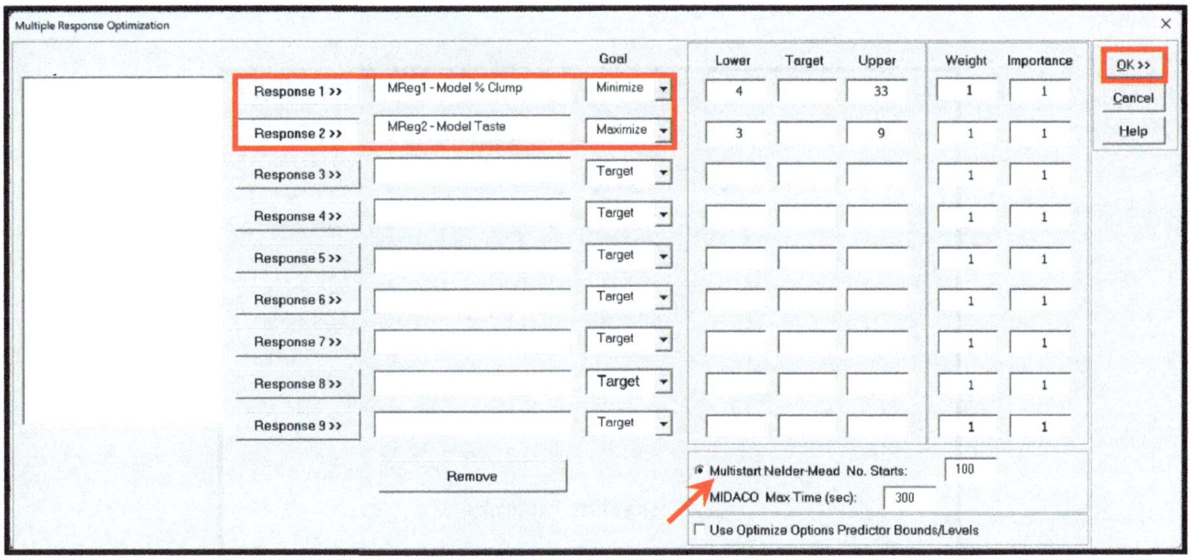

Select the **MReg Model** for each response. Determine the goal. For % Clump choose **Minimize**. For Taste select **Maximize**. The lower and upper value are automatically populated from the worksheet. These values can be manually changed. The target value is only used when the Goal is a Target value. Otherwise, leave it blank.

Leave the default **Multistart Nelder-Mead** option at 100.

The system will try to maximize a **Composite Desirability** value (**D**) to determine the best factor settings. It starts with **individual desirability** (**d**) values for each Response, based on the Weight setting. It then combines the individual desirability values using the Importance values.

The **Weight** and **Importance** information will be explained next.

Importance

The Importance value is a relative number indicating the importance of the multiple outputs to one another. The values range from .1 to 10; Responses with equal values have equal importance. The scale allows one Response to be up to 100 times as important as another (.1 versus 10).

Weight

The Weight value tells SigmaXL how to calculate the individual d value.

- .1 places more emphasis on the lower or upper values. (The d value increases rapidly once the lower or upper limits are crossed.)
- 1 gives equal emphasis to all values. (The d value increase linearly from the upper or lower threshold to the target value.)

- 10 places more emphasis on the target. (The d value remains small until the value approaches the target.)

Graphical representation of the Weight

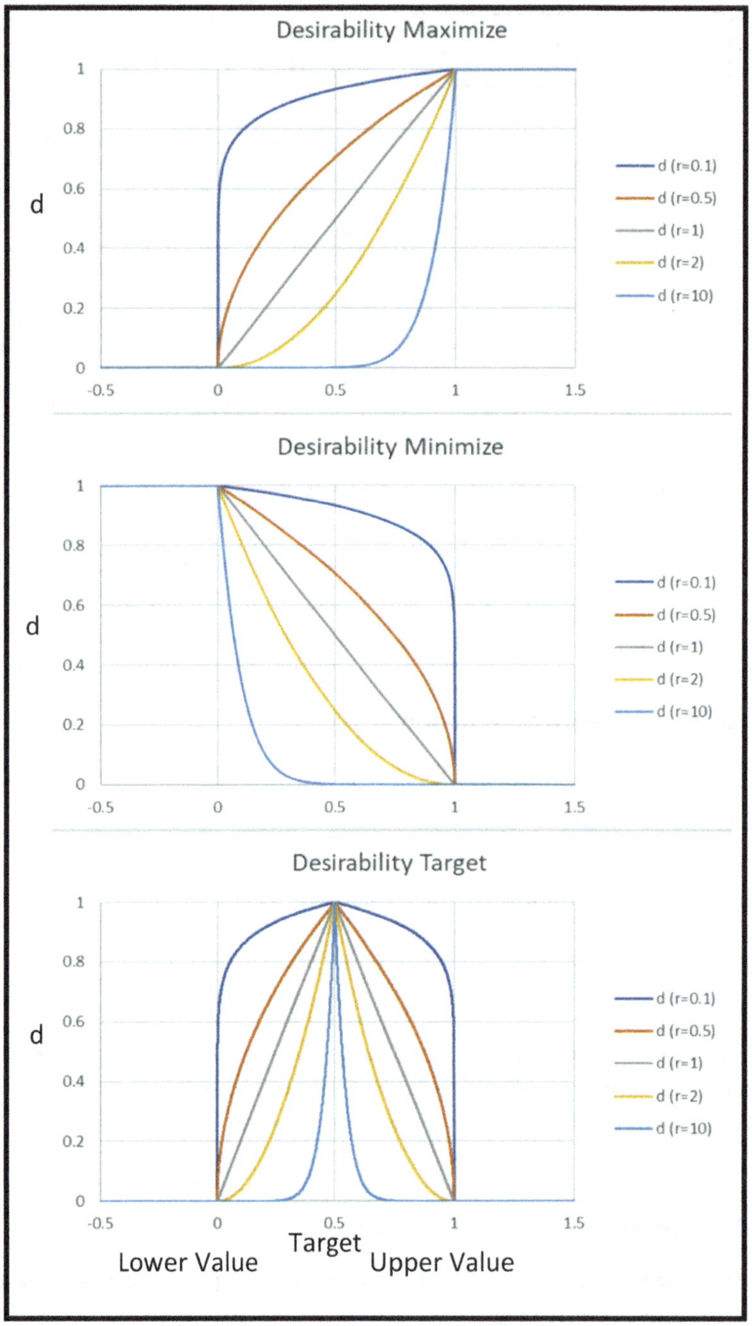

Click **OK** in the Response Optimizer window when complete.

Predictors	Settings:
A: Stir Rate	11.82764985
B: Amount _lbs_	81.00617094
C: Sugar _%_	13.72123787

The optimizer maximizes the desirability (d) value for each Y, and then combines all d values for all Y's to obtain a composite desirability value D. The larger the composite D, the closer the results are to satisfying the Y's goals.

The Optimizer produces a local (but not necessarily global) solution. Inputs can be varied to obtain a more desirable output. One method of doing this is to manually change the values of X's.

Go to the Edit Graph window and click the red **Cur** value under the factor to change its value. (For **Stir Rat** this is the value 11.7837).

Response	Goal	Predicted Response	SE
% Clump	Minimize	5.435938551	0.958655886
Taste	Maximize	7.688724526	0.191370739

Lower 95% CI	Upper 95% CI	Lower 95% PI	Upper 95% PI	Desirability
3.364888421	7.50698868	-0.215278039	11.08715514	0.950484878
7.280827452	8.096621601	6.416474091	8.960974961	0.781454088

Composite Desirability
0.861835421

Change to the desired value and click **OK**.

The red line moves to the new value and new outputs are shown.

This is the graph with updated settings (new Stir Rat of 11).

Planning Experiments

The critical step to achieving a successful result is proper planning for a Designed Experiment. Such planning should include discussion of the following:

- Outputs to be measured
- Factors to be investigated
- Design type
- Potential need for blocking
- Potential issues with training
- Potential issues with data collection

All of these issues should be thoroughly discussed and decisions finalized before proceeding to execution of the experiment.

Assuming planning and execution are properly conducted, it is still necessary to confirm results; this involves execution of confirmatory runs at conditions within the design space, but not necessarily at the axial or corner points. If the model does a good job of predicting results, then the model can be used. If it does not, then further experimentation is required.

Conclusion:

The Improve phase uses both graphical and analytical tools to determine the relationship between critical X's and Y's. This provides the necessary information to shift the team's emphasis from controlling the Y's to controlling the X's.

Control Phase

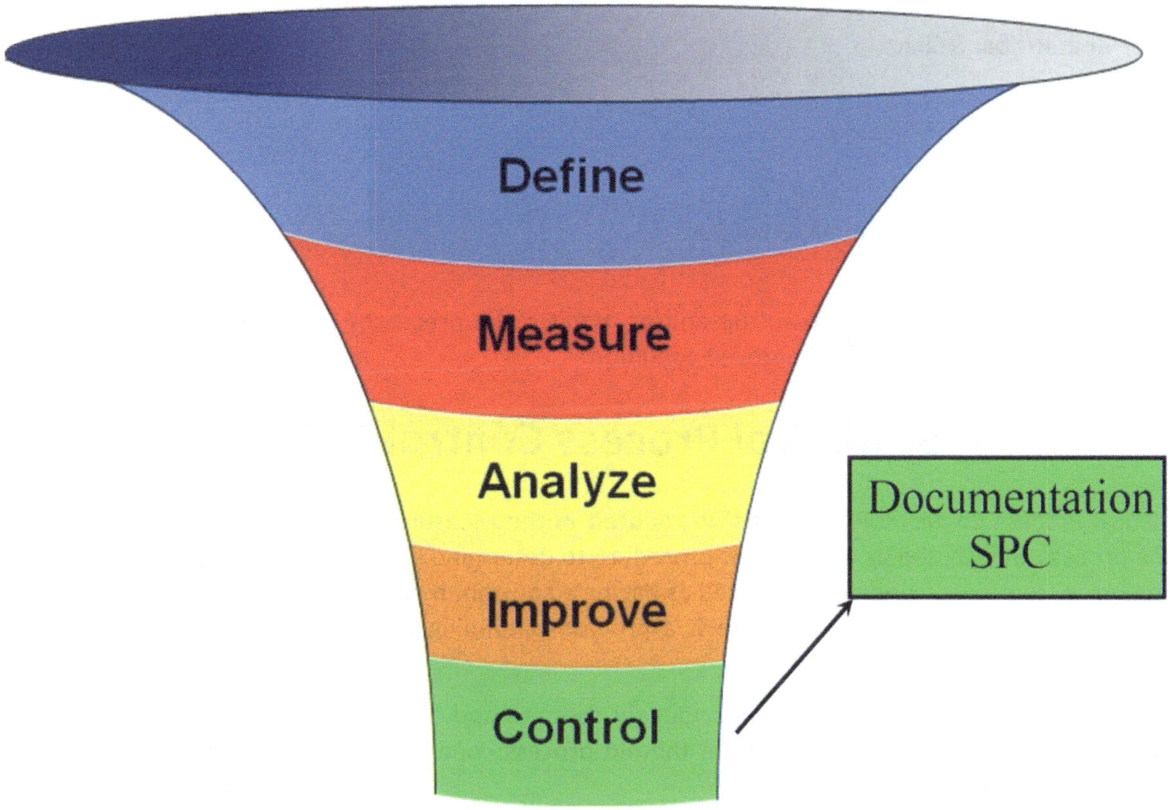

Control Phase

The Control phase of a Six Sigma process is the last step, but is by no means any less important than any of the others. In fact, it is the critical step necessary to ensure improvements achieved throughout the process are maintained over the long-term. Without an effective Control phase, the process will lose any gains made and inevitably slip back to the initial baseline condition.

Tools and Outcomes

During the Control phase teams set up the control charts and tools necessary for proper Statistical Process Control (SPC). A few examples include:

- I-MR Chart
- Xbar R/Xbar S Chart
- P Chart
- NP Chart
- C Chart
- U Chart
- Process Capability – Non-Normal Data
- Distribution Curves

All of these tools are designed to set up and/or monitor the processes and procedures necessary to maintain a process in its new and improved condition.

Statistical Process Control (SPC)

Statistical Process Control (SPC) was first introduced in the Measure chapter. At that point in the Six Sigma process, SPC is used as a diagnostic procedure to determine if a process is running in a controlled condition. A controlled condition is defined as having a constant mean and a standard deviation. In the Control phase SPC is used to determine if a process is running in a controlled condition and as a predictive tool.

When setting up control charts, it is important for samples and data to reflect the process in its new, improved condition. Never use data from the old process condition because it will contaminate the control chart findings.

Another common mistake occurs when control charts are constantly recalculated and updated using the most recent data available, rather than the new baseline data collected when the improved process was first stabilized. If the control limits are continually updated using new data, there is a risk of missing key signs of subtle changes in either the mean or the standard deviation.

The best approach is to collect 25 to 30 samples from the process once it is improved and stabilized, and then use that data to calculate control limits. From that point forward, all efforts focus on maintaining the process within those limits. The only time to recalculate control limits is when a change occurs in the process itself.

The examples presented in this chapter all assume the process in question is improved and stable. The overall concepts discussed are applicable to any type of control chart.

Control Charts for Continuous Data

Individual Moving Range Chart (I-MR Chart)

Worksheet: ***Cycle Time***

In an earlier section it was demonstrated how to construct and analyze an SPC chart. In this section, it will be shown how to set the Control Limits while constructing SPC charts.

Menu command: ***SigmaXL > Control Charts > Individuals & Moving Range***

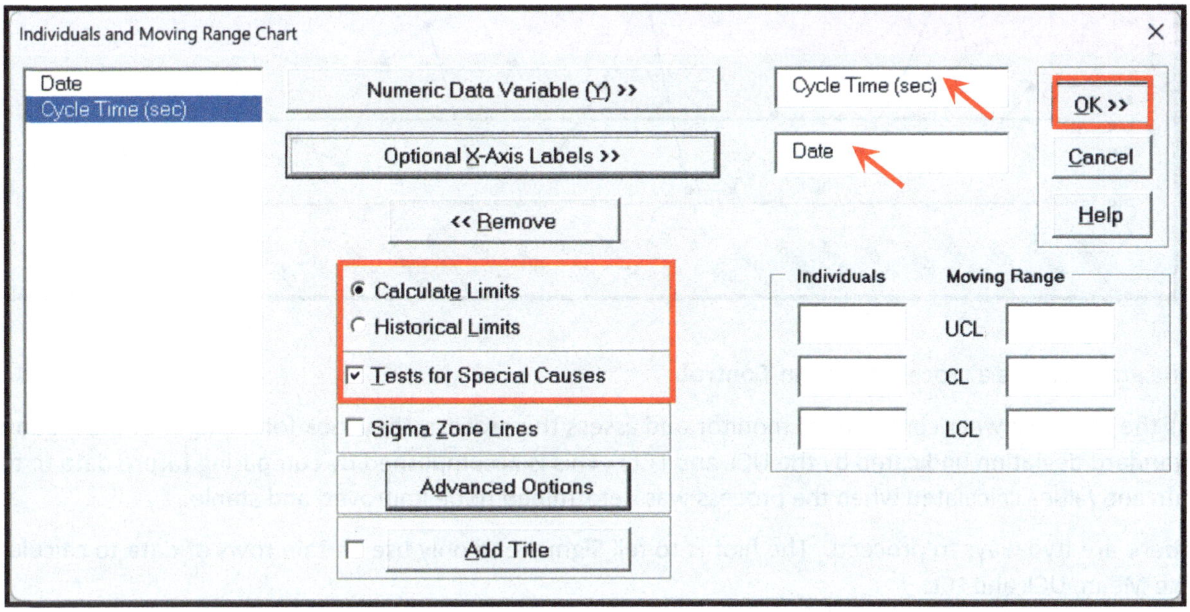

Select **Cycle Time (sec)** as the Numeric Data Variable (Y), and **Date** for the Optional X-Axis Labels.

Choose Calculate Limits and Tests for Special Causes. Click OK.

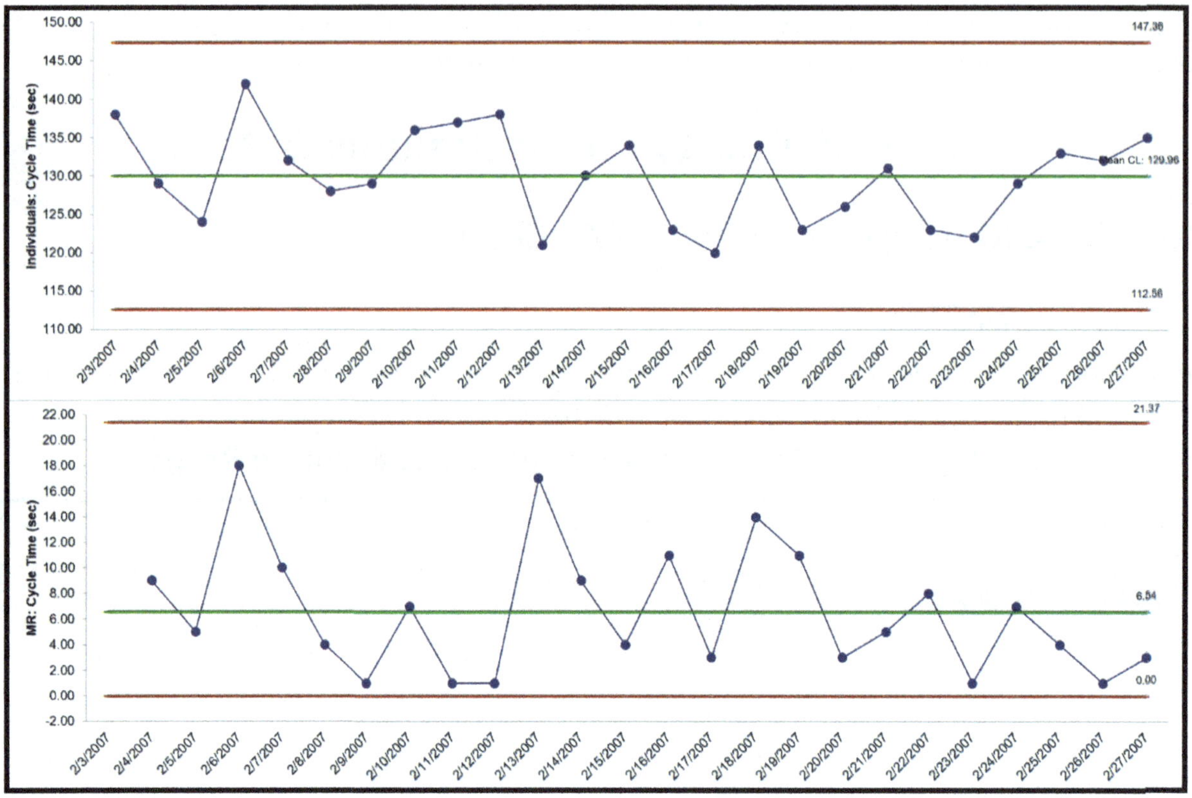

The graph shows a process that is **In-Control**.

As the process owner continues to monitor and assess the process, they look for changes in the mean or standard deviation (indicated by the UCL and LCL). This is accomplished by comparing future data to the current values calculated when the process was determined to be improved and stable.

There are two ways to proceed. The first is to tell SigmaXL to only use certain rows of data to calculate the Mean, UCL and LCL.

Select Worksheet: ***Cycle Time 2***

This worksheet contains the initial 25 data points plus 20 additional data points, for a total of 45 points.

Menu command: ***SigmaXL > Control Charts > Individuals & Moving Range***

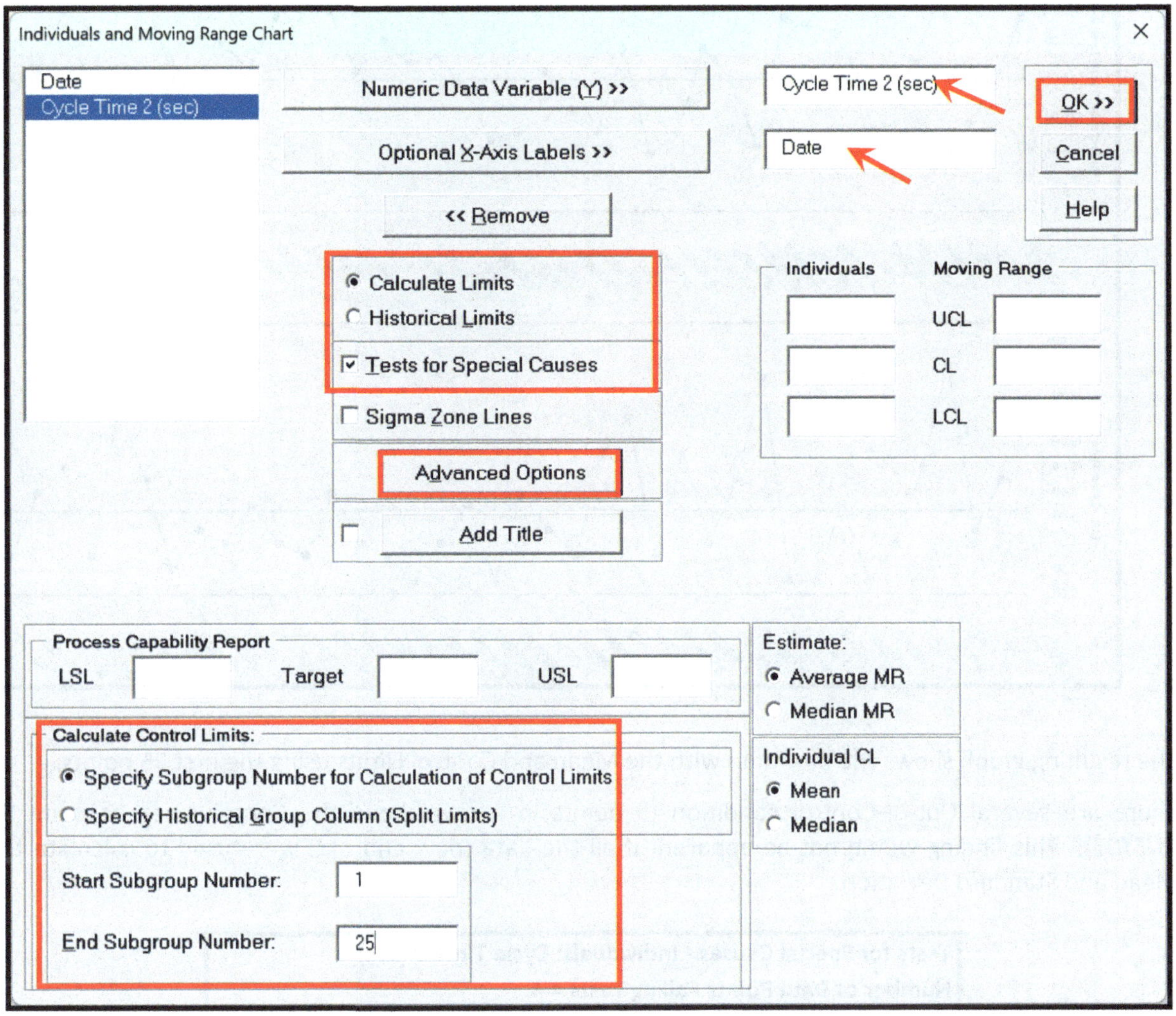

Select **Cycle Time 2 (sec)** as the Numeric Data Variable (Y), and **Date** for the Optional X-Axis Labels.

Choose **Calculate Limits** and **Tests for Special Causes**. Click **Advanced Options.** The lower portion of the Dialog box appears. Under Calculate Control Limits, choose **Specify Subgroup Number for Calculation of Control Limits**. Type **1** for Start Subgroup Number, and **25** for End Subgroup Numbers. These are the values from the previous chart. The 20 new values will not be used in the calculations. Click **OK**.

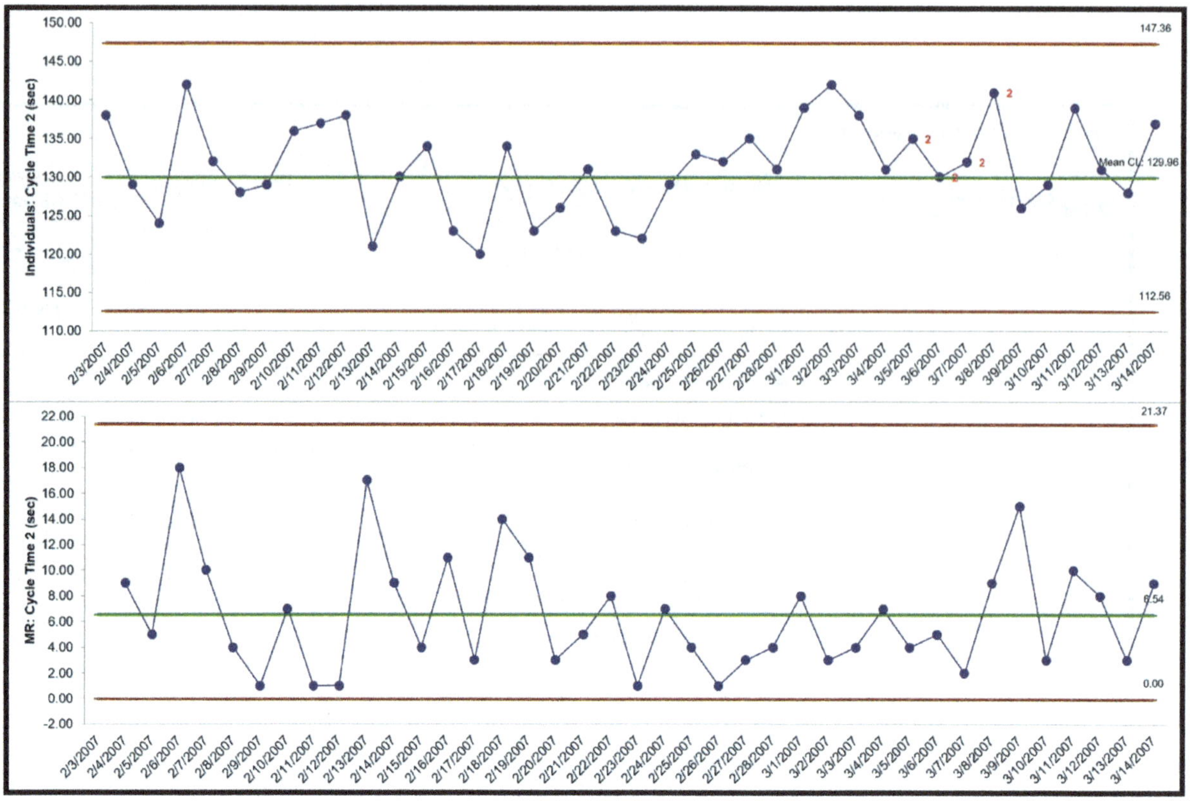

The resulting graph shows the new data with the Mean and Control Limits using the first 25 points.

There are several Out-of-Control condition (9 points in a row above the Center Line). at point 31 (3/5/07). This finding would not be apparent if all the data (new and old) were used to calculate the Mean and Standard Deviation.

Tests for Special Causes - Individuals: Cycle Time 2 (sec)
Number of Data Points Failing Tests = 4

Observation No.	Test 1: 1 point more than 3 StDev from CL	Test 2: 9 points in a row on same side of CL
31		x
32		x
33		x
34		x

If all points had been used to create the Control Chart, a different Mean, UCL and LCL would have been created. The following chart was created using all 45 data points to calculate the Limits.

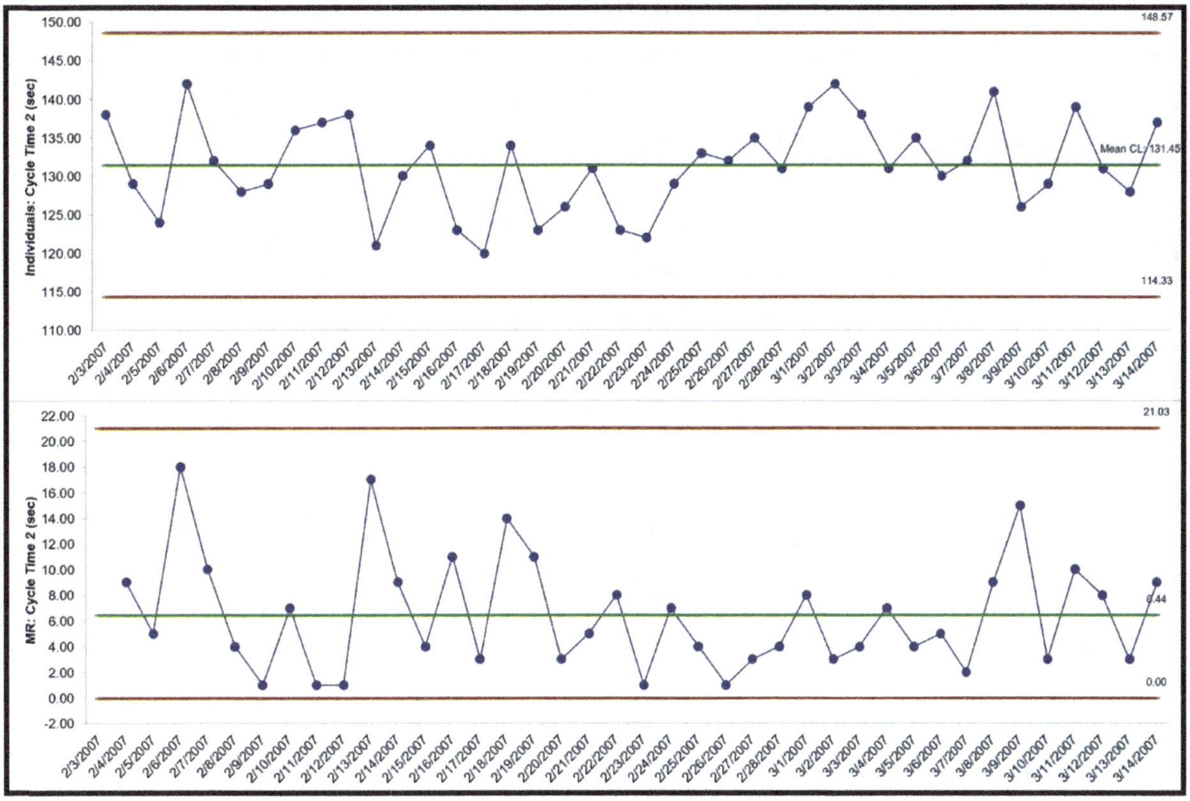

In this situation, no Out-of-Control points are indicated. This is the result of an increase in the Mean values from the last 20 data points. The first graph showing the Out-of-Control points indicates the process has experienced a slight shift during the last 20 runs compared to the first 25.

The second method is to capture the values for the Mean, UCL and LCL for both the Individuals and Moving Range charts, then input them into the dialog box.

From the original graph, the values were;

Individuals Chart: Mean (CL) = 129.96, UCL = 147.36, LCL = 112.56 (values are rounded to 2 decimal places.

Moving Range Chart: Mean (CL) = 6.54, UCL = 21.37, LCL = 0.

Return to the **Cycle Time 2** worksheet.

Menu command: ***SigmaXL > Control Charts > Individuals & Moving Range***

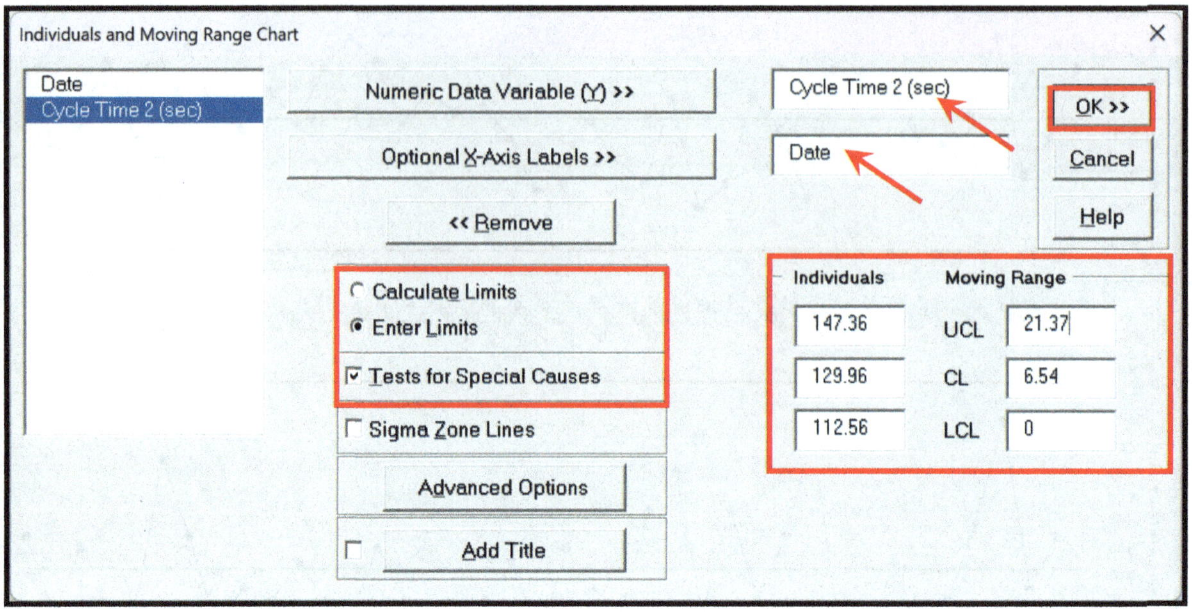

Select **Cycle Time 2 (sec)** as the Numeric Data Variable (Y), and **Date** for the Optional X-Axis Labels. Choose **Tests for Special Causes**. Enter the information under Individuals and Moving Range.

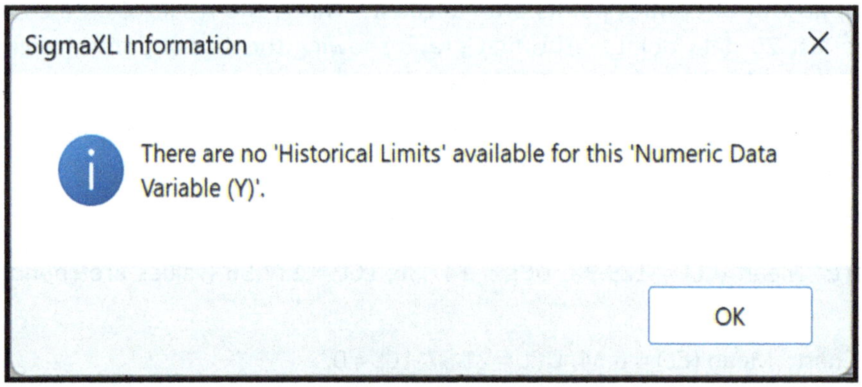

NOTE: When beginning to input the values, a warning will appear:

Click **OK** and continue with inputting the values.

The final chart appears with the Mean and Control Limits specified.

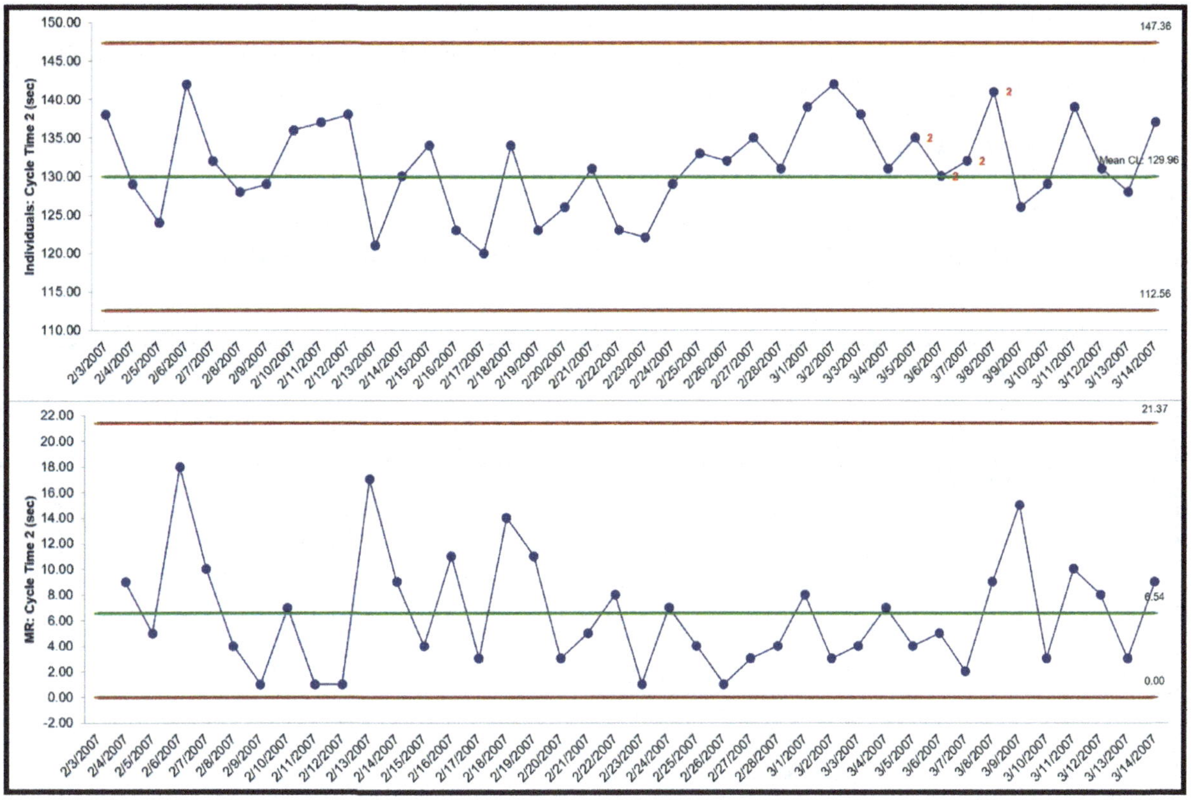

XBar-R Chart

If output data is collected as a series of subgroups (more than one item at a time) the appropriate chart to determine stability is the Xbar–R or Xbar–S.

Worksheet: ***Xbar Example***

Menu command:

SigmaXL > Control Charts > Variables Charts for Subgroups > Xbar-R

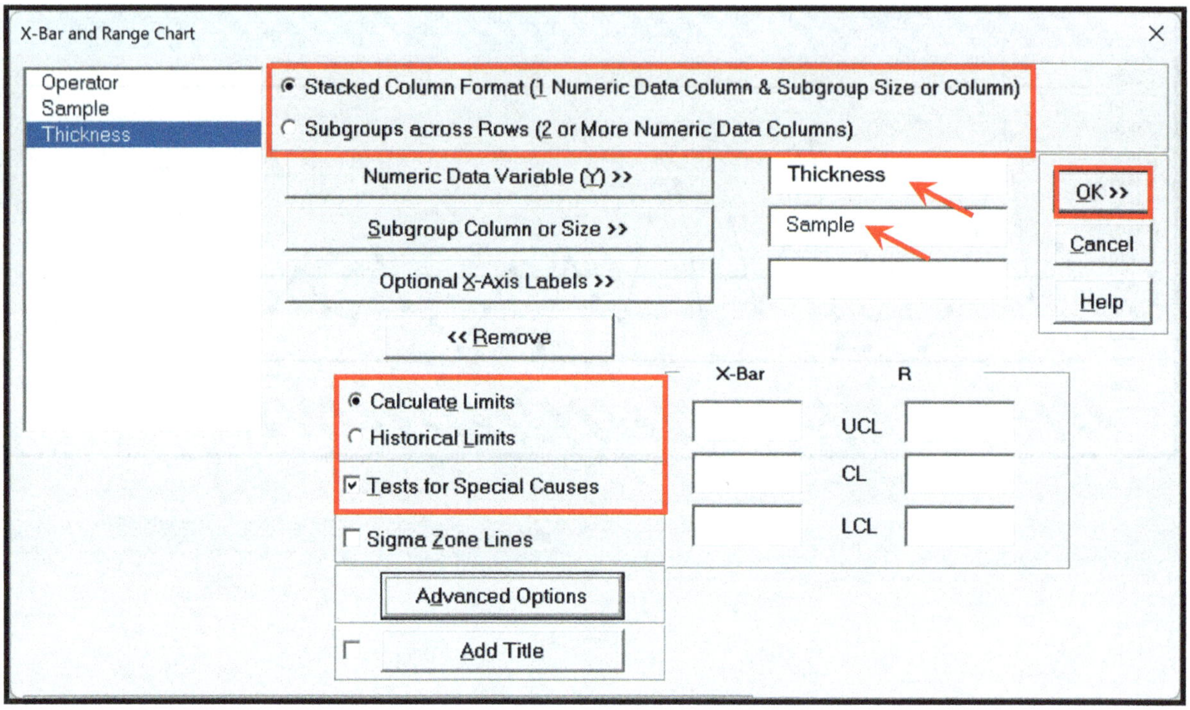

Choose Stacked Column Format, Input **Thickness** for the Numeric Data Variable (Y).

For the Subgroup Column or Size use **Sample**. As an alternative, the number **3** could be inserted.

Keep the Calculate Limits and Tests for Special Causes options. Click OK.

The graphs show one Out-of-Control Point.

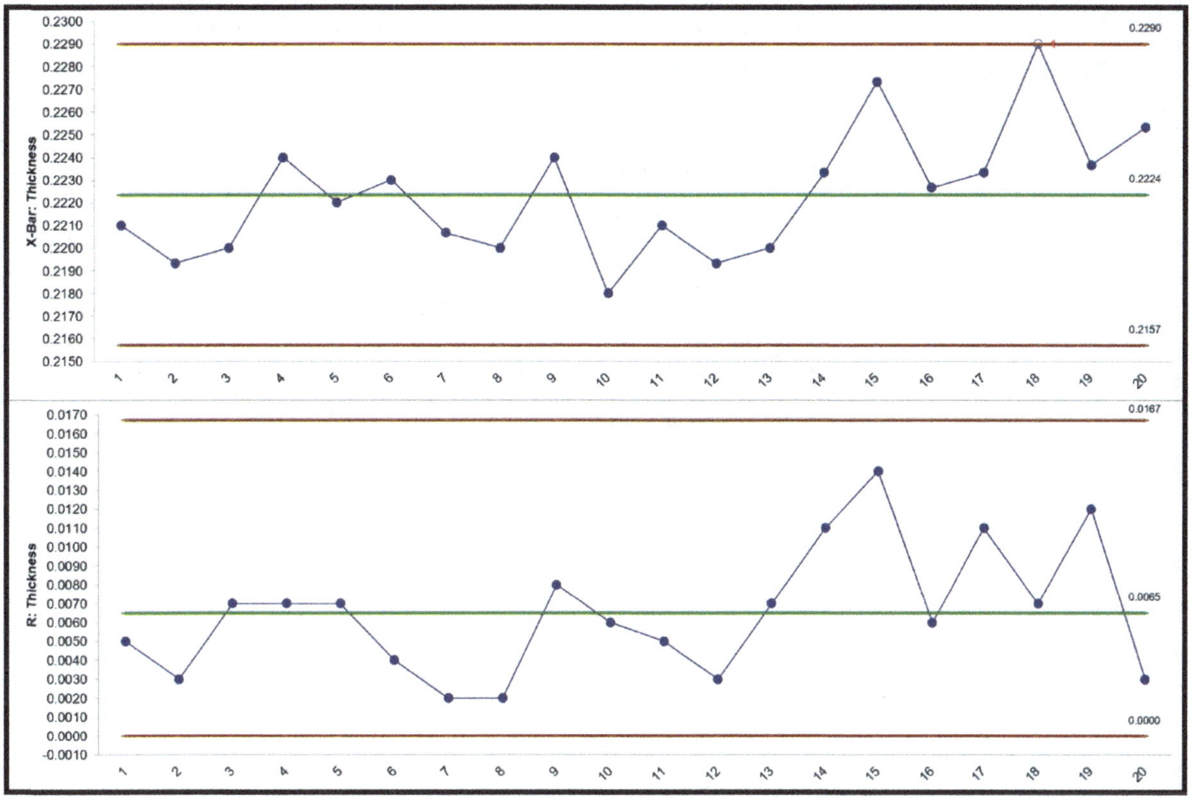

Tests for Special Causes - X-Bar: Thickness Number of Data Points Failing Tests = 1	
Observation No.	**Test 1: 1 point more than 3 StDev from CL**
18	**x**

The Out-of-Control point occurs at observation 18.

Just as with an I-MR chart, any issues with special causes should be investigated.

In this graph the last 7 points are above the mean.

This does not violate the official rule of 9 or more points on one side of the mean, but it is suspect.

Observing the worksheet, notice that the first ten subgroups were measured by one operator and the next ten were measured by a different operator. It might be interesting to see the differences between the operators. SigmaXL will create side-by-side graphs displaying information from each operator.

Return to the **Xbar Example** worksheet.

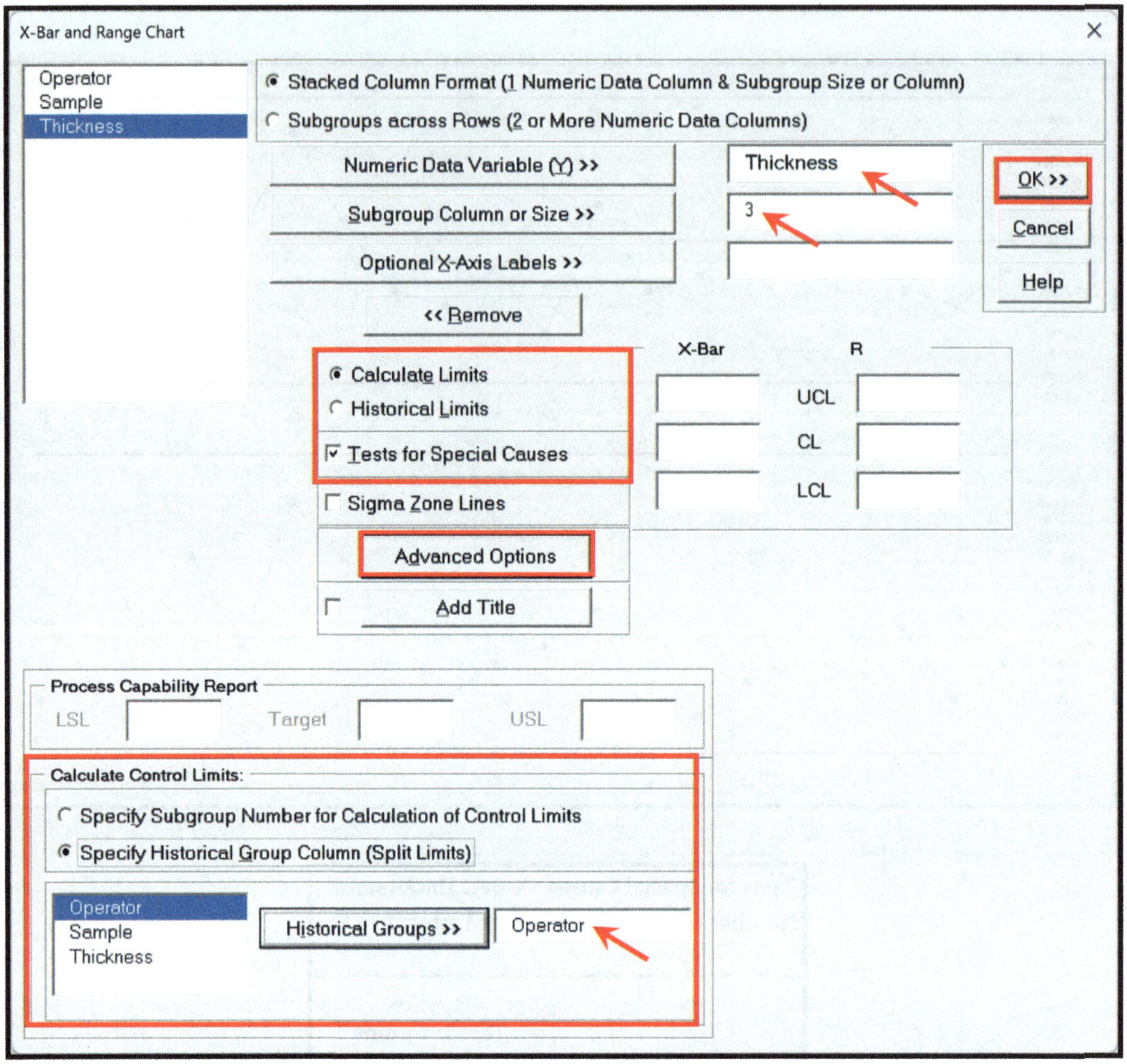

Keep the **Stacked Column Format**, and input the Numeric Data Variable (Y) as **Thickness**. Input the value **3** for Subgroup Column or Size.

Maintain the options of **Calculate Limits** and **Tests for Special Causes**. Click **Advanced Options**. The lower portion of the Dialog box opens. Choose; **Specify Historical Group Column (Split Limits)**. For the Historical Groups, select **Operator**.

Click **OK**.

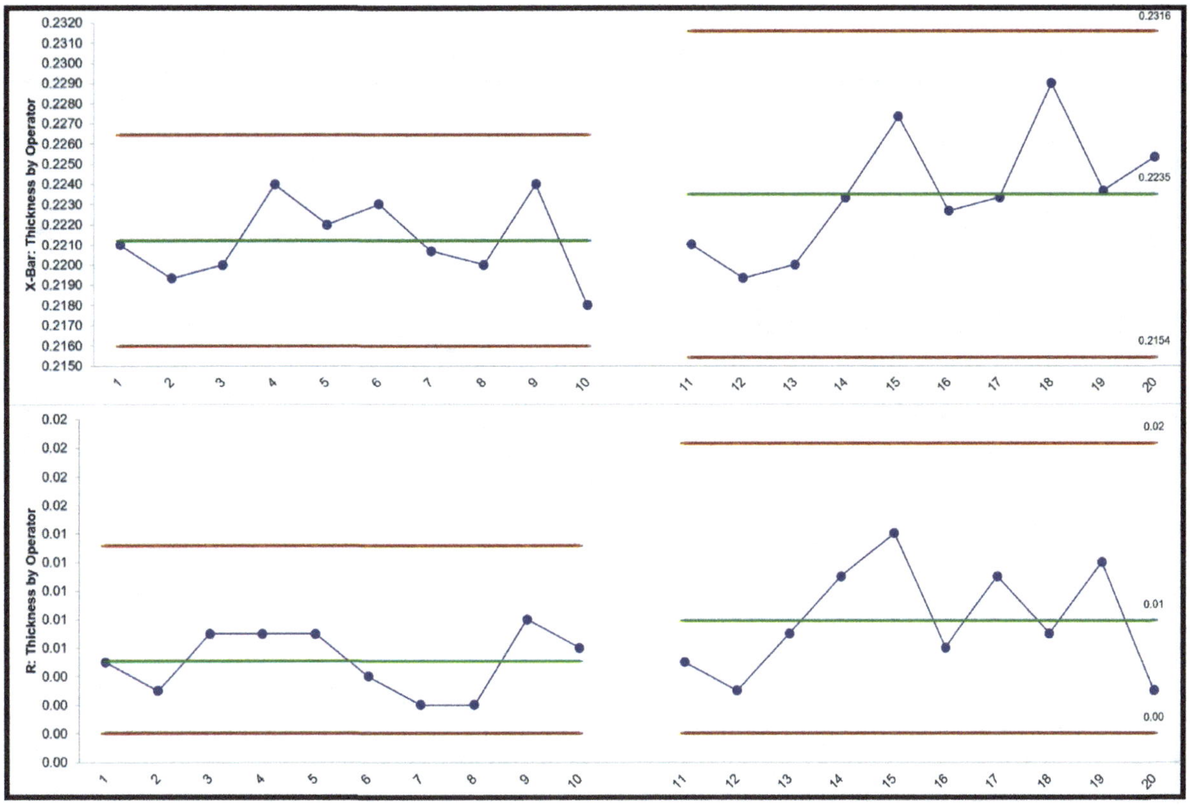

Each Group is displayed with its associated control limits. This type of graph is useful to answer questions such as, "Are differences seen in the output related to different Group variables?"

The graphs on the right have the limits listed.

> ***Hint:*** *The Control Limits for the graphs on the right are listed. To obtain the limits for the graphs on the left, hover the cursor over the line. The value will be displayed.*

The value for the Upper Control Limits is listed as 0.226417637.

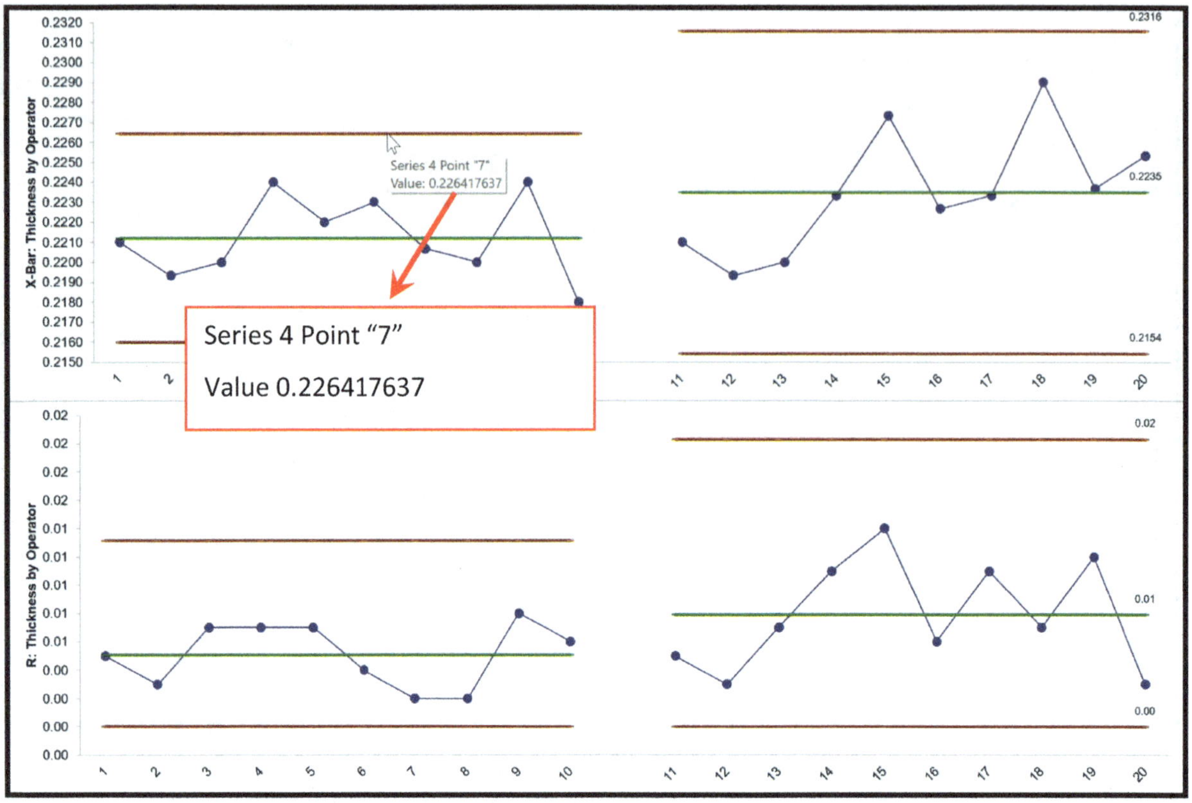

XBar-S Chart

The Xbar S is an alternative to the Xbar – R. In the Xbar S, the standard deviation is estimated using the subgroups average standard deviation. The remaining aspects of the chart remain unchanged.

Menu command: ***SigmaXL > Control Charts > Xbar & S***

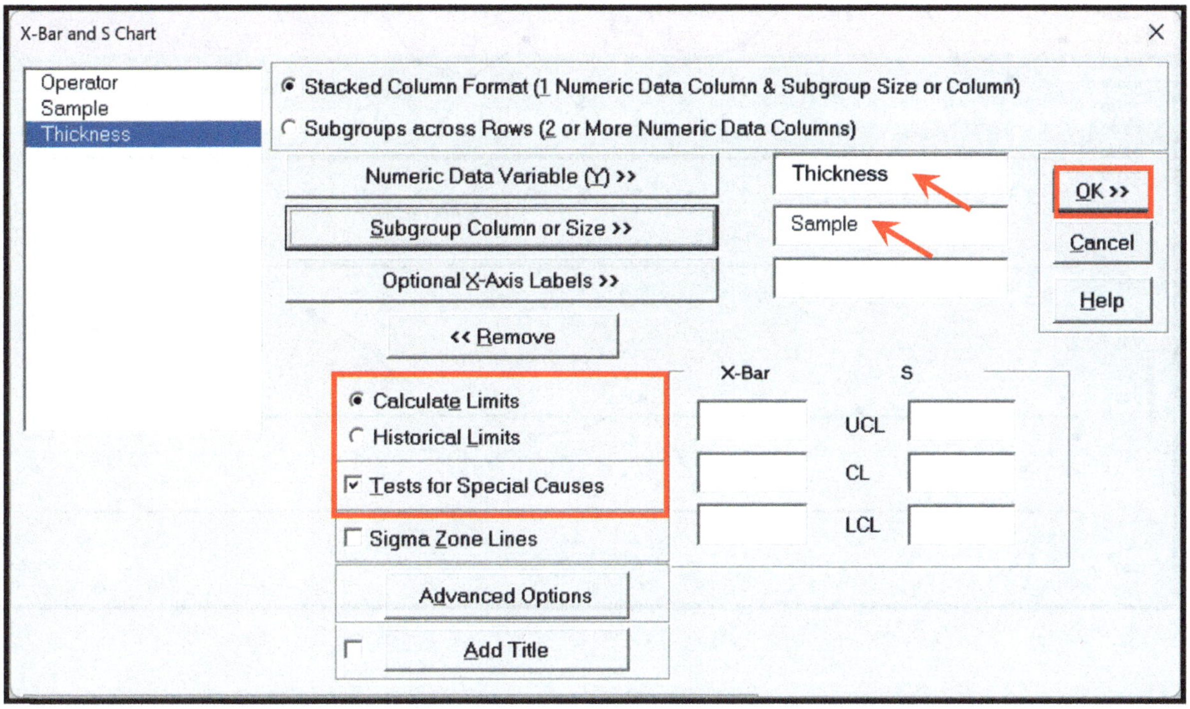

Input **Thickness** as the Numeric Data Variable (Y), and select **Sample** as the Subgroup Column or Size.

Keep, Calculate Limits and Tests for Special Causes. Click OK.

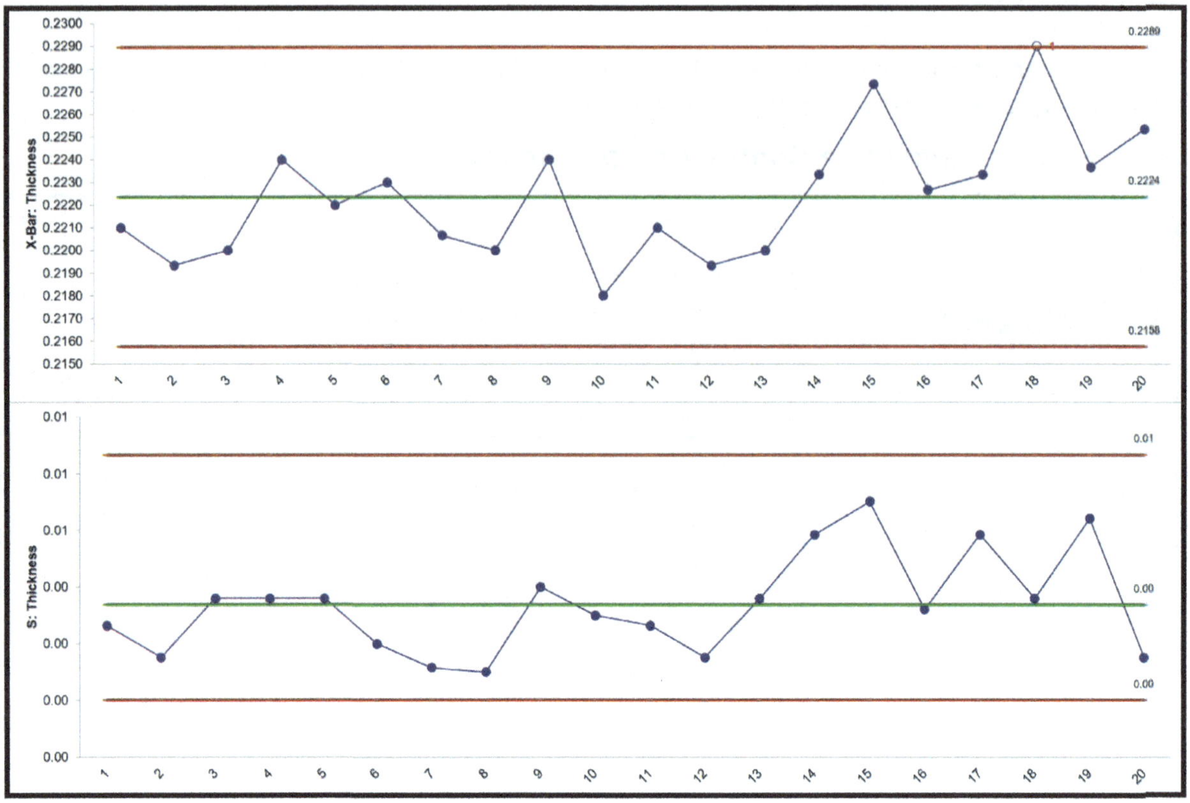

The graph looks very similar to the Xbar & R chart. But now, the lower chart is measuring the standard

Hint: When is it appropriate to use the Xbar & R versus the Xbar & S? It really depends on the specific circumstances. Six Sigma references claim the Range calculation is efficient up to a sample size of 7, and recommend using the Standard Deviation calculation with sample sizes larger than 7.

deviation of the subgroups, not the range.

Control Charts for Attribute Data

Attribute data is generally measured in terms of Defects or Defectives. For Defects, use the C or U chart; for Defectives, use the P or NP chart.

P Chart

This chart plots the samples percent defective, which is used as an estimate of the population's percent defective.

Worksheet: ***P Chart***

Menu command: ***SigmaXL > Control Charts > Attributes Charts > P***

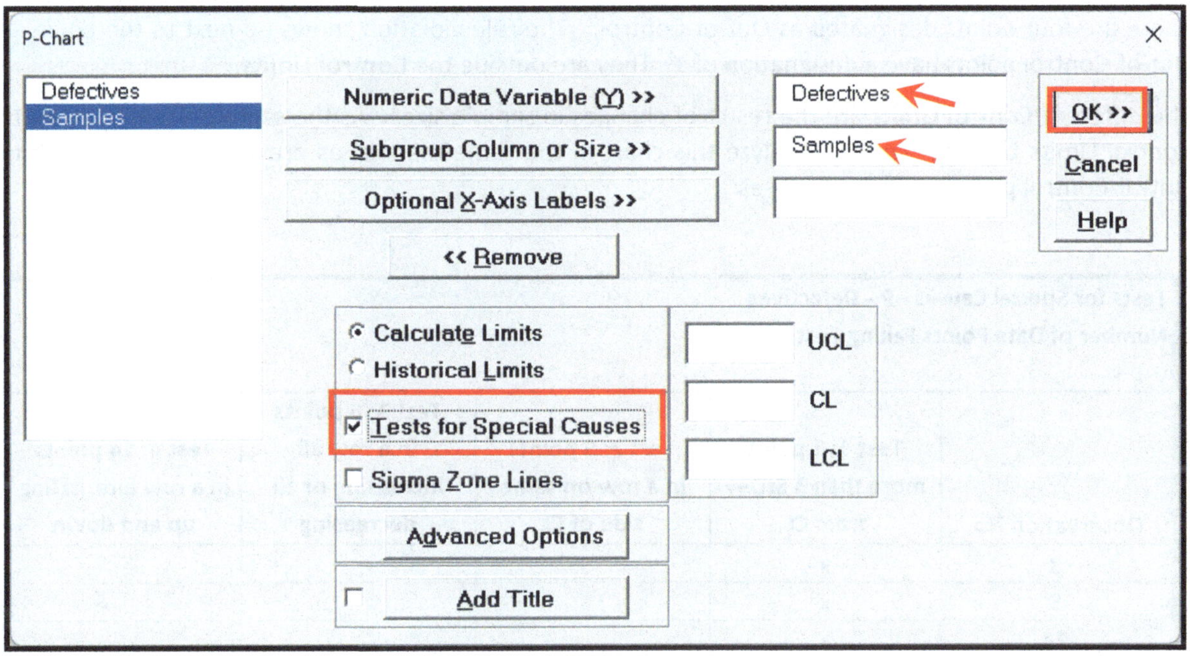

Select **Defectives** as the Variable. Use the column **Samples** for Subgroup Size. Choose **Tests for Special Causes**. Click **OK**.

Hint: Attribute Control Charts use only *4 tests.*

1. Point outside a Control Limit.
2. Nine (9) points in a row on the same side of the Center Line.
3. Six (6) points in a row either increasing, or decreasing.
4. Fourteen (14) points in a row alternating up and down.

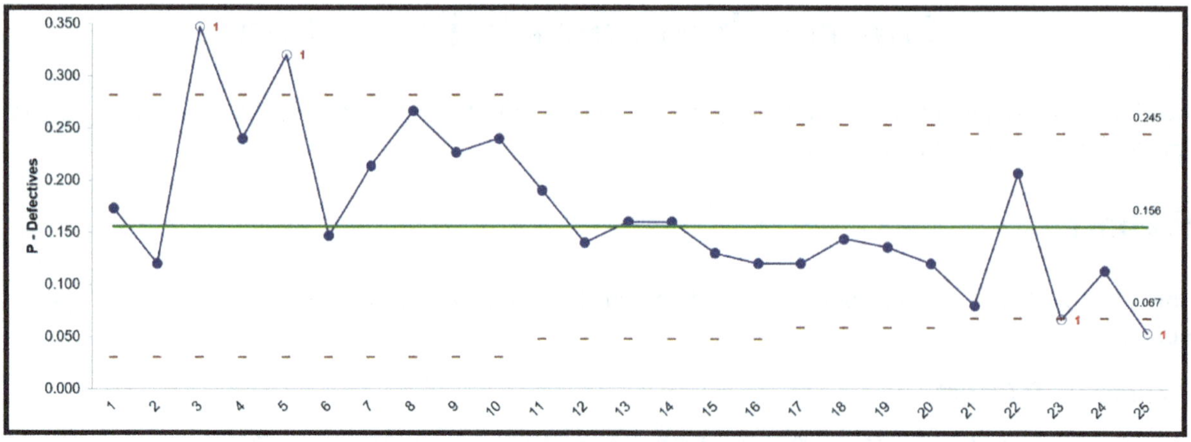

There are four points designated as Out-of-Control. The rule violation shows up next to the point. All Out-of-Control points have a designation of 1. They are outside the **Control Limits**.

The different **Control Limits** are the result of changes in sample sizes. As the sample size increases, the Control Limits become tighter. Analyze this chart in the same manner as previous charts. Check the Out-of-Control points for special causes.

Tests for Special Causes - P - Defectives
Number of Data Points Failing Tests = 4

Observation No.	Test 1: 1 point more than 3 StDev from CL	Test 2: 9 points in a row on same side of CL	Test 3: 6 points in a row all increasing or all decreasing	Test 4: 14 points in a row alternating up and down
3	x			
5	x			
23	x			
25	x			

A listing of the Out-of-Control conditions are displayed below the graph.

All four of the flagged points failed for Test 1; Point being outside the Control Limit.

The Test criteria can be changed using the following method.

While in the P Chart (1) tab, select;

SigmaXL > Control Charts > 'Tests for Special Causes' Defaults.

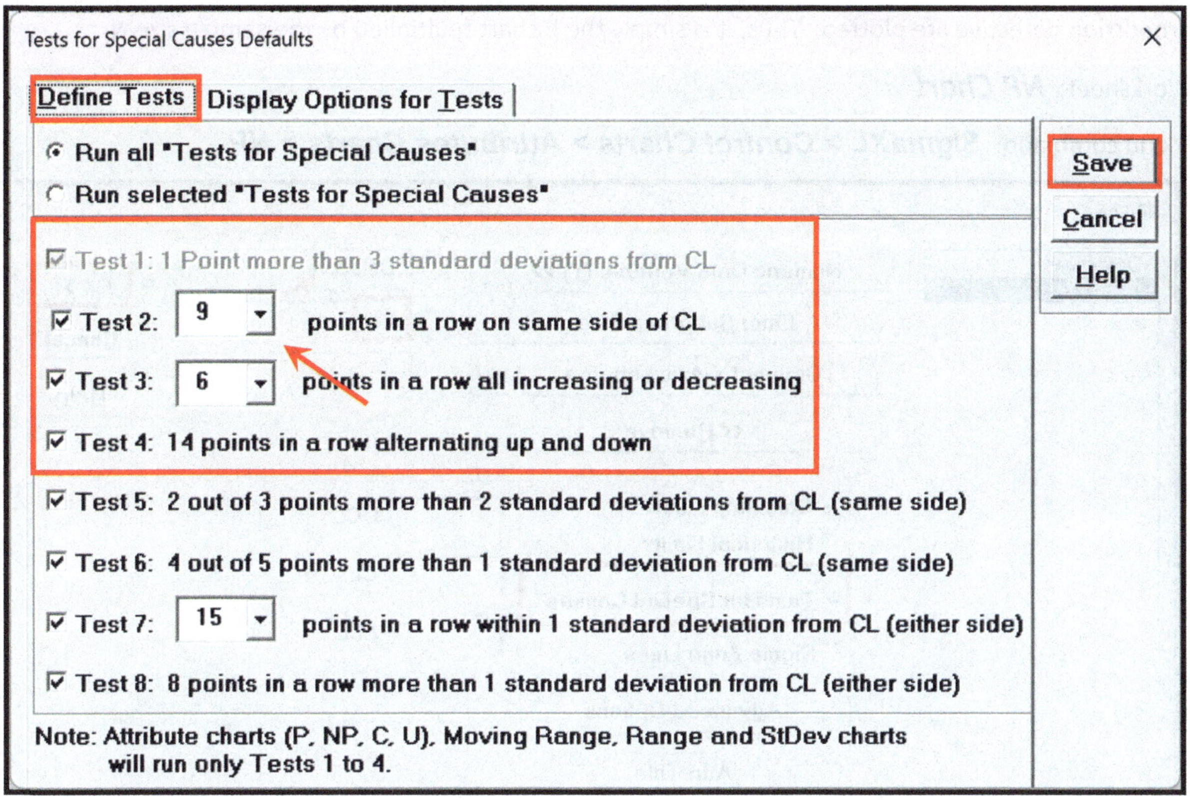

The note at the bottom states that only the first four tests are used for Attribute Charts. Only tests 2 and 3 have a value that can be changed. Make the desired changes, then click **Save**. Tests 2, 3 and 4 can also be deselected. Test 1 should always be active.

NP Chart

The NP Chart mimics the P Chart; however, with the NP Chart the number of defectives rather than the proportion defective are plotted. Thus, it is simply the P chart multiplied by the sample size N.

Worksheet: ***NP Chart***

Menu command: ***SigmaXL > Control Charts > Attributes Charts > NP***

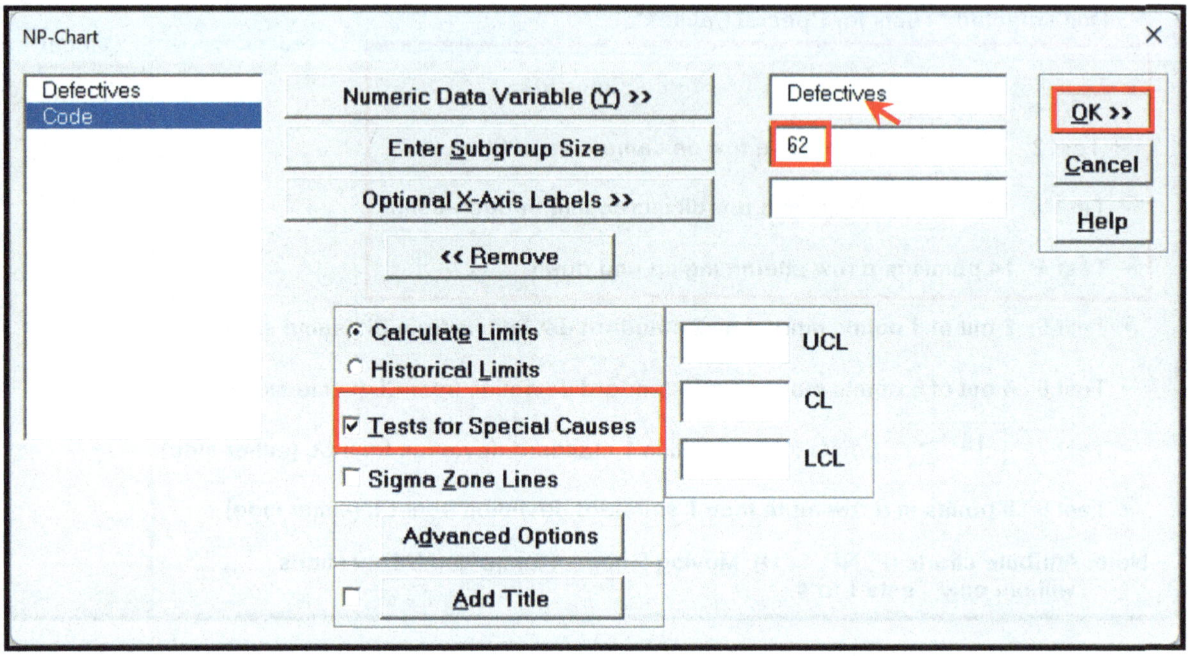

Input **Defectives** as the **Numeric Data Variables (Y)** and **62** for the subgroup sizes. This process looks at 62 items and determines the number of defectives. Choose **Tests for Special Causes**.

The NP Chart Options are the same as the p Chart options.

Click **OK**.

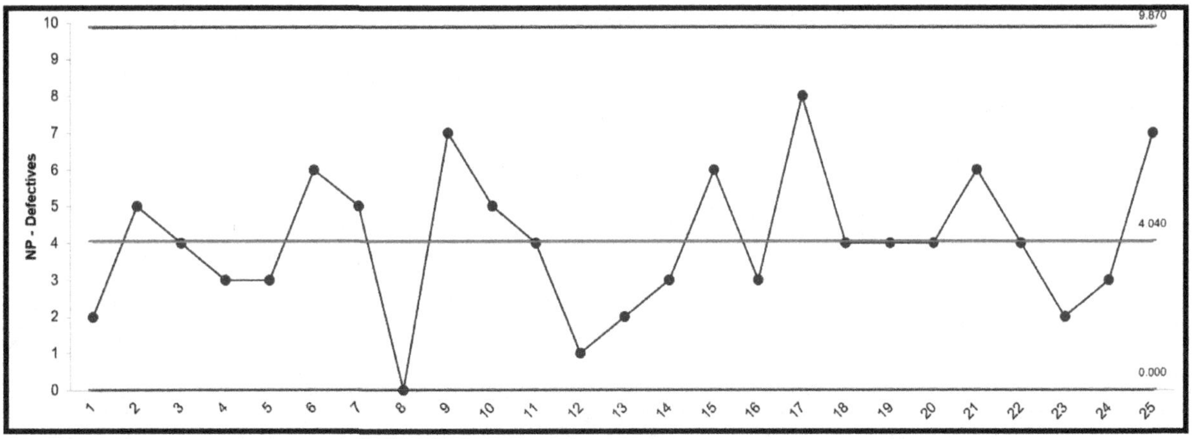

The chart shows no Special Cause rule violations. The expected number of defectives from a sample of size 62 is 4.04, the Center Line.

Anything below 9.87 defectives (upper control limit) can be considered from a stable process with an average number of defective items of 4.04.

SigmaXL does not allow for varying sample sizes. Using varying sample sizes results in a chart with varying control limits as well as varying mean values. This makes it difficult to determine the number of defectives to expect for a specific sample size.

C Chart

Use the C Chart to monitor the number of defects found in a sample.

Worksheet: ***C chart***

Menu command: ***SigmaXL > Control Charts > Attributes Charts > C***

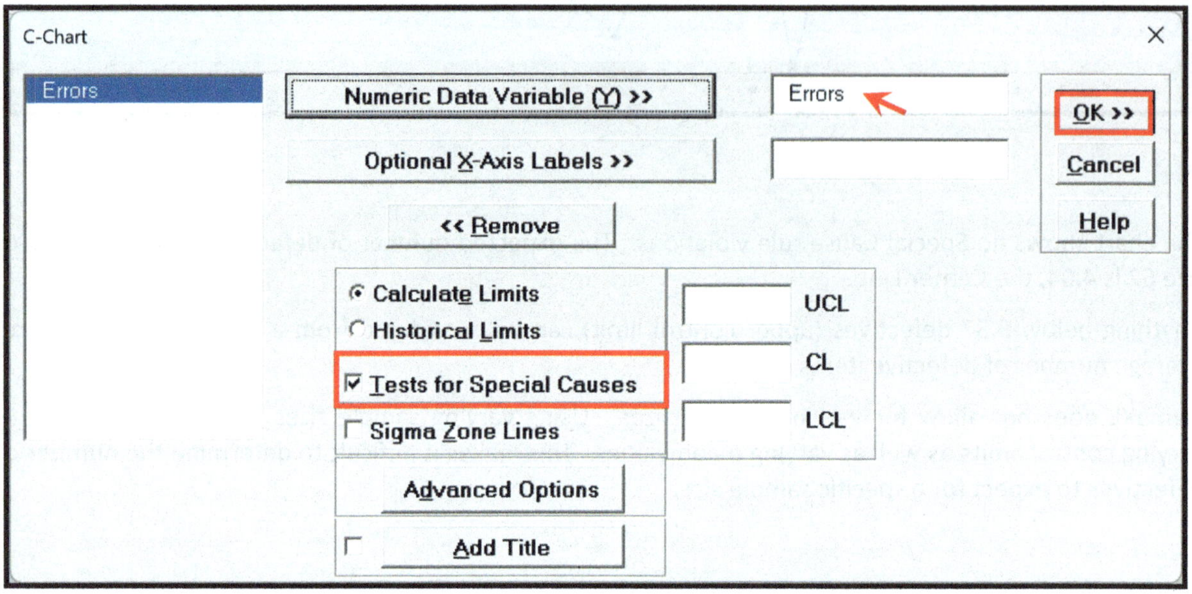

Input **Errors** as the Numeric Data Variable (Y). Select; **Tests for Special Causes**. Click **OK**.

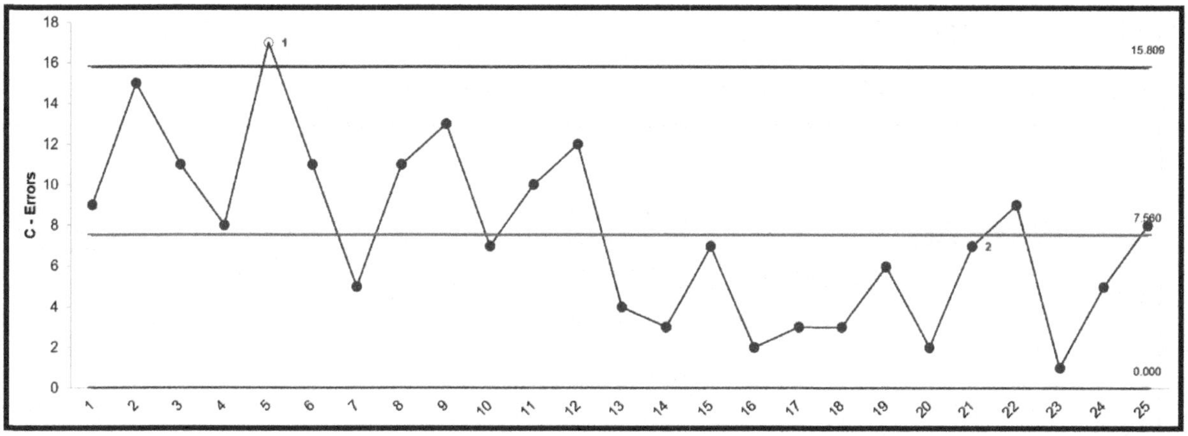

Observation No.	Test 1: 1 point more than 3 StDev from CL	Test 2: 9 points in a row on same side of CL	Test 3: 6 points in a row all increasing or all decreasing	Test 4: 14 points in a row alternating up and down
5	x			
21		x		

Tests for Special Causes - C – Errors

Number of Data Points Failing Tests = 2

U Chart

The U Chart also measures defects, but as defects per unit.

Worksheet: ***U Chart***

Menu command: ***SigmaXL > Control Charts > Attributes Charts > U***

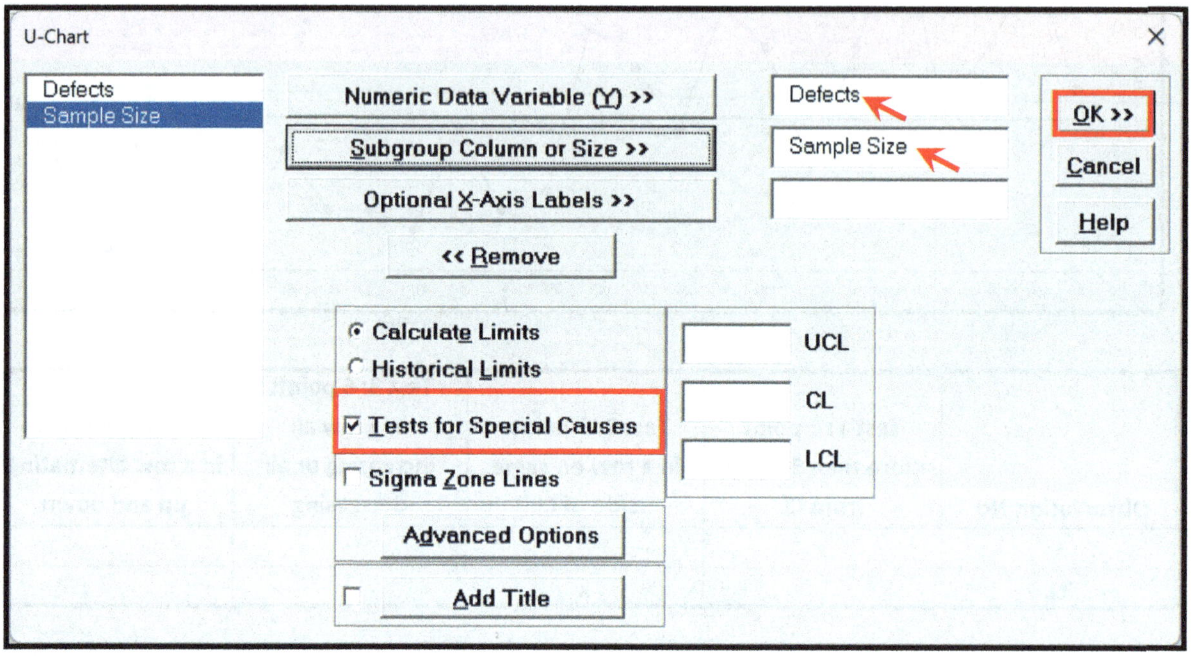

Input Defects as the Numeric Data Variable (Y). Select Sample Size' for the Subgroup Column or Size. Choose Tests for Special Causes. Click OK.

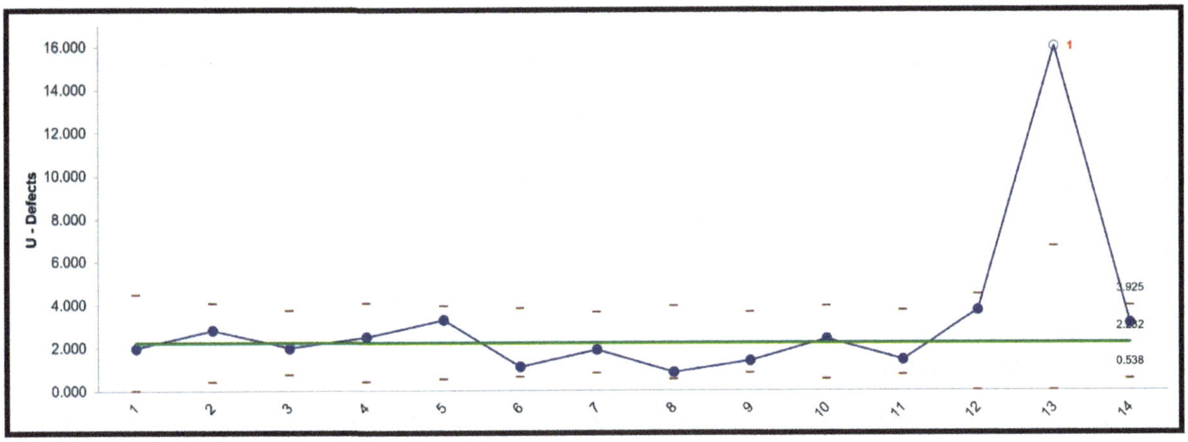

Tests for Special Causes - U – Defects

Observation No.	Test 1: 1 point more than 3 StDev from CL	Test 2: 9 points in a row on same side of CL	Test 3: 6 points in a row all increasing or all decreasing	Test 4: 14 points in a row alternating up and down
13	x			

Number of Data Points Failing Tests = 1

The control limits vary depending upon the sample sizes.

The larger the sample size, the tighter the limits. The 13th record should be investigated for a Special Cause event.

Attribute Control Charts for Special Situations

The traditional P and U charts with large sample sizes will often experience situations referred to as ***Over Dispersion*** and ***Under Dispersion***.

Over dispersion exists when noise factors cause the process to experiences more variation than is expected based on either the Poisson (for counts), or the Binomial (for proportions) distributions. Under dispersion is the opposite, here there's less variation than expected. In these cases, the regular P and U charts will demonstrate excessive **Out-of-Control** conditions.

The charts of choice in these situations are the Laney P' and Laney U' charts.

Worksheet: ***Defective Records***

(This worksheet comes from the SigmaXL dataset included with each licensed copy of the software.)

P' (Laney) Chart

Begin by creating a standard **P Chart**

Menu command: ***SigmaXL > Control Charts > Attribute Charts > P***

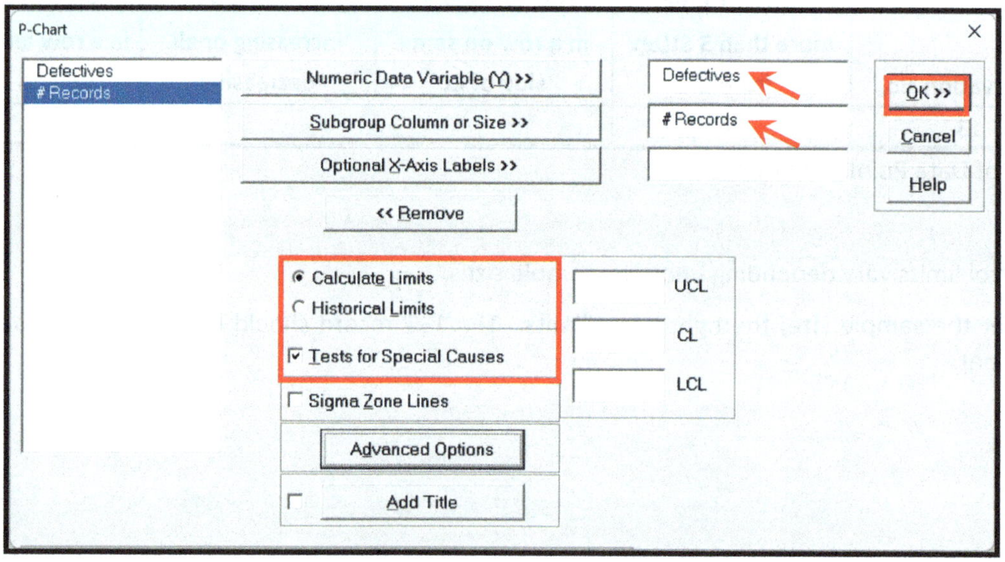

Select **Defectives** for the Numeric Data Variable (Y).

Select; **# Records** for the Subgroup Column or Size. Choose **Calculate Limits**, and **Tests for Special Causes**. Click **OK**.

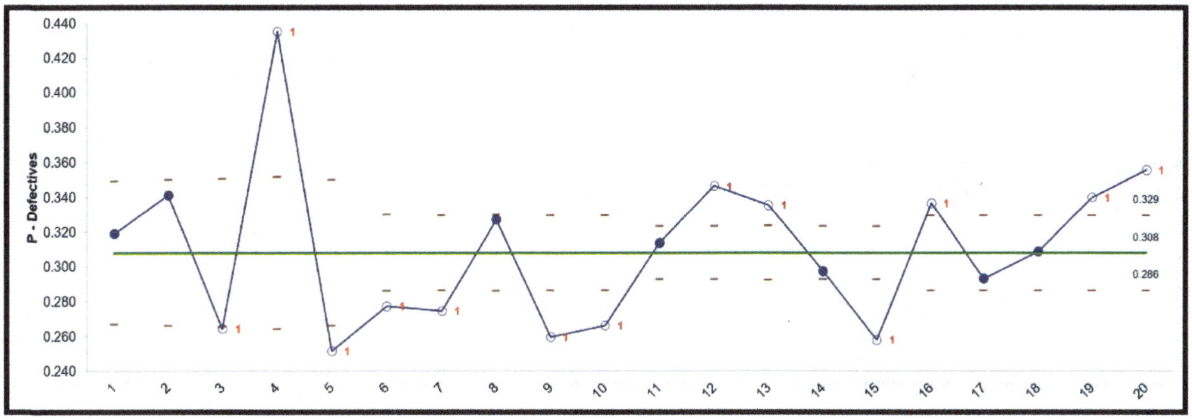

Results show many Out-of-Control points.

Multiple Out-of-Control points are caused by the large number of Records being investigated for each data point. To correct for this issue, use the **Laney's P'** Chart.

Use the same worksheet.

Menu command: ***SigmaXL > Control Charts > Attribute Charts > P' (Laney)***

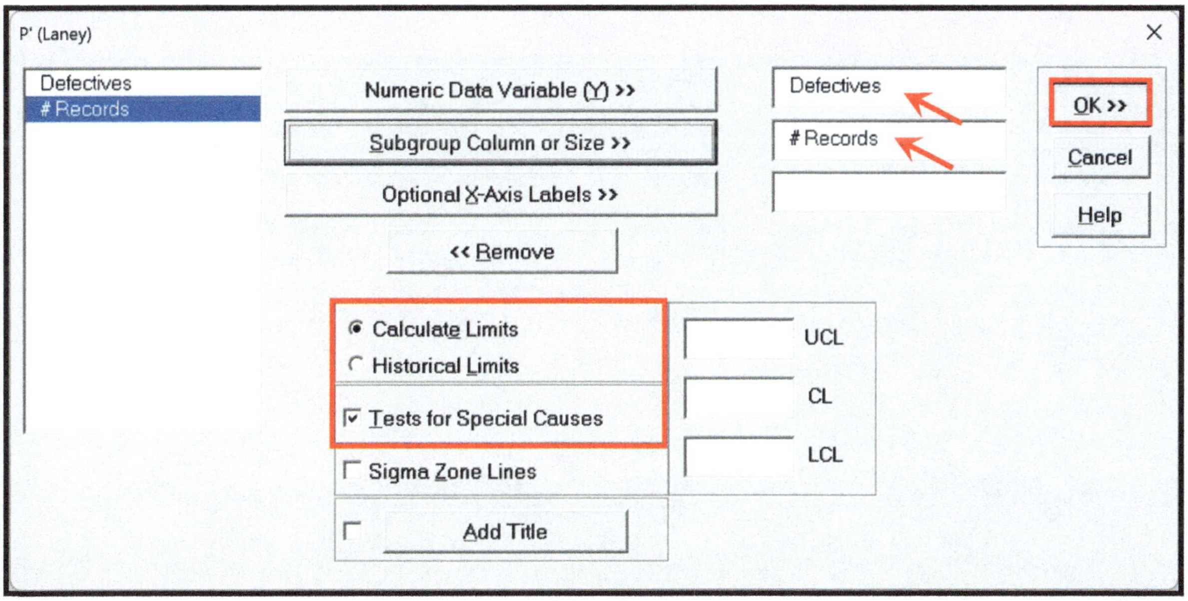

Select **Defectives** for the Numeric Data Variable (Y). Select; **# Records** for the Subgroup Column or Size. Choose **Calculate Limits**, and **Tests for Special Causes**. Click **OK**.

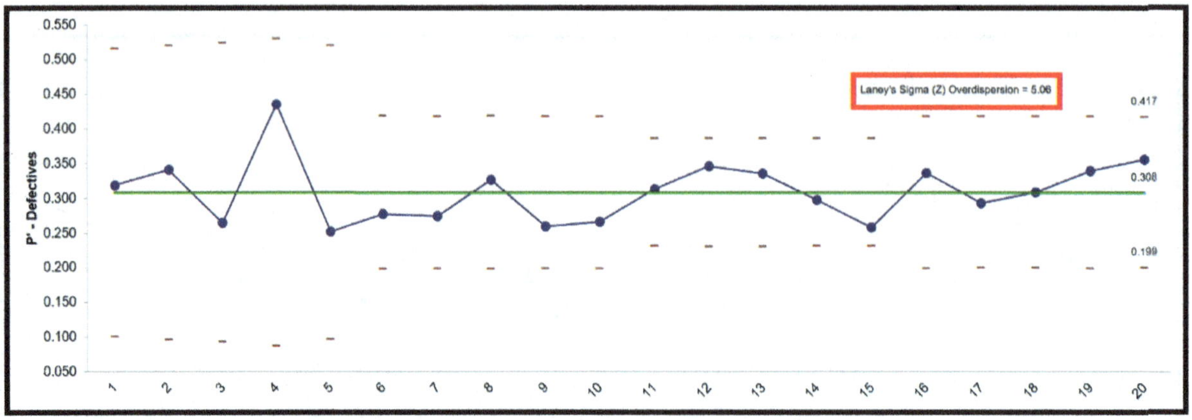

No Out-of-Control points exist. The Laney's Sigma (Z) Overdispersion value of 5.06 indicates an issue with over dispersion. Values greater than 1 suggests the Laney P' chart is the proper chart for this data.

The same procedure can be used for a comparison between the U Chart and the U' (Laney) chart.

U' (Laney) Chart

Use worksheet: ***Record Defects***

Begin with the **U Chart**.

Menu command: ***SigmaXL > Control Charts > Attribute Charts > U***

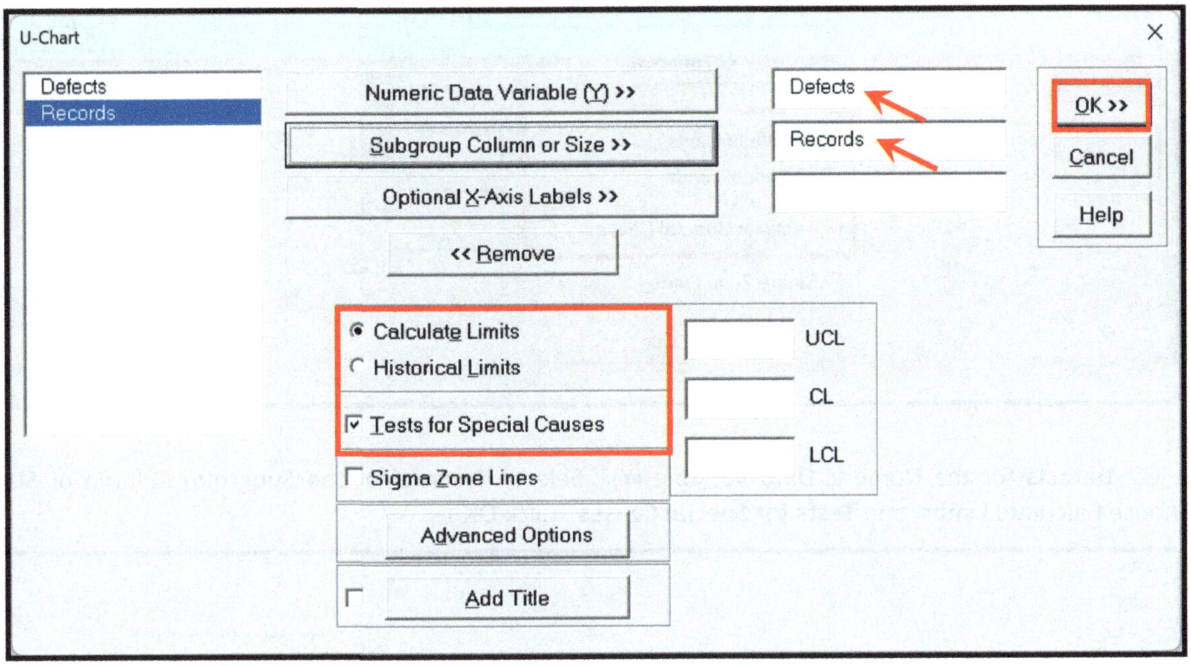

Select **Defects** for the Numeric Data Variable (Y). Select; **Records** for the Subgroup Column or Size. Choose **Calculate Limits**, and **Tests for Special Causes**. Click **OK**.

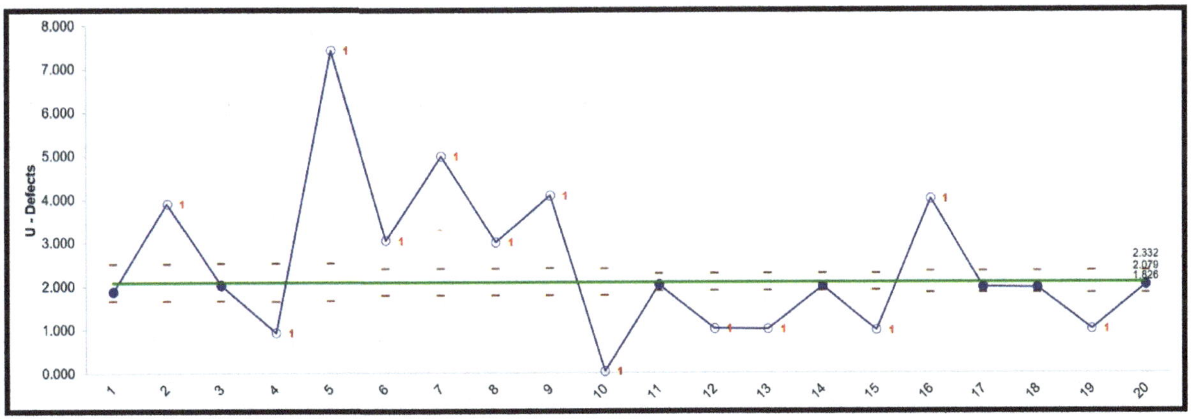

Most points are considered to be Out-of-Control. Next, check the U' (Laney) chart.

Menu command: ***SigmaXL > Control Charts > Attribute Charts > U' (Laney)***

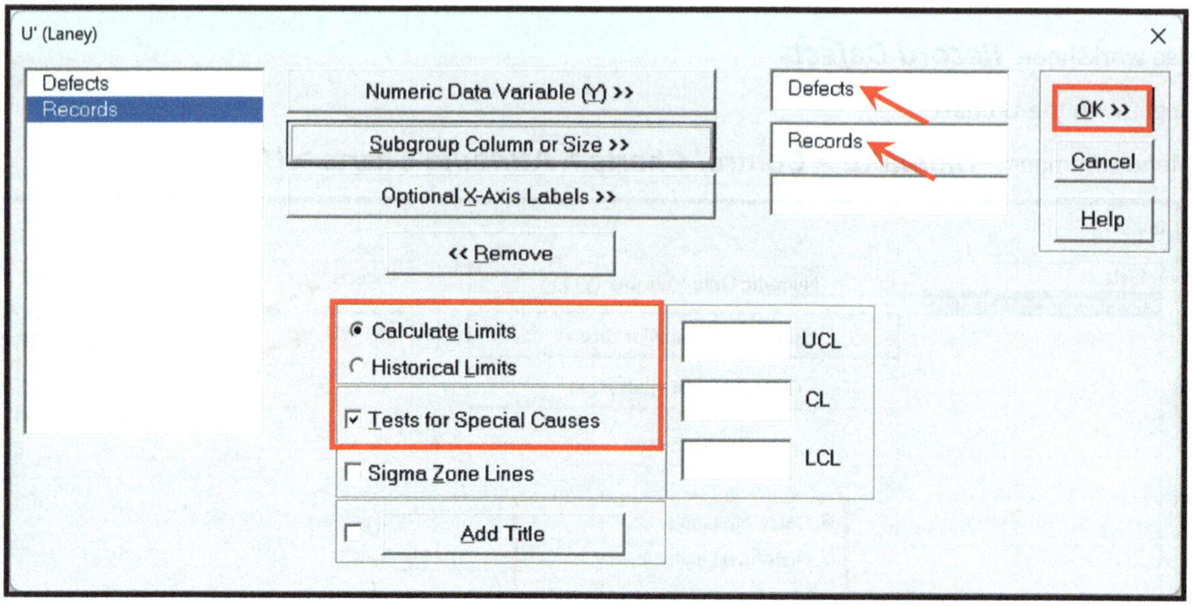

Select **Defects** for the Numeric Data Variable (Y). Select; **Records** for the Subgroup Column or Size. Choose **Calculate Limits**, and **Tests for Special Causes**. Click **OK**.

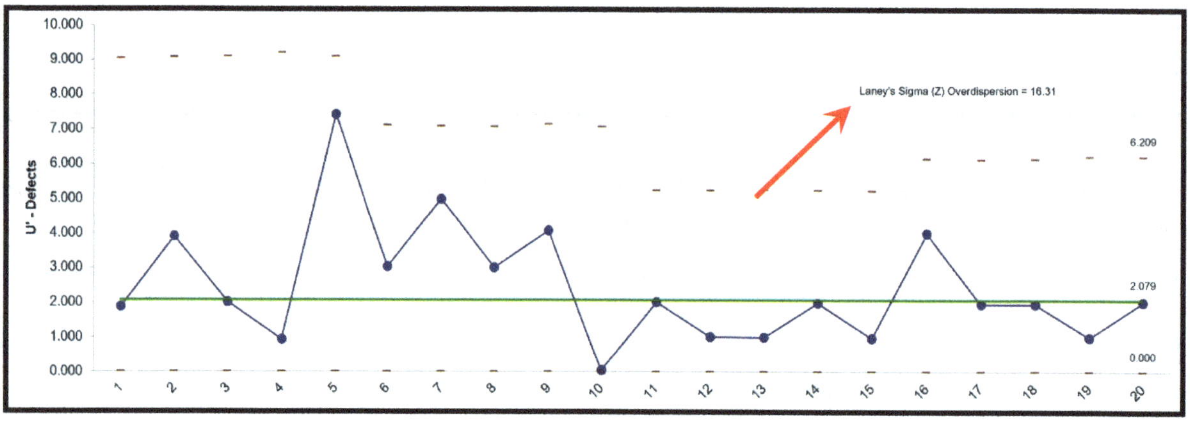

No points are considered Out-of-Control. The Laney's Sigma(Z) value of 16.31 indicates the U' chart should be used.

To learn more about the Laney P', and U' charts, see SigmaXL Help.

Process Capability – Non-Normal Data

Previous calculations for capability assumed data came from a population with a normal distribution. When this assumption is incorrect, it is important to use procedures to account for the non-normality.

Worksheet: ***nonnormal***

Menu command: ***SigmaXL > Process Capability > Nonnormal > Capability Combination Report (Individuals – Nonnormal)***

This data originated from a process that has a hard limit or boundary at zero. However, the Box-Cox transformation technique requires that all values be greater than zero. Therefore, the lower specification cannot be zero. Use .001.

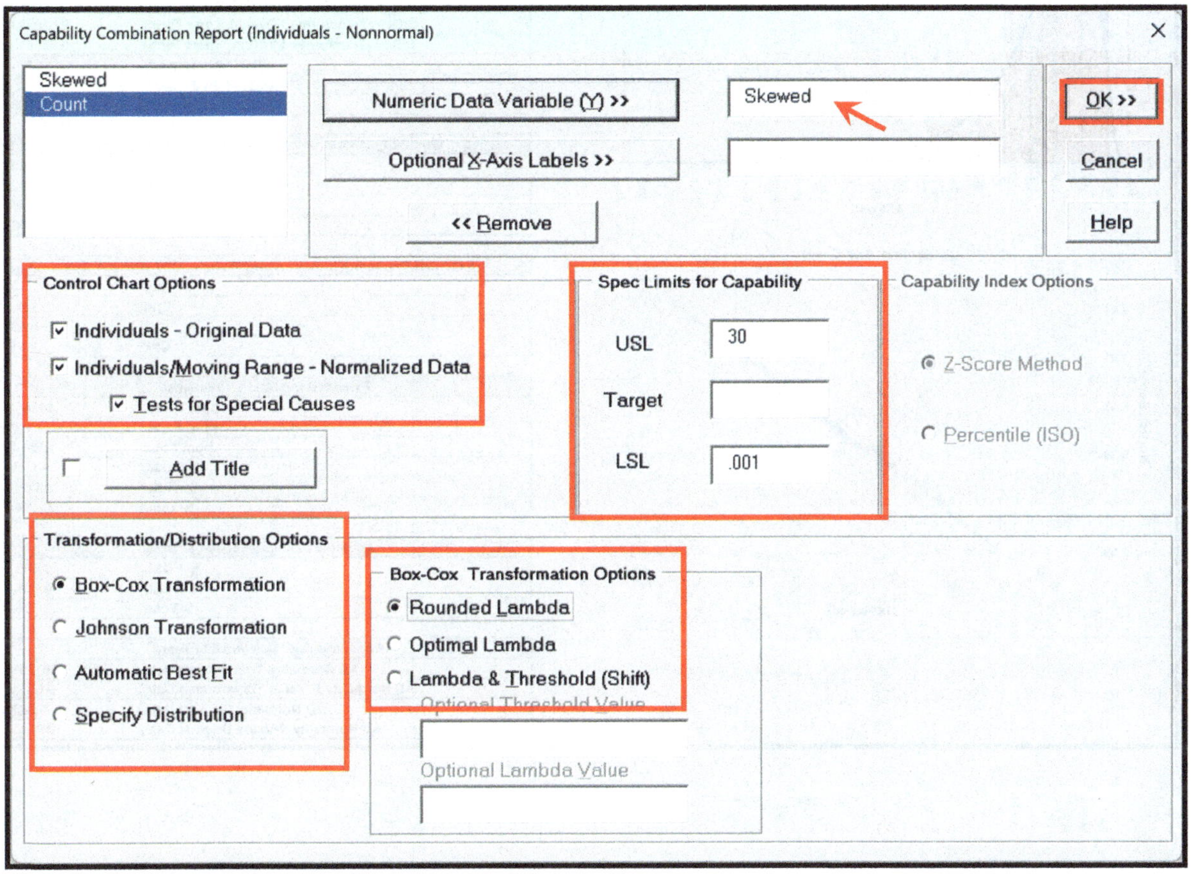

Select Skewed as the Numeric Data Variable (Y).

Under **Spec Limits for Capability**, the lower specification for the Box-Cox transformation must be greater than 0, so use a small value such as **.001**. The upper spec is **30**.

For Control Chart Options, select all three. For Transformation/Distribution Options, select Box-Cox Transformation. For the Box-Cox Transformation Options, choose Rounded Lambda. Click OK.

The two graphs on the left show the original data along with the Normality Plot for the transformed data. The Process Capability Report (Nonnormal) Skewed provides information for the original data and information for the transformed data. The rounded transform is the Natural Log (Ln). The capability values associated with the transformed data are more reliable than capability values associated with the non-transformed data. At the bottom of the report are the Normality Test results for both the untransformed and transformed data.

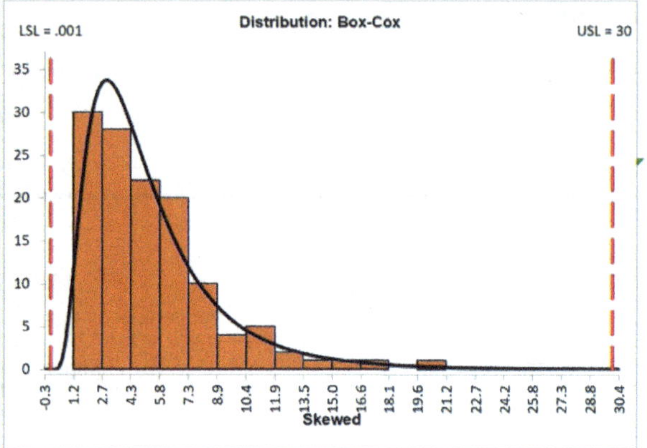

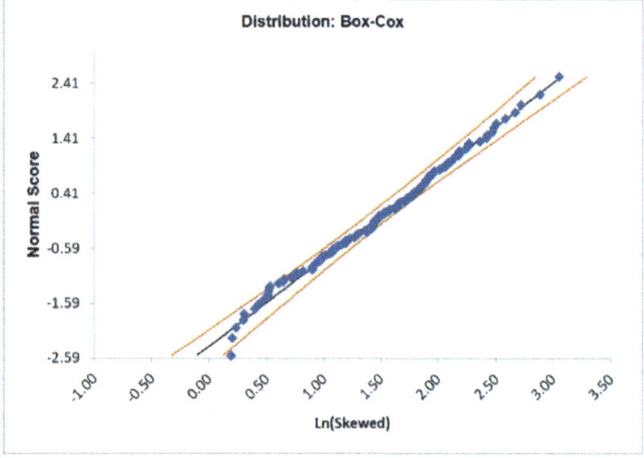

Process Capability Report (Nonnormal): Skewed	
Box-Cox Transformation: Z = Ln(Y)	
Sample Count	125
Sample Mean	5.336
USL	30
Target	
LSL	0.001
Lambda (Rounded)	0
Mean (Transformed)	1.485
StDev (Transformed Overall, Long Term)	0.625223
StDev (Transformed Within, Short Term)	0.631413
USL (Transformed)	3.401
Target (Transformed)	
LSL (Transformed)	-6.908

Capability Indices using Transformed Overall StDev	
Pp	2.75
Ppu	1.02
Ppl	4.47
Ppk	1.02

Potential Capability Indices using Transformed Within StDev	
Cp	2.72
Cpu	1.01
Cpl	4.43
Cpk	1.01

Expected Overall Performance	
ppm > USL	1088.7
ppm < LSL	0.0
ppm Total	1088.7
% > USL	0.11%
% < LSL	0.00%
% Total	0.11%

Actual (Empirical) Performance	
% > USL	0.00%
% < LSL	0.00%
% Total	0.00%

Anderson-Darling Normality Tests	
AD Normality Transformed Data	0.281759
AD Normality P-Value Transformed Data	0.6331
AD Normality Original Data	3.682
AD Normality P-Value Original Data	0.0000

Additional information includes an Individuals plot of the original data, and an Individuals and Moving Range chart of the transformed data.

Original Data

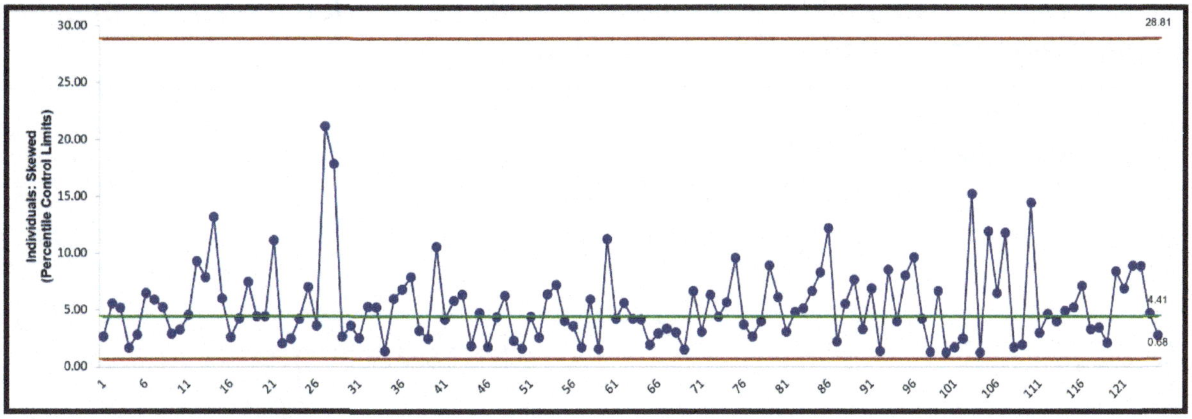

Transformed Data

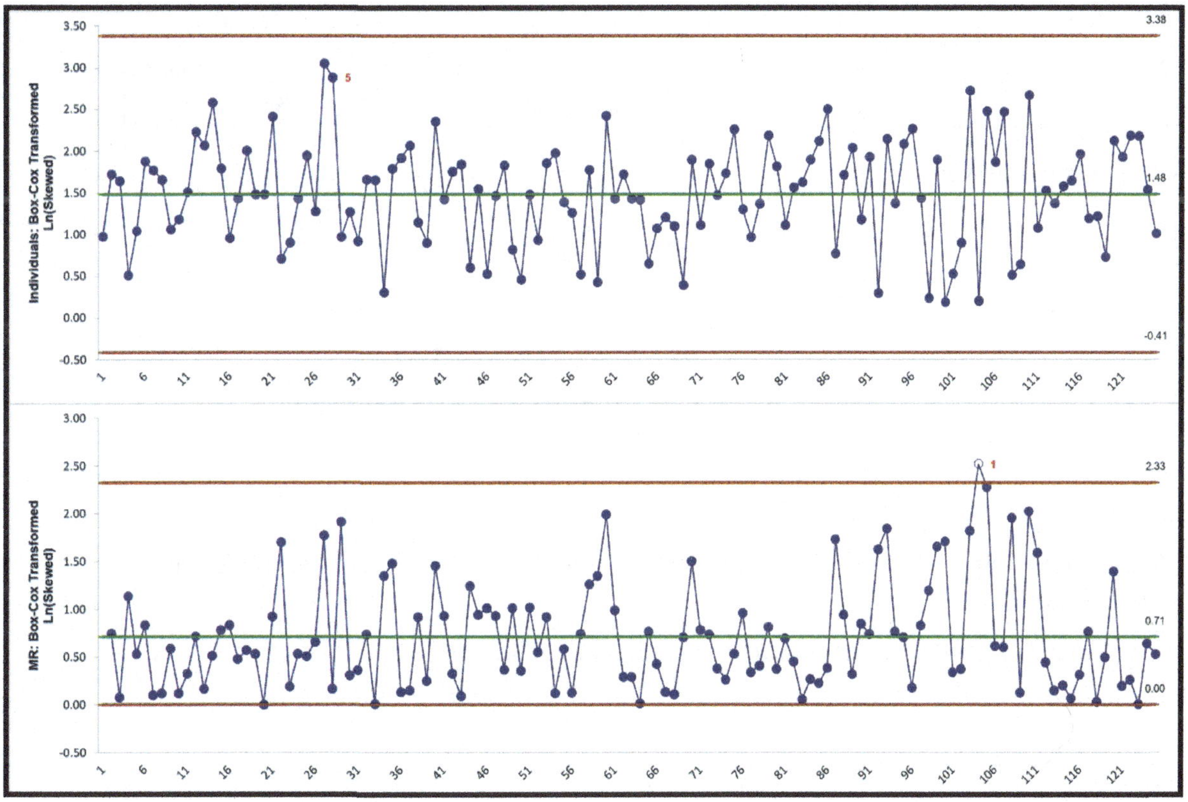

Using Other Distribution Curves

If the Box-Cox transformations are not successful, the next option is to select the distribution to use.

Menu command: ***SigmaXL > Process Capability > Nonnormal > Capability Combination Report (Individuals – Nonnormal)***

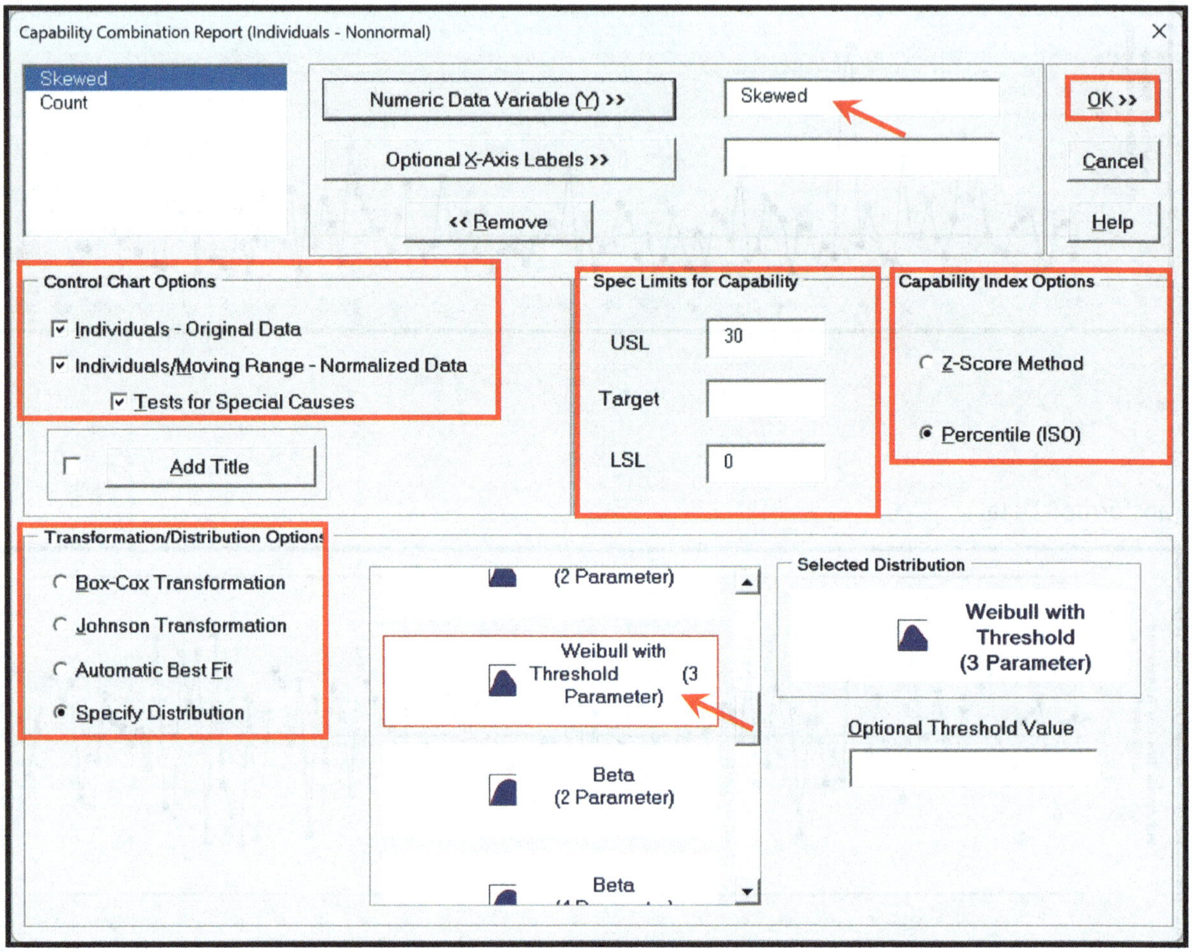

Input Skewed as the Numeric Data Variable (Y). Keep the same options as shown. Choose Specify Distribution under the Transformation/Distribution Options section.

Select **Weibull with Threshold (3 Parameter)** for the distribution. Input the Lower spec. as **0** and an upper spec. of **30**.

Under Capability Index Options choose Percentile (ISO). Click OK.

The data remains in its original form, (it is not transformed), but the capability values are now calculated based on the 3 Parameter Weibull distribution.

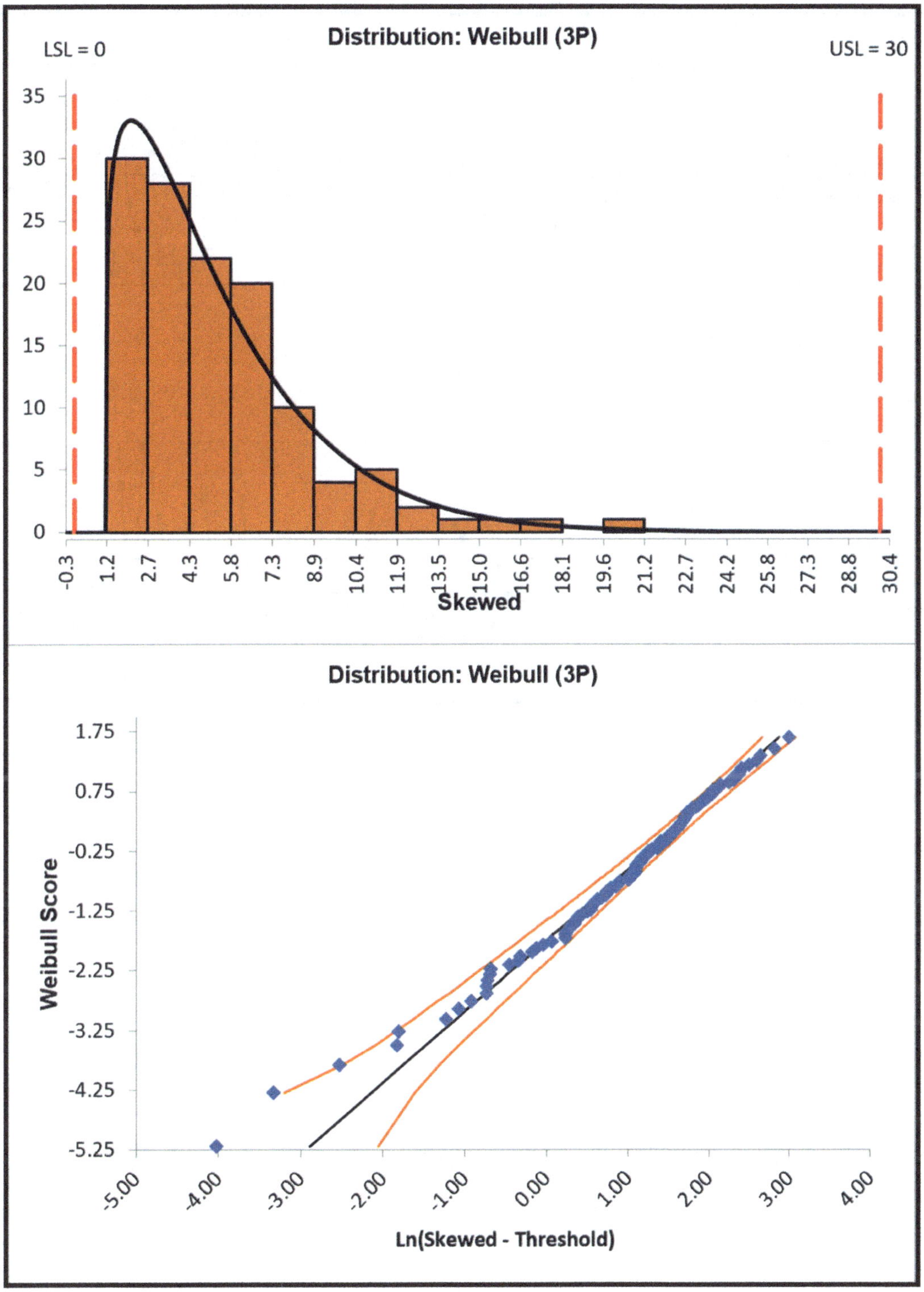

The Individuals and Moving Range charts show a few Out-of-Control points that should be investigated.

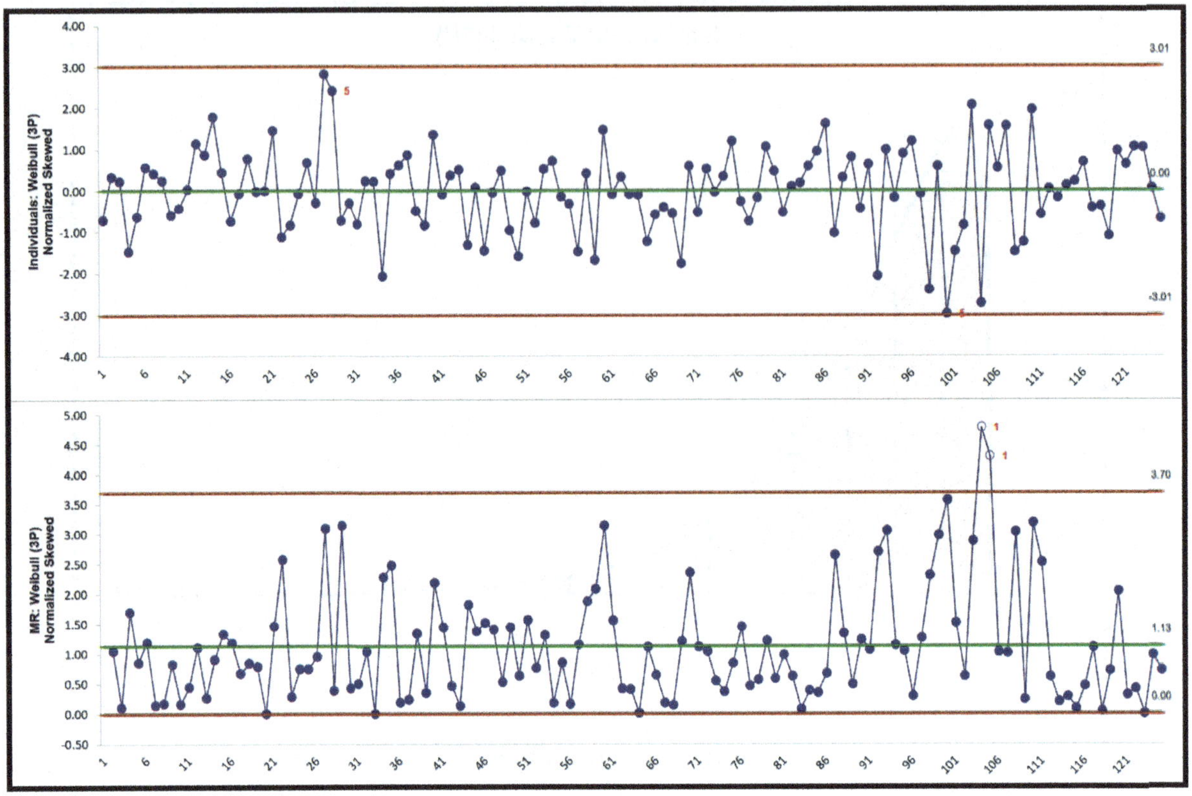

The Capability values can be trusted because they are calculated based off of a distribution that fits the

Process Capability Report (Nonnormal): Skewed	
Distribution: Weibull (3P)	
Sample Count	125
Sample Mean	5.34
Shape	1.187
Scale	4.390686356
Threshold (ML Estimate)	1.186548596
StDev (Normalized Overall, Long Term)	1
StDev (Normalized Within, Short Term)	0.985476
USL	30
Target	
LSL	0
Capability Indices (Percentile - ISO Method)	
Pp	1.393
Ppu	1.40
Ppl	1.38
Ppk	1.38
Expected Overall Performance	
ppm > USL	89.2
ppm < LSL	0.0
ppm Total	89.2
% > USL	0.01%
% < LSL	0.00%
% Total	0.01%
Actual (Empirical) Performance	
% > USL	0.00%
% < LSL	0.00%
% Total	0.00%
Anderson-Darling Goodness-of-Fit Tests	
AD Weibull (3P)	0.316171
AD Weibull (3P) P-Value	> 0.5000
AD Normality Original Data	3.682
AD Normality P-Value Original Data	0.0000

data.

The previous example simply specified a distribution. But what if the correct distribution is not known? To determine which distribution the data might fit, use the Distribution Fitting option.

Menu command: ***SigmaXL > Process Capability > Nonnormal > Distribution Fitting***

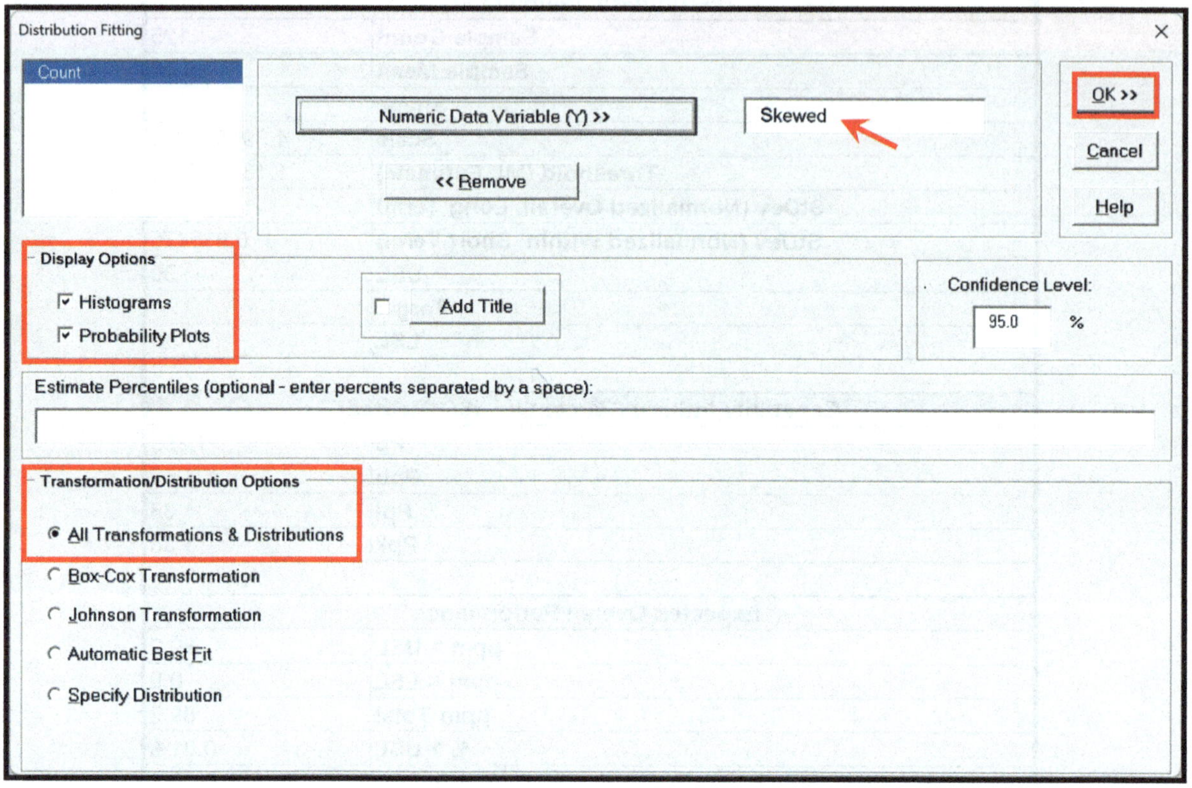

Input Skewed as the Numeric Data Variable (Y). Select both Display Options, and choose All Transformations and Distributions option under Transformation/Distribution Options.

Click **OK**.

Many different Transformations and Distributions are tested. Each will have a Histogram, Probability Plot and Summary Information. High AD (Anderson Darling) P-Values indicates the data could originate from that Distribution or Transformation. If there is more than one option, the user must decide on which one to use.

The **Lognormal (3P)** distribution will be used to demonstrate the output.

The resulting graphs will have p-values for each distribution. Any distribution with a p-value greater than .05 is a possible solution. If the process is known to follow one of the acceptable distributions, use it; otherwise, use the distribution that provides the best fit.

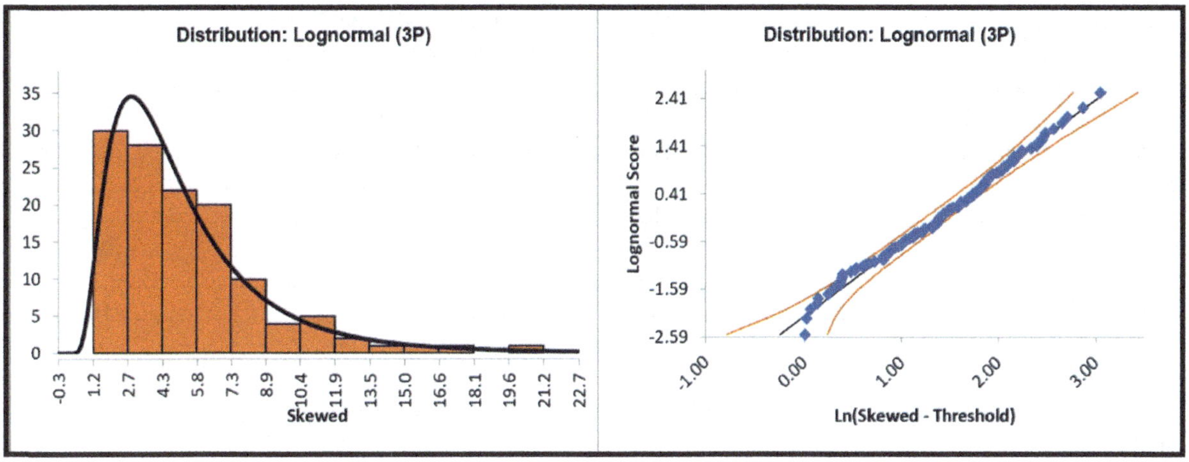

The graph on the left shows a histogram of the sample data with an overlayed Lognormal (3P) distribution. The graph on the right is the Probability plot based on the Lognormal (3P) distribution.

Distribution Fitting Report: Skewed	
Distribution: Lognormal (3P)	
Sample Count	125
Sample Mean	5.336

Model Summary and Goodness-of-Fit	
Log-Likelihood	-303.707
AD Lognormal (3P)	0.352443
AD Lognormal (3P) P-Value	0.462 (Z-Score Est.)

Parameter Estimates				
Parameter	Estimate	SE Estimate	Lower 95.0 CI	Upper 95.0 CI
Location	1.429	0.154688	1.126	1.732
Scale	0.658297	0.102998802	0.484440	0.894546
Threshold (ML Estimate)	0.196310	0.479701	-0.743887	1.137

Percentile Report				
Percentage	Skewed	SE Percentile	Lower 95.0 CI	Upper 95.0 CI
0.135	0.775540	0.246473	0.415992	1.446
50	4.370	0.272323	3.868	4.938
99.865	30.271	6.255	20.190	45.385

The Model Summary and Goodness of Fit information provides the AD P-Value. The Parameter Estimates and Percentile Report are also provided.

Index

Made in United States
Orlando, FL
04 November 2026

90200634R00175